Crossed the Game

Crossed the Game

Dino Bradley Sr. & Clyde Hayes
with Brooke Raymond

www.bossangelespresents.com

All rights reserved. No part of this publication may be reproduced, distributed, or transmitted in any form or by any means, including photocopying, recording, or other electronic or mechanical methods, without the prior written permission of the publisher, except in the case of brief quotations embodied in critical reviews and certain other noncommercial uses permitted by copyright law. For permission requests, write to the author @bossangelespresentsllc@gmail.com.

ISBN: 978-0-578-94689-4

First printing edition 2020, 2021.

Published by:

Boss Angeles Presents LLC

Crossed the Game

Website: www.bossangelespresents.com

Email:bossangelespresentsllc@gmail.com

© 2020 Boss Angeles Presents LLC

Dedicated to Marlon Bradley aka Johnny Ball

Acknowledgements Part I

Dino "Phatz" Bradley

Crossed the Game is biblical. It's not a story it's the truth. This book is dedicated to the mean streets of Boss Angeles, the hustle, and all our struggles. To all of us that are living in a cell or planted in a grave because of the hustle. To our families that never quit or gave up on us during our struggles. Just know Forever is Now! It don't start once we die! It's right now! "US."

Special Thanks: To my baby sister Denise, she told me to set them out like a Thanksgiving dinner. To my mother Kathi and my father Harry Bradley, if it were not for you I would not be able to write this book. To my big brother Marlon this story is dedicated to you. Thank you to my great grandmother Mother Dear and my great aunt Be Be. Thank the both of you for raising me to love family period! Y'all had my back 24/7. Thank you to my Uncle Kenny who told me "Ride Nephew, We All We Got!"

Thank you to my baby girl Shira J for supporting my struggle while telling this story. Thanks to Duck and Ink. Thank you to my cousins Ricky, Kenny, Tangela, and Gerald. They all told me to tell the truth and shame them devils!

Special Thanks to Ramona, my better half. She told me to make em clap for C.T.G.!

Thanks to James A. he told me, "I'm with you until we get to heaven."

Special Thanks to Brooke Raymond, who helped me & AC speak our truths. She told me they don't know "US" like that! So she sat side by side with us and was swinging her pen until it "Moved the Crowd!"

Thanks to my pal Ira Tillman. He said, "Don't let no one speak to your life, speak to it yourself. Thanks to Ronnie Moe, Pebbles, Ace, and Big Lil Dino Jr. Thanks to Sweetz who will push play at once about CTG cause they all know The Phatz & AC really bout this life!

Last but not least. Thanks to "Awful Clyde" for living this life with me. Forever is Now! To us, it don't start once we're planted. No!

This just Some Mo Of It! The truth don't need a hiding place and thanks to Boss Angeles California for putting me through the test. For them Ima stay West Coast'n in any place I land Ya Heard Me! We gotta stay active and game related !

"US"

And to all my haters stay on your jobs cause I'm 24/7 with mine!

Part II Acknowledgements

The struggle is real. All the females I held hands with - a thousand pardons. I'm not hard to find no! Breathe on me. I'm still him!

To all my frenemies', it's hard to change when everything around "US" stays the same. I'm only fighting the battle in front of me! Not behind me. Today our paths are different. So I write. Beef battles wont sweeten. No! They will only sour. Let's live. Fuck that cell. That's Not Living. Ya Heard Me!

To all the hustlers who huddled up on 42nd and Vermont at Marshals, we took Boss Angeles down through it and gave the city plenty of game. Here's to "Us" Boss Angeles finest. We did that, Yea! Show up and Show out @bossangelespresents!

To all them brothers that woke my game up on that River in Louisiana y'all forever my rounds! New Orleans, Batton Rouge, Shreveport. Y'all taught me to "have it on my mind" and play it like it go! Find me on social media. Let's Live! Leave the bodies where they lay. Ya Heard Me!

To them mean unforgiving streets from San Diego to The Bay don't call the alligator a big mouth until "we" cross the river, Don't end up in the mouth of the gator (prison). Just know that what we lose in the fire we will find in the ashes.

To all my Boss Angeles hustlers & riders! We didn't start this writing stuff, No! We lived it! So to Boss Angeles we're just speaking out loud in CTG. We seek righteousness, but we'll "Take" revenge. The Phatz and Awful Clyde avenging ourselves. It's just some mo of it!

If you cut ears off a mule it won't make it a horse! So tell the truth and shame the devil! History will remember all of us that lived in Boss Angeles and played in the streets. Cali tell your own truths. Don't let no one water down our struggles. Hit em' with the devils breath! Blow back on who lied on our lifestyle. We're not just Boss Angeles we're Cross Angeles. We are more than legends. We alive and well and active in all that we do!

We're just taking the knife out our back and making sure all candles are lit before we blow out the match. When they spoke on running "Boss Angeles" they was fanning an elephant with a fly swatter. Speak to it Boss Angeles. "US"

Acknowledgements

Clyde "Awful Clyde" Hayes

I will start off in the sandbox east of Normandie. The true dirty 30's. Getting it in every way you can imagine. Not to mention the many ways you can't. The first person I have to acknowledge is my earth Mama Redd, Rubbie Lynn my sister and my G1 Big Reg. Not to forget the Infamous Exposition Crew. Not forgetting my escapades up and down Vermont. Pitstops in every neighborhood up and down Vermont. Fast forward 38yrs here we are stretching toward The Sun. Polished by the grind. The grind has two functions: it grinds you down or it polishes you. Now it's time to Shine! I tip my hat to all that I have broke bread with on this unbelievable journey!

When Hustlers Meet

(The Phatz (left) & Awful Clyde)

It was perfect that April morning. Not too hot, not too cold. It was the kind of weather that attracted families and crowds to the clear blue waters of the Santa Monica beach they had just driven by. As AC sat in the back of the Cadillac Brougham listening to Deuce and Ray argue over their stupid plan, he couldn't stop the sweat from trickling down the sides of his face despite the windows being down. Staring at the cracked leather seat he tried to remain calm. Though he knew the longer they sat in the parking lot of the mall, the higher their chances were of getting caught. Momentarily distracted by the family of three walking past the car hand in hand, AC imagined what it felt like to live in the quaint little suburbs. It even smelled different. Like peace and prosperity.

He chuckled to himself.

Who was he kidding? He had no idea what either smelled like. Growing up in 30's Fruit Town , a L.A. neighborhood often plagued with violence and death, AC couldn't imagine a life where he didn't have to hustle to survive and oddly enough he was proud of it. At seventeen, life had taught him that he would have to take care of himself by any means necessary and ever since he was a youngin' he had been doing just that. His fingers tightened around the rubber strip of the hammer in his hand as his hawkish gaze zoomed in on the happy family walking into the mall, unaware of the chaos that was about to erupt around them.

Slapping the headrest of Deuce's seat to get his attention, AC grabbed the handle of the door.

"You niggas doing too much talking, either you wit it or not." Not waiting for a response, he climbed out of the car, surprised when Deuce followed. Apparently, the man had more sense than he had given him credit for.

"Slow down," Deuce cautioned a few steps behind as he struggled to keep up with AC's long-legged strides across the tar pavement.

Ignoring him, AC continued until he stood in front of the double doors of the mall entrance.

"What's the plan?" Deuce asked kneeling over on his knees to catch his breath.

AC stared down at him in disgust and wondered why he had chosen to invite the two along in the first place. His eyes strayed to Ray in the front seat, the answer clear as day. He needed the car. It would be hard for him to make a clean get away without transportation. At the feel of the hammer's iron head at his waist adrenaline shot through his body. His heartbeat quickened as he glanced around to make sure no one was in listening distance.

"All I need you to do is be the lookout I got the rest. If you see or hear anything give me a holler. You got it?" he asked.

Rising to his full height Deuce let out a deep breath before nodding his head.

The answer did nothing to stop the tightening in AC's stomach warning him that this was a bad idea. Glancing over his shoulder he saw the desperate look on Ray's face. It was too late to turn back now. Shoving his feelings to the side, AC pulled the doors handle, immediately chilled by the shot of cold air in the air-conditioned entrance as he stepped inside.

Anxiously scanning over the lobby, he took note of the strangely thin Friday crowd. Older couples strolled hand in hand as a family darted into a sports store with their screaming children in tow. A few workers lounged on the benches during their break chatting. *Was it luck that the mall was basically empty?* He thought to himself. It definitely would make what they were about to do a whole lot easier. Walking across the tiled floor he cast a glance in Deuce's direction. They were so close AC could see the beads of sweat that had broken out on his forehead. Fidgeting with the hem of his T-shirt Deuce nervously checked over his shoulder every few steps.

AC swore silently.

At the rate they were going his shifty posture would give them away.

Relax he mouthed when their eyes locked.

Taking a deep breath Deuce pulled himself together, his body visibly relaxing.

That's better AC thought. Continuing pass the food court he almost paused when the smell of mozzarella cheese melting on dough and marinara sauce invaded his senses, but a light giggle pulled at his attention. Shifting his head slightly he could feel the eyes of the college girls at the table boring into him. From the corner of his eye he watched one dressed in pink nudge the girl beside her. The reaction on her face was similar to many women when they saw him. Standing at 6'2 with high yellow skin, green eyes, and wavy black hair AC attracted women of all ages. His good looks and flashy style made him the center of attention everywhere he went. Dressed in a black and red Adidas sweatsuit with a pair of white K-Swiss, he never left the house looking anything but sharp, even when he was about to commit a crime. First impressions were everything to him and seemingly to everyone else being that most couldn't look beyond his handsome face to see the viciousness that lurked underneath until it was too late.

Sending a friendly smile in their direction he continued towards his destination. Nothing would get in his way of getting what he had come for, especially not a pair of titties and ass that came a dime a dozen.

Nearing their target AC glanced over his shoulder. As planned Deuce had fallen a few steps behind him. Stopping short outside of the Footlocker store, Deuce whipped his head around, when he was sure everything was clear, he touched the tip of his nose with his finger.

That was AC's cue. Tucking his shirt in the waist of his pants, classical musical reached his ears the second he stepped foot inside of the Slavic jewelry store. The red-haired attendant at the front of the store never once lifted her head to greet him. She was too busy buttering up the older couple in front of her for a sale.

Using the distraction AC took the time to glance around the store. The plain beige walls served as the backdrop to the cases of gold watches that called out to him from behind the countertop. Moving closer for a better inspection he noticed that they were all Concord and Baume and Mercier brand watches. Each one worth $20,000. He could get a nice bargain for them in downtown L.A. at the jewelry mart. Hell, he might even keep one for himself.

Lifting his head, he saw that the older couple had fallen for whatever the salesclerk had told them as she was wrapping up the sale on the cash register.

If he didn't act now it would be too late.

Nodding at Deuce who stood outside, slowly he removed the hammer from his waist. He could feel his pulse racing as he raised it high above his head, bringing it down hard.

Boom!

The sound bounced off the glass as it cracked.

Gripping the hammer tightly, AC raised the hammer again, this time bringing it down with a powerful motion sending glass shattering everywhere.

He barely had time to register the piercing scream from the salesclerk as he reached in with his bare hand removing the watches from the case, careful of the shards of glass surrounding it.

Dropping them down his shirt he ignored the screaming woman and cowering couple as he moved to the next case, repeating the same movement.

Keep going keep going he told himself. If he could make it to the third case, he would have at least a hundred grand down in his shirt.

But the hammer in his hand froze midway in the air when he noticed a blur out the corner of his eye. Quickly turning, the sight in front of him made him pause.

"Get off me!" Deuce yelled as a fat white security guard gripped the back of his shirt. Struggling to hold him still, the guard tried to wrap his thick arm around Deuce's neck.

Oh shit! The voice inside of AC's head screamed as he watched Deuce sink his teeth into the security guard's beefy skin.

A piercing sound tore from his throat, sending another guard barreling towards them.

Deuce's panicked gaze darted to AC. *Help me* his eyes screamed. Following the direction of his stare the security guard approaching halted in his steps when he realized what was going on. His head swiveled between AC and Deuce who was still struggling against the white guard.

"Stop!" He yelled fumbling with something on the side of his belt. Onlookers tried to move far away from what was unfolding. Taking two steps forward the guard gripped the stick in his hand. AC couldn't believe it. He wanted to laugh at the pitiful look on the guard's face.

"Get the fuck back before I bash yo head in," AC warned as the guard tried to approach him.

"No, no stop you don't have to do that," the guard said pleadingly.

AC eyes went above the guards' head. Deuce had managed to break away and was running away.

Abandoning his position, the other guard gave chase as they both scrambled to recapture Deuce.

Fuck it, slamming the hammer in the case AC made for his last grab before sprinting from the store.

Legs pumping fast he ignored the pieces of glass digging into his skin from the watches in his shirt as he ran through the mall.

The family from the parking lot earlier hunkered down on a bench with a look of horror on their faces as the security guards began running after him.

It was chaos as the few shoppers darted to get out of their way.

The girls from the food court cheered him on as he climbed on the wish fountain, evading the guards grasp.

Up ahead he could see the entrance doors leading to his escape. AC didn't stop until he was back outside on the tar pavement.

Wildly he glanced around for the car.

It wasn't in its original spot.

Ray and Deuce were nowhere in sight. A sinking feeling settled into the pit of his stomach. With no time to think he darted between a row of cars, lowering himself to the ground just as the security guards came bursting through the double doors. From his hiding spot he watched them argue among themselves before splitting up. He would've laughed if he didn't think they would find him.

Think think he said to himself as he rested his head against the car door, forcing his racing heart to slow down. He couldn't stay there; it wouldn't be long before one or both security guards discovered him.

Could he make a break for it? From his position he could see the Ferris wheel down on Santa Monica beach. The distance was kind of a stretch, but if he could just get there then maybe he could blend in with the crowd.

Weighing his options carefully, he decided to make a run for it. It was better than waiting to get caught.

The minute he popped from behind the car he heard tires squealing. Turning his head in the direction he watched the car barrel down on him at full speed.

It was Ray.

He wasn't the only one whose attention the sound caught. Out of nowhere the security guards appeared again.

Ray was headed right for him now and so were the guards.

The car had barely stopped when the door was swung open.

"Get in!" Ray yelled foot already on the gas.

AC threw himself across the backseat, wincing when his head collided with the opposite door as Ray sharply turned.

Rubbing the spot he'd just bumped, he raised up to peer out of the back window.

The guards had given up chase. He exhaled closing his eyes.

Damn that was close.

"What all you get?"

At the sound of Deuce's voice his eyes snapped open.

"Yeah what you get?" Ray echoed.

Rage rushed through AC's body replacing the adrenaline. Forcing himself to calm down he yanked the hammer from his pants.

"What happened to you Ray? You wasn't where I told you to be."

"And Deuce where you run too?" He asked side eyeing him. When neither of the two responded the reality of their silence began to settle in.

Baffled, AC's head swiveled back and forth, "I can't believe this shit! You niggas was gone leave me?" The guilty looks on their face said it all.

"See what happened-" Ray began but was cut off by the sound of sirens. Trailing only a few cars behind them were three police cars.

AC mentally kicked himself at the sight. He should've known the guards wouldn't give up that easy. Instead they called in reinforcement. The heist was turning out to be one big fuck up. Starting with his decision to let Ray and Deuce in on his lick. He shook his head, wishing that he had listened to his gut earlier.

"What you get?" Ray asked again in a clipped tone. His eyes never once leaving the road.

Frowning at the man's audacity, especially after they had almost left him, AC leaned forward positioning his lips next to Ray's ear, "Don't fucking worry about it, just focus on getting us out of here."

Judging by Ray's quick intake of breath he had gotten the message…for now.

Loud horns blared as they pummeled through a red light with the police hot on their trail.

Sitting back, AC tried to think what his next move would be. His eyes rolled to the roof.

God if you get me out of this one, I promise not to fuck with these dummies no more, he silently prayed.

Peeping down his shirt he stared at the watches. There had to be at least ten of them. The payout would be nice if he ever made it downtown. Judging by the sounds of the sirens closing in around them, he wasn't so sure if he would.

Feeling as though someone was watching him, he glanced up to see Deuce staring at him in the rear-view mirror. The sneer on his face was hard to miss.

"You got a problem?" AC asked, gripping the hammer at his side. He had enough reasons to bash his head in. Biting his lips Deuce shifted his attention to Ray, whose face was fixed with determination as he steered right then left. Soon the sirens began to fade in the distance. Cutting through a neighborhood, Ray maneuvered the car into an alley. It was almost too much to hope that they had gotten away.

Ray turned around in his seat and left the car running.

"Listen if I was gone leave you would I have double backed to get you?" he asked.

At AC's blank stare he shot off another lame excuse, "I parked where I could get a clear view of you coming out."

AC called bullshit. The parking spot he had chosen had been perfect. Did Ray think he was a fool? Or that he couldn't see the greed in his eyes?

"You gone show us what you got or what?" asked Deuce, who was beginning to grow impatient.

Deciding to appease their curiosity, AC pulled out a watch and held it up letting the diamonds glisten in the suns light.

"How much we getting for that?" Deuce asked with dollar signs in his eyes.

AC bit the inside of his cheeks to keep his composure. There wasn't a *We*. Before he could break the news, the sound of sirens made him whip his head around.

"Damn I thought we lost em," Ray said panicking. Throwing the car in drive he sped down the alley. Out of nowhere a police car appeared, headed straight for them.

"Back up!" Deuce yelled.

Throwing the gear in reverse, Ray hit the gas as he wheeled the car out into traffic before shifting into drive.

"Shit!" AC yelled at the sight of six police cars headed their way.

His hand closed around the watch. *All that for nothing* he thought as Ray drove wildly through the street taking every sharp turn imaginable. At this point AC didn't know what was worse. Ray's driving or the jail time he was facing.

"Slow down before you kill us," he warned.

But the warning came a second too late. Just as the words left his mouth Ray lost control of the car sending them crashing headfirst into a light pole.

The force from the impact was so hard AC swore he heard his neck snap as his body was tossed to the other side like a rag doll. The ringing in his ears was deafening. He tried to collect his bearings as he watched steam rise from the damaged hood. Blinking his eyes to clear his vision, he tried to move but the sharp pain shooting up his side made him pause.

"Uugggh!" he gritted out.

After what felt like forever, he finally managed to drag his body up into a sitting position. In front of him Ray's body was slumped over the wheel as blood leaked from a deep gash in his head.

Is he dead? The second the thought occurred, Ray began to stir. In the passenger seat Deuce groaned as he began to regain conscious.

AC released a pent-up breath relieved that neither man was dead. Gazing through the smoke haze he realized the police still hadn't reached them yet, but he could hear the sirens. The dull ache in his head and the ringing in his ears made it hard to tell if they were far off or close by. He couldn't wait around to see. At this point it was every man for himself. He winced from the pain as he pried the door open.

Barely steady on his feet AC glanced over his shoulder just in time to see Deuce stumbling from the car. The man crashed into the ground face first. Unfazed by the sight, AC set his teeth against the pain as he forced his feet to move. Picking up the pace, his entire body felt on fire as he broke out into a run. Crushing through the broken glass that littered the alley, the mangled tree branches and the trash. It seemed like he had run for miles when the burning sensation in his chest forced him to slow down. Breathing hard he leaned over to catch his breath. When his heart rate returned to semi-normal and the chest pains eased, he stood to survey his surroundings. Still in the building stages the subdivision he'd wandered upon looked almost deserted. Only a few houses were complete and judging from the looks of the house in front of him the builders were adding a garage. The cement and gravel hadn't been laid yet. Thinking quick he removed the watches from his shirt.

Next, he pulled off his socks carefully wrapping the watches in them. Using his bare hands, he dug a hole in the dirt beside the garage and placed the sock inside it before raking the dirt back over the hole.

With the watches secure, AC finally sat down on the curb to collect his thoughts. His chest heaved as he breathed through his nose. In the back of his mind, he knew he would have to get up and move again but his body wouldn't budge. Rotating his bruised shoulder for relief, he touched his throbbing head. When he pulled back his hand and there was bright red blood on his fingers, he was surprised. He must have hit his head harder than he thought. His suspicions were confirmed when he stood and swooned on his feet. Steadying himself he breathed in deeply through his nose. With his eyes closed he waited for his head to stop spinning. Then he noticed something. Silence. He could no longer hear the sirens. Maybe they had found Ray and Deuce and given up the chase. When the spinning stopped his gaze landed on the row of houses. He had to figure out where in the hell he had landed. Mustering up the strength to move, he went in search of the nearest street sign. AC had taken less than five steps when two squad cars swarmed him.

"Down on your knees!" The police shouted, jumping from the car with their weapons drawn.

Squeezing his eyes shut, AC exhaled. He had been so close. His face grimaced as his knee hit the ground. His hands were handcuffed behind his back in a matter of seconds.

"Where's the jewelry?" The cop asked as the other one searched through the trash.

At his silence, the cop repeated his question, "Where's the jewelry you stole from Slavic?" he asked angrier this time. Inwardly AC cringed at the revelation that they knew he was the culprit. Briefly he thought back to when they were in the parking lot of the mall, when their chances of escape had seemed believable. The truth was the mission had been a bust the second he relied on someone else. But it was a learning experience for him just like all the others and he was close to perfecting his plan. For now, there was only one thing left to do.

"Y'all gone read me my rights?"

15 Minutes Away

Standing outside of the pale white building on Wilshire Boulevard and Rodeo Drive, Phatz caught his reflection in the Neiman Marcus store window. He was flyer than the mannequins on display, in his white and red Ellesse sweatsuit and all white Reeboks. While the Turkish gold rope around his neck looked heavy with its diamonds, it was light as a feather, but it made a loud statement. Fresh out of California Youth Authority after six months, he hadn't missed a beat. Gently touching his permed hair, he made a mental note to go see Marshall this week for a touch up. Shedding the jacket to his sweatsuit he casually tossed it over his arm as he glanced around at the bustling traffic at the intersection and the thickening crowd.

Beverly Hills was the heart of the money. Another world full of glitz and glamour that would promise you everything you ever wanted. Most times the price turned out to be more than people bargained for.

He laughed to himself as he watched tourists clamor up the block with polaroid cameras around their necks and sun visors, hoping to run into a celebrity.

They were easy marks. Too easy. He knew it would be worthless to go after them. Phatz was looking to cash in on the big fish. He needed to get back on his feet and quick. His eyes roamed to the gold Neiman Marcus sign in the window.

Big Fish.

Just thinking about it made his pulse skip a beat. No matter how many times he hit a lick it always felt like his first. And just like a virgin who couldn't shake their first love Phatz couldn't shake his. He was in love with the hustle, the thrill of the game, and no matter the consequences he didn't plan on stopping any time soon. Absentmindedly his fingers brushed across the small scar on his arm transporting him back in time to where he had learned his first valuable lesson in the game.

"Seven!" The teenage boy called out as the red and white dice came to a slow roll on the concrete sidewalk. He didn't realize he was holding his breath until four white dots appeared on one dice and three dots on the other. He exhaled slowly as his eyes darted to the two men standing with deep frowns on their faces. At fifteen, Phatz could spot a mark a mile away and after breakin' up a dice game at school that day, he had cut class, on the hunt to make more money. It wasn't long before he stumbled upon a game being played in his neighborhood in Baldwin Hills also known as the Jungle.

"What it hit for?" he had asked in a deep voice when he approached them in front of the apartments on August and CoCo Street. They had taken one look at the ceno's he pulled out of his pocket and jumped headfirst at the chance to beat the youngin' out of his money. It was obvious they had taken him for an easy mark, never realizing that they were the ones that had been marked. Now as the reality of their mistake began to set in, he could see the regret in their gaze.
Yea, fo- tray trigger make my bankroll bigger he thought to himself, cradling the stack of money growing in his hand.
Feeling as if he were on a lucky streak, he decided to squeeze the game for all it was worth. Peeling off two ceno's Phatz tossed them on top of the cash already on the ground in the alley where they played.
"Fade that," he challenged.
The two men shared a look.
"You sure you wanna keep playing, you been pretty lucky so far don't crap out," the man who had introduced himself as Larry joked with a twisted smirk. Standing a little over six feet, Larry was brown skinned and skinny with a low haircut. Phatz had seen him around the neighborhood a lot with the older guys. Always loud.
Dismissing his taunts Phatz turned his stare to Larry's partner Tee, who had been silently watching him. He was the exact opposite. Dark skinned and short, for the most part Tee hadn't said much. Phatz knew that they both were trying to save face. Neither of them would admit that they were losing to a teenager.
"You in or what?"
Tilting his head to the side Tee pretended to think it over. With a stiff nod, he accepted Phatz challenge.
Forty minutes and three rolls later he had broken up another crap game. Phatz hid his smile as he claimed the $600 prize. This time he had been more than lucky. Already he knew that he would hit up the tailor shop B.Black and Son on Seventh and Los Angeles for new material for a couple of two piece tailored suits to add to his growing collection. While most teens his age were wearing faded ash jeans with the Kangol bucket hats, imitating the latest hip hop fashion, Phatz was stepping out suited and booted in custom suits letting people know he meant business. Today his dress code had been a little more relaxed, dressed in a pair of Tommy Hilfiger pants with the shirt to match, he was in hustler mode. Phatz was considering stuffing the money in his K-Swiss shoes when a strange feeling washed over him. Looking up he noticed that the two men had wandered a few inches away

from him. With their heads lowered, he couldn't hear their hushed whispers but immediately knew something was off. That and the envious look on Larry's face let him know that it was time for him to roll. Tucking the money in his pockets he spun on his heels, headed towards the front of the apartments.

He was halfway to the stairs when Larry's voice stopped him, "Nigga give me my money back you cheated!"

He hadn't gotten out of sight fast enough. Letting his eyes drift shut for a brief second, he turned towards his accuser.

"The doctors said take medicine, not my money!" he yelled poking his chest out. The statement drew a look of confusion from them. As they pondered his words, he clutched the pair of dice in one hand while slipping the other hand into his pocket. Relief coursed through his body at the feel of the pocketknife. Gripping it tightly he stared at the two men in front of him. Phatz had learned a long time ago that not everyone was ok with losing. Purchasing the knife from a school friend had been his way of making sure that win or lose, he was covered.

"Lil nigga you heard what I said," Larry said taking a threatening step towards him. Fast as lightning he shoved Phatz sending him stumbling a few steps back. Whipping the knife out of his pocket, Phatz pressed one button releasing the long shiny blade. Keeping it at his side, he planted his feet flat, prepared for the next blow.

"You cheated."

"No, y'all lost, fair and square."

The answer only infuriated the man more. Mistaking his lack of action for fear, Larry lunged at him. Swinging the knife through the air, Phatz aimed for Larry's neck. A second earlier and he would've hit his target, but the man brought his hand up defensively.

"Aaah!" he screamed as the blade sliced through his skin sending blood oozing down his arm.

"This lil nigga stabbed me!"

Phatz watched Larry's expression morph from shock to fury as his heart pounded. He had two choices. Either he could run for it or he could stay and fight. Phatz had never been scared even when he was outnumbered. Decision made he gripped the knife tighter in his sweaty palm.

"Use this!" Tee called out, tossing a two by four in his direction. The board landed with a thud at Larry's feet.

"Yeah, we gon' even this out," he said before snatching it up. Rearing back Phatz dodged the first swing, but he wasn't so lucky with the second. Instinctively, his arm flew to his face when he realized where Larry was aiming. The wood came crashing down on his arm sending the knife flying from his hand. Phatz howled out in pain as he cradled his arm to his chest.

He barely had time to process the pain when another blow rained down on his other arm. The sound of bone meeting wood echoed loudly through the air. Phatz knew that something was broken. Blinding pain vibrated through his body causing him to stumble. Through slit eyes he could see the sick smile on Larry's face as Tee egged him on again. If he didn't strike back, they might beat him to death.

When Larry pulled his arm back to swing again, Phatz dug his feet in the ground preparing to charge at him with full force, but the telltale sound of a click, followed by a loud booming voice made him pause.

"Leave that boy alone!"

Looking up his gaze traveled to a big, tall man standing on his balcony aiming a .45 at Larry and Tee. It was Big Walt.

"Big Walt, man this lil nigga cheated us," Tee complained.
"Yeah he gotta give us our money back," Larry followed up.
Gun still aimed, Big Walt looked down at Phatz.
"Come on up here."
Body still racked with pain Phatz moved his feet, while keeping his eyes steadily trained on Larry and Tee who stood with their mouths wide open. By the time Phatz made it up the steps he was sweating.
Waving his gun at them Big Walt jutted his double chin out.
"Get the fuck outta here." Phatz watched in relief as the two men slunk away, mumbling under their breath.
"You aight lil man?" Big Walt asked. Before Phatz could respond, Big Walt waved him inside of his apartment.
"Come in here and let me fix your lil bad ass up."
Hesitant at first Phatz took small steps as he tried not to crumble at the pain shooting through both of his arms. Big Walt was well known in the jungle. In his late forties, well over three hundred pounds, the hustler was the epitome of his name. Phatz followed him inside of his neat apartment where he led him to the small kitchen.
"Sit down right there," he motioned.
When he realized Phatz would need help with the chair he pulled it out for him. Spent, Phatz flopped down, vaguely aware of the delicious scent wafting from the pots on the stove.
"Anne!" Big Walt yelled out seconds before a small white woman with long blonde hair appeared in the entrance.
Her brown eyes landed on Phatz before she moved to the stove. Without a word she left and returned with arm full of bandages, gauze, and alcohol.
She offered him a small smile as she sat in front of him.
"Let me see baby," she cooed.
Phatz winced when her hands landed on his skin.
Puckering up her plump lips she clicked her tongue. After inspecting both arms she gave him a small pat.
"No broken bones, but a small fracture in your right arm, I'll clean up the blood and get you all fixed up." She handled him with care. First cleansing his bruised skin with a hot wet towel, then applying alcohol to the scrapes caused by the wood. Phatz endured through the pain. His eyes fixed on her small nipples pressing through the thin shirt. When she caught him looking she winked. Thirty minutes later both arms were wrapped and bandaged up.
"You can stay and eat if you like," Anne said as she cleaned everything off the table.
Politely declining, Phatz stood up but was stopped by Big Walt entering the kitchen.
"Sit down lil man let me wake yo game up," he said.
Taking a seat opposite from him he waited until Anne was gone to talk.
"I knew when I saw you go into the alley with them niggas that it was gone be some trouble." He leaned back laughing.
Surprised that he had been watching him Phatz opened his mouth to thank him, but Big Walt shook his head as his face grew serious.
Removing the gun from his waist he placed it on the table.
"If you gon' be out here hustling you need something bigger than a knife. Get you one of these and you won't have those problems," his dark eyes peered into his own.

Phatz looked at the gun. His mouth was suddenly dry. He knew Big Walt's' words were true, but naively he had thought that the knife would protect him. He knew better now. A look of understanding passed between them. By the time Phatz left Big Walt's apartment, the streetlights had come on. Scurrying down the steps his head swung back and forth, weary of Larry and Tee jumping out on him as he moved through the streets. When he made it home in one piece he headed straight to his bedroom. Inside he removed the $600 from his pocket wincing at the pain the tiny movement caused. Spreading the money on his bed, he stood back, a smile playing on his face, it disappeared just as quickly when he glanced down at his bandaged arms.

Big Walt's last words echoed in his mind.

"The tailor suits can wait, I'm getting me a strap," he declared aloud. That would be the last beating he ever took he silently vowed. Today he had gotten his first taste of the thing they called the game and to him it wasn't a game at all. They had tested his gangsta but next time he would be better prepared.

'Til this day he could still hear Big Walts' voice crystal clear, but that was a different time and a different game. In this one all he needed was his wits, a hammer, a pillowcase and voila, magic!

Looking down at the Concord watch on his arm he saw that both the minute and the hour hand were on the twelve. It was almost time.

Lifting his head, he was caught off guard by the woman heading in his direction as he passed Saks Fifth Avenue. She was a dead ringer for the famous singer Deniece Williams. It was only last week that she had sung *Free* to a room full of criminals at his YA graduation. He didn't know if it was because of her song or the fact that he was awarded most improved prisoner of the year, that he was released on probation three days later. Whatever the case, he was happy to be free.

Almost face to face with the woman now they locked eyes. Phatz winked, earning a bright lip stick smile. Her face said Deniece Williams but the tight spandex pants she wore with the low-cut shirt revealing her ripe titties screamed Pam Grier, the actress most known for her role as *Foxy Brown*.

He could tell by the look on her face that she was interested. And who wouldn't be. At nineteen, Phatz had the face of a pretty boy with his clear brown skin and deep brown eyes. Though averaged height with a stocky frame he was never short of women companions.

Maybe another time he thought to himself as he made his way around to the back of Neiman Marcus where the cars were valet parked.

The greeter dressed in a stuffy suit, smiled tightly as he opened the door for him.

Inside he inhaled the sweet scent of perfume that lingered in the air.

Exhaling deeply, he glanced down at the marbled wax floor. The chandelier's reflection above his head shined brightly.

With it being lunch time, the store lacked its normal crowd of customers, only a few browsed through the high-end shopping store.

Making his way to the front, Phatz waited patiently for the salesclerk to ring up the customer in front of him. He tapped his foot along to the elevator music coming over the intercom while discreetly scanning the cases of watches.

Zeroing in on the Rolexes he quickly dismissed them knowing that they wouldn't sell for much. Moving a little further, he stopped when his eyes landed on the Omega watches.

Bingo.

Mentally adding up the value of the watches, Phatz began to grow excited at the thought of cashing out big.

Hello sir, how can I help you today?" A voice asked interrupting his thoughts. Making eye contact with the salesclerk Phatz watched a smile flash across her face as she rounded the counter.

Noticing the direction of his stare she tilted her head. "Ah I see you're interested in our new pieces, would you like a closer look?"

Nodding, he folded his arms across his chest. Just as he'd expected, the movement brought attention to his wrist.

Her pale green eyes lit up. "That's a nice Concord you have there, we have a few of our own."

Behind the counter she removed the watches from the case, starting with the Rolexes. Feigning interest Phatz nodded on cue as she gave a detailed description of each one, including their value; something he already knew. When a customer appeared at the register, she paused her presentation and motioned in their direction.

"Excuse me for a moment while I go help them, feel free to look around some more and call me when you've made your decision," she said before returning the watches to its cases and shuffling off.

Little did she know Phatz had already made his decision. Grabbing the pager at his waist he noticed all fives flash across the screen. In his head he began the mental countdown for the things he knew were soon to come. Seconds later the clerk whose nametag read Mandy was back with a cheery smile. She pushed her blonde hair behind her ear revealing a glistening pair of diamond earrings.

"See anything you like yet?" she asked.

Playing into her sales pitch he pointed at the Omega watch.

"That one right there."

While she busied herself retrieving it for him, Phatz stole a glance at the clock on the wall. Less than thirty seconds until show time.

"Here it is," Mandy said proudly setting the Omega in front of him.

Tapping a finger against his chin Phatz pretended to mule over his decision.

"I really should check with my girlfriend about this, she's across the street in the Saks 5th store. I would hate to make a purchase without her."

"You know how you women get," he added when she raised her eyebrows in question.

"How about this? I'll head over there and as soon as she's done running up my credit card, I'll be right back over here to get that," he said pointing at the Omega.

Mandy's pasted smile waned a bit.

"I might even grab another Concord." His last statement seemed to settle her. With a jerk of her head, Mandy returned to the register as he headed for the door.

Phatz was reaching for the metal handle when he heard the telltale sound of glass breaking followed by loud screams.

Right on time.

A wide smile settled across his face. Through the reflection in the glass, he watched Sly and Master Blaster crack the side of the case just like he had instructed them to. He had seen the men enter the store seconds ago.

The remaining customers scrambled to get out of the way of danger.

Poor little Mandy stood frozen at the register. All the blood had drained from her face. Her green eyes blinked rapidly as if the image in front of her would go away.

It wouldn't. Case by case. The men slung the hammer expertly shoving the watches into pillowcases held open by a clothes hanger.

When Phatz had seen all that he needed to see he scurried out of the front door and back around the building. Jumping the small brick wall, he strolled through the apartments that were right behind the store. Earlier he had parked a stolen black Cadillac in the apartment parking lot for Sly and Master Blaster.

He continued to walk until he was a block away where his own car was parked. Hopping in, he checked the rearview mirror, watching for any signs of the police, but it was unlikely that he would see any. Phatz had done his homework. For days he had scoped out the scene noting that during lunch time the cops were more focused on the traffic and the crowd stomping through the hills, than what was going on inside the stores. The information helped him plan exactly when they needed to strike. Still when he realized Sly and Master Blaster were running three minutes behind schedule he began to worry. Drumming his fingers against the steering wheel he tried to remain calm as the minutes continued to tick off. When the five-minute mark passed, he turned the key in his switch.

"Fuck this, "he said out loud.

Just as the engine roared to life, the Cadillac driven by Master Blaster came speeding down the street in haste.

"Let's roll!" Phatz shouted, stomping on the accelerator. Making a sharp U-turn, he followed their lead as he trailed them south towards Pico Boulevard. Unwilling to let his guards down just yet, Phatz kept his eyes glued on the rear-view mirror to make sure the cops weren't behind them.

He didn't relax his grip on the wheel until he saw the familiar blue and white street signs that marked their entrance into L.A. A few blocks later he maneuvered his car into the Fat Burgers on San Vicente and La Cienega Boulevard, stopping long enough for Sly and Master Blaster to jump in the back seat.

He drove around aimlessly before crossing over into the west side.

"Y'all can get up now," Phatz said when he was sure they weren't being followed.

"Bout time," Sly the taller of the two mumbled, stretching his long frame.

"How we do?" Phatz asked gaze still trained on the traffic in front of him.

"Damn good except the last case didn't break man I tried every fucking thing," Master Blaster complained.

Phatz wasn't worried about that, he was proud of how they handled everything. They swung the hammers like they were born to do it. Besides he had already peeped that the case was plexiglass. It would take more than a hammer to break it.

Sly placed the pillowcase in the front seat next to him. Phatz smiled as he counted out seven watches. Four of them were Omegas, the other Concord and Cartier. The rest were solid gold unisex Rolexes. His big fish plan had panned out. He knew Neiman Marcus would be the perfect store to hit. The way Phatz saw it was either he would go back to jail trying to get money or he would walk out with the money. He was glad for the latter.

Neither of the men questioned him when he dropped them off on August Street in the Jungle and promised to return with their cut. They knew he was a standup guy. True to his word Phatz returned two hours later from the jewelry mart downtown with their share. His jeweler Zac had given him a good deal.

Shaking his head as he drove Phatz looked at the crisp bills in the rubber bands in the seat next to him. He couldn't believe everything had worked out so smoothly. His first week out had been a success but there would be more to come. Plenty more.

2 weeks later

The loud slamming of the gavel snapped AC out of his dreamy state. The judge had just dismissed the charges against him due to insufficient evidence since they couldn't find the watches. He was relived on the inside, but on the outside his stoic frame never changed as the guard led him down the hall to be processed out.

AC had spent the last two weeks in juvenile detention thinking of all the things he could have done different. Ray and Deuce popped in his mind. This set back had taught him a valuable lesson. No matter what happened from now on he was doing things solo.

When the guard handed him the clear sack, he wasted no time shedding the khaki jumpsuit. Happy to be back in his own clothes, AC tucked the brown paper sack containing the rest of his items under his arm. His knee bounced impatiently as he waited for all his paperwork to be processed. Glancing down at his jeans he noticed the bottom was caked in mud. A small smile spread across his face but disappeared when he saw his public defender approaching. The man wore a navy-blue suit two sizes too big with scuffed black shoes. He looked tired as he ran his hand through his brown hair. Green eyes like his own peered at him from behind a pair of wire framed glasses. AC racked his brain trying to remember his name. Finally, he recalled the man saying it was George.

George cleared his throat, "Well that's it," he said confidently sticking his hand out for him to shake.

AC ignored it, remembering during their first meeting George had urged him to take a plea deal for less time. He had ignored his legal advice and kept his mouth shut. Snitching was against everything he stood for.

After realizing he wasn't going to shake his hand George handed him a stack of papers, "Stay out of trouble you were lucky this time kid," he stated before sulking off.

Fuck you AC wanted to shout after him. Luck had never been on his side. He knew the public defender didn't care if he rotted in jail or not. He was just another name in the system to him.

When he saw his Aunt Twinkle approaching, he grabbed his things. Because he was still a minor he had to be released into her custody.

She greeted him with a hug.

"Your mom was working," she explained rifling through her purse.

He nodded halfheartedly. That was always the case.

Keys in hand the two strolled out the doors of the Santa Monica courthouse. Though he was thankful his aunt had shown up, AC already had plans.

"Aunt, I got a few things to take care of. I can handle it from here," he said once they were in the parking lot. He could tell from her uniform that she was headed to her job at Kaiser Hospital.

She gave him a knowing look. "Ok but you stay out of trouble," she said repeating the lawyer's words from earlier.

"Do you need anything?"

Shaking his head, he leaned down to kiss her cheek before sending her off with a wave. Mind set on one thing; AC struck off in the opposite direction. He didn't stop until he reached the payphone where he quickly retrieved a few loose coins from the brown paper bag in his hands.

Punching in the numbers he glanced up and down the block while he waited.

"Fat Rat," AC called out when the man answered.

"Who the fuck is this?" the voice responded groggily.

AC laughed, "Nigga who you think it is?"

Recognition caught on in Fat Rat's voice, "Clyde young nigga what's up I thought they had you locked away for good nigga."

"You know they can't keep a real nigga down," AC responded not bothered by the use of his government name.

They exchanged a few more jibs before AC got to the point "I need you to come scoop me up off of Fourth and Main in Santa Monica."

He heard the hesitancy in Fat Rats' voice. "Shit man its 8:00 in the morning," he complained.

"Yeah I know but I got a lil business to handle."

A few beats passed.

"Yea aight," Fat Rat responded.

Thirty minutes later Fat Rat pulled up in his candy apple red Regal. Climbing in the passenger side he pounded the mans outstretched fist.

"Where to?" he asked guiding the car into the early morning traffic.

"Going to get this buried treasure," AC responded leaning back in the seat. The comical expression on Fat Rat's face made him laugh. The way he saw it Ray and Deuce had forfeited their share the minute they left without him. Ultimately, he was the only one that had to face the consequences. Both had managed to slip through the system while he fought for his freedom. The payout from the watches would be compensation for his pain and suffering.

His smile widened. Doing things solo was already beginning to pay off.

****

      Summertime was approaching in L.A. and that meant half naked honeys strutting around in booty shorts and tank tops, showing nothing but skin. Nicknamed the City of Angels, it was anything but especially when the seasons changed. The weather had a way of bringing out the worst in people. To cool off, crowds flocked to Venice Beach to splash around in the teal and blue water or lounge on the white-hot sand. But the real fun wouldn't kick off until later that night on Crenshaw and King Boulevard where colorful rag top convertibles crept along the famous strip leaving the audience mesmerized by the shiny expensive cars being manned by some of the biggest players in the game. Low riding was a California tradition with its own language that only those from the West Coast could speak. And the most understood message was the bigger the grind the brighter the shine. It was Phatz first thought when he purchased his candy red 1971 Glasshouse ragtop with white interior. The car was one of a kind with its front to back side to side hydraulics ---low riding was pointless without it .Two fifteen-inch speakers for the bass were in the trunk, while the front was customized with six infinity speakers. If the car didn't get their attention the sounds coming from it would. His hard labor was paying off big time. Since his release he and a small crew of thieves had cracked over twenty cases in jewelry stores. His money was piling up and he figured now was the time to send a message to those watching. And from the looks of envy he had gotten the first time he cruised down Crenshaw in the ragtop, they had gotten it loud and clear. Phatz was claiming his spot in the game and daring anyone to get in his way.

****

By the time he pulled into the long driveway on 43rd and St. Andrews Street the sun had turned the sky into a mural of colors reminding him of orange sorbet and pink cotton candy as it eased below the horizon. Using the remaining sunlight to survey his surroundings he cast a glance at the neat one-story houses with manicured lawns on each side of the street. It was a typical day in the neighborhood as the kids played hopscotch on the sidewalk while the music teacher quietly observed them from her porch, chiming in to help when they messed up. Next door was the Asian man watering his grass while his wife moseyed around in their home-grown garden. The upper middle-class neighborhood was home to decent hardworking families who tried hard to keep the evil outside. Which was why almost every house on the block had bars on the windows. Well almost all—the gray and white house that he was raised in was void of the steel bars. An observation he had made at an early age. When Phatz questioned his uncle Kenny the man had smiled before replying in a serious tone

"Don't ever let no one make you feel like a prisoner in yo own shit." Years later the window and doors remained bare. And yet everyone in it was safe and would remain so as long as he had a say in it. Phatz would give his all to protect the ones he loved. Especially the woman who raised him and his siblings. His great grandmother Mother Dear as they called her. He couldn't recall a time when she wasn't waiting with a mouth full of wisdom and outstretched arms full of love for them. She had taken three babies in well after she was done rearing her own without one complaint. He could never repay her, but he would try his hardest. It was his job to get her anything she wanted starting with the box of Church's Chicken sitting neatly in a paper bag on the floor of the car. He could smell the scent of the crisp chicken coming through the box. Right beside it was a separate container with corn on the cob dipped in butter and the flaky apple pies the franchise were known for. It was Mother Dears' favorite. Picking the items up off the floor careful not to spill anything, Phatz opened the car door. The streetlight came on just as his feet touched the concrete sending the children playing scattering like roaches to their homes. He smiled remembering all the times he had done the same. With the food tucked safely under his arms he jotted past the blooming apple tree in the front yard and up the steps. Before he could open the door good it was flung open. Mother Dears' smiling face greeted him.

"I smelled you coming," she joked.

Moving inside the house Phatz placed the food on the large table in the dining room before embracing his grandmother in a loving hug. She laughed when he began to rain kisses down on her face. Even though she was eighty-five she didn't look at a day over sixty with her shiny brown soft skin and gray hair.

"You got my apple pies, right?" she asked pulling away from his embrace to open the container.

"That's right."

Phatz noticed the TV in the living room tuned in to an old black and white cowboys' movie. "We might have to hand him his hat," the cowboy's voice came through the television.

"Mother Dear what are you watching?" he asked pulling out her chair.

"My western," she stated before sitting down. Rummaging in the Church's bag she dug out the fresh baked apple pies. Phatz used the distraction to reach into his pocket and remove the manila envelope in it. Placing it firmly on the table he waited for her to notice it.

When her gaze finally landed on it, she paused. Desert forgotten Mother Dear picked the heavy envelope up, breaking the seal she peeked inside.

Phatz watched her eyes bulge behind her glasses.

Without a word he walked to the kitchen. Retrieving a glass from the cupboard he opened the freezer for some ice. In the background he could hear the cowboy's guns going off.

"I wanna ask you something?" Mother Dear said from behind him.

Phatz hadn't heard her approach he was too busy listening to the TV.

Facing her now he watched a worried look come over her brown face as she leaned against the countertop. Folding her arms, she pinned him with a stare, "Are you robbing banks?"

The glass in his hand almost slipped at the question. Tightening his grip on it he stared back at his great grandmother. *Robbing Banks.* Before answering her question, he gave serious thought to it. Honestly, he would if he was positive that he could get away with it, but there were too many factors to consider. Too many risks.

Still he couldn't stop the laughter that spilled from his lips. "Banks Mother Dear really?" he asked incredulously.

The laughter died when he noticed her stern expression. Placing the glass on the counter he lightly gripped her shoulders. "No, I'm not robbing banks," he answered truthfully.

Relief washed over her face. Resting her hand against his cheek Mother Dear sighed, "Good, but that's a lot of money you got. From now on you need to take it to Be Be's house we got too much here."

The manila envelope had over $20,000 in it. After picking off the money from the licks he hit, Phatz made sure to bring Mother Dear the rest which was always more than he had spent. But she was right, it was time to look for another holding spot for his cash. If he had to guess there was over $200,000 stashed away in the house. Not including the jewelry. Taking the money over his aunt Be Be's house around the corner didn't seem like a bad idea.

He kissed her cheek. "You're right, I'll start making my drop offs there."

"Good, she's expecting you," she tossed over her shoulder as she went to her seat.

Joining her at the table, he thought about how Mother Dear was always looking out for him. Always thinking ahead. He credited her for shaping his mind.

Sitting across from her he watched her bite into the crispy chicken. A loud explosion came from the TV as he grabbed a piece of corn.

"Aw man I missed it," he complained.

Wiping her hand on the napkin she shook her head, "You didn't miss anything he just got his hat handed to him."

Phatz doubled over with laughter. That night dining on Church's Chicken with his great grandmother all seemed right in his world. He had no idea that the summer of 83' would be one to remember.

(43rd & St. Andrews)

****

The strong scent of lye clung in the air at Marshalls barbershop as Phatz sat in the chair getting his hair combed for the third time that week. A weekly routine that had begun when he was fifteen. At the sound of the loud applause he dragged his eyes away from the television mounted on the wall to the growing crowd to his left. Someone was on a winning streak. It wasn't unusual for them to shoot craps at the shop. Marshalls was a safe haven where all the young criminals hung from drug dealers to hustlers. If you wanted to get in on the action or make some money Marshalls was the place to be. Marshall was a slick talking hustler himself so there was always something going on in the shop.

Like now a man was taking bets on the Rams game that would take place next week at the coliseum around the corner. He stood in front of Phatz trying to reel him in.

"Man, I know you got some money, look at that fly ass shit you got on."

Dressed in a Polo outfit, a pair of Nikes, sporting a Cartier watch, Phatz knew he looked like money, but he wasn't interested in participating in the bets so he declined and watched the man move along trying to hustle the next customer.

The bell over the door pinged pulling his attention to the tall young cat that strolled in and joined the dice game. Phatz had seen him around the shop a lot with the other young guys who should have been in school, instead they were hustling up on a buck and he couldn't blame them.

"Almost done," Marshall commented as he added the finishing touches to his finger waves.

The pager on his hip buzzed. When he saw the code, he smiled. It was Silky, a girl he'd met a few months ago after jumping in a fight for her. Phatz had no idea what the drama was about. All he saw was a small waist, cute face damsel in distress and he couldn't stop himself. The two hit it off pretty good and had been hanging tight ever since. He made a mental note to give her a call as he slipped the pager in his pocket. He was contemplating how he would kill time until later when heated words reached his ears.

"These niggas don't want no money."

Turning towards the voice, Phatz noticed it was the young cat from earlier. Assuming that he had lost in the dice game he watched him pace the floor angrily.

"Shit this nigga right here go get money every day," Marshall responded as he unsnapped the protective cape from around Phatz shoulders.

Checking out the neat finger waves in the mirror Phatz took the opportunity to size the young cat up and had to admit that he had style. The black Fila corduroys with the short sleeve Fila shirt and black suede Pumas was an outfit he could see himself rocking.

"Is that right?"

His light-colored eyes narrowed as he stopped pacing. Marshall's words had gotten his attention. Swiveling around in the chair to face him, Phatz folded his hand across his midsection revealing the Omega watch on his wrist.

"Yea that's right," he said confidently as they stared each other down. It was the young cat who broke eye contact first.

"We can get money today then," he stated in a matter of fact tone.

"Soon as I finish my business with Marshall," Phatz responded, rising to the challenge he saw in his stare.

A boyish grin came across his face as he stepped up. "They call me Awful Clyde, AC for short, I'll be outside," he said before walking out the door.

Phatz stared after him amused.

Awful Clyde.

It was one hell of a name. He hoped he lived up to it. But then again, he knew that if Marshall recommended him, he had to be serious about getting money. It was all he cared about.

****

Outside AC leaned up against the wall. This wasn't his first time seeing the well-dressed guy in Marshall's chair. In fact, they seemed to always be at the shop around the same time. Yet it never occurred to him that he was a hustler. Even though Marshalls was considered the den of thieves, AC had learned that everybody that talked it couldn't necessarily walk it. Since his release his solo act had been going good, but he noticed that he spent most of his time being the lookout than he did bashing the cases. It was slowing him down, causing him to miss easy money. So maybe it was time to give this partner thing another try he reasoned. Afterall four hands were better than two.

****

A few minutes later Phatz walked out the shop to find AC leaning up against the building. The wheels had already begun to spin in his head. He realized he had yet to introduce himself.

"I'm Phatz," he said sticking out his fist." He watched the smirk on AC's face before the man pounded his fist.

"Where you from?" Phatz asked.

"The 30's Fruit Town side," AC responded easily.

Oh, it was on. Phatz knew that the niggas from both sides of the 30's were always bout' it.

He was just about to lay out the plan to AC when he heard his name being called.

Spinning around he watched a two-bit hustler named Cheetum approach them. He and Cheetum went way back. Grew up around the corner from each other. But when the hardcore drugs hit the streets of L.A. it took a lot of his childhood friends like Cheetum with it. The man was barely recognizable now. His collar bone protruded from beneath the loose fit shirt, eyes sunken in his head, Phatz could see the bleakness in his stare as he closed in on them.

"Aye I overheard y'all in there and I'm tryna get down."

Inwardly he cringed as he wondered who else had heard the two men make plans. He was just about to refuse Cheetums offer when AC cut in.

"Shit we good playa," AC said, stepping up to him menacingly.

And they were except they were missing one important thing. While Phatz liked AC's check game, he was beginning to think that Cheetum could be of use to them.

"Yo sister still got that lil Camaro?" he asked as the final pieces began to come together in his head. The man had made himself a pawn and Phatz was going to play him like one.

Cheetum nodded eagerly.

Ignoring the questionable look AC was giving him he turned towards Cheetum. "Go get the car from her and meet us at ya mom's crib in about ten minutes."

The words were barely out of his mouth before Cheetum took off in a dash.

Phatz shook his head. Nothing appealed more to a dope fiend then an opportunity to get their next high.

If the cloudy expression on AC's face wasn't indication enough that he wasn't cool with what Phatz had just done his next words clearly were.

"What eva go down today he ain't getting shit from me."

Phatz laughed.

It was exactly what he would have said had the roles been reversed.

****

A sense of déjà vu overcame AC as he sat in the backseat of the car. This time he was at Sherman Oaks Mall off Riverside and Woodman. And instead of two dummies in the front seat one was a crackhead and the other a hustler. He honestly didn't know how things would turn out for them, but he was determined to walk away with some money.

"You hold this."

Phatz handed him the hammer over the seat.

"And be careful with it, it belongs to my great grandmother it's been in our family for over seventy years."

AC looked down at the wooden hammer with its smooth ridges. The metal head was shiny and unscratched. For a hammer that had been around for seventy years it sure didn't look like anyone had put it to good use.

He smiled. That would change today.

When they finally exited the car, his head swiveled around in alarm at the sound of Cheetum driving off.

"Where the fuck he going?"

Past experiences had taught AC not to trust the driver, especially one that snorted powder.

"Relax, I told him to park east on Riverside that way when we jump in, we can take the 101 south freeway back to L.A.," Phatz answered.

Hiding his relief, he nodded. He wouldn't admit it, but he was already impressed with Phatz preparedness.

Inside the mall the men split up. With the hammer at his waist, AC browsed around the stores like a normal shopper. When he reached the jewelry store located at the far end of the mall, he glanced over his shoulder to see Phatz paying for a pretzel at the refreshment stand. When their gazes clashed Phatz gave him a subtle nod. It was showtime.

The familiar rush of adrenaline began to settle into his veins when he spied the glistening Baume and Mercier watches inside the cases. Encrypted in diamonds with a gold band, dollar signs flashed in his mind. Sticking to the script, Phatz entered only seconds later, stopping to browse their wide collection of cologne.

Meanwhile the money bag in AC's head grew larger as he scanned over the inventory. At the sound of the clerk's voice his head popped up. She shook her brunette hair before erupting in laughter at something Phatz said as he stood at the register. From where AC stood, he could see her cheeks turn a rosy red. He was flirting with her.

Averting his gaze, AC pretended to study the watches, while Phatz made his purchase. Out of the corner of his eye he tracked Phatz movement. Cologne in hand only inches away from him Phatz spoke loud enough for him to hear as he breezed by.

"Now!"

Snatching the hammer out his pants, AC gripped it tightly before slamming it into the glass case.

Pow!

The impact of the hammer hitting the glass sounded like a loud gunshot. Behind him voices screamed loudly as the horror of what was happening began to set in. But in front of him the glass case didn't have so much as a scratch on it. Blinking away his confusion, AC went in for the second time.

Pow!

In the reflection of the case he watched his lips turn downward into a frown.

Maybe I'm not hitting it hard enough he thought.

Tightening both hands around the hammer he brought it down again.

Pow! Pow!

"What the fuck?"

AC couldn't believe his eyes. It was still intact. A fresh wave of anger surged through him as he gritted his teeth.

"Break!" he yelled as he hit the case repeatedly. His arms began to burn as he pounded away. Finally exhausted his chest heaved up and down as he stood in disbelief. Glancing down at his hands he saw the angry red marks on his fingers caused from gripping the hammer so hard, but he couldn't give up.

Hit it once more a voice in his head told him as beads of sweat began to gather on his forehead.

You got this he hyped himself raising the hammer over his head prepared to go at it again. Mid strike he was interrupted by someone grabbing him from behind. "Come on, let's go!"

It was Phatz.

Snatching away from him, AC hit the case with so much force the hammer head popped off.

"Shit!" He felt like he could explode. First the glass wouldn't break and now the hammer was broken. In all his years of hitting licks this had never happened to him. The store was empty now as all the occupants had fled. A strange sense of failure roiled through him. AC no longer cared about getting caught. He had to break that case. Using the end part of the hammer he began to beat on the case until Phatz pulled him away.

"Security coming, man we gotta go."

Resisting the urge to hurl one of the tall flowerpots through the case AC reluctantly turned away. Stuffing what was left of the hammer into his pants he and Phatz fled through the same doors they had come through, security fresh on their heels.

A part of him was relieved when he saw Cheetum waiting for them. The other part was downright angry.

"Go!" Phatz yelled at Cheetum as he pressed the gas burning rubber out of the parking lot.

AC was in a daze as Cheetum drove. He had the money right there in his hands. Never had he walked away from a lick empty handed.

In the front seat Phatz argued with Cheetum.

"Calm the fuck down before you draw attention to us! Why the fuck you driving crazy like the police chasing us anyways?"

AC was so caught up in his disappointment he hadn't realized that they weren't being chased. In fact, there wasn't a police car in sight, security had given up chase back at the mall. Maybe they knew they didn't get anything either. He sighed. Then there was the matter of the broken hammer. Lifting his head up he struggled with his next words.

"Hey Phatz, my bad about your great grandmother's hammer man I-," He stopped himself from going any further.

The tension in the car was thick as they lapsed into silence.

"Shit fuck this we gotta do something," AC stated determinedly.

Phatz turned to face him, "Do what? Nigga you broke the hammer and I'm not tryna use no weapon unless I'm catching a body ya feel me?"

"How was I supposed to know the hammer was gone break? Shit if you had let me keep at it, I would've got that shit!" AC answered defensively.

"Naw lil nigga you wouldn't have, trust me not the way you were hitting it. It was plexiglass. It's only one way to crack that shit and that's from the side with a hatchet," Phatz replied smugly.

AC shook his head in amazement. Plexiglass. Why hadn't he realized it? He observed Phatz quietly. It was obvious he knew his shit, but why hadn't he told him those details the first time when the damn case didn't break! He was about to ask, when Cheetum's voice interrupted. The man had been silent during their exchange.

"We need some gas if we keep riding around," he stated.

"Look, pull up to this grocery store on Olympic and Western," Phatz instructed him.

He didn't seem all too upset about the hammer as AC expected, he on the other hand was fuming about their botched heist.

Lost in his thoughts as they drove up to Ralphs grocery store, AC almost missed the group of Asians walking. A sinister idea popped in his mind.

"Stop the car," he stated.

Ignoring the curious looks from Phatz and Chettum, he made sure to stay a few feet behind the group of five Asians as he trailed them across the parking lot waiting for the perfect opportunity. Never mind the fact that it was broad daylight and cars whipped in and out of the parking lot. When they were halfway to the store, he made his move.

With his hands tucked under his shirt he crept up behind them unnoticeably

"Give me the fucking wallets!" he demanded.

Not worried about them identifying him in a line up AC forced them to turn around.

A look of shock covered their pale faces as they all did as told. The small Asian woman sobbing began speaking in her native tongue.

"Yeah, yeah, yeah, whatever!" he shot back as he took off with their wallets. His gaze swung back and forth as he searched for Cheetum. In seconds he spotted the man steering towards him.

Hopping into the back seat he let out a deep breath as Cheetum sped off. He couldn't believe how easy it had been. AC had seen the fake gun under the shirt trick done on a television show once. Never in a million years did he think it would have worked in real life. But it had. In the car he counted the money. Damn them chinks was loaded AC thought counting out $1200. He should have felt bad, but he didn't. If he hadn't gotten to them someone else would have. At least he hadn't harmed anyone.

While he counted, he could feel Cheetum's eyes on him. He could barely focus on driving.

"What you got back there?" Cheetum asked, licking his dry lips. The wild and crazy look in his eyes let AC know that the monkey was riding his back hard.

Instead of answering he kept counting. When he was certain Cheetum wasn't looking he slid half the money through the side of the seat to Phatz. Back on 43rd and St Andrews Phatz handed Cheetum fifty dollars.

"This it," he complained.

"Man, you know them fucking chinks wasn't walking around with all that money on them, fool this L.A." AC responded cooly.

Cheetum said a few more words underneath his breath and left.

"Clown ass," Phatz said, watching after him as he removed the real stash from his pocket. The two men split the loot evenly down to the last dollar.

AC was floating off his accomplishment when his eyes strayed to the 71'candy red ragtop parked at the curb.

You like it?" Phatz asked, stuffing his half in his pockets.

Like it? AC loved it. It was his dream car. Masking his excitement, he shrugged nonchalantly, "It's aight."

"Aight?" Phatz said not convinced. He had caught a glimpse of the dreamy look on AC's face earlier.

"Get in let me show you these hydraulics."

They drove around for a few hours getting to know each other before Phatz slowed the low rider down outside of AC's house on 39th and Wisconsin.

Shutting off the engine Phatz turned to him,"I like what you did back there."

Looking at him with a confused expression, AC motioned for him to continue.

"You refused to take a loss, see that's the state of mind a lot of these dumb ass niggas round here lacking."

AC thought about Phatz words. He knew he wasn't like most young cats his age that was out chasing a nut, money was the only thing he wanted these days. Besides, he knew that if he got the money the girls would chase him.

"Yea you right, but shit a nigga gotta get it by any means necessary know what I mean,"he replied quoting Malcolm X one of his favorite revolutionaries.

"Damn right," Phatz responded as they bumped fists.

His hand paused on the door when Phatz spoke again, "What you doing tomorrow?"

Immediately AC felt the stinging in his cheeks. Might as well tell him he thought.

Lowering his head, he answered sheepishly, "School."

"I knew you was a young nigga," Phatz teased.

Ignoring his teasing, AC hopped out the ragtop. His eyes flickered to the empty driveway and the dark house. He knew no one was home, they never were. Shifting his attention back to Phatz he realized that he had been watching him.

"You tryna get the money or what?" asked AC.

Phatz gazed at him thoughtfully.

"Meet me at Anne's breakfast spot over on Vermont and 42nd."

Now he was talking.

"Bet," AC responded before starting up the driveway.

He smiled at the sounds of *Atomic Dog* by George Clinton blasting from the speakers as Phatz pulled off. Not only did they like the same music, but they liked getting money. AC was starting to think that it was the beginning of a beautiful friendship.

The Next Day

"Are you ready to order sir?" The waitress asked standing in front of him.

Seated at Anne's, the popular food joint on Vermont and 42nd, Phatz lifted his head from the menu, reciting his order.

"Anything to drink?" she asked scribbling in a notepad.

"Apple Juice, ice on the side."

Retrieving the menu in front of him, the waitress returned seconds later with his request and ice before leaving again.

Alone with his thoughts, Phatz mind strayed to the events of yesterday. Awful Clyde was living out his name to the fullest. Seeing him jack the Asians in broad daylight only confirmed what he had already known. AC was a wild card and a man always needed one on his team. In fact, the more Phatz thought about the more he realized that teaming up with him would be a good thing. He liked AC's hustlers' mentality. Even more so, he could teach him how to perfect his swing with the hammer. At the thought of the hammer, Phatz squeezed his eyes shut. He still hadn't told Mother Dear it was broken. She wouldn't be too pleased at the news.

His stomach growled when he caught a whiff of fried bacon coming from the kitchen. Sipping on his apple juice he was just about to ask for a refill when AC breezed through the door.

Waving him over they greeted each other with a fist pound before AC plopped down in the booth opposite of him.

"A nigga hungry as fuck," he complained reaching for the menu. Like clockwork the waitress appeared to take his order.

Phatz watched AC scope out his surroundings the same as he had done when he entered.

"Never been up in here before," he said.

"You'll like it," he said, plucking the vibrating pager from his waist. It was Silky. Again. He bit back a smile. Shoving thoughts of their raunchy night together to the back of his mind he glanced across the table at AC who was rearranging the salt and pepper shakers.

"Look like you want a job here," he joked.

AC smirked. "Money too slow."

The statement made him like his character even more. He figured now would be a good time to pitch his partnership idea to him, but before he could get a word in the waitress arrived with their food. Placing the steaming plate of cheese grits, eggs, and pancakes in front of him, she grabbed his half empty glass and refilled it before moving on to the other customers.

His eyes wandered to the pile of hash browns on AC's plate. A separate plate of bacon and eggs were next to him.

"I see you got a big appetite after yesterday," Phatz said before slicing into his fluffy pancakes.

"It was wild right?"

"Hell yeah, nigga you broke a hammer! You know how hard it is to break a hammer?"

Remorse oozed from AC's tone as he spoke.

"My bad about that for real."

The silence stretched between them. While Phatz wasn't happy about the family's heirloom being broken he knew that AC hadn't broken it purposely.

"The shit just blew my mind I'm standing there like what the fuck?"

At the duped expression on AC's face, Phatz couldn't stop himself from laughing.

"And here you go ducking behind the counter and shit."

"I was scared," he joked as the two shared a laugh.

Wiping his hands on the napkin beside him AC's tone turned serious.

"On the real I know where we can get big bucks from."

Phatz was tuned in. Over the next few minutes, he listened as AC told him about the check cashing place at the Fox Hills Mall. Apparently, they were bringing in the big bucks. His ears perked up when AC revealed the amount.

"$80,000?" he repeated skeptically.

Finishing off his glass of orange juice AC placed it on the table.

"Could be more," he answered with a shrug of his shoulder.

Phatz thought on it for a few seconds. What did they have to lose?

****

Thirty minutes later he stood outside the check cashing place and answered his own question.

"Lost a lot of time," Phatz said as he stared at the closed neon sign lighting up in the window.

"So, you didn't know they would be closed?" he asked, turning to AC who gave a careless shrug.

"My bad man."

Letting out a deep sigh Phatz weighed their options as he gazed around the empty mall. On one hand they could wait until the check place opened then try hitting the lick, but by then the mall was bound to be flooded with shoppers who would further complicate their plans. Or simply put they could just leave and count today as a loss.

He was leaning more towards leaving when his eyes homed in on the big fluorescent Zales sign at the end of the mall. A smirk appeared on his face. Maybe their time wouldn't be wasted after all. As if AC had read his mind they smiled when their eyes locked.

Inside Zales, a Black man hunched over the cases as his hand moved swiftly over the glass. He was so preoccupied with his task he didn't register the men watching him.

Ahem

Startled, his head snapped up as his hand stilled. Quickly rounding the counter, light leaped into his eyes as he approached them.

"Man, I know who you are," he said excitedly.

Caught off guard by the man's reaction Phatz scratched at the nape of his neck.

"Who me?" he asked.

"Yea man I see you on TV all the time don't act like that," the man smiled before shoving his hands into his pockets.

"TV?" Phatz said puzzled. None of his crimes had been shown on TV. He didn't think he'd made it that far yet. Had their plan been foiled already he wondered. The longer Phatz stood there the clearer things became. He was dealing with a case of mistaken identity. It was the only thing that could explain the shop keeper's reaction to him.

"Who am I then?" he asked searching for information.

"You that football player that plays for the Raiders."

He would've laughed at the man's answer, but the look of awe on his face stopped him. What were the odds that he would be mistaken for a famous football player? But with his stocky build and the jewelry around his neck it was no wonder.

"That's right," Phatz said playing along. He fought the urge to laugh as the star struck clerk pumped his hand eagerly.

"I'm Earl by the way, what can I help you fellas with?" Earl asked seconds after returning to his position behind the counter.

Slipping into his role Phatz pointed to the glass counter. "Let me see the best watches you have."

"You ball players don't spare any expenses when it comes down to luxury I see." Removing the jewelry Earl placed the row of Baume and Mercier watches on the counter. Phatz eyes bulged at the collection. Knowing he could have them all in his possession with one swipe he cautioned himself to move slowly. He had to think this opportunity through, especially since it had fallen right into his lap.

For the first time he realized that AC was still lingering in the doorway. The expression on his face said that he was equally shocked by what was happening.

"Who's that you have with you?" Earl asked after noting the direction he was looking.

Thinking quick Phatz responded, "My bodyguard."

It seemed to satisfy the man because he continued to pull out watches.

Meanwhile Phatz watched AC struggle to control his laughter.

When the final watch from the collection was placed in front of him Phatz stroked his growing goatee as he pretended to think on his choices.

"I wasn't planning on buying anything today but it's a must that I have these." Picking up the watch he reveled at the weight of it in his hand. Pure gold.

Shocked, Earl asked, "All of them?"

"All," Phatz repeated still clutching the watch. Realizing that Earl was studying him, he made a show of comparing the Baume and Mercier watch to the Rolex on his wrist.

Turning to AC he winked.

"Go get my wallet."

"Yo wallet?" AC responded eyebrows knitting in confusion.

"Yes, it's under the seat," he said pointedly hoping that he would catch on. They didn't have much time. Any minute now the morning shoppers would come barging in. Phatz wanted to make his escape while he had a chance. He watched as understanding dawned on AC's face. When he turned to leave Phatz motioned towards the other cases. Obliging his request Earl chatted away about football games as he pulled a rack of Peugeot watches out. One ear tuned in, Phatz had to give it to the man, he knew his shit when it came down to football stats, which was why he couldn't figure out for the life of him how he had managed to mistake him for a famous football player. Guess it was his lucky day. Out of the corner of his eye he peeped AC returning with his *wallet*.

Sliding a watch on each arm he winked at Earl.

"How do they look?"

"Man, you know they look good you probably got a whole room full," he chuckled lightly.

Almost Phatz wanted to say.

"You have my wallet?" he asked instead turning to AC.

"Sure do," AC answered as his hand slipped to the bulge in his pocket.

Backing away from the counter Phatz waved a finger in the air.

"Pay the man."

"You got it."

Earl beamed excitedly, "Man I can't—" His words were cut short when AC shoved the .38 revolver in his face.

"Put the rest of them nice ass watches in the bag too don't be cheap," he commanded just as Phatz spun on his heels and casually strolled from the store. He didn't stick around to see the look of disappointment and sadness on the man's face as he realized what was happening.

Once outside he rushed to crank up the white two door Chrysler AC called "Moe Green."

The doors had to be unlocked from the outside. Rushing around to unlock the passenger door then jetting around to the driver's side must've been a sight to see. At the sound of AC's voice, he spun around to find the man bent over in laughter confirming his thoughts.

"Get in and stop laughing nigga," Phatz said trying to keep his own laughter at bay. He could only imagine what he looked like.

"Yeaaaaaa Muthafucka!" Phatz yelled out driving in traffic as they made a clean getaway. Rehashing the lick, the men finally released their laughter.

"Man, I don't know who that nigga thought you was but we got his ass. You may not be a football player but yo ass looked like one running around the car."

Phatz released a loud roar, while gripping the wheel.

"Now what?" asked AC when the laughter subsided.

"Now we go to my man Zac he'll get us right," Phatz responded guiding the car towards the jewelry mart.

And he was right Zac gave them $90,000 for the watches and they split it evenly.

It was late when he dropped AC off at his home with plans to meet up the next day, so he wasn't surprised to find everyone in his own house sleeping. Creeping into his mama room he saw that his baby sister Denise was in the bed with her pretending to be asleep. Leaning down Phatz placed a kiss on her cheek.

"Get back," she said playfully pushing him away. The sound caused Kathi to stir.

"Boy what are you doing?" Kathi asked in a sleep filled voice when she heard the two laughing.

"Tryna give Denise some sugar," he said bending down.

"Give this to Mother Dear in the morning," he whispered in Denise's ear as he slid $20,000 under her pillow. She nodded her head as he crept back out the house hoping that it would make up for the hammer.

****

Meanwhile AC kneeled at his bed putting his money in the shoe box. After counting it for the fifth time he slid the box under the bed and climbed on the cool sheets. He was tired but his mind wasn't. He couldn't believe the dough he had made today. It was luck that the checking place was closed, and the man had confused Phatz with a football player. For once he was thankful for the encounter he had with him at Marshalls. When his eyes finally drifted closed it wasn't darkness that he saw behind them, it was green big face dollars.

****

"We racked up at least $10K worth of shit out of the stores in Beverly Hills," Silky boasted from the passenger seat of the Volkswagen Rabbit that Phatz steered. He nodded along as she continued talking, listening to every detail. Boosting was Silky's thing and she was cold at it. Almost as good as Phatz was with swinging the hammer. Except he would never reveal all his techniques. Silky on the other hand was laying it bare. From the corner of his eye he watched the yellow tennis skirt rise revealing her smooth brown skin. Catching his stare, she winked before fluffing out her wind tossed hair. They'd spent almost half of the day in Valencia at Magic Mountain, standing in long lines in the hot sun to ride rollercoasters, but it was worth it. The day had proven to be a much-needed break for Phatz. Lately, he and AC had been putting in overtime with the hammer. It was during those times that Phatz began to realize not only was AC a good partner in crime, but he was loyal to the bone. Another characteristic that he greatly admired. When they weren't casing new licks, Phatz was spending time with his newborn son. It was still hard to believe that he was someone's father. Just shy of a month, the infant was the splitting image of him. Knowing that his son carried his namesake filled him with pride. While Phatz had always been focused, having a baby to take care of only fueled his fire. He would swing the hammer to make sure that his seed wanted for nothing. When his son got older he would teach him how to feed himself so he never needed to depend on anyone else.

"I got some nice shit for my party too," Silky voice floated to his ears as he tuned back into her words. He'd almost forgotten her approaching birthday but with the mention of the party he knew that his presence would be required.

"You're still coming right?" she asked on cue.

Phatz bit back a smile. Silky liked to show him off to all her girls and he didn't blame her. He was the man in the streets and everyone who was anyone knew it.

"Of course," he answered as he made a left turn off Martin Luther King Boulevard landing on Hillcrest.

Satisfied with his answer she returned to her rambling. Guiding the Volkswagen into the Jungle, Phatz slowed down when they reached August Street and as usual the street was full of activity. It was common of him to swing by his old neighborhood from time to time. He was just about to claim one of the empty parking spaces when a familiar face began to approach the car. Greeting the young boy with a pound Phatz observed the serious look on his face.

"So, what's up?" he asked, knowing that only something important would cause him to abandon his post and approach.

"Some dude came by looking for you," he said, shifting nervously on his feet.

"Me?" Phatz asked puzzled. Throwing the car in park he motioned for the young boy to continue.

"Yea said he was looking for you then he went to sit over there." The boy hooked his thumb over his shoulder to a set of apartment steps that were now empty. As the boy began to describe him a name flashed in Phatz mind that matched the description.

"What did he say his name was?"

"Ty," he answered, confirming Phatz suspicions.

Fishing in his pocket he pulled out a crisp bill and handed it off, "When he comes back tell him to stay here." With a stiff nod the boy fled to his post in the apartments.

Phatz didn't miss the curious expression on Silky's face. Instead of addressing it he drove them to Hamburger City where they chowed down on burgers and fries. An hour later they were back on August Street.

"Who's Ty?" Silky asked draining the last of her drink.

Ty was Phatz's childhood friend that he had grown up in the Jungle with. Together he and Ty would hit licks until they tired, even then they were always on the hunt for more. It was their insatiable hunger that would eventually lead to a botched robbery in Downey. While Phatz had gone on the run for six months, Ty had easily given up and turned himself over to California Youth Authority and received three years for the robbery. Phatz still didn't understand what made Ty surrender at the time. In his mind surrendering was never an option. One time would have to catch him and that's exactly what happened. Still Phatz had felt better about running, at least he hadn't gone out like a chump. He had taken those eighteen months at the Youth Trade School to the chin with no complaints. The last that he had heard of Ty was that he had broken out because of a girl only to be recaptured and sent to prison. Ty showing up almost a year later seemed odd to him, but he had shaken the strange feeling off. Still he couldn't help but to wonder if his childhood friend was up to his old tricks again.

Turning to Silky he jutted his chin over her shoulder.

"That's Ty."

The man headed in their direction was of average height like Phatz remembered. It was his build that had changed. The once lanky boy was now a muscled man. He had the look of someone who had utilized his time by working out. A lopsided grin split his face as he reached the driver's side. Besides his obvious growth nothing seemed to have changed about Ty. To Phatz that was both a good thing and a bad thing.

"Damn nigga when you get out?" Phatz asked him as he leaned out of the car to grip him up.

"Shit not too long ago," Ty replied happily. His eyes slid away from Phatz to Silky in the next seat. Phatz watched as he ogled her breasts that were spilling out of the tank top she wore. Noticing the same, Silky cocked her head in annoyance causing Ty to let out a low chuckle.

Ordering him to get in Phatz pulled off with Ty in the backseat. The two reminisced on old times while he drove.

"Shit it don't look like you getting money like I heard," Ty said from the back seat after they had spun a couple of blocks. Phatz smiled to himself. So that was the real reason he was trying to reach out to him. If only this nigga knew he thought. He was sure he was getting more money than Ty had probably ever seen in his life, but decided not to reveal that just yet. Glancing over at Silky he saw the frown on her face as they crossed Western Street a few blocks from the apartments where she lived on Avalon and 41st Street. Once they pulled up it took a minute for him to talk her into getting out of the car. With a promise that he would return later Phatz watched her storm into her building.

"Nigga get in the front I'm not about to chauffeur your ass around," he said to Ty before pulling off. It was time for the two to discuss business, but first Phatz needed to know Ty's intentions. He had listened closely as the man bragged about all the licks he had hit since being released and no matter what he said, Phatz knew that Ty wasn't doing it like him and AC were. No one was. But he was about to offer Ty a chance to change all of that and from the greed shining in his eyes he knew he would accept.

"Man I can't believe your grandma still lives here,"Ty stated when they arrived at Phatz crib.

On further inspection he noticed that all the lights inside were off. The sight wasn't unusual since it was well after nine o'clock but the look on Mother Dears face when she answered the door was one he had never seen before. When he requested that she retrieve the bags he kept his money in you would've thought someone had insulted her. Phatz knew he was in for an ear full once they were alone. When Mother Dear retreated to her room, he flipped the switch flooding the house with light. Emptying the Louis Vuitton bag on the table he watched Ty eyes bulge out of his head at the pile of green bills. Based on his latest count Phatz knew that it was $250K piled in front of them and that wasn't all, unzipping the other Louie bag full of jewelry, he watched the expression on Ty's face linger between amazement and disbelief.

"Now tell me what you heard again?" he asked with a smirk.

Speechless Ty moved towards the table of money. Stopping him Phatz made sure Ty understood his next words.

"You can't always go by what you hear."

"I-I--,"

His words faltered on his lips when Phatz reached down and handed him $5,000 from the stash. Reaching into the jewelry bag he removed a Turkish gold rope and keys to a brand-new Eldorado Cadillac.

"Welcome home nigga," he said and began to tell him about the stores he and AC had hit from Oakland to San Diego.

"We could always use another team player," he said when he was finished.

The statement was barely out of his mouth when Ty responded with an eager yes while his eyes darted between the money in his hands and that on the table.

"Cool."

Placing the money back in the bag Phatz thought about how Ty had played right into his hands. He had known when he came looking for him that he would want in on their licks. He watched Ty slide the chain around his neck feeling a certain loyalty to him. They both had come up in the game seeing a lot of shit that kids weren't supposed to see. Most of their old friends had lost their lives to the streets before they even turned twenty-one. Phatz was thankful to have made it this far with the risks he was taking. He knew eventually he would have to face the consequences of his actions, but until that day arrived, he would continue to take care of his family and his friends.

"Nigga go enjoy yo self you should be able to pull a few bitches with that gold chain by itself instead of looking at mine," he joked.

Ty touched the chain, "You right my nigga these hoes bout to go crazy, wait til I cop me a nice fit, bitches will think I'm the black Hugh Heffner."

They joked for a few minutes before Ty left promising to get in contact with him in a few days. Phatz was clearing the last of the bills off the table when his grandmother appeared with a frown on her face.

"Sorry for waking you up Mother Dear," he said trying to ease out of the scolding he knew was coming.

She waved his comment off, "That's not the problem, the problem is you letting people know your business."

Taken back for a few seconds Phatz stumbled over his words, "Mother Dear that's Ty you know we use to run to—"

She raised her hand up silencing him "I don't care who he is, you never let no one know what you got or where it's kept, people can't be trusted these days," she said sternly.

Phatz remained silent, letting her words sink in. Even though he and Ty had grown up together she was right, but he didn't think Ty would be stupid enough to try to rob him especially not when he was about to be getting his own share.

After Mother Dear placed the bags where they belonged, she returned to walk him to the door. Still pondering her words Phatz leaned down to brush her cheek with a kiss.

"You're right Mother Dear I won't do it again."

"I know," she said patting his face lightly with her hands.

He waited until he heard the locks click in place before he hopped into his ride. Guiding the car towards east L.A. he figured he would swing back over to Silky's and end the night with a bang.

****

Manual Arts High

Ring Ring

The sound of the school bell sent students rushing from the overcrowded classrooms out into the sea of freedom that was summer break. Eager to put the school year behind him AC made haste to his locker. Stuffing his belongings into the Louis Vuitton backpack that he carried, he was just about to make his exit when a voice behind him made him stop.

"Are you coming to the party tonight?"

Swinging around he came face to face with the brown skin cutie from his Calculus class. Popping a cherry flavored lollipop in his mouth his gaze swept over her slowly, his sudden itch to leave had all but left him before he answered with a sly smile.

Instead of answering her question he holstered the backpack higher on his shoulder before propping his arm against the locker, "You going?" he asked.

Inching closer she removed the lollipop from his mouth and inserted it into hers. The tip of her pink tongue darted out to the side of her mouth as she savored the flavor before she spoke.

"Maybe," she grinned slyly. As the noise level increased around them AC took a second to survey his surroundings. Almost everyone seemed to be posted on the lockers. He could hear their plans for the summer being made. Some of the faces were familiar others not so much. AC hadn't taken the time to make a lot of friends for the most part, mainly because he was hardly there. And when he was, he spent the time playing catch up with his school work so he couldn't say that he would miss the place or the people. When he walked out those doors that would be it for him. He had made the decision not to return to school the following year. It was the only way to double his profits. Waking up to go to school had him missing much needed money. Besides what he needed to know couldn't be learned in a classroom.

A girl in neon tights wiggled her fingers at him pulling at his attention. He would miss macking on all the girls that threw flirtatious glances and words his way, like the one standing in front of him that was rudely snapping her fingers in his face.

"Maybe you need to be talking to her if that's who you want," she spat with her lips turned up.

Focusing on her his brain scrambled for her name. Was it Iesha? No that was the chick that had just passed.

Folding her arms under her plump breast she waited with a wide-eyed stare. Shaking her head, she reached down for her backpack. The album picture of Gladys Knight and the Pips triggered his memory just as she was about to storm pass him.

Lightly touching her arm, he halted her in her steps. He recalled her telling him how she was named after the soul singer.

"I got who I want right here, Gladys." He recalled her telling him how she was named after the soul singer during one of their talks in class.

Gladys tried to bite back her smile but lost in the end when her wide lips spread. Removing the lollipop she stood on her tip toes to whisper in his ear, "My mama working a double tonight, you can come over if you like."

It was AC's turn to smile.

"We can have our own party," he said suggestively.

"That's right," she nodded in agreement just as the last bell rang.

"Alright everybody out!" the hall monitor called out ushering them out the door.

With plans to meet later that night he and Gladys went their separate ways. As he walked out of the door of Manual Arts High School for the last time, he didn't have any regrets.

∎∎∎

The voices carried on loudly in the shop at Marshalls that Monday morning as the argument grew heated with every passing second. The source of the conflict: Kareem Abdul Jabbar and Magic Johnson of the Los Angeles Lakers.

"I'll bet you every dime I have Abdul will win it all," an old timer called from the back sparking more opinions.

"I don't see why, he not doing shit, what they need to do is give MVP to my boy Johnson." Someone countered as a chorus of disapproval rose in the air.

AC listened closely, half entertained as he waited for Phatz to get out of the chair so that they could begin the day's business. So far, they had hit over twelve malls. Just last week they'd shut off the electricity at the Northridge Fashion Square mall before running in and smashing cases, fleeing with over $200,000 worth of merchandise. With each heist they reached new heights perfecting their craft along the way. Yet even with his growing love for his new trade AC couldn't keep his eyes from straying to the dice game going on in the corner. Seemed like only yesterday he had kneeled on the same floor of the shop hoping to cash in big on the growing pot of cash.

Small beginnings he told himself.

Still he had to run his tingling fingers down the white Fila suit that he sported to curve his urge to join in. Especially when he noticed the arrogant smile on the player who had dominated the last few rounds. Didn't help that the man was gambling with a crew of rookies, taking them for all they were worth. AC tried to focus on the highlights on the sports channel, but the groans pulled him right back to the game. That was it. He couldn't stand to watch the youngns get beat out of their cash by a newcomer. If anybody would take their money it would be him. Sliding over to the small crowd that had formed, AC dropped a wad of green bills in the center of the floor, sending a hushed whisper over the ban of hustlers as all eyes focused on him.

Jutting his chin forward he spread his arms out.

"I got next."

****

      Watching AC join the game Phatz smirked to himself. He knew it would only be a matter of time before his friend caved in. Just like him, AC couldn't pass up a good dice game and if not for Marshall adding the finishing touches to his hair, he would've joined himself. Speaking of hair, Phatz flinched when the heat from the blow dryer zinged his ear. Just a few more minutes he told himself. After seven years of hairdo's Phatz still was impatient with the process but thirty minutes later when Marshall passed him the handheld mirror, he admitted that the wait was always worth it. He eyed the neat finger waves made with the imprint of Marshall's finger and the comb. Winking at his handsome reflection he handed the mirror back to Marshall. Preoccupied with thoughts of his next move, he almost stood when the heavy piece of steel resting in his lap made him pause. As if reading his mind, in one swift motion Marshall removed the smock from around his neck taking with him the .38. The gun had been courtesy of Marshall, the two men both understood that in a place where every type of criminal dwelled one could never be too careful. Stepping aside for the next customer to claim the chair, Phatz brushed strands of hair off his Ellesse sweatsuit. He was about to call out to AC when the beeper on his hip vibrated.

"Damn," he stated when he saw the number flashing.

It made the third time that morning that his friend Corey had paged him.

What could be so important?Phatz wondered to himself. At eleven o'clock that morning there was only one thing that he was interested in hearing about. Strolling two doors down to the local arcade to the payphone Phatz punched in Corey's number not surprised when he answered on the first ring.

"Aye this betta be about some cash," he said jumping right in.

"You at Marshalls?" Corey asked instead.

Phatz rolled his eyes, already regretting the phone call.

"Yeah," he answered dryly.

"I need to holla at you about something. I'll be there in fifteen minutes."

Detecting the hint of desperation in his voice Phatz opened his mouth to speak only to be met with the loud beeping of the dial tone in his ear. Curious now, he replaced the receiver on the hook. Though he had plans Phatz decided to delay them this one time off the strength of their relationship.

Just like Ty, he and Corey's relationship went back to when they were just boys shooting craps and chasing girls. The two had basically grown up together, but after attending Dorsey High they'd lost touch. Years later a crap game in the bathroom of Baldwin movie theater in the Jungle would reconnect them. No longer boys, a lot had changed during their separation. These days Corey was making a name for himself in the streets as an upcoming drug dealer who didn't mind bragging about how it was paying off for him. The man spared no expenses when it came to clothes and cars. It was the exact flashy lifestyle that gained him enemies from all sides. Yet Corey embraced the hate with open arms fanning the flames. Phatz knew Corey wasn't built to play in the dangerous streets like himself, but like so many others the fast money had lured him in and refused to let go. Never being one to stop a man's hustle, Phatz had warned Corey to be careful because no matter how good things were going, the streets had a way of flipping on you in the blink of an eye.

His gaze strayed to AC as he exited out of Marshalls at the same time Corey arrived in his all black two-seater Benz. Realizing there were no parking spaces Corey continued down the long street.

Strolling to where AC stood Phatz watched the man shove his winnings in his pocket as a satisfied grin settled over his face.

"Guess that's just some mo' of it huh?" he asked him.

Dipping his hands in his pockets again,AC produced the green crumpled bills.

"You know it," he stated proceeding to straighten the bills. Seconds later with the money pressed neatly into the palms of his hands,AC tilted his head in Phatz direction.

"When you gone let me drive the whip?"

Grinning Phatz glanced at the whip he spoke of. The bright candy orange Cadillac in front of them beamed in the sun's light. He was quickly developing a fetish for nice cars. The coupe with its big grill and bumper kit and vogues and wires was his second purchase. He had only driven it a few times to get a feel of it and while it wasn't his favorite it did turn heads.

Retrieving his keys from his pockets he tossed them to AC who caught the keys midair.

The surprised look on his face was quickly replaced by a scowl.

Noticing his eyes locked above his head Phatz turned to follow his gaze when he spotted Corey coming up the street. Dark skinned with a jheri curl and standing at 6'2, Corey was hard to miss. Even more so with the Turkish gold rope resting against the V- neck sweater he wore hanging so low that it almost touched the top of his black faded jeans.

Putting two and two together Phatz suspected the expression on AC's face was courtesy of Corey.

His suspicions were confirmed with AC's next words.

"There go that nigga Corey." The disdain dripping from his words were hard to miss.

His hard stare turned to Phatz

"I can take that gold rope over his head without breaking it," he stated confidently twirling the keys around his finger.

A sneaky smile began to creep over his face. Phatz had seen the look plenty of times. AC had just marked Corey as a lick, but his friend had no way of knowing that the chain actually belonged to him. If he violated Corey it would be the same as violating him. Caught off guard by the dilemma Phatz scrambled to make a decision as Corey closed in on them.

Seeing the predator in AC about to leap out, Phatz placed a firm grip on his arm before he could move any further.

Staring down at his hand AC's voice hardened as their gazes collided. "You know him?" he questioned.

Phatz opened his mouth to speak, but Corey's voice cut him off.

"What's up Big Pimpin' I see you out in the great pumpkin," Corey stated unaware of the danger he had just walked into.

With a nod of his head Phatz released his hold on AC's arm.

"I need to holla at you real quick," Corey said looking around. There it was again. Desperation. Only this time Phatz could see it etched in Corey's face. When he suddenly spun and headed towards his car, Phatz stared after him.

"Go ahead, I'll wait." His head whipped around to AC who had stood by silently. He could tell AC was pissed that he'd interrupted his plans to rob Corey, but Phatz would explain everything to him later.

"You know a crackhead around here name Lewis?" Corey asked when he joined him in front of the arcade.

"Maybe ya boy know, you know they all run in the same circle," he rushed on.

"Who?"

Corey tilted his head towards AC who stood a few feet away out of ear shot.

A spark of anger rushed through Phatz when he realized what Corey was implying.

"Aye he's not a crackhead do it look like I'd be hanging out with junkies and shit?" he asked, coming to AC's defense.

Sensing that he'd made a mistake Corey shook his head quickly.

"My bad pimpin' it's just that I always see him around here I didn't know what to think," he explained lamely.

"Yeah whatever just hurry up and get to the point," Phatz snapped.

Uttering another half assed apology Corey continued, "Last night the nigga Lewis called me for an eight ball right, so I get there and just as we're about to do the deal he snatches it out of my hand and run, now you know them motherfuckas fast so wasn't no catching that nigga."

Listening to Corey spin the tale of how he got tricked out of his dope further confirmed what Phatz already knew: Corey wasn't built for that life. At least not the dirty part of it.

"So, I'm guessing you want me to track this crackhead down and get your money back," Phatz stated, folding his arms across his chest.

"Just this one time," he pleaded.

Standing face to face with him, Phatz let his eyes roam over his long frame. Corey was doing his best to fit into a world that he didn't belong in. It was no wonder niggas robbed him. Even dressed in the flyest gear Corey still stuck out like a sore thumb. If word got around that he was an easy mark more than his reputation would be at risk. So would his life. Never one to turn his back on a friend in need, Phatz agreed to get his package back.

Pretending not to notice the look of relief that washed over Corey's face he rattled off more words and instructed the man to give him a week before parting ways with him.

Standing beside his Cadillac, he motioned towards AC as he reached for the door.

"You driving or what?"

Dashing to the driver's side AC slid in. He ran his hand over the dashboard before sticking the key in the switch.

"I can't wait to get me one of these babies. It won't be as loud tho," he joked. While AC pulled away from the curb Phatz took a moment to decide how he would address what had just happened between him and Corey. While it had seemed like he had chosen a side, the truth was if the roles were reversed, he would have done the same thing for AC. Still he decided to leave Corey's ill mention of AC out of the conversation as he explained the history the two shared.

"…In other words he's off limits,"AC concluded as he slowed at a stop light.

"Yeah and he's cool once you get to know him."

And it was true Corey hadn't always been the bodacious bragging type. Phatz took AC's silence in stride knowing that the man needed to be able to process what he was saying.

When the light turned green AC drove in the direction that would get them to the Westminster Mall where they were planning to bash some cases in.

"Aight, I'll take yo word for it," AC stated, ending the silence.

He turned his head towards Phatz,"But I hope they got one of those chains ole boy was wearing out here in one of these cases."

Relaxing against the seat Phatz smiled.

"Shit,I know where we can get plenty of those , turn right here," he directed, leading them away from their route. The mall could wait… for now.

****

"Um what did you say you do again?" The dark-skinned cutie with the short haircut, shot Phatz an innocent smile as she squeezed his bicep.

They were seated beside each other in the booth in the crowded restaurant. A plate crashed to the floor making heads turn towards the culprit. Using the distraction Phatz slid his hand up and down her plump thigh. When Corey phoned earlier about some chick begging to meet him, he became skeptical. Racking his mind, he couldn't seem to match a face to the girl who called herself Patsy and insisted that they had met once before at one of the street races. Shit he had given his number to plenty of honey's out there. Corey's description of her got his attention and he agreed to meet them at the popular soul food restaurant Murrys on King and Crenshaw. Finally seeing her Phatz realized that Corey had left out one important detail in his description of her. Baby was stacked. Her 38DD breast almost spilled out of the lime green halter top she wore.

Inching his hand further under the blue jean skirt that hugged her narrow waist and fat ass he licked his lips before answering her question.

"A little bit of this," he said as he stroked her inner thigh for emphasis, "and a whole lot of that."

A blush crept up her neck darkening her pretty skin. She grabbed the chain hanging from his neck and said in awe, "I never seen none like this. This some Mr.T shit."

He laughed at the reference to the flashy character from the *A-Team*.

"Now see baby Mr. T playing make believe, this is me in real life."

The monster gold rope around his neck had *Phatz* encrusted in the best diamonds. It was complimentary of his jeweler Zac. Phatz knew that no one around the area had anything like it. The chain matched perfectly with the gold Polo V-neck sweater he wore, and Patsy couldn't seem to take her eyes off it.

While she swooned over the jewelry his eyes strayed across the restaurant. The crowd was growing, and no one had come to take their order yet. The spot behind his ear began to tingle like it always did when ever unfamiliar faces were around. In his mind it was never a good idea to stay in one place for too long that's how you became a target. His free hand rested on the cold steel tucked at his waist. Immediately he began to relax. Phatz never went anywhere without his weapon. A rule that he was trying to teach Corey.

The man sat across from him with his off again on-again girl Lori. She and Patsy had drifted off into their own conversation that neither Corey nor he had any interest in. Phatz and Corey drifted into a conversation of their own. Speaking in code whenever necessary. A few times he caught Lori's slanted look and wondered if Corey had been pillow talking.

"You got that?" Phatz asked.

"Damn right," Corey responded with a wide smile.

"Any word on Lewis yet?" he asked in a low whisper.

The crackhead in question was doing a good job staying out of sight, but Phatz knew eventually he would have to come up for air and when he did…

"Not yet," Phatz answered knowing it wasn't the words that Corey wanted to hear. His shoulders sagged as he shifted his head to the window to stare at the red lowrider Chevy Blazer he arrived in. It seemed to cheer him up. Phatz could see the pride beaming on his face. He felt the same when he looked at the new ice white Jaguar parked next to it. The cars were the freshest on the lot. Just like the owners.

Beside him Patsy picked up the menu. "Do you know what you're ordering?" she turned to Phatz and asked.

He nodded. He didn't need a menu Murrys had the best soul food he had ever tasted.

"Yep I'ma get me a big ass plate of chitterlings and drown them in hot sauce."

Wrinkling her petite nose, she frowned, "Ew I don't see how anyone can eat those things." Tossing his head back Phatz laughed. He and his mom Kathi would eat them religiously every New Year for good luck. It just so happened he would be having his share a little earlier in the year.

"Shit we might not be eating, no one has taken our order yet," Lori stated with an attitude.

"Relax baby you gon' eat," Corey tried to assure her, tossing an arm over her shoulder.

"Yea girl here she comes now," Patsy chimed in.

Once everyone had placed their orders Phatz was about to suggest a movie or maybe a trip to World on Wheels to really kick their double date off but the words dried up on his tongue at the sight of five masked gunmen rushing into the restaurant.

Shit. The tingling behind his ear turned into a full throb.

"Don't fucking move!" The gunman shouted jumping on top of the countertop, aiming the double barrel shotgun at the crowd.

Loud screams and whimpers echoed through the restaurant.

A whimpering Patsy huddled closer to Phatz with her head down as her fingernails dug into his skin.

He hissed before prying her death grip off.

"Relax," he coaxed.

Across from him he watched the blood drain from Corey's face. His Adam's apple bobbed hard when he swallowed. To Phatz surprise it was Lori who had barely made a sound or batted an eye lash. They seemed to be the only two calm ones in the restaurant. Everyone else cowered in fear. In the chaos, Phatz surveyed the men noticing that two of them were working their way to each table demanding money and valuables while another man collected money from the register.

The one on the countertop paced back in forth with the shotgun keeping everything in control.

The last man stood at the door with a .45 in both hands. It was the same gun tucked away in the waist of Phatz pants. Peeping out the scene more closely he had to give it to them, the heist was well planned and orchestrated reminding him of his approach to the jewelry licks. It was obvious they had cased the place a few times.

The pain radiating up his leg pulled his attention back to their table. Corey had kicked him. Turning his glare on the man he raised his eyebrows while he massaged the throbbing spot.

Leaning slowly over the table Corey motioned at the gunman closest to them.

"We can get him," he whispered just as his hand disappeared under the table.

Tilting his head Phatz wondered if he had heard him correctly.

Please don't let this nigga say what I think he said.

"Fool what?"

To his disappointment Corey repeated himself.

"We can handle this shit ourselves you got yo strap and I got mine all we gotta do is grab the one closest to us and them other niggas will fall in line."

Phatz tried hard to keep his cool. AC would never suggest no stupid ass shit like the words coming out of Corey's mouth right now. At the feel of Patsy tears soaking his arm he turned his gaze on her. The fear was undeniable. Lori was finally showing emotion. Only it wasn't what he expected. There was true excitement in her eyes at hearing Corey's plan.

"They're coming," she warned as the robbers neared them from behind. Phatz had been so preoccupied with Corey's dumb suggestion that he had lost sight of them. He had to talk Corey out of his plan before he got them all killed.

"Listen to me that shit won't work. You grab they partner and they blast both our ass. It's five men against the two of us, six guns against our two pistols. We outnumbered."

Corey opened his mouth to speak, but Phatz cut him off knowing that they were running out of time.

"All I want you to do is follow my lead. You got it?"

Reluctantly Corey removed his hands from his gun, placing them flat on the table.

Good Phatz thought to himself. Tucking the chain in his shirt he removed the diamond ring from his finger, urging Corey to do the same. Next, he removed the wad of cash from his pocket. His method was simple, give them what they wanted and there would be no problems. And he was right.

When the gunmen arrived at their table all their valuables were swept into a pillowcase without any hassle.

Just as they were moving away Phatz locked eyes with who he figured was the lead gunman. "Keep hustling man," he commented.

Pausing the gunman stared at Phatz for a few seconds before nodding his head and moving to the next table.

Corey slumped down in the booth. Phatz could feel the anger vibrating off the man. He would get over it. They could easily get the money and jewelry back, but not their lives.

Turning towards Patsy he touched her tear stained face.

"Everything is cool aight." No sooner had the words left his mouth did the robbers escape through the same door they had rushed in.

"See," he said smiling.

Corey slid out of the booth with Lori in tow. The rest of the dinners filed out in a hurry, some hysterical, others mad about losing their valuables and money. Outside next to their cars Phatz guided a visibly shaken Patsy to the passenger side.

Next to him Corey began to complain. Phatz knew it was coming. He was just hoping it would be after they made a clean getaway before the police arrived.

"Why you acting so calm them niggas just robbed us?" Corey asked pacing.

Phatz knew that the reality of it hit Corey the most being that this would make his second time getting jacked. Unbeknownst to Corey it would have been his third time if he hadn't stopped AC outside of the barbershop. Instead of airing him out in front of the girls about his stupid suggestion back in the restaurant, he pulled him to the side where neither could hear.

"First off don't ever do no stupid shit like you tried back in there, now how much cash you give them?"

"S-Shit about $1900," Corey stuttered out.

That was play money to Phatz. "Well look I gave up $3900."

Removing his chain from inside of his shirt he held the heavy metal piece in his hand feeling its heaviness. "This piece alone cost me $70,000."

Touching the chain on Corey's neck he continued, "I know for a fact Zac ran your pockets for a nice lil amount for that shit right there."

"$70K," Corey volunteered.

"Like I thought," Phatz stated. He could hear the sirens in the distance. They would need to get away soon, but not before he made his point. "We gave up the chump change so we could keep the big chain," he said tugging on his necklace.

"And our lives," he added, wanting to get his point across to Corey.

"You right, man I'm tripping."

"I know," Phatz stated when he knew he had been heard.

The parking lot was almost empty now. Almost everyone had fled the crime scene.

Heading back to the car he looked over at Corey, "Besides nigga you the one always wanna come to hood joints," he joked trying to make light of the situation.

The men shared a laugh before sliding behind the wheels.

Phatz leaned down and removed a stack of cash from his socks, glad the robbers hadn't suggested body searches, or they would have surely found it.

"Are you still hungry?" he asked holding the money for Corey to see.

"Hell yeah."

A quick glance at Patsy and he could tell that she was doing better. She had even retouched her makeup.

Turning the key, he waved at Corey.

"Follow me then," he replied before pulling out of the restaurant parking lot. Phatz would take them to Beverly Hills where they could dine in peace. He wasn't fucked up about the robbery nor was he worried about getting revenge because he knew that eventually the niggas that had robbed them would meet the same fate one day. Life always came full circle like that.

****

"Well Mr. Bradley it looks like you have been adhering to the rules and staying out of trouble like we have requested of you," the balding white man peered over the rim of his glasses at Phatz who was slouched down in the chair in front of his desk. He had been home from Y.A. for three months now and as a requirement for his release, he had to visit his parole officer once a month and give a piss test. Phatz hadn't smoked weed in years. He needed his mind to stay clear so he could focus on his only goal. Getting money. So he was never concerned that his piss would come up hot. After a few more minutes of listening to the white man ramble about curfew and future plans, he was given the okay to leave.

"Keep up the good work," the man called behind him.

Yea yea yea he said to himself slamming the door shut on whatever else he was saying. Phatz had plans and it didn't include listening to anyone tell him how to live his life. Hopping in his all white Jaguar he drove to Corey's duplex on Washington and 3rd Avenue.

Corey's black Benz wasn't in the driveway when he pulled up on the dead-end street but he decided to stick around until the man returned.

"What up Phatz!" Someone called out as he walked into Corey's brother house at the back. Phatz greeted the men not surprised to see a large amount of coke being bagged up by workers.

This was his real reason for visiting. He needed to re-up. Grabbing one of the many scales lined up on the table he proceeded to measure out a half ounce of coke. Coke was in high demand on the streets now. The money was so quick and easy to come by Phatz had to try his hand at it. Of course, cracking jewelry cases was still his specialty but for now he needed something that didn't require that much labor.

He was focused intently on the scale when he heard a voice from behind him.

"Give a pimp a blow of that shit young ass nigga."

He glanced over his shoulder to see Corey's big brother buying what appeared to be an entire kilo.

Damn that's a lot he thought to himself. "Man, I see you got all the money throw a dog a bone," he taunted before returning to his task.

He was almost done when someone tapped him on the shoulder.

"Corey on the phone he wanna talk with you."

Bagging up his last batch of coke he headed to the other room where the telephone was. Phatz wiped the perspiration off his forehead and grabbed the phone.

"What up sweet pimpin'?" Phatz answered.

But he was caught off guard by the panic in Corey's voice "Man the police saying me and you shot up Chico's low rider hang out a few nights ago in Lynnwood!"

Pulling the phone back from his ear he stared at in disbelief. Corey had never called him before about any police problems no matter how serious the situations got.

A warning went off in his head.

"Man, who on this phone?"

There was a dead silence before Corey spoke up again, "Vivian and Kenny."

Before Phatz could tear into him he heard another voice come over the line. Corey's brother had picked up the phone in the other room.

"Tell these niggas to make my pack fat."

Ignoring him Corey continued to talk to Phatz

"Big pimpin' the police tripping they think we shot up Chico's."

Leaning up against the wall Phatz spoke into the phone, "Look I don't even know where Chico's is and you know damn well we didn't do no goofy shit like that."

"The police looking for us."

"Hell, not me!" I just left my parole officer and he told me to keep up the good work if 5-0 was looking for me his ass wouldn't have let me leave," Phatz said feeling confident.

He listened to Corey ramble some more and it was clear that something had spooked him.

From the room he stood in Phatz could see his work still on the table bagged up and ready to be served to a willing buyer. Talking to Corey trying to convince him to remain calm was costing him time and time was money.

"Man, I don't know why they think we did some goofy shit like that but we both know the truth."

Growing irritated by the second he let out a deep breath. "Aye, I got some--- he was interrupted by a strong and clear voice before he could get his words out .

"Look Phatz this is Sergeant Johnson, and you can help your friend by coming to Lynwood police station so we can all talk this out."

What the fuck? Stunned Phatz pulled the phone from his ear and stared at it not believing what he was hearing. The police had been on the phone the entire time listening and Corey had known. A bad feeling settled in his stomach.

Corey's brother emerged from the other room with a look of shock on his face.

Phatz shook his head. Damn. His own friend. One that he thought of as a brother. He looked at the phone again. He wasn't about to confess to shit he didn't do, and he let it be known.

"I'm not coming to no police station to talk to no one about shit I don't know about!" He slammed the receiver down hard.

He and Corey's brother shared a knowing look and when he rushed out the house Phatz wasn't far behind pulling off in his own car.

A strange feeling rolled through his body and settled in his chest. Pulling over into a gas station he breathed deeply through his nose as the blood roared through his head. The betrayal stung. After a few seconds of sitting still his breathing returned to normal and the anger he felt began to drain. He laughed to himself when he started the car up. In the seat beside him was the half ounce of cocaine he had bagged up. Coreys' workers were in such a panic they hadn't seen him slip out of the house with it. Shoving Corey's betrayal to the back of his mind he tried to focus on what was more important and right now it was getting the white substance out to the junkies. Besides Phatz figured if the police really wanted him, they knew where to find him.

****

It took three trips to transport all the clothes into the newly furnished apartment he shared with Silky on 67th Street and Brynhurst. Locking the door, he admired his handy work. The robbery was one of the easiest he had ever planned. Hitting jewelry licks was his thing but at his weekly trip to Marshall's he'd overheard a few boosters bragging about a nice spot in the Wilshire District that was impossible to hit. The Asian owners had seemingly outsmarted all the boosters by placing bars with heat sensors inside and outside of the store. No one could get in or out without alerting the police. When he left the shop Phatz decided to check the place out for himself. He loved a good challenge. He couldn't believe all the high-end fashion clothes and shoes he was seeing when he entered the store. Top of the line Brightly colored Fila, Ellesse, and Sergio Tacchini sweatsuits were on display. Goose Feather coats of every color with the shoes to match. The store was every label junkies-like himself- dream. He had to have it. All of it.

After peeking around a little more he admitted with disappointment that the boosters were right—the store was ironclad. The owner had thought of everything to keep his inventory safe. Phatz was about to chalk it up to a loss when he noticed a weakness- something that the owner hadn't accounted for-. It was true that he would never get in through the doors or windows but thank God for walls. He smiled as he exited the store and entered the key shop right beside it. It was just as he suspected the two stores shared one wall and from his view it was paper thin. Not only that but the key shop had a basic alarm that a child could disable. Phatz returned later that night with the only people he knew could get the job done. Jungle Niggas. It had taken only five minutes to smash a hole into the key shop wall and enter through the opposite side. He and Silky shared a soda on the bus stop bench watching for police while his homies loaded everything into the cargo van. When they finished the only thing remaining in the store were the mannequin dolls and hangers. So much for impossible.

Phatz ran his hand over the canary yellow feather goose coat. The icy white one beside it would look good on Silky. Denise would probably pick the ruby red one. Flipping on the big screen TV he had just purchased he turned to the championship game. He was suddenly hungry and since Silky had decided to take a spin on the town in one of her new fits he was left to fend for himself. A cold cut sandwich with chips was the best he could do despite their refrigerator being packed with food. Washing down his food with a glass of cold water he headed back into the living room. It was time to take inventory.

With the sports announcer talking in the background he sifted through the clothes. He was checking the size of the Ellesse sweatsuits when his pager went off. It was Billy an old friend that he and AC both knew. Freshly home after a stint in the pen, Billy had once been a big-time drug dealer. He was trying to get his feet wet again. With Phatz dipping in the coke trade now, the two were in talks on where to find the best product for the best prices. Phatz transition to the new hustle had been easy. As he began to make moves he realized that selling drugs required less labor than smashing cases, but still he could never turn his back on his first love. Picking up the phone he dialed up Billy. He listened in closely as the man dropped the information that he had been waiting to hear in his lap. It wasn't long before he pulled up to Billy's trap house on Carmona off Washington, he wasted no time going inside.

"Just handle yo business with that nigga in there and we'll get to all that other shit later," Billy greeted him already aware of the situation.

With a nod he made his way to the closed door in the back of the house. Opening it slowly his eyes landed on Corey's back. Silently Phatz watched the man clumsily weigh and bag up the drugs. There had to be something wrong with the triple beam scale Corey was piling too much in the bags. Phatz had been doing it for so long he knew how a gram was supposed to look. He was cheating himself.

Corey still hadn't realized he was there yet.

"The fiends making more than you."

At his voice Corey jumped spilling white powder on the scale.

"Shit."

He tried to brush it in the bag with his hand, but it was no use. It was tainted.

Finally, Corey faced him with a look of guilt written on his face, he dropped his eyes to the ground like a child who had been caught doing something wrong.

"We gotta talk," Phatz stated.

"Yea, I know," Corey responded meeting his eyes briefly.

"Meet me in the bathroom when you done in here," he said walking out of the room not waiting for a response.

In the bathroom he leaned against the stained sink. The crack in the mirror reflected how he was feeling…torn in half. A part of him wanted to let Corey slide and move on. The other part of him had to know why his best friend had set him up. Ultimately the side that couldn't take any chances won.

Corey launched into an explanation the second he walked in.

"Big Pimping it's not what you think, the pigs picked me up on a one eighty-seven, out of nowhere. I only called you because I knew you wouldn't break no matter what."

The excuse sounded lame to Phatz ears, and he told him so. He was getting angry just thinking about it. If he had stayed a second longer on the phone, they would be having a different conversation because he had learned minutes after he had left the cops raided the place.

Corey shoved his hands in the pocket of his jacket. A jacket he hadn't been wearing before. It caught Phatz attention.

"What you got in yo pocket?" Leveling him with a stare Phatz folded his arms over his chest.

Corey shifted from one feet to another.

"A gun."

"A gun!" Phatz repeated almost hysterical.

"But it doesn't have any bullets in it," Corey rushed out in a pleading tone.

It took everything in Phatz not to lunge at him. "Give me the damn gun!" he demanded.

Sheepishly Corey handed it to him.

Phatz palmed the .357 in his hand.

"I know I fucked up," Corey admitted, tucking his chin in his chest.

"Yeah you did," Phatz said, stepping closer.

"Don't ever do me like that again with the police, you could do anybody else nigga but not me."

He let his words sink in.

All out of excuses Corey sighed. Squaring his shoulders, he lifted his head, "You right man, you right, I shouldn't have brought you into it and I'm sorry."

This time he held his stare. Seconds ticked off before Phatz let out a deep breath. He'd known Corey for over fifteen years and honestly, they were like brothers. He couldn't hold it to him. No matter how hard he tried.

"Don't do no dumb shit like that again," he repeated handing Corey the gun.

"I won't man, I was just under a lot of pressure you know how that shit be I told them we weren't killers but they looking to pin those three bodies on somebody," Corey said.

Phatz hand was on the doorknob when he paused, "So who was all on the phone?" he asked.

"The Sergeant, Kenny and Vivian."

Phatz glared at him.

"Don't be mad at Vivian I made her call you."

Eyeing him wearily Phatz scrubbed a hand down his face. Maybe Corey was right and they were just looking for the killers. With a nod he opened the door. With Corey still on his tail Phatz was halfway to his car when he remembered.

"Oh yeah I got something for you."

Corey appeared confused until Phatz opened his hands.

"My work! Damn man you got it back for me like you said you would," Corey said as he took the bag out his hand along with the money.

"That's right I got all that they didn't smoke up and I hit all of them niggas pockets."

A look of gratitude passed Corey's face.

Phatz gripped his hand, "All I need you to do is have my back like I have yours."

Shaking his head hard Corey smiled "I got you man, I promise."

It was settled.

"When you get back inside reset that scale or you gone fuck yourself," Phatz warned.

"Uh huh," Corey said half distracted by the 71' candy apple Glasshouse ragtop at the curb.

"Fool you gotta let me drive this please," he begged.

Digging in his pockets Phatz tossed him the keys. "Go ahead."

Skittering around to the driver's side Corey slid behind the wheel before the engine purred to life. Five minutes later he returned with a dreamy look on his face.

"I gotta get me one of these bitches."

Phatz took the keys from him, " Bag ya shit up right and you will."

Behind the wheel now he dapped Corey up. "Aye remember what I said fool, you gotta have my back like I got yours," he repeated.

"Big Pimpin', I got you for real." They embraced one last time before Corey returned to the house.

Phatz took the man's word not knowing how much it would cost him in the end.

****

"Your total is $2,129," the cashier behind the desk stated with a smirk on her face.

Reaching into his pocket AC produced a wad of cash watching as her thin lips set into a grim line. He smiled to mask the frustration he felt when she recounted the money in his face. She kept her blue eyes on him the entire time. It took everything in him not to snatch the bag away from her when she handed it to him.

He didn't want to draw any unwanted attention to himself but knew it was already too late for that. The moment he stepped foot in the high-end Louis Vuitton store they watched him. He could feel their eyes on him as he browsed the aisles trying to select a gift for his big sister Ruby's birthday. Instead of offering their assistance they stalked him like prey until he picked the overpriced Louis Vuitton purse. The bag was the real deal and cost a lot of money unlike the knock offs they sold in downtown L.A. He knew his sister would love it.

It was almost after 3 P.M. when he finished shopping at the Century City Mall, he thought about the jewelry store he'd spotted while browsing through the stores. It wasn't much but he saw a few pieces that was worth mentioning to Phatz to see if he had them in his personal collection already. If not he wouldn't mind returning at a later time to give the store clerks a real reason to be afraid.

When he arrived at Marshall's he wasn't surprised that the guy he was scheduled to meet was nowhere in sight. Mentally cursing himself he checked the time on his Presidential Rolex. I'm giving this nigga ten more minutes and I'm out of here he told himself. Marshall's was unusually empty for a Friday evening. Besides one lone customer in the waiting area and another in the barber's chair the place looked like a ghost town. There wasn't a dice game in sight, which made waiting around even harder. Settling on a recent issue of *Jet* magazine to pass time He was eyeball deep in the beauty of the month when Marshall appeared in front of him. Noticing the look of concern on the man's face he lowered the magazine into his lap.

"It's too hot for you to be sitting around out in the open like this," Marshall said.

"What you mean?" AC asked puzzled.

Marshall leaned in so close he could see the stubble growing on his cheek.

"At about eight this morning one time came through here flashing pictures of you and Phatz asking questions about y'all whereabouts," said Marshall.

The news caught AC off guard. He struggled with his next words. "What else did they want?" he asked already climbing to his feet. Just knowing the police had been around made him want to leave.

Marshall shrugged. "You know the usual threats, tried to get a few answers but nobody talked. They shook the place up pretty good though." He glanced around the empty waiting area.

AC shook his head. "I'm sorry bout that man."

Marshall waved his apology off. "Fuck that you boys out here getting money and they hate that, just be careful out there, lay low until all this shit blow over."

"You right," AC agreed. As he walked out the door, he was still reeling from the news he'd just learned. He didn't even notice the man standing by his lowrider.

"You ready?"

His head snapped up. It was Red. A half hour late, the man looked like he had just rolled out of bed.

"Change of plans," AC said opening the door to the driver side of his lowrider.

Red slid into the passenger seat. "What you mean change of plans I thought we was bout to go get some money?"

Checking his rearview AC cast him a side glance. "A few things have come up."

Sharing what he had just learned with Red he put the car in drive. Red had spotted a nice spot to hit earlier that week. Presenting the opportunity to AC they'd both decided that today would be the day to handle business.

That was before the police had thrown a monkey wrench into his plans.

Red continued to try to persuade him to move forward with the plans.

Inside AC wrestled with himself. The good thing was at least he knew they were looking for him. He would be a little more careful now. The police didn't scare him. He'd been in trouble with the law enough to know how they operated. It was the threat to his hustle that bothered him. He couldn't make as much money inside like he could out in the free world.

He was so deep in thought he didn't notice the car that had been tailing him since he pulled away from Marshall's.

Taking the street that would lead him to his Aunt's house he needed to warn Phatz about their current problem.

"What you gon' do man?" Red asked when they came to the stop sign.

"I-" AC's words were cut off by the squealing of tires behind him.

The dark van swerved around them before coming to a complete stop blocking their path. In slow motion he watched two white men jump out.

"Oh shit!" Red exclaimed beside him.

"Get out the car!" they yelled approaching.

What the fuck AC thought as he caught sight of the shot guns in each of their hands. Approaching quickly, they aimed the guns at them now. From the side of his eye he watched cars come to a halt at the action taking place.

Stomping his feet down on the accelerator sending the car lurching forward he cut the wheel sharply barely missing the plainclothes officer and side swiping the van in his escape.

In the rearview mirror he watched them jump into the van.

"That's the police," Red said with a look of horror.

"Duh nigga I just told you they was looking for me," AC answered trying to concentrate on the road in front of him. A glance over his shoulders revealed they were still chasing them. Laying on the horn he ran through a stop sign.

"GO!GO!" Red cheered him on.

There was a big bang behind him. Horns blared.

"Oh shit, they crashed!" Red exclaimed.

Good AC thought. He eased his feet off the accelerator as his mind raced. He barely had enough time to slam on the breaks when a telephone truck came out of nowhere and stopped in front of them.

He blew the horn to no avail. His intuition began to set in as people began to climb out of the truck.

Something wasn't right, his mind screamed at him.

Then AC realized they weren't just any people. They were cops as well. He could tell by their stiff shirts and boot cut jeans.

Reversing the car, he made a sharp turn and drove wildly down the street.

The next turn he made brought them to an alley. Stopping abruptly, he threw the car in park.

"We gotta split," he told Red who was already climbing out the car before he could complete his sentence.

Abandoning the car, the men ran in opposite directions. AC choosing the one that would take him to his aunt's house. Sticking to the loitered alleys he was halfway to his aunt's house when he realized he'd left Ruby's present in the car.

Shit he cursed himself. He would have to get another one. That one would likely be used as evidence to retrace his steps. He cursed again.

Entering his aunt's house through the back door he crept to the front window. Sirens blared loudly as black and white police cars raced down the street. He had to get away.

Tossing a few clothes in a Gucci bag he calmly walked to the new red Eldorado parked in the driveway. Seated behind the wheel, he stuck the key in the switch. Sweat poured from his forehead as he held his breath and turned the ignition. At the sound of sirens approaching he wildly glanced out the back window expecting to be swarmed by police. When the car continued down the street. He sighed. Backing out of the driveway he drove the opposite way of all the commotion.

AC knew he had to leave the city. They wouldn't stop looking for him until they found him. But he wouldn't make it easy. He settled into the drive to Antelope Valley where he knew he would be welcomed with open arms and closed mouths Noticing the gas hand he made the quick decision to fill up once he put some distance between him and L.A. When he got to his destination, he would make a call to his aunt and tell her where to find the money if she needed any. It should hold them over until he could figure something out. Then he would call Phatz and tell him the bad news. They were being hunted.

2 months later

It was Christmas in July for Phatz family. He couldn't begin to describe the joy he felt at the sight of his sister and mothers face when they learned that the Thunderbird and Honda parked in the driveway belonged to them. His ears were still ringing from Denise's loud screams. She and his mother jumped around like kids on Christmas morning before rushing outside in haste.

His big brother Marlon's reaction was no different when he arrived and found out that the gold Chevy lowrider was for him.

Phatz's chest swelled with pride. This is what it was all about. Being able to give his family any and everything they wanted. His hustling had provided a life for them that they would have never been able to obtain with a regular day job. A stress-free life of luxury. And he would let nothing get in the way of that. Not even the threat of legal actions looming over his head would stop him. It had been almost two months since AC warned him that the cops were on to them.

At the time Phatz had shrugged it off. Yet when Mother Dear became aware of the police camping out on their street, he knew he had to prepare for the inevitable. Calling Corey up they met at Church's on Western and Vernon the next day. Phatz gave the man over $90,000 worth of personal jewelry and $10,000 in cash for a lawyer. He felt better now that he had a small plan in place. He and his great grandmother even laughed now when the police camped out. No one had made their move yet and since they hadn't, they kept hustling recently hitting the mall near AC's new residence out in Antelope Valley.

Sitting at the dining table now he bit into the succulent rib that had just come off the grill. The meat was falling off the bone. Lapping the sauce up with his tongue he tried to ignore the disagreement his sister and mama were having.

"It's not fair that I don't get to drive the car that my brother bought me," Denise complained.

"Well you don't have any license," his mother responded from the kitchen.

Folding her arms Denise plopped down on the sofa with her lips poked out like a bratty child. "I just don't see the point in having a car that I can't move," she murmured.

Placing another plate of ribs in front of him his mother wiped her hands on the apron around her waist.

Phatz had seen the look on her face before she was ready to battle. And that was good because Denise wasn't about to give up.

"Well can I at least drive around the corner and back," Denise tried to reason.

"No," Kathi said firmly shaking her head. "Anything can happen from here to there."

Denise let out a pitiful whimper.

"Baby tell her the responsibility that comes with driving," she said tapping him on the shoulder.

Phatz sighed, he had tried his best to stay out of it. In all fairness they both were right. Denise did need her license to drive but at the same time the car was made to be driven.

Downing the sweet tea in front of him. He thought about what his response should be. He didn't want to take sides.

Both ladies stood waiting for his answer.

He was reaching for another rib when his mother playfully slapped his hand. "Hello, did you not hear me?"

Relenting he finally answered

"How bout this mama, since Denise can't drive the car without her license how bout we let Twin drive her around." Twin was his sister's boyfriend. Admittedly he liked the kid. He treated his sister with respect, and he hooked Phatz up with the shoe deals from the Footlocker store he worked at in the mall.

He saw the situation as a win win and apparently his mom did too because in the next few seconds Denise was rushing in the back to call Twin over.

"You know you got her like that don't you," his mother said taking a seat beside him.

"Like what?" Phatz asked feigning innocence.

"Spoiled rotten."

He chuckled. It was true. At sixteen Denise had everything a girl could want from clothes to jewelry and now she had a car. She was living out her sweet sixteen in style.

"I'm gonna go sit in my car until Twin gets here," Denise announced coming from the back. "My car," she repeated testing the sound of it.

"I have to give it a name," she said as she wiggled the keys around her finger. "Something fly," Denise said more to herself than them as she walked out the door.

A few seconds later they heard the car's alarm system followed by the slamming of the door.

Wiping his mouth with the napkin Phatz stared down at the meatless bone. Pushing the plate away he decided he would save some room for later. He wanted to take his low rider out for a spin. Maybe cruise down Rodeo drive with the top back. He was contemplating his next move when his mama voice broke into his thoughts.

"So, what did you get mother dear?" Kathi asked removing the plate in front of him.

Reaching into his bag he pulled out the Presidential Rolex. Since Mother dear didn't drive, he figured he'd upgrade the Rolex she wore. The new one was encrusted with diamonds and the sleekness of it almost made him keep it for himself.

Leaving it in his mother's care he walked to his car with a to go plate in his hands.

Twin was backing out of the driveway when Denise blew the horn. Letting down the window she waved. "Thank you, little big brother I love, you!" she yelled out the window as they pulled off.

Phatz stared after the car knowing that she was in good hands. Seeing the smile on her face made him happy. Their happiness was his happiness.

Back at his own place Phatz worked under the hood of his low rider replacing the old, corroded battery with a new one. When he had tried to crank it earlier the engine didn't budge. He was relieved that it was only a minor problem. There was over $20K in the cars' system alone.

"That ought to do it," he said slamming the hood down. At the sight of Corey cruising down his street he lifted his arms in hopes of flagging him down. When the man kept face forward without a single glance in his direction Phatz thought it was odd, especially since they had just met up.

"Maybe he didn't see me," he said out loud as he slid behind the wheel. Making a mental note to hit him up later he crank the car.

When the engine roared to life, he smiled seconds before hitting the hydraulics sending the car in a series of side to side movements.

That's it right there.

Easing out into the street he smiled at the onlookers in traffic. The lowrider commanded attention everywhere it went just like it's owner.

****

Sitting at the red light on Slauson and Crenshaw in the early morning traffic Phatz watched steam rise from the concrete street creating a mirage a few feet away. The cool air blowing in his face made him grateful that he wasn't like many of the poor souls walking around in the stiffening August heat that day. In the passenger seat his friend E-Mac bobbed his head along to James Brown *The Big Pay Back*, blaring from the wolfer speakers. Phatz had recruited the man for a job that morning and with E-Mac recent release Phatz knew that he was eager to line his pockets. The last couple of weeks had been filled with nonstop jewelry heists. Now with the summer coming to an end Phatz was thinking of expanding their hustle. He was thinking big. Real big.

He was lost in his thoughts when E-Mac tapped him on the shoulder and pointed out the window. Casting a glance in the direction Phatz watched as unmarked cars pulled up into the empty KFC parking lot. Men dressed in windbreakers with shotguns casually slung over their shoulders gathered in a circle.

"I wonder who they bout to bust?" E-Mac commented.

Phatz tilted his head, "Probably me." The men burst into a fit of laughter as the light turned green and the traffic moved along.

Almost an hour later they were driving down I-10-east after their heist at Service Merchandise. E-Mac was on a natural high as he examined the jewelry in his lap.

"It gotta be at least $50,000 in this bag," he said excitedly.

"Try a hundred," Phatz said casually.

E-Mac's smile widened even more. There would be plenty more where that came from once Phatz put his new plans into motion.

Back at E-Mac's house he grabbed the phone to call the unfamiliar number that had been blowing him up for the pass thirty minutes.

"Hello?" A panicked voice answered on the third ring.

Immediately realizing that the voice belonged to Silky's mother his body tensed.

"Wait, calm down I can't understand a word you saying," Phatz responded. Switching the phone to his other ear trying to keep an eye on E-Mac who was looking at the jewelry.

"They got Silky!" she finally blurted out.

He listened closely as the woman recalled the details. The squat team had kicked down their door and hauled Silky to jail.

"What did they find?"

Catching E-Mac's eye he shook his head at the puzzled expression on his face.

"Just a gun, they said it wasn't registered so they took her in for questioning."

Silky's mom didn't have to say what they both already knew. They were looking for him.

He rattled off a location for her to meet him at. Ending the call, he grabbed the jewelry promising to return with E-Mac's cut before hopping in his Volkswagen Rabbit.

His mind raced with thoughts as he drove down Western Boulevard. Phatz still didn't know what had triggered one-time alarm on their operation two months ago. But something wasn't adding up.

"Damn," he swore under his breath.

He'd made the mistake of thinking that since they hadn't come after them full force yet, they had given up, but he had a strange feeling that they were just getting started.

An hour later he paced the floor of the hotel room at the Ramada Inn while Silky showered. Her mom had placed the $500 bond and thirty minutes after that her bail was posted. Silky denied ever knowing Phatz when questioned of his whereabouts and when they'd asked her about the gun she replied, "What gun?"

Her fingerprints didn't match those on the weapon, so by law they couldn't hold her, especially with her not talking. Phatz had to give it to her. She performed well under pressure.

Gently easing the drape of the window back he peered out the window. Except for his Volkswagen parked underneath the light pole, the parking lot was almost empty. They were in Culver city less than thirty minutes away from L.A. He knew he couldn't return back to his old place on 67th and Brynhurst. The hotel would have to do, even though he hated the smoke smell that clung in the air and would prefer his own king-sized bed. He made a mental reminder to call the front desk and switch to a nonsmoking room before the week was over.

His eyes strayed to the bag of jewelry on the bed. Picking up the phone on the nightstand he dialed the number to Zac's shop to inform him that he would be coming with the good stuff. He had just placed the receiver on the hook when Silky exited the bathroom with a towel wrapped around her body. Shamelessly she let it drop to the floor. Any other time Phatz would have been eager to slide in between her brown thighs but he had business to handle. When she was dressed in nothing but a T-shirt she plopped down on the soft mattress.

"So, what's the plan?"

He smiled. She knew him well.

Walking over to the mini fridge he grabbed a bottle of water from it.

"First I'ma take the jewelry down to Zac and get the cash." Twisting the cap off he raised the bottle to his lip and took a deep sip from it.

Wiping at the small dribble that had managed to escape he handed the bottle to Silky.

"Then I'ma take the cash to mothers dear and-"

She stopped him.

"You don't think the cops will be parked outside?" she asked before draining the bottle.

He shook his head. "No see me and Mother Dear have a system, if they're parked outside, she'll page me. Since I haven't gotten a page then everything is cool. But to be on the safe side I'll call and check before I go that way."

Silky nodded her head.

"After that we'll just lay low around here until we can figure out something."

Bag in hand he headed for the door.

Turning back to her he said, "You know to not answer for anyone but me."

Silky rolled her eyes and stood. "Duh Phatz I'm not a little kid."

Moving towards him, he watched the hem of the shirt rise up her thighs with every step. Standing in front of him now she rubbed her body against his.

We'll get to that later."

"You promise?" she nibbled on his ear.

"Promise," he replied kissing her lightly on the lips. And he was gone. Outside in the parking lot he glanced over his shoulder. Deciding it was clear he got in the Volkswagen Rabbit and pulled off.

Zac was excited to see him when he walked in the shop with the bag.

Phatz exited the shop one hundred and ten thousand dollars richer than before. At E-Mac's when he'd dropped of his cut, Phatz had placed a call to mother dear who confirmed that the coast was clear.

That still didn't stop him from circling the block twice before going in through the back door. When the money was tucked safely away in the house, he breathed easier.

He was halfway back to the hotel when he remembered he promised a friend he would drop by his party in Inglewood. It didn't seem like a good time considering everything going on, but throwing caution to the wind he decided to proceed with his plans Who knew the next time he would be able to move around? Plus, the way he saw it he was two steps ahead of the police. He knew they were looking for him and he knew where they were looking at. None of those places would lead to him. Los Angeles was too big. It was his personal hiding place.

Pulling up outside the apartments he noticed the small dice game going on, on the sidewalk. Another group had spilled out onto the grass with cups and bottles in their hands. From where he was standing, he could hear the music. It looked like the party had already started.

Making his way through the crowd he entered the apartment. A quick scan around the room and he calculated that there were at least eighty people in the small space.

Phatz shook hands with a few Jungle niggas that were in attendance. Finally, he spotted Duck making his way over to him.

"Man, I'm glad you could make it," Duck said happily embracing him.

"Aye Phatz here,"he announced proudly to the large crowd over the music.

Inwardly Phatz cringed. He didn't need that type of spotlight shining on him. Not right now.

"You want something to drink or eat?

My baby got some good ass potato salad," Duck said sliding the woman beside him underneath his arm.

Declining Phatz mingled around a little bit.

Though it was honey's everywhere, it was the dice game outside that had caught his attention.

Returning to the group on the curb he placed his bet.

Phatz was winning when the pager on his side began to buzz. Ignoring it he shook the dice in his palm and let it roll. Five.

The growing crowd around him cheered. He was on a winning streak. The pager buzzed again. Pausing, he unclipped it from his hip.

It was Marlon. What now he wondered.

"Aye I'll be right back I need to make a phone call hold my spot, "he said handing the dice to the man beside him.

Back in the house Duck guided him to their bedroom where the phone was.

The room was leopard print crazy. There was a leopard bedspread, blinds, carpet. There was even a painting of a leopard hanging over the bed. It wasn't his taste, but at least they were matching.

Phatz lounged back in the comfortable black chair next to the bed as he dialed Marlon's number. The phone rang twice before his brother's voice came over the line,

"Hello?"

"Yea playa wat's up, you interrupting my night, I'm tryna ge---" His words were cut short by his brother's hysterical voice.

"Bro one time just pulled me over in yo shit with guns on me, they were looking for you, they said they gone kill you if they catch y'all coming out of a jewelry store!"

Phatz bolted up not believing what he had just heard. "What?" he asked in disbelief.

First, they grabbed Silky now they pulled out guns on his big brother. What was next?

You know what's next the voice in his head answered.

Marlon was still talking, "They said y'all wanted for robbing thirty-two jewelry stores."

"Y'all?" Phatz questioned.

Marlon sighed on the other end in frustration. "Yea, you and AC. They know everything," he said stretching the last word.

Phatz continued to listen to his big brother, but frowned at Marlons' next words.

"You need to go to daddy's house."

"Daddy, nigga I haven't seen daddy since the fourth grade?" Cracking the door open he looked down the hall. It didn't look like he would be getting back to his game anytime soon.

"Just go to daddy until shit blow over out here," he paused. "Dino-," Marlon said using his real name, -"you need to go."

The words erased any doubt he had about the situation He had never heard Marlon sound so serious before.

Letting out a deep breath Phatz scrubbed one hand down his face.

Still clutching the phone to his ear, he spoke "Ok look in thirty minutes I want you to meet me at the A.M./P.M. mini mart on Crenshaw and Jefferson."

"For what?" Marlon questioned.

Phatz could hear the uneasiness in his brother's voice.

"Just meet me there," he said ending the call.

Sitting back in the chair Phatz put his head in his hands. How could a day that started so good be ending so bad?

His musing was interrupted by a knock at the door.

"You aight in there?"

It was Duck.

Twisting the knob, the man let himself in.

Rising to his feet Phatz was careful to conceal his emotions. He didn't want anyone knowing anything.

"Everything's velvet, I just gotta go holla at a few people."

"Aw man, that's too bad," Duck said falling for the lie.

He walked with Phatz out the door. The dice game had swelled to twice the size since he'd left. That meant so had the money pot.

Damn he thought to himself again, getting into his rag top.

By the time he arrived at the twenty- four- seven gas station his brother was already posted in the white Jaguar.

Rushing up to him Marlon embraced him.

Noticing the bug eyed expression on Marlons' face he realized the incident with the police had done a number on him.

Pulling back from their embrace Marlon eyes darted around the parking lot.

"It's cool," Phatz said knowing the man was looking for any signs of the police.

Folding his arms in front of him Marlon stared at him. "You going to Daddy's, right?"

It didn't seem like L.A'. s finest was giving him any other choice. If he didn't leave now there was no telling what else they had up their sleeve. Today it was Silky and Marlon who's to say they wouldn't kick down the doors of Mother Dears' house. He couldn't have that. The best thing to do was get out of the city for a while. Long enough for someone else to catch their attention.

Phatz nodded his head at his brothers' question.

"Good," Marlon said sounding relieved.

On the way there Phatz had come up with the plan. The first part of it involved switching cars. He would take the white Jaguar and his brother would get the 71' Glasshouse. That way Marlon wouldn't have to worry about them pulling down on him again. This time they would get the person they were looking for, even though he was hoping it didn't come to that.

"I need you to go to Mother Dears house- through the alley- go to the safe and get me $5,000."

Money was another thing Phatz had accounted for. He would need some if he was going on the run.

He continued, "When you get it bring it to Aunt Be Be's house then we'll go to the airport."

"Sounds good," Marlon said handing him the keys to the Jaguar.

Marlon pulled away from the gas station first. A few seconds later Phatz did the same. At Be Be's house he dialed the number to the Ramada Inn. The operator put him through to their room.

Silkys' sleepy voice answered on the first ring.

"I'm going to Louisiana."

"What?" she asked wide awake now.

He quickly filled her in on all that had happened since he left the room.

"Well I'm going too I got family in New Orleans."

He was hoping she would say that.

"Ok well you need to get to my Aunt Be Be's house now."

"Now? I don't have any clothes packed or anything."

He could hear her moving around on the other end.

"Forget the clothes, we'll get everything new when we get there."

The line went silent.

"Hello?"

"Ok, I'm coming," she said excitedly before hanging up.

At his great aunt's house Phatz checked the money he stashed in the safe. It was over a quarter million there, plus the money that Marlon was bringing. He knew the police wouldn't think to look there and if they did, they would never find it. The safe was cemented in the ground. Satisfied with what he saw Phatz waited patiently for Marlon and Silky to arrive.

When Silky arrived at the house before Marlon he began to grow concerned.

"You ready?" she asked carrying a Louis Vuitton bag.

"Soon as Marlon gets here."

Silky took a seat next to him on the sofa.

"It's been a long day huh?"

"Too long," he responded before remembering what she'd said over the phone.

"Do you really have family in New Orleans?"

Sitting her bag on the floor she smiled, "My daddy and my mama side of the family lives there. That's where I was born," she added filling Phatz in on a piece of her life that he didn't know about.

The wheels in his head began to turn.

"First we'll go to my daddy's house in Shreveport after that, we head to your family's house." He paused, "We gone hit licks the whole way to New Orleans."

Silky laughed. "I knew you were up to something."

He always was.

Just then Marlon walked through the door. He greeted Silky before handing Phatz the bag of money.

"Sorry it took so long thought I spotted something, but it was nothing."

"You sure?" Phatz asked.

"Positive," Marlon responded.

"Well let's go."

Marlon drove them to LAX in the Jag. On the ride there Phatz kept thinking about how much he didn't want to go. He'd been on the run before but never like this. This was the first time he was being forced to leave. Who would bring mother dear her Church's Chicken? He worried about his mother and sister as well.

All too soon the car stopped in front of LAX airport.

Sending Silky to purchase the ticket he hung around outside with his brother. Darkness had settled over the city, outlined by the city's lights. He watched the large airplanes leave the runway disappearing among the clouds and twinkling stars.

In the blink of an eye everything had changed.

He shook his head. What was done was done.

"You know what I want when you come back," his brother said staring up at the sky.

Phatz slanted his eyes towards him. "What?"

"A Porsche," Marlon laughed.

"A Porsche, man I just got you that 63' Chevy."

"Yeah I know…" his voice trailed off.

The two were quiet for a while.

Phatz could hear the loud intercom from inside calling out flights.

Silky appeared at his side.

"We leave in an hour," she said handing him his ticket.

"Damn that was fast," Marlon said checking the pager on his hip that had just vibrated.

Using the excuse to freshen up Silky left the two alone.

"About that Porsche?" Marlon teased.

"I got you."

"For real?" Marlon asked surprised.

"You know it", Phatz answered truthfully.

His brother embraced him.

"Aight I'ma hold you to your word." The sound of another plane taking off sounded in the distance.

Phatz glanced inside the airport. It was getting full. Now was the time to go find a place for them to sit. No longer able to prolong the inevitable he turned to his brother. Phatz thought about the fact that he hadn't said bye to his mom, his sister Denise, or Mother Dear. God forbid if something happened to him or them. He shoved the thoughts away. He would be back. Nothing could keep him from returning home.

"You hold it down while I'm away, I'll be back in no time," he said with confidence as he embraced his brother one last time.

"I know and when you do, we gone ride that Porsche through the city fuck one time. What's that you and Awful Clyde be saying?"

Smiling Phatz knew exactly what he was referring to.

"It's just some mo of it."

"That's right," Marlon smiled. Getting into the Jag he turned up the sounds of *Cold Cold World* by Teddy Pendergrass, with one last head nod to Phatz he drove away.

Phatz watched the car until the taillights disappeared. The memory of Marlon driving off would forever be branded in his mind.

On the plane Silky drifted off to sleep as soon as the wheels were in the air leaving him alone with his thoughts. He stared out the small window seeing nothing but the dark sky. Eventually his eye lids began to droop as he struggled to stay woke. Finally, he leaned his head back against the seat and gave in to the darkness, knowing that the next time he opened his eyes he would be in Shreveport, Louisiana.

Family

(Aunt, Father, and Uncle)

(Phatz, Denise, and Marlon)

(Kathi (mother), on the slant nose P-car)

(Phatz and beautiful sister Denise)

Shreveport, Louisiana

With every passing second the pounding in his ears seemed to grow louder. Gripping the Louis Vuitton bag at his side his eyes darted down the dark street to the lone light pole at the corner. The cab driver told them that the area was known as the Bottoms by the locals and when Phatz arrived he realized why. Even in the dark he could tell how poor it was. He barely missed the large pothole gaping in the street when he stepped out of the cab. Without sidewalks he was left standing in the street staring at three houses surrounded by an old metal fence. The wooden house sitting on bricks in the middle looked as if a strong wind would blow it down at any second. Taken back by the sight of it he double checked the address written down hoping he was wrong. Shoving the paper back in his pocket he sighed. He hadn't been mistaken. 412 Lawrence Street was where his father lived.

Harry Bradley left Los Angeles over sixteen years ago, to return to the place he had grown up. The distance never stopped the man from being in his children's lives, even if it wasn't physically. When Phatz was young, just one threat to call his dad would straighten him out, at least for a while. As he grew older the threats stopped working, but by then he and his dad had developed mutual respect for one another. Phatz respected the fact that he took care of them and Harry respected the man his son was becoming. Knowing only a few steps separated him from the one person he looked up to felt strange. And to think, all it had taken was a panicked phone call from his brother to send him running to what felt like the other side of the world.

Once he stepped off the plane Phatz knew he was no longer home. Unlike the cool nights in L.A., the heat in Louisiana was almost suffocating, making the polo shirt he wore cling to him like a second skin. Gravel crunched under his Nike shoes as he shifted from one foot to the other pulling the shirt from his damp chest as he continued to take in his surroundings. Another telling sign that he was in no man's land was the lack of noise. Except the insistent chirping of an insect, the street was quiet. Already Phatz was beginning to miss the sounds of the lively city. Here, it sounded dead.

"You ready?" Silky asked from beside him. His gaze strayed back to the shack, with a tight nod of his head Phatz took a deep breath. Inside the rusted gate they walked the short steps that led them to the wooden door. The pounding in his ears roared even louder as he raised his fist to knock, but there was no answer. Just as he was about to lift his hand to knock again the porch light came on flooding the darkness.

"Who is it!?" the gruff voice called out from behind the door.

"It's me dad."

Phatz had taken the liberty to call him at the airport to tell him he was coming, but Harry didn't believe him.

On the other side he could hear him wrestling with the locks before the door swung open.

One-minute Phatz was staring into eyes like his own and the next he was being embraced in a tight hug.

Pulling out of the embrace Harry blinked in disbelief.

"D-Nee?"

Not trusting himself to speak Phatz forced his head to move up and down. Time seemed to stand still as he gazed at his dad. On the plane he'd calculated that his father was fifty, just a few years older than his mother and from the looks of it he was wearing his age well. Except for his rounding stomach, he still looked as he did when Phatz was a kid. Under the light, Harry's brown skin was blemish free. His wisdom filled eyes shined brightly with unshed tears. Quickly pulling himself together he ushered them inside.

Reaching for Silky's free hand Phatz stepped across the threshold into the house. Based on the house's outer appearance he knew not to expect anything luxurious inside. Two shabby couches, a floor model TV and a table were the only furniture in the room. Moving further inside, he noticed pictures hanging on the wooden wall. A younger version of himself, Denise, and Marlon stared back at him.

"You're all grown now," Harry said from beside him, his face beaming with pride.

For the first time since the door opened Phatz spoke, "I am."

Closer now, he could see the crow's feet that shaped Harry eyes. The permanent laughter marks around his mouth told him that even though he didn't seem to have much he was enjoying his life. Placing an arm around his shoulder Harry guided him to one of the couches as Silky took a seat on the other one.

Thirty minutes later he watched Harry wipe at his leaking eyes. After introductions were made Harry had entertained Silky with stories of Phatz -or D-Nee as he called him – and his mischief as a kid. Phatz was relieved that the nervousness he'd felt about meeting him had disappeared. Talking and joking with his dad had come naturally.

Silky's giggles drew his attention to her. Sometime during the night she'd slipped out of her shoes and jacket and now lounged comfortably across the couch. In the short time he'd known her he'd never seen her so relaxed. She appeared to be right at home. Not any part of her gave away the fact that she was on the run with him from L.A.'s finest. While he had filled Harry in on his life happenings, Phatz intentionally left that part out.

When a gurgling sound came from his stomach he was reminded of the pretzels and water he choked down on the plane. In his rush to get out of L.A., food had been the last thing on his mind.

Harry talked in an animated voice as he continued to entertain Silky, who seemed to be enjoying every second of it.

"I need to get something to eat I'm starving," Phatz said interrupting them.

"Well D-Nee I can whip y'all something up on the stove really quick." He tried to ease up but Phatz stopped him.

"No dad how bout we take you out to eat?"

"Yeah Mr. Harry," Silky echoed.

Even though it was approaching ten o clock, Phatz figured that there had to be at least one restaurant open in the small town.

Smiling Harry stood, "Well ok let me go put on some clothes." The flannel pajama shirt over a pair of worn jeans wasn't the ideal dress code.

When Phatz heard him rambling around in his room he turned to Silky who had a goofy look on her face.

"What?" he asked.

"D-Nee huh?" she asked before erupting into laughter.

Phatz shook his head. He was hoping she wouldn't take notice of the childhood nickname.

"Wait til I tell everyone about this."

"You won't," he dared seconds before lunging at her causing another fit of laughter to echo through the house.

****

"Listen I don't know about anything on this menu, just bring me something good to eat." Reaching into his pocket Phatz peeled off a twenty from his stack and handed it to the waitress. Her brown eyes lit up against her pale skin as she retrieved the money from him. Pushing her stringy blonde hair from her face she smiled.

"Yes sir, I know an order that's absolutely delicious, I'll be right back with your drink."

"Yeah do that," Phatz stated growing annoyed from hunger.

The minute she disappeared behind the white swinging doors Harry leaned in closer to him. "D-Nee you can't be speaking to these white folks like that," he said in a hushed whisper.

Phatz glanced around him. They were seated in a restaurant only a few blocks from Harry's house. It wouldn't have been his first choice but because he was unfamiliar with the place, he'd let his dad decide. Now confused he searched his father's face.

"What you mean don't talk to them like that I gave her my money and she's about to bring me something to eat, I don't know how country fried steak and gravy taste," he said mentioning an item from the menu.

Harry dropped his eyes "Yeah I know-" the rest of his sentence was cut short by the waitress returning.

"I got you all fixed up your order will be ready in a minute," she said smiling at Phatz.

"Now what will you lovely folks have?"

Silky rattled off her order. Next his dad did the same, but he noticed that the man included yes mam and no mam after every question the waitress asked.

Was that the way Harry expected him to talk to the waitress that didn't look to be a day over nineteen? If anything, she should've been curtseying Harry seeing that he was the elder in the situation. Phatz stewed in his seat as she jotted down their order. Louisiana was already giving him a bad vibe. Trying to shake off the sudden dark cloud that had ascended on him he began to think of his next move, while Silky told Harry about her family in New Orleans. She was still talking when their orders arrived. Biting into his fried chicken, Phatz mused over all that had happened in the last twelve hours. When he woke this morning, he never would've imagined that by nightfall he would be in Shreveport, Louisiana. Shit he was sure if not for his dad he would have no idea the place existed.

Halfway through the meal he heard his name being called.

Looking up he noticed a funny look on Silkys' face.

"What?"

He was so deep in thought he hadn't realized they were talking to him.

"Your dad asked how long we were staying?"

Pushing his empty plate to the center of the table he reached for his drink. It was a question that he didn't quite have the answer to yet.

"Why dad? Are you ready for us to leave already?" he half joked before bringing the glass to his mouth.

Harry waved him off. "Stay as long as you like, I was asking because it's a few more restaurants you can check out in the morning Freeman and Harris is not too far, there's a mall, shopping stores…"

Phatz ears perked up at the mention of the mall.

"…You know just little things, nothing like the big city, but it's enough to keep you from going crazy," Harry added.

"Ok cool, we need to hit a few stores for some clothes tomorrow you think you can take us?" Phatz asked half excited.

"I have to work, but I have a friend who can come pick you up and drop you off and take you anywhere you want," Harry responded wiping his hand on the napkin.

Across from him Silky shrugged her shoulders. He knew she was more interested in the mall than she pretended.

With plans made for the next day they all returned to the house full and tired. The jet lag was finally beginning to wear on Phatz when he stepped out of the hot shower. Quickly toweling dry he joined Silky in the small room they would be sharing. She was fast asleep after her own shower. He was pulling on his shirt when a light knock came.

"Yeah?"

The sheet that covered the entrance slowly slid back.

"I just wanted to tell you and Silky good night, but I see she's already out like a light," Harry said chuckling.

"I know it's been a long day for you both."

You have no idea Phatz wanted to say instead he only nodded.

"I'm glad y'all here."

"Me too."

Harry shook his head like he still couldn't believe that his son was there. Phatz felt the same way for different reasons of course.

"Well I'll let you get to bed, goodnight son."

"Night dad."

Climbing under the cool sheets next to Silky, he silently vowed to visit his dad more often once he returned home. In fact, next time he would bring Marlon and Denise with him. It would be just like old times. As his eyelids grew heavy with sleep Phatz thought about what the next day would bring. Once Harry left for work, he planned to find out what all little old Shreveport, Louisiana had to offer them.

****

Tears rolled down his cheek as he gripped at his stomach. Swiping them away quickly his eyes darted to the side of him. Silky was in a similar state as she doubled over. When the camera cut back to Eddie Murphy's face on the screen, the crowd in the dim lit theatre roared with laughter. The movie *Trading Places* was a hit. Stopping at the matinee movie theatre located inside the mall proved to be a nice gamble. Sitting in the theatre with a bucket of popcorn with extra butter lodged in between them a sense of normalcy returned to him that he hadn't felt since leaving L.A.

When the movie was over instead of calling up their ride, Silky decided to visit a few more stores. Inside of Robinson's she tried on clothes as Phatz browsed through the men section. Not finding anything his taste he ventured back over to the dressing room.

"D-Nee that you?" Silky's voice teased as he approached.

"Stop calling me that," Phatz warned in an annoyed voice.

Amused, Silky bit back her laughter.

"Can you hand me the red shirt on the hanger please?" she asked.

Locating the shirt Phatz tossed it over the door.

He gazed around the store as he watched the people come and go. In the daylight Shreveport wasn't much. From what he could see the mall was the biggest attraction. Phatz hadn't done much sightseeing when they walked in. Maybe it was time too.

"Hey I'ma go check out Footlocker."

Passing Silky a stack of hundreds to take care of her purchases he rushed from the store.

Instead of going to Footlocker he wandered up and down the mall, hoping that by the time he was finished Silky would be ready.

He was doubling back towards the entrance when a bright light caught his attention. The Zales sign pulled at him like a magnetic force. Phatz didn't know how he had missed it.

Inside the store his mouth watered. A tingling sensation rushed through his body as he eyed the jewelry inside of the case. Out of all the stores he'd hit back in L.A. Phatz had never seen as much jewelry as he was seeing in the cases.

Breathe he cautioned himself as he moved closer. After counting forty Concord watches, two hundred diamond rings, and sixty Omega watches for men and women in one case, Phatz began to make his way to the case beside it. At the end of his inspection he calculated that there was a half a million worth of jewelry in the cases all together. It was enough to make his heart flutter.

At the sound of the recorded voice coming over the speaker announcing that the mall would be closing in fifteen minutes he realized he'd stood there so long that he'd lost track of time. But still he couldn't seem to pry himself from in front of the cases. Five minutes later he finally forced his legs to carry him out of the store.

As he went in search of Silky, Phatz couldn't believe his luck. This right here was the motherload of all the jewelry stores. What made it even harder to believe was that it was tucked away in the most unsuspecting place ever: Shreveport. The little hank town was loaded. Phatz began to wonder if there were other stores in the area like it. With the wheels in his head spinning he knew this was one opportunity that he couldn't pass up.

He was glancing down at his arm to check the time when he remembered that earlier at breakfast after spying Harry eyeing his wrist, he had given him his Presidential Rolex. Seeing his dad's eyes light up like a kid on Christmas when he handed the watch over made him smile. While Harry gushed over what he called an 'expensive piece' Phatz considered the $15,000 watch chump change. Especially now that he had gotten a good look at an even bigger stash. If the Presidential Rolex could make Harry happy, he couldn't imagine what his response would be when he bought him a brick house. Judging by the way those nice cases were set up back at Zales, Phatz figured hell he might buy his dad a house or three.

****

"You know that rag top Mercedes Benz you wanted back home?"

The question was posed to Silky who sat under the wheel of his dads 1972 Ford LTD. They were outside the now deserted St. Vincent Mall. When Phatz filled Silky in on all that he had seen inside of Zales, her eyes rounded like saucers. And just like that they had come up with a plan to revisit the mall once it was closed.

Silky shook her head, "Yeah what about it?"

In the car's dark interior, he turned to her, "It's yours once we pull this off."

He heard the smile in her voice when she spoke, "Well let's get to it then."

Reaching in the back seat he grabbed the crowbar and the bumper jack.

"Ima bust in through the front doors," he pointed towards the doors glass entrance. "I want you to go around to the back door of the mall," he continued as he pulled out a pillowcase, he'd taken from his dad bed. "If you see the police blow the horn and go to the other end by JC Penny and wait there."

"Ok got it," she responded.

With the pillowcase tucked in his pants, the crowbar in one hand and the bumper jack in the other he climbed out of the car. Determined, he stalked towards the entrance of the mall. Inside he could see that all the lights were off. Pulling his arm back Phatz swung the bumper jack into the door sending glass shattering everywhere.

When he was sure that the coast was clear he stepped through the doors, scooping up his tools as he went. With the glass crunching under his shoes, he made his way through the dark until he was standing in front of Zales. His eyes zeroed in on the iron gate that blocked his entrance. There was no way to access the store through the front. Thinking quick Phatz sent the bumper jack flying through the display window. When the glass shattered, he wasted no time crawling inside and locating the glass cases.

Minutes before the mall had closed, Phatz had stealthily watched as the manager and a worker removed the jewelry and placed it underneath the cabinet. It was the reason he had brought the crowbar along. Getting to work he set aside the bumper jack. His heart was in his throat as the jewelry came to his mind. It was almost his.

Just a little bit more he said to himself. Forcing the crowbar into the small slot he pushed down on it. When it didn't budge. He tried the other end.

The cabinet made a creaking sound before the latch finally gave away.

Pop!

A sigh of relief rushed through him.

Immediately his hand went to the pillowcase. This was the moment he had been anticipating all night. Phatz couldn't stop the grin that spread across his face.

Pushing the latch away he reached down to retrieve his treasure only to feel something hard underneath his hands.

"What the fuck?" he whispered snatching his hand back.

Taking a step forward he peered into the cabinet.

"Ain't this bout a bitch."

He couldn't believe it. Instead of the shiny jewelry he expected to see staring up at him, there was a big steel safe.

Snatching the crowbar up he cracked the cabinet beside it only to find the same thing: a safe.

Watching them place the jewelry in the cabinet earlier, he never would've guessed that they had a way of protecting their riches. Phatz shook his head in disappointment. With his plans ruined he hurried from the store.

Busting out the back door Phatz strolled to the car where Silky waited.

Angrily he tossed the crowbar and bumper jack in the backseat.

"Go!" He yelled ignoring the confused expression on Silky's face.

Without another word she sped out of the mall's parking lot.

"So, what happened?" she asked breaking the silence.

Slouched in the seat beside her Phatz shrugged, he was still fuming from his discovery. He had underestimated them. But there was no way he was leaving the little country town empty handed. There had to be another way in. It was time he put all his cards on the table.

Staring straight ahead he folded his arms across his chest, "Ima introduce these muthafuckas to Awful Clyde."

****

The shrill ringing of the phone broke through his sleep. Beside him the warm body stirred. It was late, the numbers from the digital clock on the nightstand read 2 A.M. for a moment he thought about ignoring it. Then he decided against it. It could be his aunt calling. Reaching over he grabbed the receiver.

"Awful Clyde."

The voice on the other end made him spring up from his sleep induced state. Untangling himself from the sheets, with the phone pressed firmly to his ear AC moved into the lit bathroom. When he closed the door down, he spoke into the phone.

"Phatz, man I've been looking all over for you how'd you get this number?"

On the other end Phatz laughed, "Well here I am. Twinkle told me how to reach you."

AC leaned his head against the cool tiled wall. Still trying to stay one step ahead of the cops he had taken to moving around to throw them off his trail, occasionally popping up to hit licks with Phatz, but even then, he was careful. Though he had to admit moving around from hotel to hotel was becoming exhausting.

"I thought the police had you, I hit up all your spots, niggas couldn't tell me nothing," AC said as he cracked open the door.

"Marlon ran me out here to Louisiana two days ago said the police pulled him over on Adams and Crenshaw in my VW Rabbit pointing guns at him."

"Louisiana!" AC repeated wiping the sleep from his eyes hoping that he'd heard wrong.

"That's right one time said we needed to turn ourselves in or they would kill us."

AC was still digesting the part about him being in Louisiana when his last words registered.

"And who is we and us?" he asked straightening up. He cringed at his bloodshot eyes staring back at him in the mirror as he leaned against the sink.

"Me and you nigga," Phatz laughed.

This wasn't the news he wanted to hear especially since the task force didn't seem like they would be giving up their chase. Knowing that he had managed to allude them all this time made him even more determined to stay out of their grasp.

On the other end of the phone Phatz voiced turned serious, "I'm at my pops house in this country ass part called Shreveport and you'll never guess what I found."

"Jewelry," said AC. Even with one time on their heels they remained focused on getting money. In fact, AC had scoped out two spots in the Valley that he wanted to bash, but it looked like it would have to wait.

"Damn right, worth more than you can imagine I need you to get here at once!"

At the urgency in Phatz, voice AC knew what time it was.

"I'm on my way."

Opening the door, he walked into the room with the phone still pressed to his ear. Spying the luggage that he had been living out of, he tossed a few toiletries inside along with the few items he had hanging up.

"Who you want me to bring?" he asked as he continued packing.

"Mike out the bity."

AC nodded at his choice. Mike was always down.

When all of his things had been stored away in his luggage he slid on his shoes, listening closely as Phatz gave instructions.

"Just get a plane ticket out of LAX to Shreveport, LA and call me when you get here."

His hands paused as he pulled his shirt over his head.

"I never been on a plane before, but I'll be there in the morning."

"First time for everything, catch you in the morning," Phatz said before disconnecting the call.

Replacing the receiver, AC did a once over around the room to make sure he had everything. His eyes lingered over the woman still asleep in the bed. They had been chilling for a few days now. Nice looking honey. It was too bad he couldn't enjoy more of what they had shared. Outside the room he crept down the stairs and to his car. The room was paid up for two more nights. He didn't have to worry about it being traced back to him. As far as the man at the front desk and the woman in the room knew, he was Deontae Scott. Awful Clyde only showed up when it was time for business.

. ******** **

Loud laughter and deep southern voices floated to the back of the restaurant as the group huddled around the table. The lunch crowd filed in Freeman & Harris -- the highly appraised Cajun soul food joint located downtown on Pete and Harris Drive-- at rapid speed. In the corner an old juke box spun the O' Jays song *Forever Mine* as patronages gathered around the countertop waiting for their orders to be cooked and rung up. Given the line that was beginning to stretch out the door, it would be a long wait. But no one seemed to mind battling the crowd or the scorching heat that day. Nor did they pay attention to the fly dressed group in the back that was about to give the town the most excitement that they had seen in centuries.

"When is all of this going down?" Mike asked in a voice just above a whisper. To the left of him AC stifled a yawn. Gently shaking his head his eyes darted to Phatz who sat across from him with a blank expression.

It never crossed his mind to tell his friend no when he got the call. He knew the reaction would be the same if the tables were reversed. AC hadn't known what to expect when he stepped off the plane. It sure wasn't the small run-down airport where they landed. The view only got worse on the ride to Phatz dad's house. Long winding poorly paved streets led into even poorer neighborhoods. Phatz description didn't do justice to the country town, at any moment he expected a bale of hay to roll down the street. After meeting up at Harry's house he and Mike checked into Section and Livingston motel only blocks away from where Phatz dad lived. The motel was crawling with addicts and dealers. A true shooting gallery. Usually AC went for more upscale living arrangements, but since they wouldn't be staying long, he would bare it.

Glancing around the restaurant he noticed that the waitress who had taken their order was now working the cash register. It was too much for him to hope that the frog legs that he'd ordered would be arriving any time soon. He focused his attention back in front of him.

"Damn nigga was you even listening?" Silky asked annoyed.

Mike leaned back in his chair. "Yeah, I just wanna make sure I got everything right."

She shook her head.

AC would have laughed if he didn't think it would annoy her even more.

"Nigga Ima go over this shit one more time, listennn," Phatz said stretching the word.

AC knew Mike wasn't the brightest when it came down to instructions, but his grind made up for it. Not to mention he was nice with scooping up the jewelry.

He sat there as Phatz went over the plan again.

"We'll be on our way to New Orleans by the time they figure out what hit em," Phatz stated ten minutes later.

AC slapped hands with him as Silky bounced in her seat excitedly.

"I like it, I see you and AC been doing y'all homework," Mike commented.

Before either man could respond the waitress appeared. After she placed their orders in front of them and refilled their cups she was gone.

Too busy savoring the food, the conversation was briefly forgotten as they fell into a comfortable silence.

The lunch crowd was beginning to thin out, but sometime during the rush someone had changed the juke's box tune to a bluesy song.

"What the fuck is that playing man?" Mike asked frowning. Scrapping his chair back he walked over to the juke box where he sifted through the music selection. Settling on another O'Jays classic *For the Love of Money*, he returned to the table oblivious of the glares from the other customers.

"That's more like it," he said reclaiming his seat.

Putting his head down AC couldn't help but laugh.

"AC how the frog legs taste?" Silky asked making a face.

Chewing the meat slowly in his mouth he thought about his answer before he responded.

"Chicken."

She made another face.

Everyone had just about finished eating when Phatz stared at them pointedly and asked, "So, everyone knows their part right?"

Silky nodded her head along with Mike.

"We bout to get this money," AC responded before shoving the last piece of the frog leg in his mouth. With Mike and Silky being involved it meant they would have to split the loot four ways instead of the normal two, but he couldn't complain. AC didn't have a problem sharing. To him the job would be no different than the one's they'd done back home. Quick and easy. What could possibly go wrong?

****

"Shit!"

Phatz eyes darted around the packed parking lot. If he didn't hurry fast someone might see him. Digging his tennis shoe into the pavement he gripped the vice grips in his hand tighter. At the feel of the lock sliding back he lifted the door handle. Once behind the wheel, a heavy sigh escaped from behind his lips. Breaking into the car had taken longer than he anticipated. He was relieved when the gizmo used to break the ignition started the car with no problem.

As he eased the car out of the space, he caught sight of Silky parked a few feet away from him ready to jump into action.

Bringing the car to a complete stop he hopped out and put it into drive watching as it rolled slowly towards the store window.

He breezed into the mall seconds before it went crashing through the window sending shoppers fleeing for safety.

The loud screams sent the security guards rushing in the direction.

"We need assistance!" One shouted into the walkie talkie as he sped pass Phatz.

With his hands tucked into his pockets Phatz strolled towards his destination, a small smile tugging at the corner of his lips.

The plan was going off without a hitch. The first part: create a distraction. Controlling where everyone who could ruin their heist would be, gave them the upper hand.

A slow whistle left his mouth when another guard dashed by. He glanced behind him at the crowd forming outside the store. Security would have their hands full for a while.

When he was only inches away from Zales, AC and Mike stepped from the shadows. One behind the other they walked into the store with Phatz bringing up the rear.

Removing the stopper that kept the door open Phatz closed it just as the clerks' bright cheery face appeared.

"Hi, is there anything I can help you with?" she asked with a warm smile.

In one quick motion AC brought the hammer down on the first case, breaking it into pieces.

He turned to the woman.

"Yes, you may, now lay down."

A look of horror covered the clerks face as she kneeled on the floor with her trembling hands raised in the air.

"P-please don't hurt me," she squeaked. Tears rolled from her brown eyes staining her white blouse as she got flat on the floor. Ignoring the tears AC swung around.

"Lay down !" he ordered the two frightened customers in the store.

Checking over his shoulder Phatz could see that security was still trying to contain the crowd outside of the store the car had crashed through. He smirked all the real action was happening in Zales.

Inside, AC swung the hammer like an expert cracking all five cases.

Tossing Phatz a pillowcase he stepped over the customers laying face flat as they switched positions.

Pillowcase in hand Phatz and Mike went to work.

"Scoop!Scoop!Scoop!" AC coached from behind them as they scooped the jewelry from the cases in one sweep.

Just as Phatz was nearing the last case someone let out a muffled cry.

"Lay down and be quiet!" AC yelled again.

As long as he could hear AC's voice, he knew that everything was under control. The people on the floor had no idea that hammers were the only weapon they had. Besides who would be bold enough to rob a store in broad daylight without any guns?

"Alright, let's go and thank you all for cooperating," AC said when Phatz finished gathering the last bit of jewelry.

Handing off the pillowcases to, AC they all stormed out of the store. The job had taken three minutes top. Inside he was celebrating, but his demeanor on the outside never betrayed him.

Exiting out of the side door, that led to the back-parking lot, Phatz jumped in the driver seat of the car they'd stolen before coming to the mall. Parking it in the handicap space was his way of making sure it was accessible when they came out.

When Mike slammed the door shut, he started the car.

With his heart hammering in his chest Phatz put the car in drive. No fast movements he told himself as he pulled out of the parking lot.

"Shit that was easy as hell."

"Too easy," AC replied from his crouched position on the floor.

"Man, Phatz you didn't lie, I've never seen that much bling in my life," Mike commented. He too was crouched down in the seat.

"You—," Phatz words were cut short at the sight in the rear-view mirror.

The customers from the store were running after the car pointing.

"Damn!" He ground his teeth together. Gripping the steering wheel, he continued at his normal pace, knowing that anything too sudden would only draw more attention.

"What's going on?" AC asked.

Checking the rearview mirror again, Phatz assessed the situation. The people were closer now and looked to be writing down the license plate number.

"Fucking people from the store chasing us."

"You gone speed up?" Mike asked.

Phatz didn't answer. Instead he focused on putting as much distance between them as he could. But the cars in front of him seemed to be creeping along at a snail's pace. It felt like forever before traffic budged. Finally, he made a left turn on the street that would lead them out of the mall.

Still checking the rear view, he saw the exact moment Silky crept out of her spot keeping with the plan.

That's my girl.

Before she could get completely behind him a car cut in front of her and blew his horn. When the man began flashing his lights and pointing Phatz realized the driver was trying to draw more attention to them. He could feel his anger begin to rise.

"The fool behind us wanna be a superhero, y'all hear that blowing?"

"Yeah let me handle that," AC said beginning to ease up.

Phatz shook his head "No, I got this."

With his eyes fixed on the light in front of him, he put the car in neutral. Superhero was going all in with his antics trying to draw attention to himself and attract the security who Phatz could see had burst out of the doors. But he wasn't worried about being chased by them. The back tires on the passenger side of all the SUV patrol cars were on flat. He'd taken care of that as soon as he arrived. It was the superhero who was causing the problems. If he didn't stop him now the man might get the idea to follow them or worse.

When the light turned green Phatz shifted the car in reverse and pressed the accelerator, ramming into the would-be hero's car.

As he put the car back in drive and pulled off he watched with joy as the man hit a U- Turn abandoning whatever silly plan he had in mind.

From the back-seat AC laughed.

Five minutes later they pulled over at the plaza down the street.

Silky stopped right behind him.

One by one they climbed into the car and laid down.

Phatz suspected by now that the mall was in uproar. The police would be searching for three black men in a stolen black vehicle, but they wouldn't be searching for a black woman driving by herself in a white car.

He waited until she had safely driven away to speak.

"Next up, South Park Mall."

****

The yellow cab came to a complete stop at the curb. From the living room window Phatz watched a figure climb out. When a knock followed shortly after he snatched the door open.

"Man, where the hell you got me at?"

"Right where you need to be," he responded widening the door.

In the past forty-eight hours they'd hit two more malls striking gold each time. A wrench was thrown in their plans when they discovered that the Pierremont Mall closed on Sundays. Phatz had a hunch that the mall could make their pockets a little more fatter so he wasn't leaving until he got his treasure. Using the phone book to plot out their next move, he wrote down every mall he planned to hit between Shreveport and New Orleans. Feeling confident with the seemingly foul proof scheme, he placed a phone call back home to check on things. It was then that Billy told him that the task squad wasn't the only ones hot on their heels. Ty had been searching everywhere for him non-stop. Curious to what his childhood friend could want Phatz called him up. He heard the desperation in his voice the minute he answered the phone. The cash Phatz gifted him two weeks ago had dried up. Ty was broke and damn near pleading over the phone to come. He tossed the idea of adding to their team around in his head a few times before finally agreeing. The way he saw it, more hands meant more jewelry to grab. Now after paying for Ty's flight to Louisiana they stood face to face in his dads living room.

Ty sat his tote bag down on the couch as his eyes shifted around the house.

"Where's everybody?"

Silky and Harry were still at the family's barbecue. Earlier that day Phatz had met his extended family and the little sister he hadn't known existed. Harry was indeed enjoying the life that he had carved out for himself and Phatz would leave him with some cash to make sure he enjoyed it even longer.

Grabbing the keys Phatz fanned his question off.

"Get ya bag, Ima show you where you staying at."

Reaching for his tote bag Ty began to move towards him.

"Naw, nigga you not staying here," Phatz said pointing at the door.

"Oh, my bad."

Phatz led him out the door and down the street.

Once they made it to the corner he stopped.

"You see that motel right there?" The sky was darkening, but the remaining light outlined the building he pointed to.

"That's where AC and Mike got a room, I want you to go to the front desk and see if the man will let you in the room with them."

"Cool," Ty said beginning to walk in the direction of the motel.

"Aye!" Phatz said calling after him. Closing the short distance between them he waited until a car passed by to speak.

"Don't call me, if the man at the front desk won't let you in, just come back around here cause it's another motel right around the corner."

Ty nodded his head.

Phatz watched him until he reached the motel before sprinting back to the house. When Ty didn't return, he started looking for a good hiding place to hide the jewelry. He was contemplating putting it in the closet when Silky breezed through the door.

"Pops said he'll be in later." She plopped down on the couch.

"You had fun?"

A smile lit up her face. "Yes, ooh the soul food is so good here." She wrapped a hand around her flat stomach.

He half listened to her as he continued to poke around the house. He thought he had found the perfect spot when the telephone began to ring.

With his eyes still trained on the attic door he answered, "Hello?"

"Homeboy the man just wanna know everything cool."

Phatz paused.

"You got the wrong number."

Slamming the phone down he stared at in disbelief.

Tell me that wasn't that fool Ty.

The phone rang again.

"I need to speak to Dino Bradley," the voice said.

On the other end Phatz scrubbed a hand down his face.

"Wrong number."

Hanging up he began to pace the floor. What the fuck was Ty thinking after he specifically told him not to call his dads house. Then he had given them his government name. How stupid could he be?

"What's wrong?" Silky asked walking over to him.

"This stupid ass muthafucka keep calling around with these people on the phone."

"Who?"

"Ty's dumb ass I told him good not to call my dad's house just come back."

Soon as the words left his mouth the phone rang yet again.

"Oh my god!"

Phatz tossed his hands in the air. He wanted to ring Ty's neck.

Snatching the phone up Silky put the receiver to her ear.

He listened in silence as she answered.

"Yes, that's my nephew everything is cool," she said after a few minutes.

"Stupid nigga," Phatz said to himself once Silky ended the call. Ty was already fucking up.

"Relax," she said guiding him down in a chair. Her hands moved to his tense shoulders and she began kneading and squeezing his flesh.

He let his eyes close as she worked the anger from his body. When she finished she sat in his lap facing him.

"Don't trip by this time tomorrow this place will be in our rearview and we'll be on to bigger and better." She slipped her shirt over her head and kissed him.

She was right Phatz thought while unhooking her bra. Tomorrow was Monday and Pierremont was sure to be open. They would strike first thing that morning and be headed to New Orleans by lunch. But still Ty had put him in a bad mood. He hated when niggas didn't stick to the script. He exhaled deeply as he tried to shove Ty's fuck up to the back of his mind. Ty was lucky that there was a nice pair of titties in his face begging for his attention. Instead of racing to the motel like he wanted, Phatz decided to take advantage of the alone time he and Silky had.

****

AC twirled the flower shaped brooch around with his fingers as he cradled the phone between his shoulder and ear. The brooch's sparkling glint caught his eye in the store, and he'd wasted no time plucking it from its case. He guessed that it was worth a hundred thousand. It would make a nice gift for his mom or aunt Twinkle. Or maybe his sister Ruby.

"So why did you leave?" the woman asked loudly interrupting his thoughts. Wanting to make sure that she had made it home safely from the hotel, he'd given her a call, but from the sound of her clipped tone she was still upset about him sneaking out in the middle of the night.

"Let me call you back," he said abruptly at the sound of knocking at the door. Not waiting for a response, he hung up. Standing, AC clutched the brooch in his hand before slipping it underneath the dresser. Mike was still in the bathroom showering. At the door he peered out of the peep hole into a face that he had never seen before. Light skinned and average height with a low hair cut the man didn't look to be over twenty.

Must be the cat Phatz was talking about. Still he played it cool.

"What's up?" he asked through the door.

"Phatz sent me," the man replied.

Satisfied with his answer AC stood aside to let him in. At the same time Mike emerged from the bathroom fully dressed.

"What up Ty?" Mike asked coming over to dap him up.

AC could feel Ty sizing him up as the room shrunk in size with all three of them inside.

"Shit man Phatz called me in to get this money." Dropping his bag down on the small table his head swiveled around checking out the room.

AC frowned. From his understanding it was Ty who tracked Phatz down. But he decided not to bring that part up.

"Which one of you niggas giving me the bed?"

Mike laughed.

Returning to his bed ,AC quickly slipped the brooch in his sock as Mike and Ty fell into easy conversation. Unimpressed with their talk AC folded his arms underneath his head as he lay back. When Ty suddenly jumped up and began to pace the floor, he watched him from underneath his lowered lashes. He could practically feel the nervous energy bouncing off him and wondered how much Phatz really knew about him.

"I can't wait to run up in the store tomorrow, people betta get the fuck out my way, I'm smashing and grabbing everything in sight."

The loud siren went off immediately in AC's head.

"That's not how we do it," he said sitting up.

Ty stopped in his tracks "What you mean?"

"Look," he started, "this not my first lick I been doing this shit way before you decided to jump off the porch."

AC caught the snub to his age and shrugged it off. He may have been doing it longer, but according to Phatz, Ty only worked under the cover of darkness. Smashing cases in broad daylight was a whole other level and he had to let him know.

"I don't give a fuck how long you been doing it, the moment you enter into that store it becomes my show."

From the corner of his eye he could see Mike nod his head in agreement.

"Let me tell you how the shit gonna go so you won't be mistaken."

Ty eyes narrowed into thin slits, but he dropped into the chair nearest to him.

When he had their attention, he began, "Most times it's five cases. The first case I break is yours you clean it out, leave only the glass, then you move to the third case." He paused to make sure Ty was listening.

"Mike you know the drill case two and four is yours."

"Anything Mike leaves in the case you get it out, don't worry about looking up as long as you hear scoop, scoop, scoop, everything is good. Once we're done, we walk-not run to the car."

"Got it?"

He waited for Ty's answer. What AC had just explained was the blueprint used for every store they ever bashed. Real hustlers always had a plan and theirs worked time and time again. In the end nobody got hurt and they walked away a lot richer. But in order for it to work everyone had to be on the same page.

What AC hadn't told him was that when he finished, he would take all the pillowcases. He couldn't risk either of them sneaking something from it on the way out.

A few beats passed before Ty finally gave him a low "yea."

"Do what I just said and everybody will be happy."

Ignoring the scowl that settled over Ty's face he readjusted his pillow and turned towards the wall. He could feel the man's stare boring into his back.

Ty's attitude rubbed him the wrong way. But there was no time to focus on that where money was concerned. He removed the brooch from his sock, taking one last look he placed it in his pocket. Maybe he'd get lucky and run across another one tomorrow for his other sister April. Reaching for the lamp over his bed he rested his hand on the switch.

"And Ty it's plenty room on the floor," he said flipping off the lamp switch. Closing his eyes, tomorrow he hoped to turn all the ceno's he'd been dreaming about into a reality.

****

"You sure your dad won't be mad?"

Stuffing his last pair of shoes in the bag Phatz stood back and surveyed the room. Their time in Shreveport was up. Just as he suspected the Pierremont Mall was flooded with valuable pieces and they'd cleaned up big time. His gaze rested on the Louis Vuitton bag almost overflowing with jewelry. There was some good that had come from him fleeing L.A. and he was prepared to take it for all that it was worth.

"When he sees the money I left him, I guarantee you he won't be mad anymore," he said responding to Silky's question.

Phatz was planning to take Harry's car- while he was at work- and in exchange he would leave $5,000 underneath his pillow for a new car.

Done packing he took a seat on the bed beside Silky. He thought about phoning Marlon since he had been the one keeping his ear to the ground about their situation but decided against it. Phatz had high hopes that he would be back in L.A. laughing with Mother Dear and eating one of her home cooked meals soon. He shifted his attention to his current state. Ty and AC had gone to grab their things, while Mike parked the stolen car that they'd used during the lick. Everyone would meet back at Harry's to leave. Now all Phatz had to do was wait.

****

Something was wrong. If the strange tingling at his spine wasn't enough to alert him- when they made it back to the motel- the two sheriffs walking in his direction dressed in button down shirts with ties and cowboy boots surely was.

Cursing under his breath AC closed the door to the room. With his bag clutched tightly in his hand he spun around quickly on his heel only to almost smash into Ty.

"Mike made it back yet?" he asked oblivious.

Jerking his thumb behind him to draw his attention to the sheriff's, AC continued walking hoping that Ty would get the message.

When Ty fell in step beside him AC peeped out the corner of his eye at him.

Ty looked as if he had seen a ghost.

"Shit man where they come from?" he asked nervously as AC began to pick up the pace down the walkway.

Apart of him wanted to believe that they were there for some other reason. Maybe to bust one of the many crackheads that had taken up residence in the place When a voice sounded off from behind, he could no longer ignore the facts.

"Could we talk to you two fellas for a minute?"

Without a backwards glance AC sprinted into action, his long legs carrying him across the parking lot and away from the motel.

Ty was right beside him pounding the pavement.

When he thought they were far enough AC risked a look over his shoulder in the two sheriffs' directions. He was surprised to see that neither man gave chase. While one spoke into a walkie talkie the other just stared after them. Still he knew they weren't in the clear. In fact, judging from the look on their face's things were just getting started.

****

Damn what was taking them so long Phatz wondered as he leaned back in the worn lazy boy chair. It was going on twenty minutes now and nobody had made it back. If they didn't return soon Harry would be off and then Phatz would have to feed him a bunch of lies about where he was taking his car. Questions that he didn't feel like answering.

Kicking his feet up he tried hard to relax. After complaining of a headache Silky had gone to the back to lay down. Alone now, he could hear every creak and groan the old shotgun house made. For minutes he lay there with his eyes closed listening to himself breath. Quickly growing irritated he jumped up. Sitting around twirling his thumbs wouldn't work for him. Phatz needed to be doing something and since they were running late, he grabbed the phone book and looked over all the spots they would hit. Just imagining how much money they were about to make put his mind at ease.

The sound of sirens soon broke through the peace and quiet that had settled around him.

Sliding a finger through the slit in the blind he watched a line of deputy cars race pass the house. When he heard the helicopter above his head, he knew something major was going on. A thought began to form in the back of his mind. What if?... Before the thought could plant good Phatz quickly dismissed it. There was no way AC and Ty were involved in the circus going on outside. AC knew the rules. If anything popped off, he was to go home immediately. That was always the deal. There was no sense in both of them getting caught.

"Ugh, what's all that noise?"

Phatz turned to see Silky walking in with her hand over her head.

"Get any sleep?"

"How can I with all this noise?" she asked sliding into the chair he was just sitting in.

Returning his attention back to the window he noticed the flashing lights near the corner of the street. The police where setting up roadblocks.

Backing away from the window he moved towards the phone.

"Man, I don't know what the fuck going on out there, but these fools need to get here before they put the whole town on lockdown."

He picked up the phone then thought better of it.

"What?" Silky questioned at the look on his face.

He shook his head.

"Well can you get me some water from the kitchen?"

Setting the phone down Phatz headed into the small kitchen, from there he could still hear the loud sirens.

Grabbing a bottle of water from the fridge he was about to turn around when he thought he heard a voice.

Tilting his head to the side he listened closely. When all he heard were the sirens, he shook his head.

"Damn I'm hearing shit," he muttered to himself.

Phatz had taken one step when the voice came to him clear as daylight.

"Homeboy let us in."

He couldn't believe it. From the kitchen window he could see Ty and AC knocking on the window of the house next door.

Tell me I'm not seeing this shit Phatz thought to himself. But the sight in front of him was real. Suddenly the feeling from earlier crept back in full force.

Lifting up the window he called out to them," Y'all at the wrong house!"

He watched as they reversed their tracks back to Harry's.

"Get in get in," Phatz said hurriedly slinging the door open. Closing it shut he gaped at the two men who stood in front of him out of breath. The noise caused Silky to rush into the kitchen.

Her head swung back and forth. "What the fuck happen?" she asked echoing Phatz exact thoughts.

Sucking in a lung full of air Ty spoke first,"One time chasing us."

"And you came here?" Phatz asked bewildered. He tried to clamp down on the anger rising inside of him as his gaze strayed from Ty to AC.

"We didn't have anywhere else to go man they're everywhere," Ty began pacing the small kitchen.

"Wait where's Mike?" Phatz asked suddenly remembering they were a team of five and not four.

Finally, AC broke his silence,"When he saw us running he drove in the opposite direction."

The two men stared at each other. Phatz had so many questions for AC but realized that now wasn't the time. Right now, he had to think of way to get them out of the house unnoticed. Once one time realized they weren't in the neighborhood they would leave. Slapping his hands together he let out a deep breath.

"Ok look all we have to do is wait til the block cools down and them muthafuckas pack it up before we make a move."

A knock sounded at the door the minute he spoke the words, sending a chill through him.

"Oh Fuck!" Ty said placing his hands on the top of his head. In panic mode he reached for the door handle ready to bolt but Phatz slapped his hand away.

Lowering his voice to a deadly whisper he aimed a finger at Ty,"Look nigga if you wanna make it out of this you gotta listen to me and stay yo ass right here."

"But they at the door," Ty moaned.

Ignoring his complaint, he directed his next words to Silky who was leaning against the sink stone faced.

"If that's them they're probably just doing the routine of going door to door. You and me will go answer the knock, you niggas wait right here." Without waiting for a response, he took a step then thought better of it. Spinning around on his heel he pinned Ty with a stare,"Don't move!"

On the short walk to the door Phatz ran down the plan.

"If they ask, we tell them the truth we're here visiting my dad, I know they can't come in without a search warrant." They may have been in a new state, but some laws were universal.

"Ok," she replied coolly.

In the meantime, the knock was becoming more insistent as they approached the door. Stopping short Phatz tilted his head before his voice boomed through the house.

"Who is it?"

"Sheriff Department," the reply came immediately.

Fuck. For a split second Phatz had hoped that maybe the person at the door was a disgruntled neighbor coming to inquire about the noise going on. His hopes had been shot down with the response. Pulling himself together he turned his gaze on Silkys' steady one. With a nod of his head he opened the door.

Two sheriffs in cowboy hats, boots, and jeans stood on the steps Their shiny badges reflected brightly in the suns light.

Removing the pair of shades on his head the taller Sheriff spoke in a deep country accent.

"We're looking for Mr. Harry Bradley, is he home?"

Hiding his surprise at the mention of his dad's name Phatz shook his head.

"He's not here."

The sheriff looked to his partner then back to him.

"And who are you?"

"I'm his son."

The man's hard blue-eyed gaze scrutinized Phatz carefully before moving on to Silky who stood at his back. A few seconds of silence passed before the sheriff cleared his throat.

"Ok, well do you all mind coming to the station for questioning?"

Looking at the two men in front of him Phatz analyzed the situation quickly. Regardless of what led them there, if they had any real evidence, they would be arresting them instead of asking them to come to the station. He started to breathe a little better with that revelation. Knowing that his refusal would only set off more alarms he relaxed his face, "Let me just grab my keys."

After a slight hesitation they walked down the steps and Phatz closed the door.

"Shit why did you say yes," Silky stated turning on him.

Pulling her along through the house by her arm he explained, "They don't know shit and they don't have shit, if they did, we would be in cuffs. Besides, we don't need them muthafuckas tryna press their way inside where AC and Ty are."

Making a pit stop in the room, he grabbed the jewelry before continuing to the kitchen.

"What happened?' Ty asked jumping up from his seat at the table.

"We're going down to the station."

A groan escaped from Ty's mouth.

Dismissing him Phatz stood in front of AC. He pushed the Louis Vuitton bag full of jewelry in his arms.

"Once we leave take the jewelry and go home you got that?" Phatz glared into his eyes hoping that he would follow directions this time. With a tight nod of his head AC readjusted his grip on the bag understanding the message. A dark cloud hung over them as the reality sunk in. Their plans had been blown to pieces. It was running time now.

****

"How many times do I have to say it, I'm here on vacation visiting my father."

Two hours had passed since they first walked into the sheriff station with an invisible bull's eye pinned to their backs.

Twisting around Phatz tried to get a better look at Silky who was over in the next room answering questions.

"Afraid your girlfriend is saying too much?" The fat white sheriff sitting at the desk in front of him smirked. Phatz knew they were hitting her with the same questions they had asked him 'why you're here?' Where were you between this time? Do you have an alibi?

He knew she would give them the answers that they'd rehearsed before leaving the house. So the answer to the man's question was no he didn't think Silky was saying too much. She was saying just what he'd told her to say. He had nothing to worry about. Still he wished he could wipe the smug expression off the sheriff's face and tell him the truth. That the people they were looking for were long gone along with all the jewels. No jewels meant no case. Eventually they would realize that and release them but until then he had to play his role.

"She's telling you that we're here visiting my dad that's it."

Rising the sheriff walked a few feet to the coffee pot to refill his cup before he returned to his chair and pinned Phatz with a knowing look.

Ignoring him Phatz watched the steam rise from the cup. Somewhere in the small building a phone rang. Since arriving he'd counted three sheriffs and two police officers inside the small, cluttered office. Judging by the outdated pictures, peeling paint on the wall, and chipped tile floor he could tell that the sheriff station received little money. But being around a bunch of stiff suits muthafuckas with badges increased his anxiety yet on the outside he was the picture of cool. Crossing his feet at the ankles he clasped his cuffed hands together.

"Is this necessary?" he asked referring to the tight cuffs they'd put on him the minute he arrived.

"Standard procedure," the sheriff responded as he shuffled paper around on the desk.

"For what, am I being charged with anything. I really don't see the need for this, besides you said that witnesses described three tall African American men with afros coming out of the mall."

Phatz leaned forward, "Does it look like I fit that description?"

Instead of answering the question the man squinted his pale green eyes. "Tell me what you did with the jewelry and maybe we can work something out."

Letting out a dramatic huff Phatz rolled his eyes to the stained tile ceiling, "I don't know anything about any jewelry I've told you everything I know now when can we leave?"

He watched the sheriff's face begin to redden. His fat hands slapped the desk sending the coffee sloshing over the rim of the cup.

"Nobody's going anywhere until we get some answers!" he barreled out. Scooting closer to Phatz he squinched up his big face and asked, "You claim to not know anything about the jewelry well where did that watch come from?"

Shrugging his shoulder Phatz stared at the Baume and Mercier watch on his arm. A smirk played on his lips "My girlfriend got it for me for my birthday, don't believe me go ask her."

Sending one of his on-duty guys inside the room to seconds later it was confirmed.

"Told you so," Phatz smiled in his face knowing it would make him angrier.

The sheriff observed him from over the rim of his coffee mug. Taking a loud sip, he placed the cup down and frowned. "This ain't the city boy around here we prosecute criminals to the fullest extent, I'ma give you one last time to fess up to the truth."

The last piece of control that Phatz was holding on to snapped at the man's threat. That boy word didn't sit well with him.

"First off I'm a grown ass man I don't see any lil boys in here, secondly you and I both know you don't have shit to charge me on so tell one of ya flunkies over there ,-he nodded towards another officer, To come uncuff me before I sue this whole fucking shack!"

He was done playing. Even a blind man could see that they didn't have a case without evidence.

"This is not slavery days you can't hold an innocent man for nothing, I have rights!" He could feel his heart thudding hard against his chest as he spit out his last words.

When the sheriff requested for the keys Phatz knew he had won that round.

Standing he stretched his cuffed hands out in front of him. The sheriff roughly grabbed them inserting the key into the latch, he was turning it when his head suddenly snapped up.

"Well well well what do we have here?" the sheriff asked with his eyes locked on the commotion behind Phatz.

Turning to follow his line of vision Phatz mouth went dry at the sight of AC and Ty being led in by another team of officers who were celebrating loudly.

"Found these two up in the attic," one announced proudly as a round of cheers went up.

Attic? They were supposed to be on a plane to L.A.

"What the fuck?" Phatz said not realizing he had said the words out loud.

At that moment he felt like he was having an outer body experience as he watched them get led to the back.

I'm dreaming I gotta be he reasoned to himself. But when he turned to see the sheriff's coffee stained smile, he knew he wasn't dreaming.

Placing his hands on his belt the Sheriff sneered. "You're bout to be gone for a long time boy armed robbery carries 99 years in the state of Louisiana, shoulda took my deal. He nodded to another officer, "Book em."

His lips kept moving but the words where lost on Phatz as his mind was already plotting a way to get out of the fuck up they'd landed in. They would need the best lawyer that money could buy.

Later in the booking area the number 99 flashed in his mind.

"Face the front," the lady behind the camera said as she snapped his mug shot.

Phatz couldn't do that much time.

"Now turn to your left,"

Obeying the request his eyes immediately landed on the sheriff who stood just outside the door watching with a look of victory plastered to his face.

Holding his chin high Phatz stared the man down until he turned away.

"Last one," she called out as the blinding flash went off.

Hours after he'd been fingerprinted and issued a beige two piece county suit that was too snug on his body he sat in the concrete cell enclosed by steel bars and replayed the events that led up to that moment. His carefully thought out plan was always the same and had never failed him. While Phatz couldn't quite figure out what had led the cops directly to his dad's house. One thing was for certain. He was beginning to regret the day he ever stepped foot in Shreveport, Louisiana.

'Smash, grab' suspects have $150,000 bonds set

Their behavior in court having raised the ire of a Caddo district judge, bonds of $150,000 were set today for two men arrested for "smash and grab" thefts and robberies from Shreveport jewelry stores.

The bonds of $150,000 were set for Dino Bradley, 20, and Mark Allen, 22, both of Los Angeles, Calif. Bond for their alleged accomplice, 20-year-old Van D. Williams of Los Angeles, was set at $50,000.

They are charged with armed robbery, theft and receiving stolen goods.

Bradley, wearing leg irons, had to be taken from the courtroom by sheriff's deputies before Judge Jack Fant arrived. Deputies said Bradley created a disturbance and began cursing.

Allen appeared belligerent before Judge Jack Fant, who told Allen he did not like his demeanor before he set the bond.

Along with a 16-year-old juvenile, the three suspects are accused of burglarizing Mission Jewelers in Mall St. Vincent before dawn Saturday and returning later that day to break glass display cases and run away with an assortment of jewelry.

Authorities also have charged the group with the robbery of a Pierremont Mall jewelry store Monday afternoon, in which armed bandits smashed display cases and made off with jewelry.

The suspects were arrested after police raided an Allendale area motel Monday evening and then followed two fleeing suspects to a nearby house.

Authorities have recovered jewelry with a retail value of just over a quarter of a million dollars. Authorities in California also want the suspects for jewelry robberies there.

(Shreveport, Lousiana)

For AC, being at the detention center was nothing new. At only nine he caught his first charge for shoplifting from a local store. Hoping that a trip to juvie would scare him into straightening up his act before it was too late, the sitting judge had sentenced him to a weekend stay, but the plan backfired. Instead, the weekend punishment would connect him to more experienced criminals who would wake up his game on how to break the law. From that day forward he would never get caught shoplifting again, but each time his crimes increased and so did his time at juvie. And to him they were all the same with their rules, small cells, and overworked and underpaid staff, but something told him that this experience in Louisiana would be different especially once they discovered that he was actually eighteen and not seventeen like he had claimed when he was arrested. For now, he thought of the place as a small vacation. He needed time to get his thoughts together and determine the best way to tell his Aunt Twinkle that he'd fucked up big time.

"What you in for?" A voice asked breaking into his thoughts.

Sliding his tray down the lunch line AC looked down into an unfamiliar small face. The boy dressed in a similar jumpsuit the color of green puke, starred at him from behind a pair of glasses. From the innocent gleam in his eyes and the way the jumpsuit swallowed his pre-pubescent body he couldn't be any older than ten or eleven. Glancing around the small cafeteria he saw that most of the boys seated at the tables were younger than him. One look at their babyish faces void of facial hair and he knew that they had never held up a store while people screamed or witnessed a body be riddled with bullets until there was no life left in them. They weren't the normal hardened criminals he was used to, so instead of answering the boy he grabbed his tray and claimed an empty table far away from everyone else.

Biting into the cold sandwich his mind wandered back to their capture.

"You hear that?" Ty asked pressing his ear to the floor. They were smushed in Harry's crowded attic full of boxes and old Christmas decorations. The room was so small AC could barely stand without bumping his head on the low ceiling. So, he lay flat on the dirty floor with his arms at his side listening for whatever it was Ty thought he heard.

When only silence followed, he rose to his knees.

"What you doing"? Ty asked in a low whisper.

Before he could respond he felt a sneeze coming. The stuffy air was stirring up his allergies. Stifling the sneeze with his hand AC climbed to his feet careful not to bang his head. Lifting a foot over the box, he made his way to the small door that led them to the hiding spot. It was Ty's idea to hide until Phatz and Silky returned. And for some strange reason AC had blindly followed Ty into the attic. Now he was beginning to see that they were sitting ducks waiting around to get caught.

He sucked his teeth.

What the fuck was I thinking?

Phatz had specifically told him to get the jewelry and go home. It had always been the plan. No matter what happened they had to stick to the plan. He cursed himself as regret coursed through his body and settled like a knot in his stomach. Glancing around AC realized that it wasn't too late. He could still get home. Mind made up he edged closer, slowly cracking the lid he peered down into the house. The noise outside had died down a few hours ago. AC took it to mean that the police had given up and moved to search another area. He saw his window of opportunity to get away opening up, but he knew if he didn't move quick enough it would close just as fast.

"You see something?" Ty called from behind him.

Shaking his head AC lowered himself down, when his feet were firmly planted, he glanced up too see Ty leaning over the opening.

"Look I'm not sticking around to get caught."

"If we wait here, we can all leave together," Ty responded. "Everything will be cool once they get back, you'll see," he added.

No, AC wouldn't see because he was leaving. It was obvious Ty wasn't budging and AC was done trying to get him to.

"Throw the jewelry down here."

Ty hesitated briefly before disappearing in the attic. Returning with the Louie bag he slowly began to lower it down.

AC had just gripped it in his hand when he heard the loud sound of wood splintering at the front door.

"Oh shit!" he yelled.

Tossing the Louie bag back up, with Ty's help he began pulling himself up just as the door flew off the hinges.

Sliding the lid back he tried to calm his pounding heart.

Ty scrambled across the boxes to the window.

"Damn it's boarded up!"

AC barely registered the words; his mind was racing. He could hear them storming the house below.

Squeezing his eyes shut his only hope now was that they hadn't seen him climb in the attic. But it was quickly dashed by the next words.

"Come out with your hands in the air we know you're up there!" The voice called over the megaphone.

He and Ty exchanged looks.

"Help me break the boards off the window we can go out that way," Ty said in a panic filled voice.

He couldn't believe the words coming out of his mouth. Listening to him was the reason they were in the situation now. If only he had done what Phatz said.

AC lowered his head. It was too late for the ifs. There was only one thing left to do. Stuffing the jewelry in one of the many boxes he crept to the entry.

"We're coming out don't shoot!"

Ty's mouth dropped open as he scrambled over to him, "Man what you doing? We can't surrender we can go out this way," he pleaded pointing towards the window again.

In the small space AC turned towards him. He was mad at Ty for thinking that they could get away. He was sure the house was surrounded, but most of all he was angry at himself for listening to a stupid nigga.

"It's over," he said with finality ending any argument Ty was thinking of. The man's shoulder slumped.

"Who going first?" Ty finally asked.

"You take yo ass out there first since it was your idea to come up here."

Watching Ty slither out the attic and be tackled by the police gave AC a little satisfaction. But all too soon it was his turn. His eyes scanned over the box where he had hidden the jewelry.

They were so close.

Climbing from the attic he allowed the cops to handcuff him and lead him out the house where a small crowd of onlookers had gathered.

He could tell from their expressions that none of the neighbors recognized them, but by that time the next morning their crime spree and their mugshots would be broadcasted on every news station in the state. They would become known as the California Gang.

That was three weeks ago. He still remembered the look of confusion and disappointment on Phatz face when they were taken into the station. No one had to tell him that he fucked up. AC was bearing the weight of his mistake everyday- starting with the cold thick meat in between the slices of hard bread on his tray. He would kill for one of his aunt's fluffy pancakes or a greasy burger from Meaty Meat on Pico and Fairfax Boulevard. Neither was possible. Deciding that the banana custard on his plate would be easier on his stomach than the meat he dug into it. He was halfway through his dessert when he glanced up to see three correctional officers and a deputy with a stern expression heading in his direction. Swallowing the last bit of his food he pushed the tray away. AC knew what that meant- they'd figured out his true age. His brief vacation had come to an end.

****

"We don't know who did it ,all we know is that there was some sort of an argument," taking a deep breath she paused to gather her next words, "they wanted the car and when he wouldn't give it to them they kill—," A deep sob tore from her mouth ending anything else she was about to say.

On the other end Phatz grip on the phone weakened as he listened to Mother Dear describe the details of Marlon's murder. Inside he felt his heart shatter into pieces as the grief began to consume him. At the same time, it felt like someone had knocked the wind out of him. Pressing the tip of his thumb into the crevices of his eye he tried to swallow pass the knot of pain sitting in his throat making it hard for him to breathe. He drew in a lung full of air to force the pain down, but it sat in his heart like a burning fire refusing to be put out.

Through Mother Dears tearful account, he learned that his big and only brother Marlon was slain on Crenshaw Boulevard days earlier while out driving his 71' ragtop candy Glasshouse low rider that he'd let him borrow while he was away. When Marlon refused to give up the ride to the niggas, they shot him point blank in the chest in broad daylight, flipping Phatz world upside down. When Mother Dear began to talk about funeral arrangements, he tried to stop the image of his brother being lowered into the cold ground in a box from flashing through his mind, but it was too late. The vision almost brought him to his knees. Leaning against the wall to steady himself he squeezed his eyes shut fighting back the tears that threatened to spill from his eyes.

Damn why you didn't give them the ride Marlon?

Even as his mind echoed the question, he already knew the answer. Besides himself, Marlon was the toughest person Phatz knew. As kids growing up in the Jungle they'd learned to never back down from a fight even if they were outnumbered. When Phatz decided to jump in the game he saw firsthand how cold it was. To protect himself he became just as cold with anyone who wasn't family. Marlon on the other hand had never hardened his heart to the griminess that came with the streets because he didn't see what Phatz saw. It was the reason those niggas were able to take his life.

Managing to find his voice he asked,"How is Mama and Denise?"

Though Mother Dear attested to their wellbeing, Phatz knew that there was a permanent rift in the family now and he hated he couldn't be there to console them through it.

An image of the last time he saw his brother popped in his head at LAX. It felt like a lifetime ago. Phatz tried to recall if he told him that he loved him. Had he even said goodbye?

The questions weighed heavy on his mind even as he ended his conversation with Mother Dear. Still shaken to his core he took a few seconds to gather himself before placing another call.

Fifteen minutes later and he still didn't have any answers. Every call had led to a dead end, seemingly no one knew who killed Marlon. Just knowing that his brother killers were out roaming around while he was locked up in a cage made rage course through his body. They didn't deserve to be alive and if he hadn't been caught up in his own bullshit, he would've made sure that their eyes never opened again.

The only thing he managed to find out was that Mike made it back home safely.

At least he had stuck to the plan.

With his heart still in his throat he dialed Mother Dear again, she had just answered when a tap on his shoulder made him pause.

"Damn muthatfucka you ain't the only one that gotta use the phone."

Turning to confront the voice he came face to face with another prisoner. Dark skinned with braids the man looked to be in his late forties and from the way he was sizing him up he wanted trouble, which didn't come as a surprise to Phatz. The second he stepped foot in Caldo Parrish Detention Center or CDC as everyone called it, he knew eventually he would have to make an example out of someone. The brick building housed up to five hundred prisoners who were mostly from surrounding cities in Louisiana. The man in front of him had taken claim as the leader of the Shreveport crew.

Phatz fished around in his head until he recalled that his name was Black Jack. They lived on the same tier a few cells down. Branded a killer by the system, Black Jack tossed around the title proudly and bragged about his life of crimes to anyone who would listen.

Despite his muscular frame and hardened face, Phatz had taken one look into his eyes and knew that he was all talk. The eyes told it all.

Still aware of him lingering behind him he tuned in to what Mother Dear was saying. Considering that the other phone stations were empty, Phatz figured that if he really wanted to use one, he would move on or wait.

Except Black Jack did neither.

Phatz was in the middle of his sentence when the man's hand snaked around him and grabbed the receiver.

"My turn," he said invading Phatz space. The rage that he had been trying to keep from spilling over began to bubble up.

"Mother Dear hold on."

Putting the receiver down Phatz spun around coming face to face with the man.

Curling his lip, Black Jack let out a low laugh.

"It looks like Ima have to show you who run things around here," he said as he took a step closer.

"I—,"

In one quick move, Phatz smashed his fist into his face sending Black Jack crashing to the ground.

"Nigga I don't play!" He yelled unleashing all his rage as he punched him again. *Crack.* The blow sent Black Jacks' head bouncing off the ground. Something seemed to have taken over Phatz as he pounded away at the man with all his might sending blood everywhere. The harder he hit the more numb he became.

His brother was dead, and he was hundreds of miles away from home locked in a cage waiting on the judge to hand him his fate. There would be no final goodbyes for him. And to make matters worse some nigga wanted to test him.

Lifting his foot, he was preparing to release all his pent up pain in Black Jack's chest when he was suddenly grabbed from behind.

"I'm not done yet! "he yelled as the guards wrestled him to the ground.

Instead of focusing on the spectators that gathered around, his eyes landed on the phone. Mother Dear was probably getting an ear full if she hadn't hung up. For her sake he hoped she had.

Back in his cell where the guards escorted him, he tried to blow off steam by doing pushups, but it didn't work. He was too riled up and so were the rest of the prisoners. He could hear the noise from his tier as the guards struggled to regain control.

"All inmates report to your cell the yard is now going on lockdown, this is a warning," the voice announced over the intercom.

Gripping the bars on the cell door he watched the prisoners scurry like rats.

Abandoning his place at the cell door he walked over to the sink to splash water on his face.

He was so focused with the task he hadn't heard anyone walk up.

"Nigga I'ma kill you," the voice growled out.

His head snapped up at the words.

Black Jack stood on the tier in front of his cell. There was a deep gash in his lip and his right eye was almost swollen shut.

Phatz smiled like a wolf after its prey as he approached the barred cell door. Though he couldn't see what was happening on the tier he knew the guards had to be busy locking in the other prisoners. None of them were paying attention to Black Jack.

"You had the chance to kill me, but you didn't you balled up like a little bitch and got yo ass whooped,"Phatz taunted.

"I'ma kill you," he repeated moving a step closer.

"That's yo new job then fool, kill me."

Suddenly saliva flew through the bars as Black Jack spit at Phatz narrowly missing him.

"Can't kill me like that!" Phatz chided, wishing that the door would open so that he could get his hands on him. As if someone were reading his mind the cell door slowly opened.

He didn't know who was more shocked him or Black Jack. The mean mug the man was wearing only seconds ago quickly turned into terror.

Black Jack's bottom lip quivered as he took a step backwards.

With nothing between them Phatz stepped out on the tier. For every forward step he took Black Jack took two backwards. With his eyes bulging out his head he called out in fear,

"Get him y'all get him!" he hollered out.

Phatz didn't bother to look behind him he just kept moving. His plan was to back the man into the wall at the end of the tier, where he would have nowhere to run.

"When you hit that wall, I'm stumping yo face in."

He watched Black Jack glance behind him in alarm.

"Yeah that's right nigga time's almost up for yo ass."

Reaching under his shirt Black Jack pulled out a sharp pencil in hopes that it would hold him off.

Phatz laughed at the pitiful sight "Bitch ass nigga you gone need more than that."

Just as Phatz was getting ready to pounce, the guards stormed the tier.

A black guard that he had become cool with during his short time there approached him.

"Bradley how'd you get out and what's going on here?" A look of confusion covered his face.

Phatz shrugged, innocently.

At the sight of the pencil still outstretched in Black Jacks' hand the guard rushed him, quickly wrestling the weapon from his grasp. Seeing an opportunity Phatz reached around and slammed his fist into Black Jacks' jaw drawing more blood.

"Get Bradley!" The black guard screamed getting in between them.

Immediately Phatz was swanked with guards on either side of him.

"Nigga Ima kill you!" Black Jack screamed resorting back to his old threats as the guards dragged him from the tier.

Phatz lunged after him. "Stop all that lip boxing nigga we gone meet again!"

"Someone please restrain Bradley!"

It was the second time that day that Phatz had found himself cuffed and face down on the cold floor.

When everything settled down the guards once again escorted him to his cell. Phatz stood at the door hoping it would magically open like last time, when it didn't, he took a seat on the thin mattress. Strangely enough he was thankful for the distraction Black Jack had brought. It kept his mind off his situation, but now that it was over, he looked around at his cell in disgust. It was the size of a bathroom. An old steel sink was bolted to the wall right next to the metal toilet. On the opposite wall a small square for a window allowed the light to shine through only the sun was setting casting a dark glow in his cell. He knew tonight he wouldn't get any sleep on the lumpy mattress. Not just because it was uncomfortable, but the pain was slowly taking over again. He thought about shedding the pent-up tears he held inside but knew it wouldn't do any good. Marlon was gone and crying wouldn't bring him back. Laying down that night he wondered if he would ever be able to cry for his brother or if his death would ever get easier. As time passed Phatz would learn that it never got easier and the pain never disappeared, he just learned how to live with it.

****

Graves Thomas was the man Phatz had chosen to represent him in court. The Louisiana native was rumored to be the best lawyer in Shreveport, and they would need the best for the charges that they were facing. He sat in a visiting room with only a table and two chairs waiting for Graves to arrive. Outside the cheery laughter of children in the visiting area floated in through the closed door. It sounded strange and out of place to his ears. Behind the walls at CDC there was nothing to smile or laugh about. Every morning when he opened his eyes in the small cell thoughts of Marlon would flood his mind. Today marked a whole month since his death and yet the pain was still fresh like it happened yesterday. Phatz knew eventually the LAPD would close the case and his brother's murder would go unsolved like the thousands of others in the city. Which was why he was ready to talk business with the lawyer. The sooner a deal could be reached the quicker they could get to serving their time and get home. Phatz didn't need the police to solve his brothers murder because he would and then justice would be in his hands.

At the sound of the knock he sat up straight.

Dressed in an Armani charcoal gray suit with black leather shoes and a brief case in one hand, Graves Thomas was ushered in by a guard. Phatz felt underdressed in his blue prison uniform with state issued slippers. He stood to shake his hand and noticed the initialed gold cuff links on his sleeve. Immediately liking the man's sharp style, he hoped it matched his skills in the court room.

"I take it you're Mr. Dino Bradley?" he asked removing his suit jacket. Placing it on the back of the chair he set his briefcase on the floor before taking a seat across from him.

"The one and only," Phatz responded as he watched him loosen his tie and begin to read over the file he'd placed on the table.

Graves wasted no time getting down to business.

"Look I'm not gonna lie to you, the District Attorney wants to throw your whole gang away for a very long time."

"Gang?" Phatz shook his head at the word.

"We're not a gang."

Graves gray eyes regarded him carefully before he spoke, "Did you hear what I said?"

"The DA doesn't want you to see the light of day outside of these walls."

This time Phatz stood up and leaned over the table getting so close in the man's face that he could see the gray stubble on his face "And did you hear what I said, we're not in a gang," his voice rising slightly.

A knock came at the door.

"Everything ok in there?" The guard outside asked as he ducked his head in the room.

The two men were having an intense stare down. Graves caved first.

"It's fine," Graves said. Seconds later the door closed shut.

Returning his attention back to Phatz he sighed. "Ok fine I get it you're not a gang."

Now that he'd gotten his point across Phatz reclaimed his seat.

Running a hand through his salt and pepper hair Graves eyed the file in front of him. After a few seconds he began to tap his knuckles against the table.

"Did you in any way use the hammer as a weapon to threaten anyone?"

Phatz knew the question was coming and was proud to answer it.

"No that's not our style we don't wanna bring harm to people we just want the jewels." It was the truth.

Graves scribbled something down in the file.

A few more standard questions and he seemed satisfied with Phatz answers.

Underneath the table Phatz leg bounced up and down impatiently.

"Look everybody in here told me you were the best which is why I hired you, I need to know that you can get us the lightest time possible I'm not tryna hear what the DA wanna do. It's your job to make sure he doesn't railroad us."

Graves placed his pen down on the rusted table. A smile played at the corner of his lips. "It's nice to know they regard me so high in here." He leaned in closer, "And they're right I'm the best which is why I think I can strike a deal for five years for simple robbery since no one was harmed. Not to mention the fact that the hammer was used as a tool and not a weapon, so we should be good."

"That's what I'm talking about!" Phatz exclaimed, slapping the table in excitement. Five years would be over in no time, then he and his crew would be back in Boss Angeles where they belonged.

The lawyer held his hands out in front of him, "Don't get too happy the DA is up for reelection and with the way y'all terrorized the town he'll want to send a message to the people that they're safe. He went on to say, "So first we'll have to let the publicity die down from this case since this is the most any stores have been robbed in the history of Louisiana."

Phatz smirked at the news of them making history.

"Just make sure we all get the same deal," he stressed to Graves. Ty and AC were both at CDC now while Silky was being held across the yard in a dorm for women. He wasn't leaving or striking a deal without them.

Sliding the file in his briefcase signaling the end of their meeting Graves nodded. "If this works you and your codefendants will be offered the same deal."

"Good," Phatz said out loud.

Graves was still talking as he packed up.

"…But for now, I need you to keep this between us only, there's still a few things we need to iron out. We don't want everyone to know whats going on get what I'm saying?" His dyed black eyebrows formed an almost straight line.

Looking at Graves squeaky clean image Phatz realized that it was just a front. He wasn't the best in the state because he played by the rules, it was the exact opposite. Whatever deal the man would make would be done under the table away from the public's eye and opinion.

With everything squared away Graves began putting on his jacket to leave.

"When I first heard of the robberies, I knew for certain that you guys were from out of town and were long gone after that weekend," at the door he paused, " then boom you strike again Monday I said to myself then that it wouldn't end well."

Phatz rolled his eyes at the statement.

"You wanna know what tipped the cops off?" Hitching his brief case up he checked his gold Rolex.

The question had been weighing heavy on his mind since their arrest. Phatz examined every angle and still came up short. Sliding to the edge of his seat he nodded at the man, mentally bracing himself for his response.

The words that tumbled out of Graves mouth were dipped with humor.

"They traced the only number called from the Section & Livingston hotel back to your dad's house and it led them straight to you."

Phatz squeezed his eyes shut as he processed the news. When Ty called his dads house even after he told him not to, he unknowingly sealed their fate.

"Shit."

"Yep," Graves said with a look of pity on his face as he reached for the door knob.

"I'll be in touch."

Then he was gone. Meanwhile Phatz sat stiffly in the chair. He accepted his blame in their ruin. He should've never invited Ty along. But it was too late to dwell on the should've's and could've's. Graves would get them the deal and they would do their time and move on. Five years sounded a hell of a lot better than 99 years and a dark cold night.

He could breathe a little easier knowing that his entire life wasn't gone. Pulling himself together he let the guard lead him to the visiting area where his mom Kathi stood at a table with a smile.

"My baby," she said embracing him in a warm hug.

Her signature white diamond fragrance wrapped around him reminding him of everything sweet and good.

After what felt like hours of hugging, they finally took their seats across from one another.

Kathi wiped at her eyes, "It's so good to see you," she said squeezing his hand.

"You too mama, how you doing?" he asked.

In the days after Marlons' murder Phatz made sure to call to check on everyone. It was the only support he could offer in his situation. Over the phone Kathi sounded strong, but he needed to see for himself. With her sitting in front of him now he was glad her appearance matched her voice.

"Your dad was supposed to pick me up from the airport, but he never showed." The disappointment was evident in her voice.

Phatz tried to make an excuse for him, "He probably got caught up at work or something."

But he knew the real reason why his dad hadn't shown up. He was embarrassed. Harry wasn't the man that Kathi married and had children with. His simple lifestyle was far from the one he led back in L.A. Since Phatz arrest Harry had only visited him once. Though he never asked any questions, he warned him to stay out of trouble when he found out about the Black Jack incident after it had become front page news. It was then that Phatz realized that while Harry knew the little boy he once was, he knew nothing about the man he had become. Phatz wanted his dad to know that he was just as bad as any other nigga in there. He told him straight up that he would hurt them before they ever got the chance to hurt him. Harry hadn't been back since and Phatz didn't hold it to him.

"Your sister is driving the wheels off that car," Kathi remarked changing the subject.

For Phatz it felt good sitting across from something familiar. They laughed and talked like old times. When the visit ended, he hugged his mother with a strength he hadn't done since he was a little boy. She had one son in the ground and one behind bars. He knew that was hard for her even if she didn't say it. They would never get over Marlon's death but together they would get through it. With promises to visit soon Kathi was whisked out the door and all too soon Phatz had to return to his new reality. Tucking away the good memories of his visit, he slipped back into survival mode. Cold and lethal.

****

"Here she comes," Phatz said.

Glancing up AC spotted the old white woman who ran the commissary store walking down the cemented path. He could see her wide smile from where he stood. It was rec time on the yard along with commissary day. He had been at CDC all of two weeks now and already he was learning the lay of the land. Like the fact that commissary day was like payday for the rest of the inmates. At the same time, it separated the hustlas from the bustas. Those who claimed to be getting a lot of dough inside the walls could barely afford the good soap the store sold and instead had to use the thin flaky kind the jail provided. Even now in the line behind him he saw a few familiar faces that he knew didn't have much money and he knew this because he had beaten them out of it while gambling that week. They were either there to leech or jack some unsuspecting victim of his goods. He didn't have to worry about either.

"How are you boys doing?" the white-haired woman asked with a friendly smile.

"We good just ready to shop," AC responded in a friendly voice. He liked the woman because she had a grandmother's vibe to her. His answer brought another smile to her face.

Stepping aside he waited for her to unlock the door. Briefly his eyes scanned over the crowd of prisoners scattered on the yard and he wondered where Ty was. Trying to spot him out was almost impossible. Everyone wore the same color uniformed in the maximum-security prison no matter the offense. While the two hadn't spoken since being captured AC wanted to let him know that there were no hard feelings especially since he'd learned that Phatz lawyer was getting them a sweet deal. He would be twenty-three when his sentence was over. There would be plenty of time for living.

"I need you to do something for me," Phatz said breaking into his thoughts.

Turning in the direction he watched him shove a piece of paper in his jacket.

Moving out of the line the two walked over to the fence. AC could feel the glares on them as they navigated through the yard. As soon as he made his arrival at CDC he learned that Phatz had sent a loud message with his hands when he beat down some clown nigga. And any enemy of Phatz was an enemy of his. The next day AC found himself in a similar situation when an inmate tried to test his gangsta. Wasting no time he two pieced the man, sending his own message to everyone that he wasn't to be fucked with. Black Jack and his crew seemed to be the only ones who hadn't listened. Every day during rec time Black Jack and his crew would make threats through the fence. Inviting them to sick call where there would be little to no guards around was AC and Phatz way of getting them to make good on their threats, only they never showed up.

"I can't wait to catch that nigga slipping," AC stated when he realized the heated stares were coming from Black Jack.

"And we will," Phatz said confidently.

He removed the paper he was holding earlier from his pocket. Noticing the familiar handwriting AC peeped that it was a letter from Silky.

"In a minute Silky and the guard come down that sidewalk to go to sick call." He pointed towards a closed door.

"I need you to give em some game, know what I mean?"

AC knew exactly what he meant.

"I got you."

Together they began to move across the yard.

"Yeah don't worry bout that bitch ass nigga Black Jack he gone get his soon enough… again," Phatz said pulling his cap down over his ears.

With every threat the man made, AC silently tucked it away in his mind. He planned to bring it back to his attention right before he put his fist in his mouth.

A few feet away from the door Phatz nudged his shoulder.

"They should be coming out right now."

On cue the metal door opened. A female guard stepped out with Silky right behind her.

The male inmates on the yard began their usual cat calling through the fence at Silky, but with eyes only for Phatz she ignored them all.

Dropping down to one knee Phatz pretended to tie his shoe.

Knowing that was his signal AC jumped into action. Walking towards the women he winked at Silky right before jumping in front of the guard.

"Hey Ms. C you look really nice today you do something different with your hair?"

The white lady appeared startled for second before her face eased into a tight smile. She brushed a flat brown strand behind her ear.

"Uh not really," she said.

Blocking her view of Silky and Phatz he eyed her up and down.

"And you smell good."

A hint of red began to creep up in her cheeks as he laid the compliments on thick.

"You know who you look like?" he asked.

AC snapped his fingers as he pretended to think hoping that it would distract her.

"That really pretty actress…"

"Farrah Fawcett!" she blurted out.

Hell no.

Instead of saying the words he went along with her ridiculous answer.

"Yep, that's her."

Her skinned turned an even darker shade of red.

"I get that a lot."

He was getting ready to spit her another line when the yard erupted into loud cheers.

"Hey stop that!" she suddenly yelled out.

Before he could jump in front of her, she snaked around him and sprinted towards Phatz and Silky.

"Damn," he said at his failed attempt to draw her back in.

Turning to see what all the noise was about he suddenly found himself cheering along with the others. Silky and Phatz was giving the yard a mild X-rated show. His homeboys' hand gripped a handful of her ass as they kissed.

In the blink of an eye the show was over. One minute the woman was yanking on Silky's arm trying to pry them apart and the next she was underneath Silky on the ground.

Racing towards them AC stopped beside Phatz.

"Yeah that's right beat her ass baby!" Phatz yelled.

Ms. C screamed out in pain when Silky wrapped a fistful of hair around her hand and slammed her head into the ground. Her panicked filled blue eyes searched the crowd gathering around before landing on AC.

He shrugged. Wasn't nothing he could do for her.

Once Silky had landed enough licks to the woman's face Phatz began to pull her up.

Moving to help untangle Silky from Ms. C limp body AC almost missed the male guards creeping up behind them. He turned just in time to see one lunge towards Silky. Throwing himself in front of her, AC delivered a blow of his own watching the guards body drop to the ground with a soft thud.

When his partner tried to get away Phatz hemmed him up against the fence and began to beat him senseless. The other guard managed to crawl away before AC could do any more damage to him.

Facing each other AC and Phatz shared a knowing look when more guards began to rush the yard.

They seemed to be coming from all directions and with one target: them.

****

The burning sensation was like nothing he'd ever felt before. With every breath his throat constricted making the pain worse. It felt as if he had swallowed a ball of fire. And if that wasn't bad enough, he could barely see. What little he could see through swollen slits was blurry. The ground moved back in forth in front of him. He tried to steady himself as he swayed on his feet.

"AC I'm hit man," he choked out, "punk bitches maced me!"

Using the back of his hand Phatz wiped at the saliva dripping from his mouth.

Suddenly AC was beside him.

"I got you, go this way." With one hand on his shoulder, AC guided him away from the tainted air.

Though Phatz couldn't see, he could hear and from the sounds of the loud horns blaring on the yard the jail was calling in the big dogs: the goon squad. He figured they had a few minutes before the guards came storming out with their batons and glass shields to restrain them and restore order back on the yard. Well at least they would try too. Phatz was so angry he considered handing out a few more ass whooping's. It wasn't just getting maced that had him upset, it was that he knew it would be a while before he would get to see Silky again. Her attacking the guard wouldn't sit well with the warden. The man would be even madder if he knew the attack had been planned. The female guard Ms. C had been causing problems for Silky since she arrived, but unknowingly to her Silky was the wrong one to fuck with. In her last letter to him she mentioned that she would take off on Ms. C the first chance she got. That chance had come today. Seeing Silky handle her business like that made him proud. She was hundreds of miles from home still representing. Just like him and AC. They didn't give a fuck that they were the only ones of their kind in the jail or that they were outnumbered. When it came down to it like it already had before with Black Jack and the rest of the sorry niggas, they would step up to anybody. Silky just proved that as well. He only hoped she wouldn't get shipped out because of it.

"You guys get in here," he heard a familiar voice call out minutes before they were ushered into the store.

He bumped his knee on something as he walked in. "Shit!" Rubbing the spot he'd hit, he tried once again to open his eyes, but the light inside only made the burning and stinging worse.

"Man, I can't see nothing," he complained.

Something scraped loudly across the floor.

"I got just the thing you need," the old woman called out. "You sit right here I'll be back."

With AC's help he eased down into the chair.

"Did you see where they took Silky?" he asked AC. Touching his swollen eyes he flinched at the tender skin surrounding it.

"Yeah they took her to the infirmary. They should've taken that other bitch."

Even with a sore throat and swollen eyes Phatz couldn't help but to laugh. Silky did a number on her while he and AC worked the guards over.

A sweet smell drifted in his nose reminding him that they were in the store. Vision still blurry he could identify the outline of boxes.

"Ok get him up and bring him over here," the woman said when she returned.

Moving slowly this time he let AC guide him.

His hand reached out for something to hold on to t. The cold steel sink underneath made him frown.

"Why we at the sink?"

"Lean your head back," she ordered instead.

Figuring she was about to soak him with water he was surprised when cool liquid splashed on his face and dripped down his chin before spilling into in his mouth.

"Lady you pouring milk on me!"

She shushed him.

Opening his mouth to protest more milk seeped in. He spit. Blinking furiously, Phatz realized that the burning and stinging in his eyes was suddenly gone. He could open his eyes without pain.

"Old wives' tale," she chuckled at the incredulous look on his face before handing him a towel when she was done.

Patting his face dry Phatz eyes landed on AC who sported a lopsided grin.

"Shits wild out there," he joked peering outside the window.

Handing the woman the towel, Phatz made his way over to the window. From what he was seeing their day was about to get a whole lot wilder.

Just as he predicted the goon squad was on the scene. He counted twenty lining up as the gates surrounding the store was locked, shutting them in. A few plain dressed guards were rounding up the other inmates marching them inside.

"They'll be coming for us next," he said turning. With his sight restored he glanced around the small store. The shelves held boxes of paper and envelopes stacked to the ceiling. Beside it was the hygiene products and across from it was boxes of every kind of snack imaginable. The store was every prisoner's paradise. Walking over to a jar of suckers he had become fond of, he unwrapped one and stuck the caramel and green apple sucker into his mouth to help erase the bitter taste left from the mace.

"Well don't just stand there looking, get what you need before they come banging down the door," the woman encouraged.

Never the one to have be told twice he grabbed two brown paper bags and began to fill it up. AC did the same. One thing he could say about his jail stint was that they always had money. Just earlier he had spoken with Corey by phone to insure he didn't fuck up his commissary money. Last time Corey had given his $300 for commissary to that trifling bitch Patsy at World on Wheels and instead of sending it to Phatz she had done God knows what with the money. Which was why he didn't feel any way about his son's mother beating her ass for it or Corey making her pay him back with sex. It wouldn't be the first time they had tossed up a woman.

Grabbing a few hygiene products, he continued to browse around when her voice made him pause.

"You boys come and spend the most money out of everyone, you're part of the reason I'm still in business." With a head nod she turned and headed towards the door leaving them.

Fifteen minutes later with two bags apiece filled to the top they walked out of the store. Outside the gates the goon squad was already lined up waiting for them. Phatz glanced around. A few inmates still remained on the yard, but the spot where Black Jack and his crew had stood was now occupied by more guards watching… waiting for them to make the wrong move.

Phatz eyed the goon squad in their gear. He could barely see their faces for the large helmets covering them. Twenty men with batons, shields, and helmets for the two of them.

"What you thinking?" he asked AC who stood to the side of him quiet.

"I'm thinking these hillbilly's not as bad as they look."

Phatz laughed. Sitting his bags on the ground he slowly approached the gate.

"So how y'all wanna do this?"

He was giving them a choice to do things the peaceful way or his favorite the rowdy way. One thing was for certain though, he nor AC would cower. If it was a fight they wanted, then it was a fight that they would get.

"Yeah how y'all wanna do it?" AC chimed in from beside him. He had taken out a bag of chips and was eating them.

A guard stepped forward. Now that he was closer Phatz recognized him as Popeye. He was one of the cool ones.

Re-holstering his baton Popeye lifted his helmet, "Hey man look we wanna get things straightened out with as little force as possible," he sighed. The movement caused the fat under his chin to jiggle. "But if you guys can't cooperate, we'll have to use force."

Phatz shook his head at Popeye's words.

"Listen we're ready to go we been ready to go just unlock the gate."

Popeye eyed him wearily, the mistrust evident. Finally, he nodded.

Lifting his finger he motioned for the. keys to the gate.

From the corner of his eyes Phatz noticed a guard grip his baton.

Wanting to make sure everyone heard his next words he spoke slowly. "If any one of you hit me with that stick," he paused to run his eyes down the line. "When I catch you by yourself in the hallway I'ma beat the shit out of you .Now we ready to go, but y'all got sticks and mace and shit. Just remember what I said."

Stepping back from the gate he let them ponder his words.

A nervous look passed over Popeye's face as he inserted the key into the hole.

"All we want is your cooperation sir," he stated with a twist of the key.

Picking up his bags Phatz nodded,"Let's ride."

Once on the other side, the guards stayed a safe distance as they were led across the yard. Loud cheering could be heard from the girl's dorms as they passed. He and AC took the applause in stride.

To the inmates, the scene that had just transpired was unheard of. Most of the inmates were too scared to even jump at the guards out of the fear of being beaten. Now seeing the shoe on the other foot and watching them fear retaliation was bittersweet even if it did come from a couple of out of towners. Everyone that witnessed what went on that day learned something important: Phatz and AC were a different breed, almost of a different world and in their world violence solved everything.

****

It was pouring down raining when the guard came to escort Phatz from his cell into the visitor's room. On the walk there he could hear the soulful sound of *Stairway to Heaven* being played by the church band that was full of inmates. The weather had forced them inside from their normal stage on the yard. He quietly hummed along to the lyrics. The song had become stuck in his head and honestly, he enjoyed listening to the inmates sing it. Recalling that the choir only sung on Sunday made him realize what day it was. Sitting in a cell for most of the day he sometimes lost the concept of time. The days and night blended one after the other. He wasn't interested in keeping up with the time either, it was a harsh reminder that the world kept turning even in his absence.

Stopping just short of the door to get buzzed in he realized that his visitor could only be one person. Inside the small lit room Graves paced back and forth. His head snapped up when he noticed Phatz standing watching him. A scowl settled over his face before his gray eyes locked over Phatz shoulder.

"Leave us!" he barked at the guard.

Pulling the chair at the table out Phatz dropped into the seat as Graves continued to pace.

He wondered what was ailing the man. Today he was dressed in a tan Versace suit with a chocolate tie and matching Versace shoes. Instead of his signature initialed cuff links he wore a Presidential Rolex like the one Phatz had given his father. It was roughly $20,000 on his wrist alone.

"You know I thought you were smart," Graves said. Leaning up against the wall he folded his hands across his chest.

"What you mean?" Phatz asked still distracted by his watch. $20K was nothing to him, but it had been a long time since he'd seen something flashy behind the walls. It brought back to memory the lifestyle he used to live before the prison suit.

"I mean," he sprang off the wall, "I told you specifically not to tell anyone about the deal and you go and do it anyways!"

Confused to what the man was yelling about Phatz raised a hand. "First stop yelling at me I'm not a kid. Secondly, what are you talking about? I didn't tell no one shit."

Graves tossed up his hands in defeat. Grabbing the chair, he slid into it. Seconds passed before he spoke again.

"Yesterday I get a call from some shithead public defender-"

Phatz sighed at the last words, the rest couldn't be good.

"…Asking me about the deal being made for my client. Not only that,but they reached out to the DA about the deal.Do you know what this means?"

"The deal is off," Graves said stating the obvious at Phatz silence.

The words rang loudly in his head. Phatz didn't have to guess who had called their lawyer and ratted them out. There was only one person stupid enough to do something like that: Ty. Time and time again he questioned why he bothered with the man especially since he could never seem to do anything right. Phatz told him specifically not to mention the news to anyone including his public defender. And what did he go and do? His fingers curled into tight fist. He'd only told Ty because he didn't want the man to be in the dark about their sentencing. It was his way of showing solidarity. Everyone in the jail was aware that they had come together, and you couldn't fuck with one without the other and he wanted to keep it like that. Falling out with one another only left room for weaknesses to be exposed, but Ty's fuck ups were beginning to push him past his limits.

"Look my bad," he exhaled deeply. "You're right I wasn't being smart, I was just tryna put my boys' mind at ease about how much time we were facing. My bad."

He reared back in the chair staring Graves in the eye. Phatz was a man who could admit when he'd fucked up.

Reaching down into his briefcase beside him Graves slid something folded across the table. On closer inspection Phatz saw that it was a newspaper. He hesitated.

"Go head open it," Graves urged.

Flipping it open his eyes read the big bold print on the front page: *California Gang Assaults 3 Guards.*

"Shit!" he slung the paper across the table. Any other time Phatz wouldn't have minded the publicity but now wasn't the best time. They were being tried in the public's eye before they even had a chance to explain their side.

Graves clasped his hands in front of him, "So you get it?"

"Yeah, we're not a fucking gang."

Graves shook his head and huffed out, "You don't get it."

He reached for his briefcase before standing.

"Whoa, whoa, whoa, where you going?" Phatz asked rounding the table on him suddenly.

He could tell Graves hadn't expected him to move that fast. The man took two steps back.

"I know all that shit don't look good in the public's eye, but I just paid your ass fifty-seven thousand, which you probably took half and brought that Presidential Rolex on your damn wrist."

Graves glanced down at his wrist. A guilty look crossed his face. Phatz knew he had the man cornered.

Deciding to give him some room, he stepped off and walked back to the table.

"I don't care about none of that shit they are saying about us. We had damn good reason to do what we did, I just need you to get us another deal."

"I can't."

"You can."

Graves sighed and sat back in the chair.

The man seemed to be weighing his options before he spoke, "It won't be the same deal as before."

"What are we looking at?"

Fidgeting with the edges of the newspaper Graves gazed at him, "Eight maybe ten, I can't say for sure."

Five flashed in his mind right beside the number ten making him silently curse Ty.

"Cool," Phatz shrugged after giving it a little more thought.

Returning the newspaper to his briefcase Graves stood to leave.

"I need you to do something for me," Phatz said as the man moved towards the door.

"The deals, not enough?"

"I'm paying you," Phatz shot back.

Graves tossed his hands up, "You're right what is it?"

"Put me and my codefendants on a dry run tomorrow to the courthouse."

The man's brow crinkled, "For what?" he asked almost to the door.

"I need to see how my girl doing she was involved in the fight."

At the door Graves pretended to think it over. Finally, he gave in, "Ok, just keep your mouth shut from now on and please stay out of trouble," he said before leaving.

Alone now Phatz thought about his words. He would keep his mouth closed. He couldn't say the same about the trouble part because if things worked out the way he wanted them to, that deal could kiss his ass. His life was at risk of being lost in the system every day that passed. Though he was paying Graves to get them free, he knew he couldn't count on it especially with the new developments. Spending all that time in a cell made him envision freedom, the kind that he wouldn't have to wait five or ten years to experience. Taking matters in his own hand seemed to be the only way things would get done.

∗∗

A few playas from L.A. owed him a favor and he was cashing in on it. Graves too had come through on his end by placing them on a dry run to the courthouse. He and Silky sat in the van with eight inmates being driven by a fat white guard under the wheel and one on the passenger side. Behind them another van carried Ty, AC, and more inmates. Except for the country music coming from the speakers it was silent. Phatz guessed everyone was thinking about the sentences they were about to be given, but not him, he was about to be set free. One call to Corey had set things in motion. Even now as they rode down the bumpy street in route to the courthouse he knew that Baby Boy, E-Mac, and Ski were lying in wait for them to arrive. Three days ago, they'd hopped on a plane to Shreveport after Corey paid them $3,000 for plane fare and to get rooms.

The instructions were simple. They were to wait at the small bus station beside the courthouse, the second the van pulled into the parking lot of the courthouse and Phatz stepped off Baby Boy would draw down on the two guards, take their guns and lay them face flat on the ground. Ski and Mac would handle the other two guards. When they were all off the van and away from the courthouse it would become a race across state lines. A race that he was sure they would win.

The closer the van got to the courthouse the more anxious Phatz became. He couldn't wait to be out of the handcuffs and prison suit. Turning around his eyes locked with Silky's. She was against the plan at first, but she also didn't want to be left behind. The fear that was etched on her face earlier had been replaced with a look of determination. He winked at her. It was almost showtime. Nearing downtown Shreveport, Phatz could see the clock tower connected to the old courthouse. Up front the guards began to talk among each other. Seconds later one spoke

"When we get to the courthouse please remain in your seat until Officer Whitley opens the door then line up in a single file to be escorted inside."

A few mumbles of agreeance came from the inmates' mouth as the van eased into a stop at the red light.

The courthouse and bus station were in full view now. Glancing out the window Phatz took a moment to survey the downtown area. Planted trees lined either side of the streets encasing the shopping stores. It was lunch hour, so a stream of people flooded the sidewalks going to and fro. His dad had been right, it wasn't much to see. The only good thing about the place was its jewelry. It was too bad he wouldn't have a chance for one last lick. Shaking the thought away, he focused his attention ahead on the crowd gathering outside of the bus station. When the light turned green the van slowly eased into traffic. Baby Boy was the first one Phatz spotted in the crowd followed by Ski and E- Mac. Baby Boy had seen him too because he nodded his head causing a shiver of anticipation to shoot through him.

"Alright ya'll know the rules," the guard said as they rolled into the parking lot.

Filing out of the van one by one chained around their waist, hands, and feet, Phatz felt like they were being marched in front of a jury with the crowd of spectators from the bus station looking on. He silently hoped that Ski had remembered to bring the bolt cutters to free them from the chains or it would slow them down.

Any minute now he thought as they began lining up. He could no longer see Baby Boy or Ski so he figured they were about to make their move. Minutes later when the front of the line began to move forward, he brushed off the voice in the back of his mind that told him something was wrong.

They were just waiting for the right time he reasoned. Dropping down pretending to tie his shoe he tried to stall the line. Phatz bought all the time he could before the guard commanded him to move with the line. Still nothing. Feeling as though he was being watched Phatz turned to see AC staring at him. The man's eyebrows crinkled in confusion. He shrugged in response. They all knew of the plan to escape even Ty. After Phatz had chewed him out about opening his mouth to the lawyer he begrudgingly told him about the plan. But this time Ty wasn't to blame.

When they reached the elevator inside the courthouse Phatz finally had to admit what he didn't want to. Baby Boy, Ski, and E- Mac weren't coming. The niggas had backed out. His plan to escape was over. He shook his head to himself. Depending on others had always been a hard thing for him for that very reason. You couldn't count on people to do what they said they would. Phatz knew of only a few people he could count on and ironically, they were in chains together- minus Ty. If Silky and AC had been in Baby Boy's and Ski's place he would've been out with no hesitation. He risked a look in Silky's direction and saw the questions in her gaze. Questions that even he couldn't answer right now.

Inside the holding tank where they were being held Phatz grabbed a bench by the window that overlooked the street. Surprisingly, the bus station that was packed only minutes ago was now empty. He was so busy waiting on the plan to jump off he never noticed people boarding the bus. His mind raced with all the possible things that could have gone wrong.

Fuck this he thought getting to his feet. He needed to know.

"Excuse me I need to make a call," he said to the guard.

At the phone he dialed the number to the room they were staying in.

The phone rang continuously on the other end, but no one answered. Slamming the receiver, he returned to the bench where he settled in for the long day ahead of him and what he figured would be even longer years.

****

"You not gone like what I'm about to say."

AC stood at the steel sink brushing his teeth. Cupping water in his hand he swigged it around in his mouth before spitting it out. Next, he used a lukewarm towel to wash his face. In the stained mirror his eyes connected with the man standing outside of his cell. Schoolboy was an older Cali brother from Oakland that was facing charges for murder, the result of a drug deal gone wrong. Possibly facing life behind bars, he was never going to see the streets again. At forty-one, the jail didn't see him as a threat and made him a trustee, giving him freedom to move around the jail as he pleased. Lately, he and Ty had gotten close which was why AC couldn't figure out why he was outside of his cell. He hadn't spoken more than two words to the man since meeting him.

"And why is that?" he asked pulling a clean T-shirt over his head. It was barely six oclock. After breakfast they would be going to the courthouse for a possible sentencing. He was ready to get everything over with. First he needed to know what was on Schoolboys' mind. Schoolboy motioned for him to move closer to the cells' door.

"Say what you gotta say," AC said growing frustrated. On the other side he could see the guards leaving the tier after their morning count.

Schoolboy leaned in closer, his lips almost touching the bars,

"Black Jack in the court holding tank, some nigga gave him a knife."

Drawing back AC searched the man's face for any sign that he was joking. The serious look on it let him know that he wasn't.

"Thought I would let you know," he said backing away.

An image of Black Jack lying in a pool of his own blood flashed in his mind, then just as quickly disappeared.

Grabbing his shoes AC stared at Schoolboy who was still lingering around.

"He gonna need it."

****

AC noticed that Phatz had been unusually quiet on the ride to the courthouse. He wondered if he was thinking about the news, he'd just delivered about Black Jack or the failed escape a few weeks ago. If he had to guess, it was the escape. Even he was a little disappointed when things hadn't gone as planned. But Phatz was taking it personal. Ski and E-Mac betrayed him. Babyboy had revealed to them that the money Corey had given them was smoked up. At the bus station that day they got cold feet and fled back to L.A. and on the way there they had went on a reckless bashing spree. The way AC saw it, helping them escape was never in their hearts to begin with. Ski and E- Mac were just two crackheads who saw an opportunity to feed their habits and in doing so his and Phatz plans of freedom had gone up in smoke right along with the crack they smoked.

He watched Phatz shake himself out of the daze he was in when the van stopped. The man's next words erased all doubt from his mind.

"Black Jack wanna play bad huh? We gone handle this clown today!"

Relieved to know his friends head was in the right place, he followed the guards off the van and into the holding tank in the courthouse where the other inmates waited.

Immediately his eyes landed on Black Jack who stood against the bars talking to another man on the outside of the tank. At their presence he stopped and stared them down.

Pretending not to notice him, AC followed Phatz to the other side while Ty took a seat on the bench. The tank was almost full with it being a Monday and everyone having to see the judge. The cell was a lot bigger than the one they lived in. Three benches, two steel toilets, and one sink was supposed to service everyone. Outside the tank two police officers stood close checking off the names of the inmates as they were called to court.

Keeping an eye on them AC waited for the moment when they would walk off. It came seconds later. When the guards disappeared around the corner, he nudged Phatz.

"It's show time."

Side by side they headed towards Black Jack.

He must've sensed their presence because suddenly his back was no longer facing them. A deep frown settled on his face.

"Let's get it nigga ain't no fence separating us now." Spoken with a deadly calm Phatz spread his arm wide.

His words caught the attention of the other prisoners in the tank and now all eyes were on them.

"Fuck you!" Black Jack spat.

He was so focused on Phatz he never noticed AC edging closer to him. Careful not to get too close, AC watched Phatz back with hawk eyes. There was a chance that the other inmates would try to jump in to defend Black Jack. After all he was one of their own.

"Let's get it nigga!" Phatz repeated louder.

Taken a menacing step towards Black Jack he feigned surprised when the man whipped out a knife from under his shirt.

It was the moment that AC had been waiting on. "Oh, so its two against one now," he said moving in.

"Guess that means I got to even it out."

Black Jack looked startled to see him so close. Gripping the handle of the ice pick knife he held it out in front of him.

"Get back!" he yelled slashing at the air.

AC could see the fear in his eyes.

"You only get one swing before I take it from you and show you how it's done so you better make it count," Phatz warned.

Suddenly it was so quiet you could hear a pen drop.

Still focused on Phatz, Black Jack never saw the punch that AC threw coming. Striking him with one blow he watched the man stumble against the bars. His foot slipped from under him, regaining his balance he clutched the knife with a death grip as his wild stare landed on AC.

True to his words AC recalled Black Jack threats, "Yeah nigga that's right remember you said you was gone kill me, now's your chance."

"Come on mother—,"

His words were cut short by another blow, this time from Phatz. AC smiled at the blood now dripping from Black Jack's nose.

Wiping at the blood with the back of his hand Black Jack swung his head in both directions unsure of who to focus on as the two men closed in on him.

AC thought about knocking the knife out of his hand so they could really get down to business. The second he made up his mind to make a grab for it the door of the tank was slung open.

"Against the wall!" the guards yelled as they forced their way through the crowd to get to them. From the corner of his eye AC watched relief sweep over Black Jacks face. It was just another reminder that the man was all bark and no bite.

Standing in between them the guards tried to diffuse the situation. As the knife was wrestled away from Black Jack, AC could feel his chance of punishing him begin to slip away.

He tried to ease around the guards.

"You stay there," the guard warned. Ignoring the man AC spoke over his head, "Nigga it's not over."

People from outside the tank rushed over to see what was going on. The huge spectacle was causing chaos in the courtroom. More guards entered trying to get the situation under control.

Standing right next to Phatz now AC followed Black Jack with his eyes as the guards attempted to walk him out of the cell.

"You California boys always into something." The words had come from a short white guard in front of him. Dismissing his comment AC focused his attention on Black Jack who was being escorted out by the same guards that had driven them to court. It was written all over his face that he thought he would get out untouched but he underestimated the situation. The second he got close Phatz broke loose of the guard holding him and punched him in the face.

Caught off guard Black Jack screamed as he scrambled to get away.

Lunging forward AC grabbed him by the collar of his shirt pulling the man down to the floor.

"Told you it wasn't over," he taunted. Tightening his hold, he tried to cut off his breathing circulation.

He laughed at the shocked expressions on everyone's faces. The poor guards thought their presence would stop them. He'd waited too long to get his hands on him to be stopped. He continued to choke Black Jack with his own shirt while the guards looked on helpless. Through the haze he heard someone call for back up.

Crack! At the sickening sound AC snapped out his haze only to realize that while Black Jack was trying to get up Phatz had kicked him the jaw with his booted foot.

The man collapsed onto the floor. Satisfied with the damage AC finally released his hold on his shirt.

The inmates who would normally come to Black Jack's rescue shrunk back in fear as the man thrashed around on the floor before curling into a fetal position.

"Get him out of there!" A voice yelled.

The guards peeled a battered, incoherent Black Jack off the floor and once again tried to remove him from the tank.

AC shook his head at the pathetic sight. The leader of the Shreveport crew had been brought down and everyone knew it, but for some reason Black Jack was always the last to catch on.

At the front of the cell assumingly away from danger he turned towards them. Cupping his broken jaw in one hand a long unsteady finger pointed at them.

"Ima kill you niggas in Angola."

The words were barely out of his mouth before Ty struck like lightening and socked him in the jaw sending him down to the floor again.

"It's never over!" Phatz shouted.

AC tried to hide his surprise at Ty's response. He'd almost forgotten the man was there. He hadn't moved from his spot on the bench since he arrived. In fact this was the first time he had ever got in their fight with Black Jack, though aware of the beef, he had managed to separate himself from it until now.

Joining them now he nodded his head.

Maybe he was trying to make up for his fuck ups AC thought.

When the guards and Black Jack were finally out of the cell, a deathly silence fell over it.

AC was glad that they were finally able to put hands on him the right way. He hoped the ass whooping would make him think twice before opening his mouth again. Yet he knew attacking the leader of one of the biggest crews in the jail was sure to earn them even more enemies. Even as he stood facing the rest of the inmates with Phatz and Ty by his side he could sense the anger and hate. A few sported scowls and hard stares.

"Let's get to it if you don't like what just happened to that weak ass nigga."

At his challenge no one moved. He looked at Phatz and Ty.

"That's what I thought."

****

"You understand what I'm saying Mr. Bradley?"

Momentarily distracted by the kid drawings hanging on the wall in the office, Phatz mind drifted to his son Dino Jr. He was almost one now. Last he spoke with his mom he was walking and getting into everything that he could and Phatz was missing it. He wondered if the man in front of him had ever missed any of his kid's firsts. Looking at the weary expression on his face he doubted it.

"Mr. Bradley?" The warden repeated pulling his attention back to him.

"No, I don't," he said finally responding to the question. He watched as the warden rounded the desk and perched himself on the edge closest to him. Crossing his legs at the ankle he spoke

"Mr. Bradley we can't afford to move the five hundred and something inmates that we house here, now the most likely solution would be to move you guys downtown to the county jail until we can get a handle on the situation."

The situation that he was referring to, was the increase of violence that had been occurring since their arrival. The latest one was the altercation they'd gotten into on the yard once returning from court. Word spread fast about Black Jack getting his ass beat and as expected his Shreveport crew was out for revenge. On the yard Phatz, Ty, and AC found themselves facing off with a gang of niggas. When a wooden locker box was hurled at them Phatz would be the one to knock it out the way before heading in the direction it had come from with Ty and AC following right behind him. It didn't matter that it was a gang of twenty niggas versus the three of them. Backing down was never an option, but before any blood could be shed, they were quickly intercepted by the guards.

Now inside of the warden's office the man was asking him to do something he had never done in his life.

"I'm not running from none of these niggas."

"I know, but I think you've made your point."

Sucking his teeth Phatz looked the warden up and down. "No I don't think I have, look let me tell you something if these niggas think we running from them whenever we get back it's gonna be more problems, so moving us won't solve shit."

With an almost defeated sigh the warden returned to his seat behind his desk. "The entire jail is on lock down because of y'all I assure you nobody thinks you're running." Picking up the phone he pressed a button and spoke into the receiver no sooner had he hung up, Ty and AC were marched in. Each man took a seat on the side of Phatz. When everyone was settled the warden cleared his throat

"I was just telling your friend here that getting the three of you downtown to the jail would be best."

"We not running from these clowns," AC said echoing Phatz words.

Seeing that plan wasn't working the warden switched his tune.

"I'm willing to do anything other than give you guys freedom cause obviously that choice isn't up to me," he waved his hands, "name it."

At his words a plan began to form in Phatz mind. Phatz started thinking of the bigger picture. It was obvious the warden was desperate to get rid of them. They'd gotten Black Jack so maybe a change of scenery was needed. Maybe he could talk Dino Jr's mom into visiting with his son since she didn't like the idea of the baby visiting at a maximum-security prison like CDC. The county jail was much smaller with less restrictions.

He eyed Ty and AC when both men nodded, he put his negotiations skills to work.

"First we want radios and TV's in each of our cells…"

"Done," he quickly replied.

Encouraged by his response, Phatz continued, "Longer yard time for all of us."

The warden cringed at the suggestion. He held his hand up as if he were painfully thinking it over. After a long pause he gave in "Ok but look only fifteen minutes longer anything else and the other inmate will expect the same and I can't have them thinking we negotiate with inmates. He paused to stare at them "These are just special circumstances."

"So we have an agreement?"

When Ty and AC both said yes, the warden sighed with relief.

"I can have the three of you out of here today," he reached for the phone again.

Phatz had been holding the last card in his hand for this exact moment. His ace of spades.

"Warden you might want to wait until you hear this last part."

The man paused mid dial.

"Last part I thought we had an agreement?"

Phatz smirked, "They agreed, I haven't."

Slamming the phone down he glared at him "Let me hear it."

Still cuffed around his ankles and legs he slid to the edge of his seat.

"Earlier you said the three of us," Tilting his head towards AC and Ty Phatz smiled.

"Its four of us and I'm only willing to go under one condition."

"Four?" the warden sputtered in confusion.

"Four," Phatz stated.

Standing up from the desk he shoved his hand in his pocket in disbelief that he was actually negotiating with inmates.

"Whats the condition?" he finally asked.

"The fourth one is Silky, if we go, she goes."

At the wardens defeated expression Phatz leaned back he had just played the winning card.

****

To AC being at the county jail was no different from being at CDC. He was still locked away in a concrete box surrounded by bars with one shitter and a thin cot for a bed. Picking up a pair of dice he ran a finger over the dots. While his location had changed his hustle hadn't. His eyes darted to the clock outside of his cell on the wall. Big Jim's shift would be starting soon. The white country guard with the dark suntan and red hair loved to gamble. Most days he came in with a pocketful of money only to lose it all to AC. Easy going with a friendly personality the guard was the coolest that they'd come across. Big Jim was also their connect to the outside world, anything that he could get in for them he did, like food. Good food that put the county jail meals to shame and made AC crave freedom even more. Standing, he walked over to the pizza box on the metal table, lifting the lid he scarfed down the last two slices from yesterday and it was just in time because Big Jim came bouncing through the door with brown paper bags in his hands.

"How's it going it guys?"

The keys on his side jingled with every step he took.

He slid something to Phatz who was in the cell next to AC as he made his way down the tier.

"Big Jim you got my smokes?" AC heard another prisoner ask. Though he didn't hear Jim's response he knew from Jim's loud laughter that he had come through for the inmate.

Finally, after making his rounds he stood in front of his cell.

AC could smell the grease coming from the bag in his hand and despite eating pizza only minutes ago his stomach growled.

When Jim passed the bag between the bar's AC wasted no time reaching inside. Pulling out a handful of fries he shoved them in his mouth. Next, he unwrapped the aluminum foil. Hot melting cheeses dripped from the burger sandwiched between two toasted slices of bread. Taking a huge bite, he couldn't stop the moan that left his mouth.

"This good as hell," he said around a mouth full of food.

In the cell next door, he could hear Phatz gobbling down his own food.

Big Jim pulled up a chair. "Best burger ever, got it from Freeman & Harris a nic-,"

"You talking 'bout that soul food joint downtown right," AC finished.

A look of surprise crossed Big Jim's face as he hiked his pants up before sitting down.

"Yeah man how'd ya know?"

"We ate there every day when we were in the free world."

He polished off his meal as Big Jim talked. The husband and father of three took pride in his job he was even employee of the month, but AC could see right through him. Big Jim had a unquenchable gambling addiction. Even as he talked his eyes would stray to the dice on the table ever so often. His hands drummed on his knees impatiently. It was crazy to AC because the man almost never won. Like so many others with a gambling addiction Big Jim never knew when to cut his losses. AC never felt bad about taking his money either because no matter how many times the man loss he would come back the next day ready to lose it all again.

Deciding to put him out of his misery, AC washed the last bit of burger down with a coke and signaled towards the dice.

Eagerly Big Jim nodded and went to check the door, when the coast was clear he returned with a smile on his face.

"I'm feeling lucky, today."

Kneeling in front of the bar's , AC shook the dice in his hand.

"You always say that and then you lose."

Big Jim shook his head.

"Not this time."

Reaching into his pocket he pulled out a stack of money.

Biting back a smile AC called out to Phatz, "Fool you playing or what."

"Not right now," he replied.

With that settled the game started. Flicking his wrist AC sent the dice rolling across the tiled floor.

Excitement leaped into Big Jim's eyes as he peeled two crisp twenties from his wad of cash.

"Hey Phatz if I win this round, I'll buy your girl that nice perfume she wants," he teased.

He got down on one knee careful not to scuff up his steel toe boots. A voice came over the intercom temporarily distracting him. When the announcement ended, he turned his head back to the game.

"Six," AC said leaning back on his heels. On his second roll he crapped out.

It was Big Jim's turn. The man blew into his fist as he shook the dice up.

"Feeling really lucky today," he called out before releasing the dice.

Thirty minutes later AC stood up from his position. Gripping the green bills in his hands he couldn't stop the chuckle that slipped from his lips.

"Well Big Jim it was nice doing business with you as usual."

He risked a glance at the man. A loose red curl dangled from his low hung head. With his shoulders slumped forward Big Jim looked as if he had lost his best friend. Instead it was only half of his paycheck.

Shoving the money in his pocket AC stuck his hand out through the bars.

"Can I have my dice back?"

Flustered Big Jim placed them in his hand just as another guard opened the door.

"Hey Jim, they need you out front," the guard called out.

Waving a hand Big Jim looked at AC, with a wild look in his eyes.

"Maybe I can come back later and win my money back."

He never knows when to quit AC thought to himself.

Draining the rest of the drink from the can he shook his head.

"No man I'm done for the day why don't you take what you have left and take the wife and kids out tonight."

Returning to the bed AC sat up against the wall, hoping that his suggestion would work.

"I think that's what I'll do," Big Jim replied soberly.

Deciding to take a nap he stretched out. Closing his eyes AC listened to the sound of Big Jim's keys jingling as he walked away.

"Phatz next time it'll be you and I," he said at the door.

"Man, AC took it easy on you Ima take your whole check," Phatz responded seriously.

AC smiled when the door finally closed. Another day another dollar.

****

Slamming the phone down Phatz fumed at the news he had just learned. The warden was refusing his calls. It was further confirmation that the man was still ticked off after getting sued. But the way Phatz saw it, it was the warden's own fault. Three months had gone by without them receiving the TV's and radios that he promised. His days of giving them lame ass excuses had finally run out once Graves got wind of what was happening. After filing a class, A lawsuit accusing the penial system of violating their rights to access to the outside, each of their cells now had a TV and a radio inside of it. With that problem behind him Phatz had focused on getting through his stay at the jail, but the rumor mill back at CDC was working overtime. He was about to dismiss the gossiping guards who stood outside as he showered when the mention of their moniker The California Gang caught his attention. Apparently, the rumor circulating at CDC was that out of fear for their lives they had asked to be transferred to the county jail until sentencing. The lies made him regret accepting the wardens' deal. And the longer he stood listening to them talk the more he felt like he had been played. After his shower he hurriedly put on his clothes, requesting to be taken to the phone instead of back to his cell. No matter how untrue it may have been Phatz couldn't let anyone play with their reputation. With that thought he knew there was only one thing left to do. Demand that the warden place them back at CDC, but he should have known it wouldn't be that easy. Even more so now that the warden wasn't taking his calls.

As he stood by the phone puzzling his brain, he thought about calling Graves, but decided otherwise. The lawyer was bleeding him dry. Getting him to file the lawsuit alone had cost him a pretty penny.

All out of options he motioned for the guard to take him to his cell.

The chains of his shackles drug behind him as he walked down the tier. His mind scrambled for a way to get them back to CDC.

He was still deep in thought when Big Jim appeared at his cell.

"Psssttt."

Phatz wanted to ignore him, he wasn't in a gambling mood.

Beckoning for him to come to the bars Big Jim looked both ways before he pulled something from behind his back.

"What's that?" he asked standing.

Moving closer he saw that it was a book. Phatz had almost forgotten he'd asked the man to bring him something good to read, but it was actually for Silky who was growing bored.

The hardened face man on the front of the book cover looked like he was a part of the mob. Flipping it over he read the synopsis before turning it over again to read the title.

"*Scarface,* what's this about?"

Big Jim bounced on his heels like an excited child.

"That's some really good shit there man, I know you'll like it."

He tapped on the cover of the book with his finger. "Listen this guy here Tony Montana doesn't take shit from anyone. Kinda like you guys."

The words resonated with Phatz. Big Jim was right, they didn't take shit from anyone not even a two-faced ass warden and it was time the man learned that. At the table he grabbed a piece of paper and pencil and scribbled a note down. He placed it inside the book and gave it back to Big Jim.

Disappointment masked his face.

"What don't you want to read it?" he asked confused.

"Yeah, man but I want Silky to read it first, we like reading books together so we can write to each other about them. Keeps things interesting," he added hoping the man would fall for the lie. In reality, Phatz just wanted to get the note to Silky.

Big Jim tapped the book against his head. "Why didn't I think of that?"

"The wife would love the idea."

Phatz nodded his head in hopes of getting the man moving along. After a few seconds Big Jim checked his watch.

"Ok its almost chow time I can get this to her now, she'll love it" he said already beginning to walk off. Glancing over his shoulder he started up again, "Since my dice partner is still sleeping," he said referring to AC, "I'll be back later."

"Aight," Phatz responded returning to his bed.

Pressing the button on the TV he turned the knob until it picked up a local station. He was just in time for the popular soap opera the *Young and the Restless*.

He wondered what Silky's response would be to his note. He'd written it in code just in case Big Jim got curious. Only Silky would know what the words "show time" would mean. He was giving her a heads up and although he wasn't quite sure what he was going to do he did know that sitting around in a cell letting the niggas at CDC think they were run off the yard wouldn't fly. It was time to make their return.

Slowly his eyes refocused on the television, the show had cut to a public service announcement about wildfires. Flames eating through the forest appeared on the tube. The fire left nothing in its aftermath but smoke and burned trees.

Phatz eyes shifted to the lighter Big Jim had snuck in for him when they wanted to smoke weed and like a lit match he was suddenly struck with an idea.

****

The first thing AC noticed when he woke from a deep sleep was the slit of moonlight shining through the small paned window in his cell. He'd slept the day away. The second was the absolute stillness on the tier. It had never been that quiet. There was always something going on whether it was niggas arguing back and forth from their cells or music playing loudly. Tonight, he couldn't even hear the keys jingling on the guard's waist that signaled they were coming to do count. Pulling himself up into a sitting position he let his eyes adjust to his semi dark cell.

An unexpected wave of peace washed over him as he sat there. With the sentencing date looming over their head's AC had begun to think of worst-case scenarios like what if the lawyer couldn't make another deal. Ninety-nine years was life. Jail was hard enough but those four letters threatened his sanity. He thought about his Aunt Twinkle and his mom, and siblings. A life without seeing his loved ones again would become unbearable. For weeks he tried to prepare himself for the possibility that he would die alone in a cell far away from home and family. Nothing worked. But in that moment, he was glad for it cause suddenly there was a burst of hope pulsing through him. Deep down inside he knew that everything would be alright. In the case that it didn't they could always try to escape again. He smiled to himself at the thought.

With a newfound attitude a familiar feeling began to gnaw at him. His gambling bug was back. His latest dark mood had caused him to turn down Big Jim's last few offers, but now he was ready to take the man for all that he was worth. Leaping from the bed he stuck his feet into his jail issued slippers and made his way to the bars. Still not a sound. When minutes passed by with no sign of Big Jim, he turned to flip on his TV hoping it would entertain him until the man arrived.

A voice next door made him pause.

"What's going on?"

Reversing his direction AC stood at the bar. Though it wasn't Phatz he could tell by the way the man talked that he wasn't from Louisiana.

"Who's that?"

A deep baritone laugh met his question.

Not interested in playing games he shuffled back to his bed.

"Y'all them niggas they call the California Gang right?"

Trying to focus on the show on TV, AC remained quiet. The man was fishing for information.

Meanwhile Detective Tibbs was getting ready to crack a case as always. The sharp actor black skin glistened as he talked. In the *Heat of the Night* had quickly become one of AC's guilty pleasures to indulge in. It was the only time he rooted for the cops.

"What part of Cali you from?"

The question came just as the credits of the show began to roll. He considered not responding but with the jail as quiet as a graveyard at night he figured it couldn't do any harm.

An hour later he couldn't stop laughing. The man -who he learned was Frank O- was not only a native of California but he was a Jungle nigga through and through. He was being extradited back to Cali after being busted in Mississippi. The world really was a small place.

"Then the country ass niggas brought me to this shit hole, I'm up out of here at first sunlight.," Frank O said wrapping up his story.

A stab of envy shot through AC. Frank O was lucky to be returning home to serve out his sentence. Pushing it to the side he asked the man about a few more players from back home.

They talked well into the midnight hours catching up on the latest hood news. Nothing had changed.

Stifling a yawn AC flipped off the TV fluffing his homemade pillow up that consisted of his prison jump suit and a roll of tissue he could hear Frank O getting ready to retire for the night as well.

"Hey Frank O," he called out as he lay flat on his back.

The man answered but his voice sounded further away now.

"When you make it back to Boss Angeles tell all the haters the Phatz and AC will be back soon and it's gonna be some mo' of it."

"On the B," Frank O replied.

Rolling to his side he pulled the thin cover over him. Saying those words out loud gave him even more peace than before. Louisiana couldn't hold them, hell the prison system could barely handle them.

As his eyes began to drift shut his final thoughts rested on the day when he would finally be home in his own bed with a girl of his choice right beside him.

****

The flames crawled up the paper devouring it quickly before burning out.

Tearing the old newspaper a part Phatz rolled up as much as he could until it resembled a long stick then he lit it and pushed it out his cell.

Next,he grabbed the can of air freshener. Holding it away from him he struck the lighter with his thumb igniting a high flame.

"Ooooh shit!" he yelled out in excitement.

He was tired of playing the silly games that they wanted to play with him. It was time they got back to business. The Warden didn't want to answer his calls, but Phatz would see if he answered the calls from the fire station when the jail burned down.

Laughing, he threw more paper out to make the flame grow. The scent of smoke clung in the air.

"Fire!" a panicked voice yelled down the tier.

In a trance Phatz stood back and watched the paper burn.

Fire.

****

AC thought he was dreaming when he heard the words. Burrowing deeper under the thin cover he drifted back to sleep.

The shrill ringing of the fire alarm made him jump up. Putting his hands to his ears he tried to block out the sound. Seconds later it went off but now he was wide awake and could smell the smoke.

Glancing out of the door he saw the orange and red flame burning through the tile. "What the fuck?"

A little to his left there were balls of paper on fire.

"Phatz wake up man this shit bout to burn down."

When he heard the man's laughter, he knew something was up.

"Relax it's not gonna burn it down I just need to get their attention," he said before flinging more flaming paper out of his cell.

Phatz quickly rehashed to him what the guards said.

Angry at the news AC, found himself ready to burn shit down as well. The warden had set them up to look like punk bitches. They couldn't have that.

"Slide me the lighter."

On cue Phatz slid the lighter down to him.

Carefully picking it up AC grabbed the bag the hamburger had come in.

"Fools not gonna never learn," he said under his breath.

Lighting the bag, he flung it out in the hall just as Big Jim burst in.

"What are you guys doing?" he asked in disbelief.

"It's nothing personal Big Jim, we're about to get you the day off."

Big Jim stood speechless, his face turning a blanche white.

AC shook his head. He sure had been looking forward to beating the man out of his money.

The alarm went off again. Sticking one finger in his ear he continued with his task.

When Big Jim realized he couldn't talk them out of it he spun around on his heels in search of a fire extinguisher.

But it was too late. Outside AC could hear the sirens from the fire truck arriving. Peeping out the small pane window not only was the fire department there, but the entire police squad had surrounded the building.

"Phatz that fool will listen now."

****

"All rise," the bailiff announced.

Standing to his feet Phatz watched as the judge strolled in dressed in a black robe. Thin and old Judge Reed had a no nonsense look about him.

"You may be seated," he said after the bailiff called the court to order. Settling into the hard-wooden chair next to Graves, Phatz cast a sideways glance to his left. Ty, AC, and Silky were at the next table with their public defenders. Behind him the rows of chairs that were normally filled were empty. Graves had arranged a closed sentencing for them.

"It looks like the defense and prosecutors were able to come to an agreement correct?" the judge asked. His mouth set in a thin line as he peered at them over his glasses.

"Correct," Graves answered.

Lacing his fingers together Judge Reed gave them all a hard stare. "I've had more trouble out of y'all these past few months then all my years together on the bench."

"Your honor my client had a hard time adjusting to his conditions in our small town , being from the big city and what not but he understands the consequences of his behavior and works towards improving them," Graves countered.

Phatz remained quiet. Graves would say anything to defend his client, but even the judge could see through his lies. After almost burning down the jail they had been transferred back to CDC. It was too bad that Black Jack had been sentenced and shipped off by the time they arrived. On more than one occasion they'd caught one of his flunkies slipping and stuck it to em. If they couldn't get the man himself then they would get the one next to him.

Staring at the judge Phatz realized that the man would sentence them to one hundred years if he could, but it wasn't up to him. The deal had already been made. Though it wasn't the usual five that he initially got comfortable with, Phatz was glad that Graves had come through on his end.

While the judge talked Phatz gaze darted back to the table where everyone sat. AC and Silky were the epitome of calm and poised. It was Ty's who looked as if he was about to shit himself at any moment. Phatz had kept the news of the deal they'd reached from him. He couldn't risk him opening his big mouth and risking their lives again.

From his view he could see the beads of sweat on Ty's head.

Good. Nigga deserved a whole lot more for fucking up the first deal. But it was almost over now. Or rather it was just beginning.

The bailiff handed Judge Reed a piece of paper. After a few minutes of going over it he nodded at the bailiff.

"Please stand for the reading of the sentence."

Rising, Phatz tried to remember the exact moment his life changed for the worst. Was it when he decided to pick up the hammer and get to it? Even though Kathi, his mom, had done all that she could to provide for him it just wasn't enough. He'd ran the streets most of his teenage life and he knew what he wanted. The money, the cars, and the hoes that came with it. A 9 to 5 couldn't get that for him so he did what he had too for the lifestyle he wanted, swinging the hammer every which way. And like everything in life, his choices had come back full circle and it was time to face the consequences.

"I hereby sentence the defendants, Dino Bradley, Deontay Scott, and Ty Willis to seven years of hard labor at the Louisiana State Penitentiary at Angola. The sentence will start immediately."

To his left Ty sagged down in the chair. He and AC locked eyes. The two were already aware of how much time they would be doing so it didn't come as a surprise to them but hearing the words "hard labor" made Phatz cringe inwardly.

The judge wasn't finished, "Silky Smith, I hereby sentence you to three years at the St. Gabriel's Prison for Women."

He banged the gavel once.

"Court adjourned."

Graves began tossing papers in his briefcase as the public defenders celebrated. Phatz didn't understand why especially since they didn't do shit.

Silky sat with her hand on her head. When he first told her how much time she was receiving she was shocked at the low number. Being the getaway driver didn't carry as much time as those doing the crime and when she refused to roll on her partners, she figured it was over for her. Graves talked the DA down: young with a clean record ,Silky would be out in no time. She had proven that she could handle herself so Phatz had no worries.

"Well Mr. Bradley this is where we say our goodbyes," Graves stuck out his hand.

Pumping it quick Phatz stepped back.

"You'll probably be processed out of CDC later today or early morning, where you'll then be taken to Elayn Hunt, the reception center until your paperwork is done."

He paused to give him a glance.

"You be careful down there on that River and if you need anything else you know how to reach me."

"Preciate all you did for us man." Phatz said shaking the man's hand once again.

"It's my job," he paused "I like the Concord watch that was in the collection of things, you wanna loan it to me," Graves half teased.

Smiling Phatz shook his head, "I'll send you one once I'm home."

Winking Graves strolled out of the courtroom whistling. Years later when Phatz was in Angola he would read about Graves freak boating accident in *Jet* Magazine.

The guard arrived to escort them back to the van. The day that he had been anticipating was finally over. But Phatz wasn't fooled by a long shot. As he arrived back at CDC he understood that the violence he'd witnessed and engaged in at the jail was only a small sign of what was to come. The real test was waiting for them behind the thick concrete walls of Angola.

Down The Walk

Angola

      The scene in front of him was like something out of a movie. Phatz watched wide eyed as the chestnut brown stallion trampled down the dirt row, leaving behind a cloud of dust in its wake. The man perched in the saddle reminded him of the gun slinging cowboys Mother Dear liked to watch, except this wasn't a movie and the man on the horse wasn't a cowboy. He was a Corrections Officer, but for some reason Phatz couldn't get the word overseer out of his head. He knew it was because it felt like he had been transported back to the 1800's. A month's time had passed since he had arrived and began to settle into what would be the next seven years of his life at one of the deadliest prisons in America: Louisiana State Penitentiary or Angola as everyone called it. Cradled by the Mississippi River on both sides, the penitentiary sat on an expansive amount of land that used to be a plantation, earning it the rightful nicknames "The Farm" and " The River". With its barbed razor wire stretching as tall as the sky Angola looked as if it held the deepest secrets of those lost to the system inside.

      In the short time that he had been there Phatz had quickly come to the conclusion that he was now living on another man's time and that man told him when to eat, sleep, and shit. While his new conditions unsettled him, the mental shift that he had to make hadn't been hard. It was only a matter of locking away the good inside of him. Angola wasn't the place for it. There was nothing but bad apples in prison and Phatz would fit right in. As fucked up as it was, he had made his bed and the time had come for him to lay in it. Every morning before the crack of dawn, dressed in jeans and a prison issued shirt, he rose and made his bed alongside the other seventy men that were being housed in Camp C- Bear dormitory. After a hearty breakfast they were marched three miles to the fields where they would do back breaking labor in the cotton fields. Phatz found it crazy that he had gone from earning thousands of dollars a day when he was in the free world, to picking cotton for a half a cent a day. Yet even he had to admit that Angola's system was flawless. See Angola was a labor camp and to save tax dollars, they made the prisoners grow everything they needed from corn to cotton. Even the catfish they had for lunch was farmed on the land. Almost every camp on the premises was responsible for something. Some raised pigs, others herded cows, chickens, or worse picked cotton. The prison was making a fortune off their cheap labor and Phatz hated it. To take his mind off of the pain that racked his body as he worked that day, he thought of ways to make money on the inside. Yeah that's right the hustle never stopped. He needed to show Angola that he was more than just inmate #108164.

 He was lost in deep thought when the CO that the inmates had dubbed Boss Nigga came barreling down on him. Pulling the horse in by its reins he reached for the Remington shotgun at his side.

"Why are you sitting down boy?" he asked.

With his mind preoccupied with the idea of getting cash, Phatz had absentmindedly planted himself on the ground, breaking one of the main rules, no sitting. From his position he tilted his head back to get a good look at the man as he thought about his answer. He was tired, hungry, and his feet ached, but he knew none of those answers would satisfy Boss Nigga who waited for his response with an expectant look on his black face. Known for being mean and ruthless Boss Nigga was over Camp C- Bear and thought that because of his position he was better than the other CO's. Judging by the look in his red rimmed eyes he was itching for a fight. But Phatz was too tired to give him one.

Climbing to his feet, he grabbed the burlap bag that held the cotton in it. His sore muscles tensed up underneath his jacket with every movement. He could feel the CO's gaze on him as he shuffled down the dirt row. After what felt like forever, he finally heard the horse hooves pounding the dirt, carrying the Boss Nigga back to his post

Out of habit he glanced down at his wrist. Instead of the Omega watch that once adorned it, there was a cheap small one he'd purchased from commissary. With only three more hours left in the workday he hoped they would pass fast. Wiping his hand across his damp brow he reached for the soft, white ball in front of him.

"Ssss", he hissed when the sharp thorn sliced through his finger.

He watched as bright red blood began to ooze from the cut. Dipping his uninjured hand into the sack Phatz used a swab of cotton to soak up the blood on his now pulsing finger. He cursed to himself as his hard gaze landed on the rows of cotton. Trying to separate the cotton from the spurs without slicing himself was almost impossible. His swollen and pricked fingertips bore the proof of it. Until Angola, Phatz had never seen cotton up close and personal before, but now it was all that he saw, even when he closed his eyes at night. A sickening feeling settled into the pit of his stomach; he didn't know how much longer he would last.

At that moment, a strong breeze blew through the field causing the dirt in the field to rise.

Phatz blinked once then sneezed.

"Here you go," at the sound of the voice he spun around.

An older man by the name of Lenny stood behind him holding out a scarf. Phatz looked at his outstretched hands then to his face. He hadn't made any friends since arriving at Angola nor was he trying too. When he wasn't catching up on sleep he kept to himself,but every now and then he and Lenny would play a game of chess. Despite his old appearance Lenny's mind was still sharp. Dust covered almost every inch of him from his hair to his clothes. Looking around him Phatz noticed that Lenny along with the rest of the prisoners out in the field looked worn and tired and he suspected he didn't look any different.

"Tie it around ya face, it'll keep the dust and shit from getting in your mouth and nose, and don't sit down unless you want them guards to put a bullet in yo ass and take you to Point Look Out."

Grabbing the scarf from Lenny's hand,Phatz nodded his head in acceptance, "Appreciate it." Tying it securely around his nose and mouth he lifted the bottom half to speak, "What's Point Look Out?"

Lenny tilted his head to the left. Confused, Phatz turned in the direction to follow his gaze. At first all he saw were tall stalks of cotton, but then his eyes zeroed in on the wooden crosses in the next field over and suddenly a somber feeling settled over him.

Point Look Out was a graveyard for the prisoners.

His eyes cut to the CO's who were guarding them, hands clutching the shotguns in their hands.

"Damn just for sitting down?" Phatz asked, shaking his head wondering how many men had met their deaths for being tired.

"Yep and trying to cross the gun line."

Lenny expertly grabbed a cotton branch and pulled the cotton off before stuffing it into the bag. At the stunned look on Phatz's face he grinned.

"Youngin when you've been here as long as I have you learn how to work smarter, not harder."

Phatz tried to mimic the movement but gave up after he wound up with more cuts.

Lenny chuckled before moving past him, "You'll get it, just don't sit down again."

He stared after the old man as he maneuvered down the cotton row. Lenny may have been able to pick cotton without shedding blood, but his slow footsteps and slumped back let Phatz know that the cotton field had beaten the man down over the years. Raising his tingling fingers up to eye level Phatz shook his head. He didn't plan on "getting it" as Lenny had suggested. As he dragged the burlap sack down the dirt row Phatz made a decision. He had to get out of the fields and fast.

****

AC could feel the restlessness beginning to settle deep in his bones. His stomach growled in protest as he moved around. It had been three days since he had eaten any solid food. Placed in a small cell the size of a bathroom, with one small window, and sleeping on a hard mattress for twenty three hours with only an hour of free time ,AC was getting his first taste of what his sentence at Angola would be like. Or so he had thought. When Phatz and Ty had been shipped out, he had waited patiently for the day that he would get to join them at Angola. Only that day never came. AC had spent the last few weeks questioning the front desk about his transfer, only to be met with silence and blank stares. He had a sinking feeling that something else was going on behind closed doors and he intended to find out. Going on a hunger strike had been his only way to get answers and after three days he had finally gotten the warden's attention.

Throwing his legs over the bed he stood to stretch his long frame and wondered when the meeting would take place. No sooner had the thought formed did two guards appear at his cell door.

"I see you're still not eating Scott," the white guard commented.

Ignoring the smirk on his face, AC walked towards the barred door, stretching his hands out to be cuffed. He knew that the guards had an ongoing bet on how long it would be before he caved and gave up his hunger strike. Despite the hollow feeling in his stomach,AC was willing to bet he could go a few more days, hell even weeks if he had too. But at the thought, his stomach began to cramp. He balled his fingers into a tight fist to stop the slight tremble in his hand- all side effects of having gone days without eating. Inhaling deeply, AC forced himself to focus on his plan to get out of Hunt, instead of his gnawing hunger pains as the guards led him down the tier. A few minutes later he stood outside of the warden's office. The guard beside him knocked softly on the closed door.

"Come in," a gruff voice answered.

Slowly the door opened revealing a fat white man with blonde hair and pale skin sitting behind a wooden desk. Judging by the loose skin hanging around his saggy jaws and his balding head, AC guessed that the man was in his mid-fifties. The name inscribed on the metal plate on his desk read Warden Gibson. AC had only seen him once when they first arrived at Hunt. Apparently, word had gotten back to Gibson about the hell they had raised at CDC and the destruction they had left behind. As a precaution the man had opted to place Ty, AC, and Phatz in the hole instead of sending them into the general population. Gibson had tried to play smart and stay safe, but he had no idea just how close he was to danger with AC still being there.

Stepping further inside the office, AC took a seat in the metal chair in front of the desk. Drawn to the wooden grandfather clock on the wall, he watched transfixed as the silver pendulum swung back and forth, seemingly keeping with the steady hum coming from the air conditioner. The clock appeared out of place in the small junky room. Shifting, he found Warden Gibson studying him from behind the coke bottle glasses he wore.

"Nice clock," AC commented, noting the hint of surprise in the Warden's brown eyes.

Flustered, Warden Gibson cleared his throat before nodding his head towards the open manila folder in front of him. "I take it you're the one keeping up all the fuss with the hunger strike," he mumbled in a southern drawl. His head swayed back and forth as he began to read the papers. When his face began to contort into a deep scowl, AC smiled. Pushing the folder away Gibson wiped at the perspiration under his eyes. His voice sounded tired when he finally spoke.

"Mr. Scott, I understand that you're requesting a transfer to Angola to serve your time at the Louisiana State Penitentiary."

"That's where the courts ordered me and my brothers to serve our time, and that's where I need to be," AC stated firmly.

Leaning back in his chair the Warden clasped his hand together on his round stomach and stared at him with a thoughtful look on his face.

"Son, I don't think you understand the type of place Angola is," he started slowly.

Here it comes AC thought.

"If I sent you down there, I would be personally handing you to the wolves." Tapping on the folder he glanced up, "This file says that you're only eighteen. Now Mr. Scott I don't know if you know this but here's the God honest truth. There ain't nothing but cold-blooded murderers, rapists, and any other horrible criminal you can think of at Angola. The average man won't survive in there. 'Specially not a nice looking fellow like your'self."

Gibson shuffled a pile of paper around on his desk before continuing.

"Hell, I doubt if your partners will make it out, so understand me when I say I can't do that in good conscience," he said with finality.

Except for the swinging sound of the clock's pendulum and the air conditioners low hum the room was quiet.

Inside AC was boiling with rage at the Wardens' refusal.

"You need to look at that file again, all the evidence you need is in there. I can handle myself," he said in a steely voice.

Gibson shook his head. "You're only eighteen ain't nothing, but heartless killers on that river now I--"

"Don't act like you give a fuck about me you don't even know me!" AC barked.

The words made Warden Gibson sit up straight. Just then the air conditioner made a clanking sound before shutting down.

"Got dammit!" Gibson exclaimed, jumping up. The guards rushed in at the sound.

"Warden everything ok?" they asked with their eyes trained on AC.

Before he could respond the phone began to ring.

Holding his hand in the air as to put them on pause he walked back to his desk and snatched the receiver up.

"Elayn Hunt Correctional Center, Warden Gibson speaking."

While he talked AC, realized with disappointment that he wasn't going to Angola, at least not now. He also saw right through the warden's false sense of care, straight to the heart of the matter. Greed. He had been in and out of detention centers long enough to understand that the longer he stayed at Hunt the more money the state would send for him to be housed there. The truth was that the warden was only worried about lacing his already fat pockets.

Hanging up the phone Gibson scrubbed a hand down his face before motioning to one of the guards. "Get the repair crew in here, damn air went out," he ordered, lowering himself back in the chair.

With a fake look of empathy, he turned back to AC.

"I'm sorry Mr. Scott but I can't grant your request."

Even though he had already accepted the situation for what it was, at that very second AC wanted to lunge across the desk and wrap his hands around the man's fat neck but he doubted if he could get to Gibson quick enough with the guards standing right behind him.

"The best thing for you to do now is to cut out the hunger strike and wait until we find somewhere suitable for you to go understand?"

Not answering, AC stood indicating he was ready to leave. A guard immediately came to his side.

"You'll thank me for this son, I'm doing you a big favor," Warden Gibson called out to his back as he was led out of the office.

Back in his cell AC lay down on the thin mattress seething at the Wardens rejection of his transfer. They were going to try to separate them, but he wasn't having it. They had come together and they would leave together. He was getting to Angola… by any means.

"Scott, you eating? I got you a nice healthy meal here?" the guard called teasingly, breaking through his thoughts.

At the mention of food his stomach growled, normally he would turn his head toward the wall but not this time.

Retrieving the tray and cup of water he sat on the metal stool and ate the mashed potatoes and meatloaf. He was shocked at how good it tasted. Either that or he was really hungry. Once he was finished he placed the empty tray in the slot. With his stomach full for the first time he reclined on the mattress.

"He's eating boys," he heard the guard yell down the hall when he came to retrieve the empty tray.

The food that he had just eaten suddenly felt like a lump of betrayal in his stomach as reality began to settle in around him. AC had played his last hand and lost sorely. Silently he cursed himself for giving in so easy. His mind replayed all of the things he should have done or said back in the office. Then he wrote it off. It was obvious the warden's mind had been made up long before he arrived. AC came to the harsh conclusion that he was being held hostage against his own will.

2 months later

"Mail call!" the guard's loud voice boomed down the tier. It wasn't until AC heard him approach his cell that he finally glanced up from the March issue of the *Sports Illustrated* with Los Angeles Lakers Magic Johnson on the cover. He'd won it from another inmate during a dice game. Magic had been his favorite player when he was a kid and he promised himself that one day he would get to see him play. Then again, he was also supposed to be living out in Malibu in a mansion with a beach view by the time he was eighteen. But with less than three months before his nineteenth birthday AC's living arrangements included a six by eight feet dark cell encased in steel bars with a metal toilet, a hard cot, and three meals a day. It was a far cry from a mansion.

When the guard slid two white envelopes through the slot, he marked his page in the magazine with a pencil, before going to retrieve them. A faint smile touched his lips when he read the first sender's address. It was from Shauna , a pretty girl that he had met at Carson Mall, the two had spoken a few times over the phone before his mishap in Louisiana and he was surprised that she stuck around despite his current circumstances. He and the suburban girl had been exchanging letters since he first arrived at CDC. The second letter was from Ty. The two had been writing back and forth through farm mail- the system that let the prisoners write to each other- to keep up with what was going on. AC learned that both Ty and Phatz were now in different camps in Angola. Tucking Ty's letter away to read later, he focused on the letter in his hand.

He let out a deep sigh as the flowery scent drifted from the envelope as he ripped it up. It was the simple things like a woman's scent that he missed the most. Scanning over the neatly printed handwriting he could hear Shauna's soft voice in his head as he read. After he was done, he took out a piece of paper and pencil and began his reply.

Halfway through his letter he was interrupted by a familiar tapping on the steel bars. A lieutenant and a guard stood outside.

"Time for your shower, Mr. Scott you have a big day ahead of you," one of them spoke.

Confused, he placed the pencil down and stood. AC had been at Hunt long enough to know that they were only allowed three showers a week. Today wasn't one of them.

"Y'all a day early," AC replied as he studied the men's faces. Something was up. He could tell by the sly grin on the fat black major's face. The shiny metal badge clipped on the front of his shirt looked like a toy, but AC could tell he took pride in it by the way his hand stroked it as he talked. In his late forties the man reminded him of the character Virgil Tibbs with his black shiny skin and permed hair but looks was where their similarities ended. The major was a slimy dirty motherfucker. AC had heard about him from the other prisoners and how he beat them, but up until now their paths had never crossed.

When the cell door slid back the major stepped in, his eyes darting around the small cell before settling on him.

"Mr. Scott you have orientation today, so the warden instructed us to come take you to the shower and escort you down."

Orientation. The word set off the alarms in his head. Orientation only happened when a prisoner was being transferred. AC wondered what Warden Gibson was up too. His question was quickly answered by the man's next words.

"Since the Warden thinks Angola is not the place for you, he's looking into a few more options," the major said, picking up *Sports Illustrated* Magazine.

"You like Magic huh?" he asked, leafing through the pages.

"Don't touch my shit," AC warned, feeling the anger pulse through his body. The major clicked his tongue before dropping the magazine on the floor, careful to step on it as he inched forward. He was baiting him.

"You know boy you got a smart mouth for someone who's at the mercy of the warden right now."

"I'm not at the mercy of no fuck-"

"Watch your mouth," the major gritted out closing the distance between them.

His hand flying to his toy badge again.

166

"Do you know who I am?" he growled. He was so close now AC could smell the stench coming from his breath. Taking advantage of their height difference he purposely stared down his nose at the major when he spoke, "I don't care who you are," he answered truthfully.

The major drew back with a murderous look on his face.

Tightening the grip around the pencil that he managed to slip into his pocket when no one was paying attention, AC willed the major to make a wrong move, so that he could sink the pencil deep in his chest, right above the spot where his fake badge rested.

One more step he urged silently as they sized each other up.

Just when he thought the man had read his mind the guard outside stepped into the tension filled cell. The already small cell shrunk in size with three bodies crowded inside.

Averting his gaze AC read the CO's name tag. Harrison. White as a ghost with black hair and an innocent face Harrison appeared to be in his late twenties. His uniform was different from the majors. Instead of a white shirt, Harrison wore a powder blue uniform shirt with black jeans. No badges or patches covered his arm.

Immediately AC knew he was a new recruit. It was probably his first day as well he thought.

Harrisons blue eyes shifted nervously around the cell before he spoke,

"Think of it like this Scott you get to shower one day early and you still get your other ones as well, heck they might start calling you the shower king around here."

An uncomfortable silence hung in the air at the man's lame attempt to break the tension. Seeing that his joke had fallen flat Harrisons white skin began to turn a bright red.

AC directed his attention back to the major who he could feel shooting daggers at him with his eyes.

Dismissing the look, he grabbed his toiletries and moved towards the open cell, purposely brushing into the major as he did so.

At the contact the major jumped back as if he had been touched with fire. Breathing hard through his nose he screwed his face up into a grimace "You betta watch where you going or-

"Or what?" AC asked swinging around so that he was facing him again. He shifted his toiletries to one hand so that he could easily reach into his pocket if he needed to. But again, Harrison intervened.

"Whoa whoa whoa, come on Scott let's get you to the shower, then orientation," Harrison said putting his body in between them.

"You heard the CO," the major smirked.

"Let's go!" Harrison commanded in a firmer voice that didn't quite match the scared expression on his face.

Fuck this AC thought to himself. Standing around going back and forth with the major wasn't solving anything. He needed time to think and the shower was the perfect place. Walking away from the major when all he wanted to do was beat the shit out of him was hard, but he managed to make his feet move forward.

Fifteen minutes later he was freshly showered, but still without a plan. The correctional officers had refused to take him to see Warden Gibson. AC felt like they were backing him up against a wall and in that case, there was only one thing left to do.

"You're new here right?" he asked Harrison who escorted him down the empty hall when he was finished showering.

A cheesy grin split his face.

"Is it that obvious?"

They turned a corner leading them down another hall. "It's my first day," he added.

AC had suspected as much.

Harrison was about to launch into another sentence when AC stopped him just as they approached the office.

"Next time some shit like that go down in my cell you stay out the way if you wanna make it back home, got it?"

AC didn't know the first thing about Harrison, but Big Jim came to his mind. Not all the correctional officers were corrupt Big Jim had taught him that. He was giving Harrison the benefit of the doubt and a chance to escape his wrath.

Flustered Harrison jerked his head up and down.

The door to the office swung open, inside another white man sitting behind a desk motioned for him to come in. AC tossed a glance over his shoulder and saw the fear on Harrisons face.

Good.

If he had any sense he would listen.

By the time the psychologist finished with his examination AC was hungry and tired. He'd lost track of time a long time ago. Hopefully, his food tray would still be waiting for him when he returned to his cell.

Wiping at his eyes with the palm of his hands he stifled a yawn.

"Do you attest that everything here is true?" the psychologist asked still shaking his head.

AC had spent the last hour detailing his life of crime to the man. Phatz had warned him before he left about the physical and mental exams that determined where to house prisoners. AC figured since Angola was the place for hard core criminals giving them a little insight to his life of crime would help them see that he was no different. From the look of disgust on the psychologist's face he knew he had done a good job of convincing the man.

He left the office feeling a lot more confident about his transfer. If the warden didn't believe he could handle himself then, he sure would now after talking with the psych. He was one step closer to Angola.

"What's it like in California?" Harrison asked as they walked back to his cell.

AC didn't know how to answer the question. One side of L.A. was struggle, dead bodies, pain, and crime. The other was money, success, happiness. Experiencing the first half was enough to make him push for the latter.

"Is it all sunshine and girls on the beaches?" Harrison asked innocently.

AC laughed.

"You've been watching too much TV."

Harrison gave a boyish shrug. "I'm from Mississippi so my view of things is limited."

They continued to make small talk on the walk to his cell. Rounding the corner both men stopped short at the sight in front of them. The major and two more guards stood a few feet in front of them blocking the entrance into his cell.

A sinister smirk crossed the majors' faces as he slowly approached with his flunkies in tow.

AC senses heightened; he could feel the danger circulation in the air.

When the man stopped in front of them his icy stare flickered over AC before landing on Harrison.

"Why don't you go and grab some disciplinary forms, a few inmates got into a scuffle earlier."

Hesitating Harrison shifted from one foot to the other, "W-well,ok let me just get Scott back in his cell."

The major shook his head,"I'll watch him just go and do what I asked you," His tone left no room for argument.

Harrison shot him a puzzling look before starting off down the hall. Twice, the man glanced over his shoulder with worry lines on his face.

AC hoped they weren't for him. Harrison should've been more worried about the major.

The man in question stretched his hand out to lean on the wall, preventing AC from moving any further. With his guard dogs behind him AC knew the major felt like he was doing something. Seconds ticked off with the two staring at each other. It was the major who finally broke the silence.

"It's little pieces of shit like you that make my job harder."

And just like that AC was ready to pummel him, instead he clenched down on his cheek reeling in his anger. Though it was the middle of the day there was little to no movement in the halls, AC knew it had been on purpose. Sucking his teeth, he pretended to stare off into space but the truth was that he was biding his time.

"And I'll tell you something boy," the major continued in a hard voice, "if a piece of shit like yourself disappeared round here in these woods nobody would ever find you." Pausing he nodded to his guard friends who tried their best to look intimidating.

To AC they resembled Alvin and the Chipmunks. Never mind the fact that his life was being threatened, the image in his head made him smile.

"What the fuck so funny?" the major asked growing furious. Pushing off the wall he stabbed at the air with his finger.

"I can make your life a living hell, you hear me boy!"

"The only boys I see are you and yo lil bitch ass chipmunks," AC responded breaking his silence. The chipmunks head swiveled back and forth at the chill in his voice.

"I don't give a fuck about you being the major I will beat yo ass, you just another Uncle Tom motherfucker working for the white man. You a sellout, if you really want some problems just take these cuffs off or better yet follow me to my cell."

An evil laugh erupted from the majors' throat as excitement leapt into his cold flat eyes. He was enjoying the exchange. Slowly he began to circle AC, like a predator did its prey when they were ready to attack only he had mistakenly assumed he was the predator.

"Oh, see I've already heard about that silly shit you and your clown ass crew did back at CDC and I guarantee you won't do none of that shit down here."

Unfazed by his empty threat's AC shrugged a shoulder. "Like I said," he moved his attention to the chipmunks, "Y'all gone let me in my cell or take the cuffs off?"

"They don't have to do shit!" the major bit out. Face to face now his nostrils flared as his eyes narrowed into thin slits. AC's skin tingled in anticipation of what was to come as the two men squared off.

At the sound of footsteps approaching the major took a few steps backwards putting space in between the two.

Harrison had returned. He glanced at the two men who looked like they were ready to rip each other apart.

Sensing the threat, he quickly handed off the papers before walking over to AC. "Everything ok?" he whispered in a low voice.

"The fuck is you whispering to him for, you forgot whose side you on CO?" the major scolded.

"No, sir I--"

"Get over here now!"

Like a battered puppy Harrison slinked over to the major.

AC strained to hear their hushed voices, but from the way Harrison was rubbing the back of his neck it wasn't good.

When Harrison returned to his side, he couldn't meet his eyes. It set off the alarms in his head again. That and the smug look on the major and the chipmunks' faces.

Guiding him back to his cell, Harrison slammed the door shut without a word.

Angrily AC yanked at the cuffs. When they didn't budge, he began to pace his cell. His breathing sounded harsh and loud to his own ears. Catching a glimpse of himself in the mirror he stalled. His yellow skin had darkened to a deep shade of red. He could feel the heat coming from his face.

The major and his chipmunks were going to try to come in and catch him off guard. With the cuffs on his hands they knew he wouldn't be able to defend himself.

"Be damn if them niggas get me," he said out loud to himself.

His vision landed on the pencil. He quickly dismissed the idea. It wasn't strong enough. Then suddenly he remembered something. Plopping down on the metal stool he searched underneath the table, cringing as his fingers brushed over what felt like globs of chewing gum and God knew what else. He smiled the second he found what he was searching for. Raising it to eye level he squinted at the thin piece of metal in his hand. Just days earlier he had removed it from the headband of his headphones before filing it down to the size of a bobby pin. So small that only a trained eye would spot it.

Working fast he stuck the pin in the hole of the handcuffs. A few twists and he could feel the cuffs begin to loosen around his wrist. He was glad that Harrison hadn't snapped them on tight or else he wouldn't be able to move his fingers.

Just a few more he thought to himself. The sound of footsteps broke through his concentration.

Shit. It was them.

"Come on come on," he chanted twisting the metal even faster.

Click.

The handcuffs popped open.

"Yes!" he exhaled as he rotated his wrist in circular motions trying to get the blood flowing.

The footsteps were upon him now. Steadying his racing heart AC placed his hands in his lap with the cuffs loosely around his wrist.

He could feel the adrenaline racing through him as the cell door slid back.

"Remember me?" the major asked as he stepped inside.

"I see you decided to take up my offer," AC responded coolly.

Handing his badge to one of the chipmunks standing on the tier, the major stepped further into the cell.

AC could see the muscles straining in his neck. He carefully watched his rigid posture. The major was like a rigid dog ready to attack. Sizing him up not only was the major shorter than him but he was overweight. Even from where he sat, he could see his big belly move with every breath he took. How long did the major think he would last against him?

A chuckle slipped from his lips.

"Glad you think it's funny," he stated angrily as he rolled his sleeves up. Tucking his chin in his chest AC laughed knowing that it would anger the man even more. Truth was he wanted him to make the first move. And he did.

Charging at him in rage the major came to a sudden halt when AC jumped up from the table and threw the cuffs at him.

He watched as the majors' expression changed from shock to horror when he realized what he had been hit with.

"Yeah that's right bitch."

The first punch he landed to the major's jaw sent the man flying backwards. He looked comical as he flapped his hands around to stop his fall, only to meet the hard-concrete floor. Not giving him time to get up AC jumped on top of him.

"Punk bitch," he spat, hitting the man with a solid jab to his nose. AC noticed the blood immediately when he pulled his hand back.

"Get off me," he grunted out, grabbing his shirt.

"Fuck you!" AC replied before head butting him.

Shit why I do that he thought to himself as a wave of dizziness washed over him from the impact. Shaking it off he watched blood leak from the major's face.

"Wait til I get up," the major gasped out in pain.

"Aight get up, nigga get up," AC taunted. Slowly he climbed to his feet. He swayed back and forth as he put his fist up. Spitting out a hunk of blood on the floor the major opened his mouth,

"I-"

His words never made it out as AC hit him with a right hook, and a clean upper cut sending him crashing back down. Wrapping his forearm around the major's neck he dropped to the ground on one knee.

"This what happens when you fuck with a real nigga and not no lil boy like these other cats in here."

AC felt like he was in a wrestling match as they tumbled around in the small cell. He cringed when his shoulder banged against the sharp metal end of his bed. Still, it wasn't enough to make him let up.

Ignoring the majors hand digging into his flesh

AC tightened his grip, hitting him with a powerful blow to his rib cage.

"Aargh!"

"What's all that shit you was talking now, boy" AC taunted as the major writhed around in pain trying to get away. Except they were now dead locked in what looked like a full nelson; AC had seen the move done in the wrestling matches he used to watch as a kid. Forcing the majors face to the ground the man screamed when the concrete scrubbed against his skin.

"Yeah how that feel?" he asked amused.

"Get off him!" The chipmunk yelled out seconds before AC felt hands pulling at his arms.

Through the blur AC managed to catch a glance of Harrison on the outside of the cell. A stricken look covered his already pale face the next time AC looked around he was gone.

Now it was three against one.

"You motherfuckers next!" AC yelled out refusing to loosen his grip. The more they tried to free the major the tighter his grip got.

He wasn't surprised by the pepper spray that came next, catching him right in the eyes. His lungs were on fire as he struggled to breathe, his grip finally loosened.

"Put the damn spray down you maced me you dummy," the major choked out.

AC's eyes were beginning to swell. Still trying to maintain his hold on the major he tried to reverse their position.

"Let go!" the major pleaded.

AC could feel his grip beginning to weaken, the pepper spray had thrown him off balance. It burned like a bitch!

Finally, they were able to pry his hands away from the majors neck. The man stumbled blindly out of the cell.

Sprawled out on the concrete floor, AC tried to gulp in what clean air that he could as he resisted the urge to rub his eyes with his palms knowing that it would only make it worse.

"I'ma beat yo ass soon as this spray clear!" the major threatened from outside on the tier as he sagged against the rails.

"Yeah right like you just did," AC responded through bouts of coughing. The door slid shut and he was left alone.

It felt like hours had passed before he finally moved. When he thought it was safe, he gently touched the skin around his eyes noting the puffiness of it. Standing up he stumbled to the sink and splashed cold water on his face. The relief was instant. A few more splashes and his skin began to cool off. Wetting a wad of tissue, he carried it back to his bed where he placed it over his eyes.

After a few minutes the stinging in his eyes and burning in his lungs began to ease. He could breathe normal again.

At the sound of voices and footsteps his body shot up straight.

"Oh they want some more huh," he said through half closed eyes.

When the footsteps continued pass his cell, he lay back on his mattress again. Through slit he spied his abandoned magazine and Shauna's letter. It would be a while before he would be able to write to her, already he could feel his dominant hand swelling. Still a small smile played at the corner of his lips. The major had gotten what was coming to him. In that moment AC made a silent vow to himself that until they sent him to Angola no one would be safe.

****

He was free. Well not technically, but Phatz was free from the cotton fields and he couldn't be any happier. Slinging the heavy mop across the concrete floor for what seemed like the hundredth time. His mind traveled back to that day in the field when he launched his plan into action. The prison was aware that he suffered from asthma they just didn't know how bad. Two hours into the workday Phatz collapsed on the ground, his fingers clawing at the dirt as he gasped for air. A panicked Lynwood alerted the CO, who came bounding down on his horse yelling out orders. Fearing his plan hadn't worked well enough when the CO told him to take a five minute break, Phatz lapsed into another performance, this time he fainted as the men tried to help him to his feet. Next thing he knew he was being loaded onto a stretcher and carried away. Once in the infirmary, where he pretended to regain consciousness, the doctor had taken one look at his husky frame and his medical chart and declared he had suffered an asthma attack. Inwardly, Phatz gloated at the news. His act had been so convincing that even the medic had fallen for it. On doctors order he was assigned to light duty work, a task normally assigned to the elderly and sick prisoners. It was the best news he's heard since being sentenced. Now his days were spent picking up trash and cleaning the administration building he was currently in.

When he reached the end of the hall, he scrubbed the mop over the floor again only slower before pushing the bucket to the side. Standing back, he surveyed his work and smiled at the shiny floor.

For the most part Phatz liked being in the building because it meant he could roam around and do what he wanted.

After he was done mopping, he walked outside to the almost empty rec yard. It was well after ten, so everyone was still working in the fields. That was another benefit of the job, it gave him time to workout, a habit he had picked up to help pass time. Removing his jacket and his shirt, he figured he would squeeze in a light workout before it was time to return to work. Years of rust covered the barely intact equipment. Picking up the pig iron he launched into a set of arm curls, thankful for the cool breeze blowing as he built up a steady pace.

Almost ten minutes into his workout a figure loomed over him creating a shadow on the ground.

He didn't have to turn around to know that it was the captain of Camp C that had invaded his space. Ignoring the man, he continued his arm curls.

"Boy you supposed to be workin' this aint play time, na get your ass up and get back to work!" the captain ordered in a heavy southern drawl.

Lowering the weights down to the ground Phatz turned to face the man not bothered by the scowl that was on his reddened face or the green veins pulsing from his neck.

"First off I'ma grown man understand that and secondly I'm just taking a lil r and r, ya know."

He shrugged and flexed his muscles knowing that it would get under the captains already flushed skin. The captain had it out for him badly and to prove it he would order Phatz to do things like moving heavy boxes that clearly went against the doctor's orders. He hated out of state inmates, especially the ones like Phatz who he thought always seemed to be up to something. The city boy was proving impossible to lock down no matter how hard he tried.

Pushing the brim of the Stetson hat on his head back he sneered revealing his tar stained teeth. "You're finished when I say you are ,If I catch you messing with these weights again when you supposed to be working I'm sending your ass back to the fields, I want that building spick and span. Do you hear me boy?"

With his fist clenched at his side Phatz contemplated laying him out right there. A few days in the hole or the dungeon as they called it-- would be well earned after he beat his ass. Decision made he was getting ready to send his fist into the side of the captain's lean jaw when a voice came from behind him.

"Don't worry bout it captain I'll make sure he gets back to work."

Glancing over his shoulder he watched Bates cross the grass. Dressed in a similar uniform as Phatz in jeans and a white T-shirt, Bates subtly shook his head as he came to a stop beside him.

The captain glared at Bates suspiciously for a few seconds.

"Yeah you do that."

Returning his attention to Phatz he leveled a finger at him, "Don't forget what I said."

Phatz watched the man strut off with his shoulders squared and his chest stuck out like a proud rooster unaware of the ass whooping Bates had just saved him from.

The two waited patiently as he rounded the corner of the building disappearing out of sight. "Fornia nigga you crazy, was you really about to hit the captain?" Bates asked turning to him with awe in his voice.

Walking over to the weight bench Phatz dropped down and leaned back. Once the bar was in his hands, he brought it down to his chest quickly before extending his arms pushing the weights back up.

"Was about to lay his ass flat," he said through labored breathing.

Adding weight to the bar Bates threw his head back and laughed.

Serving a life sentence for murder, Bates who was from New Orleans had entered the system when he was only twenty-two. Now at forty he knew all the ins and outs of Angola and how it worked. Bates was responsible for all the inmates calling Phatz "Fornia". While it was just a nickname to them, for Phatz it was a constant reminder that he was far away from home and outnumbered and it could quickly change to him vs. them. If it ever came down to it, he would take out as many of them as he could. So, he always made sure to keep his guards up.

Working alongside Bates in his new position surprisingly the men had formed somewhat of an alliance.

But Phatz knew that aligning himself with Bates could send the wrong message. Even though most of the prisoners were from Louisiana he noticed that there was a constant power struggle between the prisoners from Baton Rouge, Shreveport, and New Orleans. It reminded him of the beef that had been occurring for centuries back home between L.A. niggas and Oakland. Nobody really knew why it started only that once sides were chosen somebody was bound to lose. With the New Orleans crew being the largest of the bunch it wasn't much that they didn't control from the drugs to the commissary. In the pen there was strength in numbers. Yet, Phatz didn't respect numbers only hustle and money. Bates had shown him he was willing to get to the money at all costs.

"You know that thing we talked about the other day?" Bates asked adding another weight to the bar.

"Uh huh," he responded, trying to focus on the increasing weight.

That thing that Bates was referring to was Phatz plan to start his own hustle. Since he was no longer in the fields Phatz could focus on the one thing that mattered. Money. Like most penitentiaries he knew that Angola had a high contraband problem. The number one being drugs. From weed to powdered cocaine it all got in one way or the other and there was a high demand for it. Phatz saw how prisoners were willing to pay anything to have something that would help ease the pain from all the time they were doing. He wanted in on the money flowing through the place. All he needed Bates to do was get the product inside and he would handle the rest. If he had to serve seven years, he would do it in style and with power.

"Well I think I have a solution," Bates responded. It was music to Phatz ears. He listened as Bates filled him in.

"As long as the money is right, she'll do it," Bates ended as he wrapped up the conversation.

Finishing his last set, Phatz placed the iron bar back on the rack. Raising up he used a towel to wipe the sweat off him.

"The money right," he said in response to Bates' statement.

Quickly calculating the cost. He stood to make the most profit, so money wasn't a thing. After giving Bates a few more instructions to get the show on the road the men went their separate ways.

Grabbing his jacket Phatz threw his shirt on and returned to the building. Pausing outside of the captain's office He eyed the captain's name carved on the door. Hocking a wad of spit from the back of his throat he watched it smear the letters in amusement.

"It's spick and span now."

****

"Are you a homosexual and or have you ever engaged in sexual activity with a man?" the hard-unflinching gaze met AC's bewildered one.

Not believing what he was hearing, AC moved to the edge of the plastic chair, his hands curling into tight fists as he did so.

Maybe the Lieutenant sitting in front of him had the wrong file he reasoned to himself. There were over fifty men crowded in the small cold room all from different parishes around the state. Groans and moans of complaints rose every few seconds as they were rotated from one check in desk to the other. The lumpy cold oatmeal that AC had eaten that morning was long digested. It had day full of tests and evaluations, but finally AC was at Angola. His transfer hadn't come as a surprise, after beating on a few more of the guards, Warden Gibson had gotten the message. AC could handle himself. Finally, he would be reunited with his partnas.

His lighthearted mood changed the minute the steely gates of Angola closed. He could almost taste the hopelessness and despair that clung to the air like a thick cloud as they were marched into the prison and issued their prison uniforms and toiletry bag. AC had a feeling that he had just landed in hell. Yet he wasn't concerned in the least, his motto was simple: Play it how it go. Whatever they threw at him he would give back twice as hard. He expected that they would try him to see what he was made of; he just wasn't expecting it to be so soon.

"What you say?" AC asked leaning forward.

The man who had identified himself as Lieutenant Bill removed the thin glasses from his face. His brown eyes scanned over AC before he spoke,"Listen don't pussyfoot around with me, it's been a long day and as you can see," he nodded to the line of prisoners behind AC waiting for their turn, "we still have a ways to go."

Putting on his glasses and picking up the pen he muttered, "You wouldn't be the first to admit it."

"Admit what!" AC said standing. Nigga done lost his mind he thought to himself.

"It ain't shit to admit, furthermore you don't ask a grown ass man questions like that, it's disrespectful."

The noise in the room came to a screeching halt.

"Everything ok over there?" a voice asked.

But AC was too focused to heed to the voice. All of his attention was directed on Lieutenant Bill who was now standing on the opposite side of the table. The older black Lieutenant clenched his teeth together as he spoke. "This is for your protection, not mine, it don't have shit to do with respect so either you answer the question or I'll make my own assumptions," he shrugged and sat down with those last words.

AC could feel his skin begin to heat- he was embarrassed. Embarrassed that another man could ask him something so foul. Behind him he heard the light chuckles from the other prisoners. He knew the game if he let the Lieutenant get away with disrespecting him in front of everyone, he could kiss his manhood goodbye.

"Sit down so we can get this shit over with," Lieutenant Bill pointed at his seat.

Putting aside any regret he would have about hitting an old man, AC lunged over the table instead grabbing Lieutenant Bill by his shirt.

The room exploded in chaos as he took the Lieutenant down with one punch.

Lieutenant Bill was in so much shock he neglected to defend himself as AC got off a few blows. Seconds later he found himself restrained by the correctional officers that had come to the Lieutenants defense.

"Are you crazy! That's the Lieutenant you just attacked!"

"And?" AC responded as he struggled against their hold on him. His answer was met with an eye full of pepper spray.

****

"Fornia, we got a problem."

The expression on the man's face standing in front of Phatz said it all. Skin as black as tar Spooky Black was a twenty-three-year-old New Orleans native serving time for armed robbery. 5'6 with a mouth full of gold, Spooky Blacks' take no shit attitude and the fact that he was one of the commanders over the New Orleans crew was the reason Phatz had chosen to add him to his operation. For the past six months Phatz had been supplying the prisoners with the finest California weed. Even now at his bed he could smell the familiar scent on some of the guys walking past.

He and Bates' plan was seemingly fool proof. While Bates was responsible for getting the weed inside of Angola, Phatz took credit for getting it to Louisiana. Twice a month he had a pound of weed shipped to Bates sister's house, who then packaged the weed into balloons the size of jawbreakers.

Then came Bates role. While Phatz was eager to get the weed in his hands and his operation running, it was Bates who had explained to him that Saturdays were the best days for her to visit. Bates knew that on the weekends the visiting room was always filled and the prison became relaxed on how many people were allowed to visit. In the packed visiting room, it was hard for the guards to see everything.

Bates not only filled him in on that, but he also told Phatz how his sister only wore long skirts and frumpy shirts to hide her curvy shape. Tight and revealing clothes drew attention from the other prisoners and the guards. Two times out of a month on Saturdays dressed in a long skirt she visited with Bates right hand man Carnell. She would discreetly slide him a zip lock bag full of balloons underneath the table.

Phatz had instructed Carnell to drink a sip of water after every balloon he swallowed so that they could easily pass through him. After visitation it normally took Carnell three to four hours to shit the balloons out or throw them up. It was a messy job, but it was worth it. Once the weed was out Phatz divided it evenly with Bates as a part of the deal.

Because it was top notch weed Phatz sold his supply for fifty dollars a packet. In no time he, Spooky and a few other foot soldiers had sewed up the yard.

Knowing that not even concrete walls and iron bars could stop his hustle filled Phatz with pride. He wanted to celebrate with his crew by giving each man a sack of weed for free, but from the murderous look on Spooky's face, it would have to wait.

"What's up?" Phatz asked, sliding the white K-Swiss with red stripes on his feet. Even locked down he had to keep his appearances up dressed in blue Levi jeans and a crisp white shirt with a gold chain around his neck He refused to go to waste like so many other prisoners he saw.

Like the guy cowering behind Spooky. Phatz rose from his bed to get a better look at him. His cornrowed hair was splattered with strings of gray and his prison uniform had seen better days. The shirt he wore underneath the button-down denim shirt had a yellow tint to it and his shoes looked as if he worked in the fields. Phatz tried to recall if he had seen him around the dorm before, but his mind kept drawing a blank.

He watched the man's shifty eyes and fidgeting hands. Maybe he was a customer.

"Hey homeboy wat's up," he called out to the man grabbing his attention. "You need something?"

Instead of answering the man looked to Spooky as if needing his approval to speak.

"This what I'm tryna talk to you about", Spooky explained. Just then the men from the field began to file back in the dorm. The guard in the command booth suddenly stood watching.

"Say my nigga we need to handle this now, meet me in the restroom," Spooky said turning on his heels with the fidgeting man trailing right behind him.

What the fuck going on Phatz thought to himself as he eyed their retreating figures.

Although him and Spooky were cool, he never let it overshadow the fact that he was in their territory by himself. With that in mind he slipped the six-inch screw he'd found while cleaning up, in the waist of his pants before walking out the dorm. It wasn't much but it was sharp and would do damage if he hit the right spot. And he always hit the right spot.

Inside the restroom the strong scent of the disinfectant the prisoners cleaned permeated the air. Spying Spooky casually leaning against the off-white walls, his eyes took in the now empty stalls. The restroom was the only place where they could hide from the guards' prying eyes and the other inmates' listening ears.

"Tell him what you told me," Spooky said as Phatz nodded his head.

"I-I don't want no trouble," the man stuttered.

"Nigga didn't I tell you shit was cool," Spooky said taking a threatening step towards him.

With his eyes bulging he turned towards Phatz.

"Fornia I know you and Bates jam I just don't want no shit."

Phatz could sense the fear coming from him. Snitching in prison was like hanging yourself with a rope. He didn't condone it but if it was something, he needed to know then…

Placing one foot up against the wall, he folded his arms in front of him, meeting the man's nervous look with a serious one. "Go head and say what you gotta say nobody gone fuck with you." The words seem to do the trick. He watched the man's shoulder slump in relief.

Still he swiveled his head back and forth like he was being watched before speaking.

"This really ain't my business I just thought you should know. "Reaching into his pocket he pulled out a lint covered plastic package.

Lunging forward Phatz snatched the plastic out of his hand. Just to make sure his eyes weren't playing tricks on him he held it up to the light.

Motherfucker!

The green seedless weed was California's signature strand. He had requested only the finest weed from his connect back home. It was the reason why his shit was selling so fast in Angola. Everyone knew that the strongest weed were the batches without the seeds.

"Bates boy Carnell sold it to me."

Phatz eyes locked with Spooky's yellow ones. Suddenly he understood the reason for Spooky's look. Bates was cutting them out.

"That's what we had to talk about," Spooky responded cracking his knuckles.

Phatz glanced back down at the package he now held.

"When did you say he sold it to you?"

"Today."

Phatz nodded his head as he sucked on his teeth.

"Today huh? Aight cool." He handed the weed back to the man who looked at him in surprise.

"Man, I can't keep that, it's yours" he tried to wave it away.

Shaking his head Phatz shoved it in his hand,"Don't worry bout it , you paid for it right?"

He nodded slightly.

"Then it's yours, enjoy."

Back at his bed in the dorm he closed his eyes and drew in a deep breath.

Knowing Bates betrayed him left him seeing red. It was just this morning when Bates delivered a message that only four of the balloons were smuggled in. Phatz had taken the man at his word. Now he knew it was a mistake. Bates was running his own operation using his products.

"So what's the plan?" Spooky asked.

He was so deep in thought he almost forgot Spooky was standing there like a soldier ready to receive his orders.

Grabbing his laundry bag Phatz began stuffing his clothes inside. Next, he placed his hygiene products in a box.

" I see what time it is," Spooky commented with laughter in his voice.

Spooky knew the game.

"Damn right, look I'm beating both of them niggas ass." He paused to make sure he had packed everything. All that remained were the sheets on his bed.

"Gotta let em' know I'm the wrong nigga to fuck with."

"All you gotta do," he said stopping to stare at Spooky. "When I beat them niggas ass make sure all my shit right here- he patted the full laundry bag - is sent to the dungeon with me."

Spooky smirked "I'ma do better than that, when you go after Carnell, I'ma handle Bates" he said, rotating his shoulders.

Phatz peered over at the guard at the table whose eyes were locked on the TV. He would have to be careful if he didn't want his plan interrupted.

"Ok, cool but listen don't let him get away cause I gotta put my hands on him too when I'm done with Carnells' bitch ass, so we gone switch."

"Double the ass whoopings" Spooky joked.

"That's right, leave em laying in they own blood."

Sliding everything under the bed, he was ready. Gazing around the dorm he wondered how many of his supposedly customers were going behind his back buying from Bates.

"Let me show you a trick," Spooky's voice interrupted his thoughts as he moved across the room.

"It'll help you pack some power behind yo' punch. Niggas gone feel like a brick hit em."

"A brick?" Phatz shook his head. "I'm knocking they ass out with one punch nigga I'ma show you how we get down where I'm from."

Grabbing a battery off the small steel table Spooky nodded. "No doubt but use this, ball it up in yo fist and when you hit that nigga its gone feel like you hitting him with a brick."

Phatz eyed the battery. He wasn't fond of weapons unless it was a hammer but in this case Bates and Carnelll deserved everything that was coming to them.

"Let me see that."

Spooky handed the battery to him. Curling his fingers around the cool battery Phatz squeezed it in a tight grip.

"Ok bet, but I'ma need my other hand because I already know he'll try to run."

He glanced back down at his fist "They always do after the first blow. "

• •

Ding.

The bell sounded signaling the second round of the fight. On TV was the replay of the match between the undisputed champion Marvin Hagler and Tommy Hearns at Cesar's Palace in Las Vegas. It was a bloodbath as the two men pounded away at each other blow after blow.

A group of inmates crowded around watching the fight in the day room. In the corner an old man held a cup up to his mouth as he tried his best to narrate the fight.

"Shut the fuck up, we can barely hear!", One of the prisoners called out but the old man ignored him continuing his entertainment.

Sitting in the back of the room Phatz pretended to watch the antics. Though he had already seen the fight when it first aired, the second showing gave him time to check out the crowd around the ring. He knew for a fact that he would've been ringside with a few honeys on his arm had he been out. But the fight was just a distraction for his real reason for coming down to the area which he rarely ever visited.

For the past hour he waited patiently for a sighting of Bates. Briefly he entertained the thought of going to find the man, but he knew Bates was smart and would know something was up.

Phatz wanted to catch him off guard like the news of him crossing him out had. He wouldn't have to wait much longer as Bates filed into the day room with Carnell trailing after him. Through slit eyes he watched Bates shake hands with a few New Orlean guys including Spooky as Carnell stood close by, surveying the room.

He wondered what could have been going through Bates mind when he decided to cross him. Did he not think that he would find out? Or did he just not give a fuck?

Admittedly Phatz was so focused on lining his pockets that he turned his head to the bullshit that happened daily. Still he didn't miss the fact that the inmates played mental gymnastics with each other to spot out weaknesses. Little by little they would test you to see how far they could go. He had been in the streets long enough to know that if someone tested you by knocking at your door with drama or disrespect you had to answer. To not answer in prison was like a death wish; it left you open for predators of all kinds who would pick away at you until you caved. It was the reason why Phatz couldn't let Bates crime against him go unpunished. Bates knocked and Phatz answer was about to be real loud and clear.

Carnell must've gotten bored with Bates and his conversation because he began to wander around. His timing couldn't be more perfect. Jumping up from his seat Phatz intercepted the man halfway across the room.

"What's up man you good?" he asked.

He noticed saw the surprise flash in Carnell's eyes, but there was something else lurking beneath.

Before Phatz could identify it, it was gone.

"I'm good," Carnell replied with a gapped tooth smile.

Not for long Phatz thought. He couldn't believe the man had the audacity to smile in his face after he had stolen from him.

Behind him the bell sounded on the TV again.

"Aye man you watched this fight yet?" he asked, getting into character. He knew that Carnell didn't suspect a thing.

Looking at the TV Carnell shook his head. "Naw this my first time seeing it," he replied.

"Nigga you gotta see this shit, sit down on the bench," he instructed not surprised when Carnell did as told. He had always been a 'do boy.'

Across the room he locked eyes with Spooky. Nodding in his direction Spooky began to move closer to Bates who was still running his mouth.

Phatz stared down at Carnell whose eyes were glued to the TV.

"Ayye watch this," he said tapping on Carnell's shoulder pretending to be excited.

"Watch now," Phatz repeated as he wrapped his hand around the battery in his pocket.

He had timed it perfectly. When Hagler landed a lethal blow that sent Hearns careening to the floor in knock out fashion ending the fight, Phatz mimicked the move and punched Carnell square in the face. Like Hearns he fell to the floor only he wasn't knocked out. The man screamed out in pain. Pouncing on him Phatz began to unleash a fury of lethal blows on Carnell's face. Eventually he managed to squirm from under him breaking out in a sprint as he escaped from the room.

Refusing to give chase Phatz searched the room for his next target.

Bates lay curled up on the floor as Spooky pounded him with his fist.

Wanting in on the action he made his way through the crowd.

Grabbing Spooky by his shirt he shouted, "Go get that other nigga it's my turn now!"

The crowd surrounding him faded away as he kicked Bates in the face sending blood gushing everywhere.

Bates eyes began to roll in the back of his head as he began to lose consciousness.

That didn't stop Phatz.

Grasping a fist full of the man's shirt he shook him violently.

"Bitch ass nigga you wanna try to steal my shit huh? So now you gone pay in blood."

With the battery still clutched in his hand he drove his fist in Bates face repeatedly.

"Come on California u gone kill him he had enough." At the voice Phatz paused long enough to look in the face of a Muslim guy he worked out with.

His chest heaved up and down as he stood up. Rage pulsed through his body. Here he was trying to help a few bum niggas out and they had tried to play him. He stared down at the blood on his hands as Bates lay unmoving on the floor. That would teach him and any other nigga a lesson. Disgusted at the sight of Bates, Phatz shoved his way through the crowd.

In the dorm he washed the blood off his hands in the sink basin.

"Ayye CO's coming!" someone shouted in warning.

Spooky appeared out of nowhere breathing hard, his shirt covered in blood. Tossing him a new one Phatz placed the now clean battery back on the table as he changed.

"That nigga fast," Spooky breathed out taking a seat on his bed across from Phatz as the CO's stormed the dorm.

Phatz tossed his head back and laughed as the anger began to leave his body. "Nigga what I tell you."

They both glanced at each other and repeated in unison "They always run" before bursting out in a fit of laughter.

****

"What the fuck?" At the feel of something hard landing on his shoulder AC jumped up. Brushing what looked like balls of dirt from his shoulder his eyes went to the spot where he was just sitting. He blinked once then twice not believing what he was seeing. Above the spot where his head rested only seconds ago, was a gaping hole. what he thought was dirt was crumbling cement. Piles of it now lay on the bed.

Tap

Tap

At the noise his brow wrinkled. He was certain it was coming from the other side of the wall. and he had no idea who or what it was.

AC had been in cell block A or the disciplinary unit for over a month now for assaulting Lieutenant Bill. The good news was that he was in Angola- away from Hunt like he wanted. The bad news was he was back on lockdown twenty-three hours a day, with only one hour spent on the outside and his living quarters had gotten worse. The cell was the smallest he'd ever been in, so small in fact that if he stretched his hands upward he could touch the ceiling with his palms. The bed was so close to the toilet that one wrong move and his lips would be touching the steel bowl. He'd complain about the sink not working more than once and the small crack in the window that air blew through at night forcing him to sleep in both of the prison issued uniforms he was given. His complaints went unanswered. AC figured it was because of his pending assault charges against the Lieutenant. Still, he had no regrets about his actions.

When the tapping came again, he edged closer, noticing the problem. The buildings at Angola were so old there was no rebar in between the walls which explained the concrete on his bed. Someone was chipping through the bricks. The thought had just registered when AC found himself staring at the whites of an eyeball.

Jumping back, he watched as more cement tumbled down onto his bed.

"What the fuck you doing?" he asked while his hands searched for something that would serve as a weapon.

The only thing that came close was a can of shaving spray.

"Aye?" he called out again noticing that the tapping had stopped.

When a long stretch of silence followed, he thought it was the end of that.

"You gone help me out or what?" the voice asked, sliding a thin piece of metal through the hole.

There was only one reason why someone would be digging through a wall. "Help you do what, escape?"

Silence followed his question. Then the voice was back.

"Naw we not tryna escape nigga. I just need to get into the cell next to yours. I got some business to take care of with that nigga and I need you to help me take the rest of these bricks down to get through."

We?

AC shook his head peeping game and not missing how the man had said we. Up until recently he had thought the cell next to his was empty.

If AC let them in through his cell, he would be a part of whatever sick shit they had planned for the unsuspecting victim. Walking over to the hole he bent down so that he was eye level with the man on the other side. He spoke slowly wanting him to hear his every word.

"The shit you tryna do does not concern me. It's not my beef. So, what I need you to do is put that brick right back the way you got it and find another way around cause you not coming in here."

He could feel himself begin to grow irritated.

Through the hole he watched the man stand. He was no longer staring at his eyes but his clenched fist.

"It's like that huh?"

"Damn straight," he responded clutching the can of shaving spray out of sight. He wanted to spray the man then beat his ass except they had only dug a hole small enough for a hand to fit through.

The man called out to someone else. That's when AC noticed it was two people in the one-man cell.

They had already chipped through one wall and were making their way through his. He shook his head in disgust.

"Y'all some cowards if you wanna handle some shit you do it yourself. You muthafuckas need help," he said edging away.

"No need for all that, we see you won't help us out so ok," the man responded.

"Fuck that nigga," he heard the other occupant in the cell say before the brick was placed back in its place filling the hole.

If he hadn't seen it for himself, he would have thought he had imagined it all. He could hear the faint sound of tapping resuming. They were breaking through another wall.

Shrugging his shoulders, he sat back on the bed, careful not to let his head get too close to the wall. He noticed the metal scraper left behind. Quickly retrieving it AC tucked it in his shirt, it would make a better weapon than the can of shaving cream. Grabbing one of the books he was allowed to check out from the book cart he lost himself in the words, but still he listened for the rhythmic tapping on the other side. He felt for the scraper,if they decided to go against his wishes and chip through his wall both the men would be in for a rude awakening.

****

The moment Phatz stepped off the bus in front of the main prison he knew Spooky hadn't bullshitted him not one bit, Down the Walk was everything he said it would be. Phatz tried to take in his new surroundings as he was escorted down the buff concrete slab with over twenty other prisoners. Unlike the camps that were scattered on the prison's ground "Down the Walk "was a thirty dorm building that housed over twenty four hundred prisoners. At the sight of the other inmates moving freely through the halls, his mind began to think of all the things he could do with the extra freedom without the correction officers watching. In the small camps CO's seemed to be around every corner he turned, making it hard for him to conduct his business, but being Down the Walk where the prisoners clearly outnumbered the guards Phatz didn't anticipate having this problem. When the line stopped outside of a dorm Phatz readjusted his hold on the blanket and pillow he carried in his hands along with his belongings.

"This shit taking too long," a voice behind him said.

Turning slightly Phatz stared into the face of the man who had sat beside him on the ride from camp C. The man had tried to make conversation with him, but Phatz hadn't been in the mood then nor was he now.

"You need help wit yo bags?" he asked.

He eyed him wearily as he tightened his hold on his bags. Fools in prison never offered anything unless they wanted something in return. It was never a good idea to borrow or ask for help from anybody, otherwise you might find yourself in a tight situation. Lucky for him though Phatz never needed to borrow or ask for anything. Shaking his head, he refocused his attention in front of him.

"Hey, you the guy they call Fornia right?"

He turned again trying to place his face now. The man in question had a bearded face with an afro, and was only a few inches taller than him, yet Phatz couldn't recall seeing him before.

"I'm Marvin, yo boy Spooky used to get me right with the smoke, some of the best shit I ever had, you got anything on you now?"

That explained it.

At the mention of Spooky's name Phatz regretted that he wouldn't be able to shine with him for a while. After beating Bates and Carnell, both he and Spooky had been sent to the dungeon - the hole and being that it was Phatz first offense they shipped him to the bigger unit Down the Walk. Spooky on the other hand had a list of offenses and because of it he was shipped off to one of the outer camps. Spooky would eventually make his rounds and end up down the walk and when he did, they would be back on.

"Naw, I'm out of commission for a while," Phatz half lied. There were over five small sacks of weed sewn in between the socks he had on that he was planning to sell, just not to Marvin. Business was on hold until he got settled in.

"Aight cool, maybe next time," Marvin said with a hint of disappointment in his voice.

The line was moving again. The CO called out a name as they approached another dorm.

"This my stop, I'll catch you later," Marvin said as he passed him.

He watched the man disappear into the dorm before the line started again. Maybe they would run across each other again. Maybe not.

"Bradley you're in Walnut 2 follow me" the CO called out. Stepping out of the line Phatz followed closely behind the CO.

He didn't know much about Walnut 2 other than Spooky had a few partners there that had been alerted of his coming. Still he wasn't too eager to make their acquaintance. All he wanted to know was how he could keep his business going.

"Here's your stop," the guard said seconds later, before walking off. Leaving him in the middle of the dorm.

The dorm was lined with over seventy-five beds and the noise was almost ear shattering. Somewhere inside a boombox blared Doug E. Fresh's hit song *La Di Da Di*. Phatz eyes swept across the room taking it all in. Some inmates lounged lazily in their beds while others slept. A group of inmates gathered at one end watching an intense game of chess. From where he stood, he could see that the rest were either reading or lost in their own world. The CO sitting at the table at the front of the dorm, who was supposed to be watching the area, was fast asleep. Every now and then he would jerk awake only to return to his slumber. There was a lot going on but one thing that was unmistakable was the tension. Tension was the prison's natural climate no matter what.

Place men from different walks of life who felt like they had nothing to lose in a cage together and watch the bodies begin to pile up. Any little thing could make a person snap, which was why Phatz stayed on alert and from the looks of his new living arrangements he would have to be a fool to ignore the dangers that were jumping out at him and he wasn't a fool by a longshot.

Phatz understood the difference between being in a cell and in an open room. In a cell he could easily watch his back because it was just him and one other person, even in the camps he felt more secure because the number of people inside the dorms were always low. But how was he supposed to feel safe in a room with seventy-five niggas and no barriers to separate them?

He couldn't.

In fact if he was being honest there was no such thing as 'safe' in Angola. Every waking day was a fight for survival and Phatz would do anything to make sure his family never had to receive a call from the prison about him being injured or worse dead. Unlike the CO up front Phatz didn't think he would be getting much sleep while in the dorm.

As he scanned the room looking for the bed he had been assigned, he could feel the stares on his back. Ignoring them, he spied his number as he began to move towards the empty bed without a sheet on it near the wall. It was the perfect spot for him to watch everything and everyone.

He was halfway there when a body blocked his path.

The light skin man in front of him towered over his 5'6 frame forcing him to step back to look in his face. Sizing him up Phatz pegged him to be about 6'5 and at least fifty pounds heavier than him. Tattoos covered his bulging biceps.

He noticed the gold teeth in his mouth as he spoke. It was a signature look for Louisiana inmates.

"You Phatz?" he asked. Phatz noted how funny his name sounded coming out of the man's mouth. But he didn't let that distract him. He could be one of Black Jack's or Bates people sent after him. Once Spooky learned of his beef with Black Jack he informed him that he too was Down the Walk. The man in his way now could be in cahoots with either of his enemies.

Dropping everything in his hand Phatz widened his stance. He was ready to get to it.

But the man's laughter caught him off guard.

"Naw my nigga I'm Big D, didn't Spooky tell you bout me."

Phatz let out a deep breath at the news.

"What up playboy," he said stretching his fist out in a peaceful gesture.

Bumping his fist lightly against Phatz, Big D shook his head "My round Spooky ain't neva lied about you, man you was ready to go to war with me ya heard me."

"Gotta stay prepared at all times," Phatz replied reaching down to gather his things.

"I feel you on that my nigga you got a bed yet?"

Phatz angled his head towards the empty bed near the wall. On the opposite side a man lie curled up in the thin sheets.

"That's the best spot right there ya heard me," Big D commented falling in step beside him.

Placing his bag on the bed he turned towards Big D who was stroking his goatee thoughtfully.

"Check this out, let's go to the hobby shop. I got you a dirk."

Being around Spooky had hipped Phatz to the native's language so he knew that a dirk meant knife. It was exactly what he needed to make himself a little more comfortable in the unfamiliar place.

"You rollin'?"

Hesitantly, Phatz eyed the man in the bed next to his. Wondering if he should take his things with him. As if reading his mind Big D spoke up, "You good my nigga ain't nobody gone fuck wit yo shit ya heard me, unless motherfuckas want problems ya heard me!"

He said the last part loud enough to draw a few stares from the men in the room. They had heard him loud and clear.

Feeling confident Phatz followed Big D down the walk to the hobby shop stopping every couple of steps to be introduced to the rest of his New Orleans crew along the way.

The Hobby shop was an actual wood workshop where the inmates made all kinds of things from small tables to headboards for beds. It was also the perfect place to make a weapon.

The room was empty when they walked in, but the smell of fresh sawdust made the hairs in Phatz nose tingle. A few seconds later he sneezed into his hands

"You aight my nigga?" Big D asked, glancing over his shoulder.

"Yeah but I can't stay in here too long this shit fucking with my asthma and allergies." The words had barely left his mouth before he launched into a fit of sneezing.

Big D moved around the heavy machine they used to sculpt the wood "Shit if you got asthma I can get you a nice ass job with me doing simple shit ya heard me?"

Phatz nodded before snagging a piece of paper to wipe his hands on. He sniffed trying to clear his nose watching as Big D maneuvered around the room. Taking a step back he surveyed the shop.

A table surrounded by wooden chairs that needed to be polished and sanded down took up an entire wall. Stylish leather belts and hats hung loosely on a coat rack for shipment to local and high-end retail stores. That was the thing about prison: the inmates provided high quality work for cheap labor. It was legal slavery. It had taken Phatz a while to wrap his head around that conclusion. Prison was a business that benefited off the mistakes and wrongdoings of others. But he'd be damned if the system would squeeze anything more than the three cents a day they made out of him.

Which was why he couldn't wait to get his business back in order.

First thing first though he needed protection.

Big D had disappeared behind a door leaving him alone.

He wondered what was taking him so long as he continued to browse through the crafty items.

In front of him a wooden clock that was almost taller than him set on display. Running his hand over the smooth surface he noticed the detailed carved brass numbers on the face of it. He could hear the timer ticking with each move of the hour hand. Phatz knew without a doubt that his great grandmother would love it. A wave of nostalgia hit him for the first time when he thought about her. He could see the clock so vividly in the dining room of her home. It had been a while since he had spoken to Mother Dear. His sister Denise kept him informed about what was going on in the outside world. It was how he learned that the rumor on the street was that they had gotten 99 years plus a dark day. He never bothered to correct it because he couldn't wait to see the look on everyone's faces when they touched down. It would be priceless.

His hands grazed the clock again.

Cuckoo Cuckoo. A small stuffed bird lurched forward.

Jumping back, he fell against the table behind him escaping the birds long thin beak by mere inches. A second later and he might not have had an eye.

Big D rushed out the room with his fist balled up, "My nigga what's going on?"

Pushing off the table Phatz walked around the clock, careful not to get too close.

"Fucking cuckoo clock almost poked my damn eye out!" He spat as his hand immediately went to his eye.

Big D waved him off "Ay dawg you gotta be careful in here niggas lose limbs and shit fucking with all this heavy artillery ya heard me."

Phatz glanced at the machine in front of him.

"Anyways I think I found something you might like back here follow me."

Behind the door was another room with even more belts and hats. Weaving through the clutter he made his way to where Big D stood with his back facing him.

Phatz stopped short when he glimpsed the knife at Big D's side.

Doubts began to plague his mind. Was this a set up to lure him back and kill him?

Seconds ticked by as he watched Big D oblivious to his presence.

Spooky had told him that he could be trusted but could he really? Phatz didn't know if the man in front of him was who he claimed to be. Hell, he was having a hard enough time separating the New Orleans niggas from the Shreveport ones. He didn't know who the real enemy was.

He wished he had thought of all this before he eagerly followed him. Could it be that Big D- if that was his real name- had caught him slipping? He could have just blindly walked into his own death.

Facing him Big D stretched out the knife "Come see."

Approaching slowly Phatz pretended to be interested in the knife. Though mentally he was trying to decide what his next move would be if shit went left.

"That's cool right there," he commented examining the long blade. Suddenly, a noise sounded behind him. As soon as Big D turned his head to check it out Phatz made his move. Grabbing the knife in Big D's hand he pointed the sharp end towards the floor.

Startled by the move Big D's brow furrowed as he looked down at his hand.

"What you doing my nigga?"

In response Phatz tightened his grip. Seconds later understanding dawned on Big D's face.

"Naw it aint even like that."

And to prove his point he released his grip on the knife, dropping it into Phatz hand.

"That's yours."

For a second there Phatz thought things were about to get bloody. Gripping the knife in his hand he tested the weight of the sharp blade that was duct taped and welded between two cylinder blocks of wood.

He glanced up at the sound of Big D's voice, "This mine, right here ya heard me, state of the art custom made shit." Big D held a knife almost the length of Phatz arm in his hand.

Shit, he thought to himself.

Next to Big D's knife his weapon looked like a stick.

"Spooky said you got some clown you gotta punish for running his mouth."

Big D had turned his back again. Phatz knew that the man was testing him this time. He had purposefully let his guards down to see if he could trust him.

He stood his ground. Besides, he would never stab a man in his back. That was for cowards. He preferred to look his victims in the eyes.

"Yeah that's right," Phatz answered tucking his knife inside the waist of his pants.

A look of respect passed over Big D's face as he silently acknowledged the move.

"Aight let's get out of here," he said, turning in the direction in which they came from.

Stopping a few feet outside the dorm Big D turned to him.

"The nigga you talking bout from Shreveport and you know we don't fuck with them niggas."

Clocking a group of inmates behind him Phatz waited until they were alone again.

"I don't give a damn where he from all I know is every time I see the nigga ima bring it to him."

A light chuckle shook Big D's shoulders "Phatz I like you I can tell you bout that action. I'ma show you where to hide that dirk and we'll go visit your friend from Shreveport tomorrow ya heard me."

Phatz nodded. In his mind he decided to take Spooky's word about Big D. Only time would tell if he had made the right decision.

****

"You the one they call Solo?"

The question sounded more like a statement. Spinning around on his heel AC stared into a pair of cold flat eyes. The same pair that had followed his every move from the second he set foot on the rec yard that day. Instead of letting on to knowing he was being watched, AC pretended to be interested in the basketball game happening on the court between the prisoners. When a light scuffle on the court broke out, he used the distraction to slowly canvass the yard, as the other prisoners rushed to break up the fight.

His eyes flickered over the field of cotton, that would be replaced with stalks of corn as tall as him in the summertime, before scaling up the tower where the guard appeared entertained by the fight. AC would've missed the man's leering stare if he hadn't taken the time to admire the CO who was collecting bets on the game, instead of breaking up the fight. With his face twisted up in a sneer, everything about the man everyone called Busta screamed snake. From his scaly cracked skin that dried out no matter how much Vaseline he used, to the way he slithered to the back of the crowd once realizing AC had noticed him.

He wasn't surprised by the hateful look he'd seen on Busta's face. He seemed to be getting a lot of those lately and it was due to one reason: cash. No longer in the hole, Camp C Tiger had been his home for three weeks now and in that short time he had discovered that the inmates in the unit ran an underground gambling ring. It was just his luck that he'd stumbled up on a game of poker being held in the back of the chow hall.

Known as only Solo to them, AC became a regular at the poker spot. He was hustling so much money from the games that the CO's started to shake down his cell. Already he'd been hit twice that week. Still they found nothing. Unbeknownst to them his stash was hidden safely in between the bricks of the wall-compliments of his time spent in the hole but being searched more than usual alerted him to one thing. Someone was snitching. And it was probably some hating ass nigga whose money he'd pocketed during a game.

Someone like this nigga.

He let his gaze settle on Busta who was openly staring now. "Who wanna know?" AC asked letting his shoulders rest against the pole he was leaning against.

Pulling hard on the long menthol cigarette, Busta squinted his eyes through the film of smoke "Shit I wanna know."

Giving the cigarette one last pull, he flicked it on the ground before stubbing it out with the toe of his run down sneaker.

"You probably don't know me, I'm Busta," he said inching closer.

Oh but he did in fact know of him. Ole loudmouth Busta - as everyone called him- talked a good game, but talking was where his talents ended because he couldn't play wortha shit and he knew it. Still it didn't stop him from frequenting the gambling ring all riled up ready to lose. AC had beat the man in a game of craps once or twice, but it wasn't his loudmouth that had caught his attention. He had peeped the man way before he ever got the balls to approach him that day. See Busta didn't just wander down to the chow hall to gamble, he came looking for prey. Known as the worst kind of predator, Busta would choose his victims based on whether he could intimidate them during a game. If a man showed even a drop of weakness, he was all over him. It was like he could smell the fear in their blood and the scent only attracted him more. He would stalk them aggressively then do shit like rob them to make men even more fearful. Never knowing when he would strike fucked up his victim's head, but all that was leading up to the grand finale. When he was done playing mind games Busta would violently rape the man repeatedly until he found another weak victim to prey on. The sick bastard was so feared that even the CO's avoided him and turned their heads when he violated men. Sentenced to life for murder Busta had nothing more to lose after trading his manhood, so he took theirs.

As AC gave him the once over, he had to silently question if Busta had a death wish. It was the only thing that would explain why he was standing in front of him.

"Man you hit those cats so hard in the game the other day they didn't know what hit em," Busta tossed his head back and let out a sound that resembled laughter.

"Pure luck," he responded coolly.

"Shit it looks like to me you one lucky mothafucka," Busta stated, licking at his dry lips. The small movement drew attention to the caked-up spit at the corner of his mouth. AC let out a slow breath at the repulsive sight.

Above them a round of thunder shook the sky followed by a flash of lightning.

"Damn and I had good money on this game," Busta complained, shifting lightly on his feet.

AC remained quiet as he feigned interest in what was happening on the court, all the while aware of Busta's nearness. They were so close now he could almost feel the nervous energy bouncing off him.

Two things struck him at once. The first being that Busta had marked him to be robbed. The man had mistaken his clean half breed look for pussy. The second thing was that Cell Block A was about to become a permanent stay during his sentence.

"That's what the fuck I'm talking about, them young cats out there balling!" Busta yelled while clapping his hands loudly as the ball swished through the net.

Casting a sly smile in AC's direction he reached in his pocket and pulled out another cigarette.

"You bout the same age as them right?" Striking a match, he lit the end of his cigarette.

AC stared at it until it glowed a fiery orange. While the man pretended to care about the game AC had wrestled with the question of whether he should kill him or not for what he knew the man was about to try. First Busta would try to rob him and if he succeeded… AC squeezed his eyes tight against the thought as a wave of rage hit him. When he finally opened them, he let his gaze settle on Busta again. At that exact moment he decided not to kill the man. If he did then he would never leave Angola or make it back home to his family. Instead he would teach him a lesson. One that he would likely never forget.

"I'm nineteen," he answered confidently, setting his bait.

Like the storm that was brewing in the afternoon sky AC felt the moment the atmosphere shifted. The friendly expression Busta had sported only seconds ago transformed into a hard one. He like many others, thought his young age made him an easy target but if they only knew.

Grounding his teeth together he waited patiently for Busta to play his next hand.

He didn't have to wait long. In a move so smooth that he didn't think AC noticed, Busta pulled out a small pocketknife, hiding it in the palm of his hand. He flicked the cigarette away.

"I want my money back," he said in a steely voice. Opening the palm of his hand he brandished the knife.

Show time AC thought springing into action. Moving away from the pole he positioned his back to the tower, not worrying about the guards interrupting because they never broke up fights.

"Since you showing weapons you gotta use it today or somebody getting stabbed," AC stated.

Just like Busta never knew when to fold during the games he didn't realize that he was in over his head.

"Pretty boy this ain't a game," he said through clenched teeth. "I want my money and something ext--

Busta never saw the two piece and uppercut coming at him, leaving him no room to react. The blows were so powerful he tumbled to the ground hard. Before he could even blink AC began stumping him all over his body. He felt like something inside of him had snapped as a low growl left his mouth. Wrestling the knife from Bustas hand AC sliced it across his scaly skin slicing it open until the bone underneath was exposed.

"Aaaahhhh!" Busta yelled as his uninjured hand flew to the wound to stop the blood from gushing out.

Landing a solid lick to his rib cage the cracking sound echoed loudly through the air. AC was putting in work when he heard feet approaching. Gripping the knife in his hand he spun around coming face to face with Busta's weak ass crew.

"Come on Cali, he on the ground at least let him get up and defend himself," one stated motioning towards a writhing Busta on the ground.

Glancing back at the pitiful sight AC shrugged a shoulder.

"Cool, get up!" he yelled.

After a few seconds Busta climbed unsteadily to his feet, a look of hatred etched to his face.

Yeah, he fucked with the wrong one AC thought. A small crowd had gathered around them abandoning the game on the court.

"Get your head clear we not done nigga!"

At his words, AC watched the fear leap into Busta's eyes. The look of hatred slowly turned to one of pleading. But with his reputation already hanging by threads Busta tried to put up a front by taking a step forward.

Wrong move.

Throwing an overhand punch, AC dropped him to the ground again.

"He had enough Solo."

Cutting his eyes sharply towards the man that was speaking, AC sized him up. He was probably one of the niggas whose manhood Busta had taken. A feeling of disgust washed over him.

"No, you should've been here before he stepped on his tongue with that sick homo shit he had on his mind."

He paused at the sound of Busta groaning.

"Now look at him all hungover and sick with his ass whooped."

He stared at Busta a little while longer. When his crew rushed over to help him up this time AC didn't object. Still clinching the pocketknife in one hand he flexed his other bruised hand.

Around the yard it looked as if things had calmed down as the ball game picked back up and the crowd began to disperse.

Lifting his head, AC caught Busta moving towards him again. He knew Busta was coming to offer peace, but he'd crossed that line a long time ago.

Stopping a few inches in front of him Busta stuck his hand out.

AC glanced down and smirked before delivering one to his chin sending him careening backwards. The wild look on his face let AC know he hadn't expected it.

Ignoring the pleas this time he went all in. Blow after blow. He was so set on tearing Busta apart he hadn't noticed that it had begun to rain. Chest heaving up and down AC stood up as the cold water began to soak through his clothes.

Grabbing a hand full of wet grass, Busta tried to stand.

"Naw punk bitch you stay down," AC said before delivering a swift kick to his head that knocked him unconscious.

Swaying on his feet he took note of all the wide mouth expressions, even the guards seemed to be shocked. All but the one in the tower who stood with a proud look.

Stepping over Bustas' limp body he moved through the thin crowd that had gathered again. He could feel the icy glares on his back as he sloshed through the wet field soaked down to his clothes.

His hand slid over the thin blade he had taken from Busta.

Try me he silently dared locking eyes with a few. When no one budged he continued without a backwards glance.

****

Angola was like a state, the camps were the cities and Down the Walk was the capital, the center of it all. A brand-new world, Down the Walk had proven to be a paradise for hustlers and Phatz couldn't believe it had taken him so long to reach it. He'd spent too much time in the outer camps fighting for scraps when he could have been eating steak and shrimp and making so much money that even the high-ranking correctional officers envied him. While prison was supposed to rehabilitate criminals Phatz knew that he was beyond saving. He did what he had to in order to survive, even if it meant getting his hands dirty and before he exited Angola, he would give the system some game they'd never seen before. It was the conclusion that he came to as he strolled across the yard careful to avoid puddles in the grass left by yesterday's storm. The stiffening heat in the storm's aftermath caused beads of sweat to roll down his face before he could make it to his destination.

"You think the rain slowed down the package?" Big D asked when Phatz reached him.

Big D and a few other guys were posted up near the weight pile. Using rags, they eagerly wiped off the water residue left behind on the work out equipment.

"No, it's still on track to arrive tomorrow," Phatz answered.

Taking a seat on the dry bench he watched a customer saunter up to Big D. The two shook hands, exchanging drugs for money.

"My nigga the shit barely makes it to my hands before its gone again. It's crazy," Big D said shaking his head as he smoothed out the green dollar bills.

Another customer appeared. Briefly Phatz let his gaze travel around the rec yard. Almost every crew occupied a certain section of the yard with their hustle. There was the New Orleans crew in their schoolboy shades who dominated the west end, with their homebrew made from apple cores, orange peels, potatoes, sugar and yeast. They let the light orange liquor sit under the buildings for three days, by that time it was so strong that just one sip of it could knock a man flat on his ass. Then there was the Baton Rouge crew who in their Blues brothers glasses, took up over half of the east end section of the yard selling weed . The Baton Rouge crew dabbled in a little of everything from drugs to weapons. Then it was them. Phatz and Big D were the game changers on the yard because there was a new product in demand. Cocaine. When cocaine hit Angola, it changed the game. While the BR crew sold weed, they were barely hanging on by a thread. Niggas wanted something stronger. Something that would numb the pain of having to wake up every day to four concrete walls. Phatz was the man for the job. He had the biggest supply of cocaine being smuggled inside Angola twice a month and all the addicts knew it. Phatz even recruited workers from other dorms and those worked in the plasma banks to help him get his product to the outer camps. There wasn't an inch of the prison that he wasn't touching.

Wiping the sweat off his forehead with a towel he turned to Big D who was serving yet another client. The man had become valuable to him in his operation. Big D moved dope like he was born to do it. Phatz never had to wonder if he was skimming money off the top or keeping a few bags for himself, like Bates. Big D was loyal and true to his word. He'd even recruited a few foot soldiers in other dorms to work for them. While he wasn't AC, Big D had proven his loyalty in more ways than one. At the thought of his friend AC, he made a mental note to send him a letter through farm mail and update him on the business. Once AC made it down the walk, he knew they would be unstoppable, it would be like being back on the streets of L.A.

He eyed the junkie who was up next.

Shifting his feet, the thin man rubbed his hand up his arm. Phatz stomach turned at the sight of open sores and pus caused by the needle they used to shoot the powder cocaine in their veins.

For a split second his bleary eyes met Phatz skeptical ones before he cast them down. There was something familiar about him.

His pants being two sizes too small should've been Phatz first clue, his clean-shaven face the next. It wasn't until Phatz saw the red bandanna tied on his head that the pieces began to click together.

Back in Boss Angeles red flags were the symbol of the notorious blood gang, but in Angola it represented one of the largest populations in the prison: the homosexuals. Behind the walls they were called hoes. And the hoes were everywhere on the yard with their tight pants. Some even wore make up and long nails.

Not new to gay men because L.A. was full of them still the culture of it in Angola left him shocked. The hoe game was a way of life in Angola. The more hoes a prisoner had the more powerful he was viewed. Phatz realized that in Angola there were two types of prisoners, men, and hoes. There were those who chose the hoe game willingly and then there were those who didn't. A real man would kill about his manhood and the one who wouldn't become a hoe. Knowing this he never let a nigga slide on nothing because the worst thing you could be seen as in prison is weak. Anyone who tried to test him would get left lying in a pool of his own blood and that fact was well known by now.

Big D was almost finishing up the exchange when the customers identity finally came to him. About thirty pounds thinner with no beard the junkie hoe looked almost unrecognizable. Phatz almost wished he was wrong, but he knew he wasn't.

"Marvin?" The name escaped from behind his lips before he had a chance to think about it.

Marvin's shoulders hung forward with his head for a few seconds before he picked it up.

"What up Phatz, I see you got back on your feet," he answered. There was almost a vacant look in his eyes.

Marvin's gaze darted to Big D then back to Phatz. He could feel the shame emanating off the man. He thought back to those few seconds where they had exchanged words outside of the dorm. A lot had changed since then. Marvin was pussy now!

Marvin's voice cracked as he fixed his mouth to say something else but gave up when the words wouldn't come out. With a defeated and broken look on his face he walked off and into the arms of his lover.

Phatz stared after Marvin. Something told him that Marvin didn't choose the hoe life. But he quickly corrected the thought in his mind. Everyone had a choice. Even if it meant dying behind it.

Phatz had wandered off into his own world when Big D's voice brought him back to reality.

"That cat been staring over here for a minute now?"

Assuming that Big D was talking about Marvin, Phatz eyes darted to the hoes.

"Who?"

Big D pointed his finger towards a man across the yard.

Following the direction, pass the group of hoes, sure enough an old man with gray hair sat on the bleachers. Like the rest of the Shreveport crew on the yard that day he wore shades. Though Phatz couldn't see his eyes, but with his head looking straight in their direction, he could feel his stare.

"So who is he?"

"Hold on," Big D waited for the signal that the coast was clear before he went to retrieve the coke wrapped in small plastic from the weight pile.

Checking his watch Phatz noticed that they only had a few more minutes remaining on the yard. Big D's stash was low and he needed to make a call home. The rain hadn't slowed down the package, but the way the junkies were running through it he would need more soon.

"Sin, he's the leader of them Shreveport niggas if anybody know where Black Jack is its him," Big D answered when he returned.

With everything that was going on Phatz had managed to let thoughts of Black Jack slip into the corners of his mind. But they were always there, reminding him to be cautious. Phatz had been down the walk almost two months now and still there was no sighting of the coward. It didn't take a rocket scientist to figure out that Black Jack was hiding. He had done everything in his power to bring him out of hiding yet nothing had worked. Phatz didn't want to spend his time having to look over his shoulder wondering when the man would strike. He wanted it over and done with so that he could concentrate on his money.

"You got that dirk on you?" Big D asked.

Phatz hand touched the long knife that was tucked in his waist. He never went anywhere without it.

"All the time."

Reaching into his pocket Big D discreetly handed him the small bags.

"I'm going over here to see what's on his mind."

A frown covered his face. He didn't like the idea of Big D going over alone anything could pop off.

"You got it?"

"That and some mo shit."

Big D touched his waist. Instantly Phatz relaxed. Big D had the biggest knife of them all and was known for stabbing niggas up. In a few steps Big D's long legged strides had covered the short distance to the other side. The Shreveport crew all stood from the bleachers like they were protecting their leader. After a signal from Sin they reclaimed their seats.

With his eyes trained across the yard Phatz tried to interpret what was going on but it was no use with Big D's back facing him.

He swore under his breath. Clients were beginning to stream through again and for the next few minutes he busied himself serving them.

Phatz was smoothing the money out like he'd seen Big D do, when he spotted Big D coming back across the yard and he wasn't alone.

Sin trailed behind him.

Handing off the next transaction to a foot soldier, Phatz stood as they approached.

"Sin you already know who this is," Big D announced.

Sin nodded once. Phatz raised his eyebrow at the greeting.

"I told Sin you been looking for Black Jack and he wanted to meet you," Big D responded.

Directing his attention back to Sin, Phatz could still feel the man's piercing stare from behind the shades. Sin was old. His receding hair line and graying hair was evidence enough, but it was his brown skin that was beginning to wrinkle and show signs of aging that made Phatz guess that he was in his late sixties. Old enough to know how things went in prison. Black Jack was going to have to come out of hiding or he would go find him. With a few minutes remaining before they blew the yard Phatz cut to the chase.

"Where he at?"

Taking a peep over Sin's shoulder he noticed the entire Shreveport crew was focused on them…well rather him. Most of the movement on the yard had slowed down as everyone homed in on the two crews. Even the CO's were watching but they wouldn't budge from their posts if anything happened. As long as no one was trying to escape it was fine with them. They just let the niggas kill each other off to make their jobs easier.

Sin shrugged a thin shoulder. "Like I told your friend over here," he said pointing to Big D "Black Jack is his own man, and I'm not responsible for looking after no grown man."

Immediately Phatz didn't like the tone of Sin's voice. Still trying to give him the benefit of the doubt before he knocked him on his ass he asked another question.

"You think you'll see him anytime soon?"

"Why?" Sin shot back.

"Look Sin cut the bullshit we know he down here we just need to talk to him," the words were spoken from Big D whose patience was a lot thinner than Phatz. Sensing his friend was about to snap Phatz knew it wouldn't end well for no one mainly Sin and his Shreveport crew. Over twenty of Big D's New Orleans soldiers took up camp near the weights watching and waiting for his signal. Twice as many would be alerted in the other dorms. Any other time Phatz would have been all down for blood shedding, however he wanted Black Jack and since he was nowhere to be found starting a war now would only result in more casualties, while the real target escaped.

Sin seemed to understand this too because he finally gave an answer to Phatz. "Black Jack don't want no funk," he said.

"Even if he don't we both here now so we need to get a clear understanding or get to it cause I got it on my mind and I'm not bout to be watching my back when I know it's on my mind so let's get to it."

"Ya heard me!" Big D echoed beside him.

After a few long beats of silence passed Sin threw his hands up in surrender, "Listen he's the barber on the trustee side and he don't want no trouble but I'll bring him on this side."

"Good you do that cause if I have to go find him, we not doing any talking," Phatz stated staring the man right in the eyes through his shades.

"How old are you?" Sin asked running his hand down his graying beard.

Phatz rolled his eyes towards the sky.

"Old enough for the reason and young enough for the situation why?"

Sin smirked before removing his glasses. The move done to unnerve Phatz made him stand taller. The hazel eyes that stared at him softened the old man's face making him appear thin and fragile but Phatz knew that looks were deceiving.

"I see you bout it youngn but no need to prove yourself to me I got kids your age." He slipped the shades back on his face.

Phatz let the "prove" remark slide. He knew Sin was trying to get under his skin.

"Ask Black Jack about me." Giving Sin a dismissive look he returned to his business.

"What you think?" Big D asked minutes after they'd watched Sin go back to his crew.

"I think Sin is full of shit." He said standing as they blew the yard.

"Black Jack gone slip up and when he do I'ma be right there waiting on his ass."

"And you know I'm down ya heard me?" Big D responded. "But I'ma catch up with you later."

The two men dapped up before Big D disappeared in the crowd. Phatz pretended not to know that his friend often messed with hoes, like Marvin. It didn't concern him and as long as it didn't interfere with his business he would continue to pretend not to know. His main concern now was getting to Black Jack, he had to eliminate the threat.

Back in the dorm thoughts of AC flashed in his mind and he wondered how his partner was fairing in the hell hole called prison.

****

AC watched with a rush of anticipation as the last dice lolled on its side before landing on the flat surface of the concrete cell floor.

The once quiet cell interrupted into groans.

He'd won again.

"I feel like we need to start calling you Lucky Solo," one disgruntled player said as the crowd began to file out of the cell.

The name was catchy, but AC preferred the one he had now and made sure to let them know.

"Just Solo," AC responded as he kneeled to pick up the money off the floor. Making sure to keep his back facing the wall so that he could see everything, he was almost finished collecting his earnings when he caught sight of a guy who owed him money from the last game.

"Hey!" AC called out as he stuffed the money in his pocket and maneuvered out of the cell.

Out on the tier the man stopped in his tracks.

"You got something for me," AC asked towering over him. The man looked like a weasel with his beady eyes and long nose.

"Nahh man my family-"

AC held up his hands ending any excuses he could come up with. The weasel looking man had intentionally been avoiding him. Now it was time to pay up.

Understanding the seriousness of the situation the man reached around his neck and unpinned the gold chain hanging from it.

"This all I have," he said stretching out his hand.

AC bit back a smile. He had been eyeing the necklace since the first game when he'd noticed it around the weasel's neck. It was worth way more than the twenty dollars the man owed him.

Gripping the shiny gold chain in his hand now AC, nodded.

"This'll work," he said as he placed the chain on his neck and watched as the weasel scurried off.

Tucking the chain in the inside of his shirt he liked the way the cool metal felt against his skin. His stomach growled as he made his way back to his cell forcing him to take a detour to the chow hall. He almost abandoned the idea to eat when he saw how long the line was, but the smell of the fried chicken lured him to stay. The line crept at a snail's pace. AC silently prayed that the chicken would still be hot when he got his tray. Inside the chow hall the loud chatter from the prisoners spilled out into the hallway. The noise was so loud he almost didn't hear the voice behind him.

"Can you step out of the line please?"

Slowly he turned in the direction of the voice. Coming face to face with a CO he squeezed his eyes shut.

What now he thought to himself as he completed the CO's request.

From the corner of his eye he saw another CO began to head in their direction.

Shit! The bells went off in his head. Two always meant trouble.

He watched the men lower their heads in hushed whispers. Leaning against the wall AC, tried to come up with a reason why he was being targeted.

Were they there about the dice game? Or had they raided his cell and found his money?

He shook his head at the last thought. That was almost impossible.

His mind scrambled for answers. The answer came to him as if a switch had been turned on his head.

Busta

Last, he'd seen him he was on the ground clinging to life. At the memory of Busta, AC remembered the knife that he'd taken from the man, now tucked discreetly between his shirt and his pants. He liked to carry it to the dice games just in case someone got out of line but since the Busta altercation most of the prisoners either gave him praise for his actions or ignored him completely. Either way it didn't matter but having the knife on him now complicated the situation.

"Shit!"

The word meant to be said only in his mind slipped out of his mouth drawing attention of the two CO's who still stood off to the side whispering.

At the sight of the CO's slipping on the white latex gloves AC knew what time it was.

He tried to stall as they came near him. He had to find a way to get the knife off of him. "What's going on?" he asked innocently as they led him further away from the chow hall.

The rightful owner of the necklace passed by casting a curious look in AC's direction to which he shrugged.

The young black CO folded his arms across his chest "We have direct orders to search you."

Direct orders. The answer put him on edge but confirmed what he already knew. Busta had to be involved in the grand scheme of things. Still AC tried to buy himself some time. He knew it was a losing battle and regretted not being able to have a taste of the fried chicken.

"How you gone search me and you don't even know my name?" he asked looking from one CO to the other.

The two men wore a look of annoyance on their faces.

AC suddenly got the idea to make a run for it. His eyes scanned over their heads. If he could make it to the end of the hall, he could get rid of the knife.

"Don't even think about it," the CO responded as if reading his thoughts.

He frowned at the man's hard stare as the other CO chuckled.

"There's nowhere to run so why don't you make this easy on yourself and cooperate, young fellow, this won't take no time. He reached a gloved hand towards him, but AC slapped it away.

"Hey!"

"Don't touch me!" AC warned as the black CO began to speak into his radio.

He tried to listen to the response, but the static interference made it hard. When one of the CO's stepped away he thought about making a run for it again. But then a voice came over the walkie talkie loud and clear.

"Search him."

AC reeled backwards. He'd heard that voice before. It belonged to the captain of Camp C Tiger. The captain never missed a chance to let AC know how much he disliked him. His reputation for attacking Lieutenant Bill hadn't gone over well for the ranking officers. They'd taken it personal and AC normally didn't give a fuck except for this time, he'd grown content with his hustle at Camp C. The money was good, but Busta had fucked that up for him when he tried to test his gangsta and AC had no regrets about punishing his ass.

"Raise your arms, this is just a quick pat down it'll be over before you know it," the CO said.

Ignoring the urge to resist he raised his arms. silently Seething at the feel of the guard's hands on him he counted to ten in his mind to keep from breaking the man's nose.

"Nothing," the guard stated as he raised up.

"We have a witness that there is a knife so Search him again, take him somewhere else, I want that weapon!" The voice over the walkie talkie demanded.

AC only had to take one guess as to who this witness was. It was just his luck that he had beaten a pervert who also turned out to be a snitch.

"You heard him we're gonna move you to the schoolhouse," the CO stated thrusting his head forward for him to move. A plan began to formulate in AC's mind as they walked him behind the canteen. The first chance he got he would get rid of the knife. Scanning the ground carefully he thought of dropping it but decided against it. The guards were too close not to notice it and it would undoubtedly make a splash in the wet grass.

"I don't know why yal fucking with me," he said still trying to distract them.

The old guard smirked as they continued their walk "Oh really," he paused, "so you don't know anything about how Busta ended up in the hospital?"

The news made AC want to smile instead he shook his head no.

"Yeah I bet," the guard said removing the keys from his pocket.

"Well somebody worked him over real good, had to get a few stitches in that cut he got. You know the captain wasn't too happy about an inmate being assaulted on his watch."

AC wanted to ask what about all the men Busta raped on his watch but decided against it. Fuck the captain, besides, he was still trying to figure out how to get rid of the knife.

As they neared the shed the two guards became distracted talking about the latest football game. They were still debating the plays when they arrived at their destination.

This is my chance AC thought as the officer opened the door.

From his position he could see that the shed room was full of boxes.

He reasoned that If he could get in there first, he could toss the knife behind one of the boxes.

"Let's get this over with," he said rushing ahead of the guard who held the door open.

"Wait!" the CO yelled. He tried to grab at the back of AC's shirt.

In a fluid movement AC flipped the light switch off and slung the knife. The sound of it landing echoed loudly in the room. He squeezed his eyes shut. He hadn't expected that.

With a fist full of AC's shirt now clenched tightly in his hand the black CO turned around with a look of amusement on his face. "Did you hear that?"

The CO standing outside scratched at his balding spot.

"Yeah I heard it he must have thrown something."

AC tried to pull away, "Man let me go I didn't throw shit."

The guard eyes narrowed into thin slits. "I know what I heard" he said stealthily.

He flipped the light back on before walking into the room.

"Lieutenant! Get in here!" he called out.

AC could feel the beads of sweat break out on his head as he began to perspire as they moved the boxes around.

He let out a small breath when they didn't find the knife.

"Wait I got an ideal," the old white guard said turning his smiling face towards AC.

He didn't like the mischievous glint in the man eyes.

"We'll be right back," he said as he reached for the handcuffs at his waist. Grabbing AC by the arm he placed the handcuffs around his wrist.

"Until then you sit tight," he said before shoving him in a chair.

The minute the door closed AC stood up in a panic. With his hands cuffed behind his back he could only use his feet to move the boxes.

"Shit!"

He couldn't find it.

The sound of footsteps made him sit back down in the chair. Seconds later He was temporarily blinded by the sun when the door opened. When his vision cleared, he couldn't believe what he saw. The CO's had fetched two inmates.

"Boys I want you to find that knife," one said.

AC stood up in disbelief. His vision drifted to the black inmate. I know he ain't gone sell a brother out he thought to himself before posing the question out loud.

"Tell me you not about to help these police ass niggas."

The inmate averted his gaze before he spoke, "We just doing what they told us."

AC's mouth dropped open. Real niggas didn't go against the grain no matter what.

Then it dawned on him. He was in a place where the grain didn't matter. It was every man for himself.

Against his better judgment he tried to have hope that the knife wouldn't be found maybe it had slid in the deepest crack. Maybe the inmate would wise up and keep his mouth closed.

The door opened. And all hope vanished as the black man walked out carrying the thin knife in his hand like it was a prize.

"You wanna tell us how that get there?" the CO asked with a knowing look.

His thoughts from earlier came back to him. Cell Block A was about to become his home indefinitely.

****

Over in Camp D Falcon Phatz was still steaming from a betrayal of his own.

"I was set up."

The clanking of the heavy iron striking the metal echoed loudly on the yard as he shelved the barbell weight back into position. Grabbing the water bottle off the ground he unscrewed the cap and took a long swallow from it. His eyes closed briefly as the cold water slid down his dry throat quenching his thirst. Using the back of his hand he swiped at his mouth before wiping the sweat from his face.

"And what's so fucked up about it" he continued as he moved towards the free weight pile, "Is that Black Jack stood in my face and looked me dead in the eyes and admitted he was wrong."

Shaking his head Phatz drained the last sip of water from the bottle as his mind tried to make sense of his current situation. Against his better judgement instead of shoving his knife deep into Black Jack's exposed skin when he and Sin had approached him on the yard two weeks ago Phatz had calmly walked the yard listening to Black Jack's half assed apology. After thirty minutes the two had come to an agreement. Black Jack would stay out of his way while Down the Walk. The two men were letting bygones be bygones for the greater good. Or so he had thought. When the captain approached Phatz his mind automatically assumed the worst: his drug operation had been blown. Imagine his surprise when he learned that he was being transferred off the Walk. Someone had put a note on Phatz claiming that his presence was a threat on their life. That was the excuse the captain had given as he ordered him to pack his belongings. It didn't take a rocket scientist to figure out who that someone was. Phatz had gone against his own instincts and took Black Jacks words. In the end it earned him a new home with the last person he expected.

"Yeah that's fucked up, but this camp not so bad."

He stared at the man in front of him like he had grown a second head on his shoulders.

Not so bad? Camp D Falcon was a hideout, mainly for low class offenders. Most of the prisoners in the seventy-dorm building were weak ass niggas who were afraid of going Down the Walk. For excitement they spent their days arguing over the television in the day room. But what really made matters worse for Phatz was that the dorm was drier than the Sahara Desert. The only drugs that made it inside were the ones he had managed to slip in, and they were long gone. No drugs meant no money and he couldn't live where there was no money… unlike some people he knew.

Seeing Ty's face the second he walked into the dorm came as a shock to him. The two hadn't seen each other since the ride from Elayne Hunt reception center. Now, Phatz realized why it had taken so long for them to be reunited. Camp D Falcon was the perfect place for Ty. His childhood friend had gone soft.

"It's more than bad, there's no money here all the money is Down the Walk," Phatz said trying to explain to Ty. He stretched his hands out at his side.

"Take a look around, it aint shit here."

Moving towards the wall Ty began to pull weeds out of the ground and stuff them in the bag at his side.

"How you been surviving?" he asked once Ty was standing still again.

"You know me, I been making ends meet," he responded avoiding eye contact.

In other words, he was begging. It was what he did when he got desperate. Ty must have noticed the look on Phatz's face because he lapsed into a longer explanation.

"My girl back in L.A. takes care of shit for me, I had a little money stashed away for hard times."

Yeah right Phatz thought to himself but he let the lame excuse pass.

"You gone help me get this shit up?" Ty asked after a few seconds.

He looked from Ty to the building they had been assigned to clean up around.

"When I'm finished," Phatz responded returning to his workout. He lost count of how long Ty stood waiting for him but by the time he completed his last arm curl Ty was nowhere in sight.

Deciding to go find him he circled around the building.

His steps faltered at the sight of Ty crouching low near the ground with a joint in his mouth. No doubt it was one of the two joints Phatz had given him when he arrived.

"Nigga is this why you so anxious to clean up?" he asked approaching.

Releasing the smoke from his mouth Ty shook his head before standing.

"Just a lil victory smoke for the bet I won last night," he said before offering the joint to Phatz who declined. As a rule, he only smoked on the weekends.

Pursing the joint between his lips Ty pulled hard until smoke came out of his nose and a loopy smile settled on his face.

"Better enjoy it while you can cause that's the last of it."

Snatching the bag off the ground Phatz began to pull at the weeds with a vengeance as his mind swirled. He had come too far in his drug operation to just give everything up. Of course, he knew Big D would keep things flowing in his absence but how long would that last? The truth was that without Phatz there was no business. And that was bad news because keeping the drug game afloat and his pockets laced was his way of taking the pressure off his family. Even though he could get whatever he needed from them with one phone call, he was a man and he prided himself on being able to take care of himself without their help. When they threw him in Angola he'd landed on his feet and that's the position he planned on staying in.

"Maybe we could get our own shit going down here."

Glancing up from his task Phatz realized they were almost near the end of the building, closer to the CO's checkpoint.

His voice went up a notch when he spoke.

"There are only four dorms back here and seventy inmates, that's too wide open for the shit I got planned. I'm not risking it. I gotta get back Down the Walk."

He lowered his voice with his next words "If you would stop arguing with those fools over the tv and bust one of them upside the head so that you get sent down the walk you'll have plenty of that," he said motioning to the pocket where Ty had just placed the joint in.

Again, Ty shrugged.

Fuck it Phatz said to himself as he returned to pulling up the weeds. After work call, he strolled across the brittle grass headed for the dorm eager to rinse the sweat and dirt from his body.

"Everything ok down there boy?"

The question caught Phatz off guard as his head jerked up to meet the intense stare of the captain who had positioned his body between him and the door.

Remaining quiet, Phatz stared at the captain's hawkish nose and small lips as he spoke.

"Seem like things were getting a little heated between you two," he nodded his head towards the edge of the building where Ty was now at.

Phatz wanted to tell the man to mind his fucking business instead he took a page from Ty's book and shrugged his shoulder. The move seemed to further irritate the captain.

"I've read through your file and I know all about you," he said stalking closer the grass crunching underneath his snakeskin boots.

"Good."

Crossing his arms in front of him Phatz waited for him to reveal more.

"That's right and I'm watching you because we won't tolerate any of that at Camp D Falcon, we have a nice system going on and it won't be disrupted by you."

It always amused Phatz when the captain's tried to keep up with him. As if they could. Many had tried to hold him back with their rules only to fail in the process. The one thing that none of them seemed to understand was that he was his own man who lived by his own rules.

"Well captain I don't know what you want me to say," he said goading the man.

"Don't say shit just stay in your place!" the captain spat.

"My place?" Phatz repeated the words as if he'd heard him wrong.

"That's right you're the prisoner and I'm the man in charge, the one who run things around here you do what I say, when I say and as long as you understand that we won't have any problems."

Oh, but they would.

Phatz had spent the last two weeks trying to figure out how to get out of Camp D when the answer had been staring him in the face the entire time. He would get out the same way he got out of everything: Violence.

He started off with a smile when he spoke to the captain. "Captain I think you talking to the wrong person so Ima give you a few seconds to get the fuck out of my face before you find yourself buried underneath the ground you standing on."

The captain reared back like he had been slapped. His face turned a bright shade of red. "Who do you think you're talking to boy!" he screamed still trying to hold on to his false sense of bravery.

The smile slid from Phatz face.

"I'm talking to yo ass."

He watched the captain eyes bulge in disbelief.

"Yeah that's right, I said it, I'm not one of these weak inmates you push around."

At that exact moment Phatz wished for a camera to capture the expressions on the captain's face. He looked as if he had swallowed a mouth full of bones.

Not giving him time to respond Phatz pounded his finger against his chest "So what you wanna do Mr. Man in charge?" he taunted causing the exact reaction he was hoping for.

The captain walked off so fast Phatz barely had time to blink. One minute he was standing in front of him and the next he was scurrying across the yard calling out to the other guards.

At a safe distance, he pointed towards Phatz and yelled,

"I want him out of my camp right this instant. He's assaulted three officers in the past already get him out!"

On command the CO's all headed in Phatz direction.

He wanted to jump for joy instead he held his hands up in surrender.

The shocked look on Ty's face as he approached was hard to miss.

"Nigga close yo mouth you know the get down, I told you this shit wasn't for me, I belong in the wild."

As the CO roughly placed his hand behind his back he glanced over his shoulder at Ty,

"When you ready you know where I'll be."

****

Chop.

Chop.

The sharp blade sliced through the long stalks of grass falling in a heap at his feet.

Raising the blade above his head he repeated the motion until his arms began to burn.

"Alright, speed it up, we gotta get this side done before the rain comes in," the field officer instructed from his horse.

AC peered up at the cloudy sky wishing that it would open and cool him off.

Just as he'd predicted he had landed back where it all started: working cell block Camp A.

His eyes scanned the field until he located the water bucket. It was a long distance from where he stood. By the time he made it there and back he would be twice as hot and still thirsty.

Ditching the idea in his mind he adjusted his tight grip on the blade, wincing at the irritation it caused his bruised skin. Raw to the touch callouses had begun to form in the palms of his hand. Ignoring the pain, he focused on getting through the workday. If the rain held up, they would move to clearing the corn from the field on the other side. Secretly he hoped the rumors of the warden having the sugar cane plucked up and replaced with soybeans and okra was just that. Rumors. The crop made for good homemade knives when shaved down correctly. But the warden had gotten word of it, not only that, but there were a few inmates laid up in the infirmary as the result of being stabbed with sugar cane. So, he seemed even more determined to get rid of it. As his shirt became drenched with sweat from clearing the rows, AC hoped that he would get to add a sugar cane knife to his own collection before they were destroyed. Shielding his face from the sun that had begun to reemerge from behind the clouds he reached up to touch his hair. He'd entered Angola with a low fade, now his cornrowed hair reached his shoulders. The braids were so soaked he could wring the sweat from them. Because He couldn't imagine sitting between another man's legs -like he had witnessed some cats do when they needed to be styled up- he had taught himself how to braid hair. Still he sighed at the task of having to redo them.

A splash of water landed on his forehead sending a short warning right before the sky opened with a downpour of rain followed by a round of ear roaring thunder.

Relieved he scrambled to the other side of the field to place the blade on the back of the supply truck. The workday was ending three hours earlier than the normal eight they were forced to work.

His arms felt like rubber at his side as he marched back into the camp alongside the other inmates.

He looked more beaten down than he felt, but still he couldn't wait to lay his aching body down.

A line of inmates stood in the boot wash area.

Glancing down he noticed the chunks of mud that clung to his own boots. They needed to be washed.

Later he thought continuing through the building, dreading walking up the steps that would lead to his cell. The closer he got the more his muscles protested.

One step at a time he coached himself.

AC was working up the strength to climb the twenty-eight steps when a voice made him halt

"Aye boy you need to go wash your boots."

Boy.

There was that dreaded word he hated to be called again. His hands clenched at his side as he tried to reign in his temper.

"Boy didn't you hear me I said you need to wash off them boots you're tracking mud all over the got damn floor!"

The little control AC was trying to hold on to slipped.

Spinning on his victim he noted the pinched expression on the black CO's face.

"I'm not a boy so watch who you talk to."

"Come again inmate what you say because I thought you said something?" The man tilted his head as he drew closer.

When AC remained silent, he began clapping.

"That's what I thought now boy—he accentuated the word --- go wash them damn boots!" he repeated louder this time.

In two strides AC was in front of him with his hand around his neck. He watched the look of surprise jump into his eyes as he squeezed tight. Struggling against his grip the CO clawed at his hand to get loose with no success.

"Stupid motherfucka I told you I'm not a boy."

Slamming him against the wall AC wanted to choke the life out of him. It was a damn shame how they treated the prisoners. Like they were wild animals in a cage, granted some of them where but the ones like AC just wanted to do their time, yet someone was always testing him.

When the CO's eyes began to roll in the back of his head AC snapped back to the present. Releasing him he watched the man struggle to gulp down air as he slid down to the floor.

"Don't call me boy again."

"Alright, alright you got it," he choked out.

He tried to climb to his feet only to slump back down. Using the wall as aide he pushed himself to a standing position. One look at the storm of emotions on AC's face and he began apologizing.

"L-listen man I get it I'm sorry I won't say it again." Stretching his palms out in front of him in a peaceful gesture he looked over his shoulder. "This never happened ok nobody saw it."

For the first time AC glanced around. There wasn't a soul in sight, not even the regular CO who manned the tier.

Eyeing the man wearily he began to move towards the steps just as everyone began to file into the building.

The CO's tough mask was back in place as he straightened his uniform shirt. Averting his eyes, he rubbed his neck before taking a seat behind the desk.

There was no question that AC had choked the word boy out of the guards' vocabulary. Taking the steps two at a time he returned to his cell where he tried to put the entire incident behind him.

The next day the rain didn't save them. For eight hours straight they sliced and chopped the grass clearing almost an acre of land as the temperature reached record breaking numbers.

When the workday finally ended he felt just as worse as he had the day before but once inside he made sure to wash off his boots this time despite the fact that another guard was on duty.

In his cell he began to take his hair down, a task that he had put off until that moment. Reaching for the comb, the corner of his mattress caught his eye, the sheet was pulled back a fraction. Forever the neat freak there wasn't a thing in his cell that was out of place he made sure of that every morning before he went out into the fields. Maybe he'd missed the corner when fixing the bed this morning he told himself. Too exhausted to go back and forth in his mind, he fixed the sheet and focused back on his hair. When he was finished, he tried to rest his body but the sunburn underneath his clothes made it uncomfortable. Even his hands were hurting from the blisters.

His eye lids had just shuttered closed when the opening of his cell door made them snap open.

Three CO's stormed inside.

"What's going on?" he asked even though he knew it was another shakedown because they didn't have shit better to do.

"Get over here and let us do our job," the CO called out, securing cheap latex gloves on his hand.

Upset about the interruption of his sleep AC rose from his bed, once out on the tier he watched them tear his cell apart. His carefully organized items now lie strewn on the floor. It would take him hours just to fix it back the way he liked. Seeing his possessions tossed around like they were meaningless made him angry, but he got a small sense of satisfaction knowing that they wouldn't find anything. They never did. All the guards did was give him new ideas on where to hide his contraband.

"Got something here," the CO kneeling beside his bed announced.

*What the fuck!! t*he voice in AC's mind screamed. Moving to the opening of the cell his eyes widened when the CO produced a knife from underneath the mattress.

"What the fuck?" he said this time out loud. "That shit not mine." He had never seen the sad excuse for a knife the CO was holding in his life. AC made sure all his weapons were strong and lethal enough to defend himself against any enemy. Thin wrapped in one layer of duct tape the knife in question would break the second it came in contact with anyone.

At the feel of a hand on his arm he stared down into the face of the CO.

"Turn around and face the wall inmate," he commanded.

"I'm not doing shit."

Snatching his arm away AC tried to walk into the cell but was pulled back as the guard continued to search around the bed.

"This is some bullshit. Why would I hide a weapon in plain sight?" he ranted.

"I'm not stupid."

The CO glared at him. His face twisted like he had smelled a foul odor.

"Could've fooled me."

As they stared each other down he realized one thing In their eyes he would always be guilty. Turning his back to them AC hung his head as his hands gripped the rail. Biting the inside of his cheek he forced himself to calm down as his mind worked overtime to put together the pieces. A vision of the flipped corner of the mattress popped in his head. Shit! He wasn't going crazy. He'd fixed his bed perfectly before leaving that morning for the fields. Someone had slipped the knife under his mattress when he was out but who?

Suddenly he had the feeling that he was being watched. Lifting his head his gaze clashed with the CO from yesterday who he choked. The man stood on the first floor wearing a sinister smirk.

Motherfucka!

AC opened his mouth to say something but felt movement behind him. Risking a glance, he watched the CO approach him with the knife found in his cell.

When he turned back around to confront the CO that had undoubtedly set him up the man was no longer there.

"That's not mine."

"Yeah yeah that's what they all say," the CO responded as he placed the handcuffs on him.

***§

Phatz tried to hold it in but the feeling that had started deep in his chest spilled out of his mouth as he kneeled over with laughter. The sound blended in with the loud cries of a baby and voices floating in the air of the visiting room that day.

Straightening himself up he wiped at the corners of his eyes with his thumb as his laughter slowly died down.

"Uncle Kenny is really something serious," Denise said from across the table.

Phatz gazed at his sister seated across from him. The past three days that they'd visited with him had shown him that his little sister had matured a lot over the years. Nothing was off limits as they talked about the brutal street war going on in L.A., rumors circulating on the street of their life sentence, family and his uncle's latest antics with his girlfriends. Just sitting across from her made Phatz realize how much he'd missed out on her growing up. She was sixteen when he fled L.A. now at nineteen Denise had blossomed into a beautiful young woman. Still there was one thing that hadn't changed, his sister's fly style. Dressed in an off-white stylish Gucci two piece suit with a pair of black Manolo pumps and 24 karat diamond earrings in each ear, she was the flyest in the room. He'd caught the appreciative stares from both the CO's and the other inmates thrown their way and even now he could tell that they were still watching.

"You know why everyone looking over here right?" he asked teasingly.

Shaking her head Denise pursed her red ruby lips.

"You have on white after Labor Day."

She rolled her eyes dramatically before brushing at the invisible lint on her suit "Listen bro-ski when you look this good, you can wear anything."

Her head swiveled around the crowded visiting room, "Besides what the hell do these country ass people know about fashion?"

"They probably never even heard of Gucci," she added.

He smiled. She was definitely his sister.

"I'm going to the snack bar anyone want anything?" she asked, looking first to him then Twin.

Phatz shook his head. The candy wrappers and empty food containers on the table was evidence of how much he'd overeaten. His body would pay for it during workouts.

As Denise got in line for the snack bar, Phatz directed his attention to Twin. Like his sister, Twin wasn't a boy anymore, but a grown man and from what Phatz knew he was handling his business back in L.A.

"Man, I wanted to thank you for that favor you did for me," Twin said clasping his hands together.

Phatz eyed the ring covered in diamonds on Twin's pinky finger. The favor he spoke of happened years earlier during his time at CDC. Tired of the square nine to five life Twin was ready to step up in the game. Setting things in motion Phatz had placed a phone call to Corey to front him some work. Now two years later Twin was one of the biggest players in the game and it was all thanks to him. Phatz had warned him to be cautious and smart, the dope game wasn't for little boys. It was a cold and ruthless game and one mistake could cost him his life. Judging by the looks of things Twin had taken heed to his words and was handling things well, not to mention he was taking care of Denise and not just with money. Phatz knew that when Marlon was killed Denise had cried on her boyfriend's shoulder because he hadn't been there to lend his own. A pang hit him in the chest at the thought of Marlon. Two years later and it still hadn't gotten any easier.

He looked Twin in the eye as he said his next words,"No matter what happens you make sure my sister stays safe you heard me."

Twin sat up straight "I got you, I don't even involve her in this shit."

"Good," Phatz responded. He could see Denise making her way back to their table now, but before she could a fat toddler waddled in front of her blocking her path.

Squatting eye level with the toddler, a smiling Denise began to coo earning squeals of delight from the child. Exchanging a few words with the mother she stood and began to stroll towards them again. Phatz was about to turn to Twin when the stylish dressed woman and the kid caught his attention as they sat down at a table. No longer wearing tight pants Marvin occupied the seat across from the mom and baby now. His beard had begun to grow back in leaving stubble on his face and his normally slicked down hair was braided in neat braids to the back. He looked happy as he sat with the baby that resembled him so much. Phatz guessed that the kid was his child, and the woman was his girlfriend. It was confirmed when Marvin leaned over and placed a kiss on her lips.

Black Gal.

The voice in Phatz 'head corrected because once you became a hoe, everything changed including your name and Marvin was now known as Black Gal.

Hoes were allowed to visit with their families sometimes to keep them from worrying, but it was all just a front. The minute they stepped behind those doors again they were back in tight jeans with clean faces acting like real girls.

Phatz didn't realized he was shaking his head until Denise appeared in front of him

"What's wrong?" she asked.

"Nothing," he answered, averting his gaze to the arm full of items she was carrying.

"I guess some of these people know what Gucci is after all," Denise said. "The woman with the baby recognized it from the fall catalog."

"Catalog, so you balling like that huh?"

"I get it from you," she said smiling playfully.

"You heard me," he joked back.

Twisting her lips Denise erupted into laughter.

"Ima tell mama how country your ass talk now." He had been in Angola so long that he was beginning to sound like them. Grabbing the pack of gum on table he ripped it open. "Did you and mama like the leather belts I sent?"

Stuffing the gum in his mouth his eyes watered at the strong minty taste.

"Yep."

Every time he needed a new knife Phatz had his friend Pocket who worked in the hobby shop to make Denise and his mom belts made from real leather with their names carved in it. He hid his weapons all over the buildings whenever he had to go through metal detectors so that there was always one in reach.

"She won't like this new look of yours though" Denise joked, pointing to the sprouting fro on Phatz head. Not only had he picked up on their words, but he had adapted to some of the natives' ways and began to grow his hair out using burnt motor oil and sulfur 8 grease. It was the style in prison.

He patted his fro. "Girl I look good."

"Tell him what he really looks like," Denise said turning to Twin who laughed.

Phatz soaked the laughter and love all up and before he knew it, it was time for them to leave.

The voice over the intercom loudly announced the end of visitation.

Standing, he embraced Denise in a big hug.

"Next time mama is bringing Dino Jr." she said, face muffled against his shirt.

Pulling back Denise wiped at her tears.

"Tell Mother Dear I'm getting her the biggest box of Church's Chicken when I make it to L.A., he joked trying to keep the emotion out of his voice.

She kissed him on the cheek. "I will."

Twin stepped up. He had remained silent for most of the visit only speaking when he needed to. Phatz could tell that being in the visiting room made him uncomfortable, but he hoped the idea of prison made him even more careful.

He was surprised when Twin removed the pinky ring from his finger and handed it to him.

"You keep this until you make it back to Boss Angeles."

Phatz gripped the ring between his fingers. He knew expensive jewelry when he saw it and the ring was worth at least $20K. He smiled as he slid it on his finger. His crew in Walnut unit would go crazy when they saw it.

"It's the least I could do."

"You just remember what I said."

"I got you," Twin replied as the two men gripped hands.

Phatz watched them walk out the doors of the visiting room with the other visitors and wished he was leaving out with them.

But with three more years left on his seven-year sentence he knew that wouldn't be happening. He tried not to think about the remaining years because he knew it wouldn't make the time pass any faster. He realized he needed a plan for when his release came. On the way back to the dorm, thoughts of ways to put a ring on every finger when he made it back to L.A. filled his mind.

****

The phone rang on the other end. Cradling the receiver between his neck and shoulders, AC propped his hand on the wall as his eyes scanned the empty lobby area. After the knife fiasco in the working cell block, he had now been moved to Camp J- another dungeon with even more restrictions. But today he got to use his phone privileges. Calling home had been the first thing on his mind that morning when he woke. It was just his luck that no one was home to answer for him. A feeling of disappointment settled in. He had almost replaced the receiver back on the hook when a raspy voice came over the line.

"Hello?"

Immediately recognizing the voice his face split into a grin, "Unc Leslie this is Clyde how you doing?"

"Hey nephew, I'm glad I came back to the house when I did."

Mindful of the time AC chatted back and forth with his uncle about almost everything. From sports to what was going on in prison. When he was younger Leslie was always the uncle that he could go to no matter what. He was glad to see that things hadn't changed.

"The Lakers looking good this year." His uncle was a diehard Lakers fan just like Phatz.

They talked about sports for a while until Leslie jumped to another topic.

"Your sister is having another baby," Leslie beamed from the other end.

"Really?"

In his head he did a quick calculation. When he left, his sister Ruby had only two kids. That was two years ago.

"This is baby number three?"

"That's right," His uncles' deep chuckle came over the phone

His uncle talked aimlessly for a few more seconds. AC knew that his time was winding down as he listened to the man. It felt good hearing his uncle' voice and in an odd way it made him feel closer to home despite his reality of being over a thousand miles away.

He almost hated to end the conversation but with the little time he had left he wanted to stretch his legs down the tier at least once.

"Aye Unc," AC tried to interrupt but his uncle continued to talk.

He tried again.

"Unc."

"And your grandmother Dorothy passed away," his uncle said casually before diving into another conversation.

On the other end AC's hand froze on the receiver.

Dead! Grandma? The words echoed in his mind.

"Wait, wait," he said in a firm voice gaining his uncle's attention.

A faint buzz sounded in his ear as he spoke again silently praying that he had heard wrong.

"Did you just say my grandmother died?"

The disbelief in his voice was evident.

Leslie cleared his throat. "Yeah, son I'm sorry to be the one to tell you."

Feeling the air rush from his lung's AC stumbled against the wall hoping that it would hold him up because his legs had suddenly gone weak.

The buzz in his ear grew louder as he struggled to pull himself together.

Swallowing back the lump of emotion forming in his throat he exhaled loudly before asking,

"When did this happen?"

Squeezing his eyes tight he tried to brace himself for the answer, but nothing could prepare him for the words that left his uncle's mouth.

"About ten months ago."

The news hit him so hard his vision blurred and for a split second he felt faint.

Not now get it together he scolded himself. Even though he was the only person out on the tier, he knew the prison was not the place to show any weak emotion—no matter how bad the news was.

Trying to slow his heart rate down he breathed deeply through his mouth. Seconds later he could feel the rapid thud begin to return to normal, but it would be a long time before the ache in his chest would go away.

"Unc, I gotta go," AC said, abruptly stopping the man in mid-sentence before disconnecting the call.

The pain he felt was slowly drowned out by the anger flowing through him.

His grandmother had died ten months ago and no one bothered to tell him. He had been in and out of lockdown and losing his phone privileges didn't make things better but still that's what paper and pen was for he reasoned to himself.

With five minutes remaining he punched in a number he had committed to memory. His thoughts raced as he waited for someone to answer.

He couldn't remember the last time he had spoken with his grandmother Dorothy, but she always supported him even in his wrong. His uncle had dropped a bombshell on him. He didn't know what was worse, the fact that he hadn't known or the helplessness that followed when no one answered.

He slammed the receiver down when he realized his time was up. The CO shackled his hands and legs before escorting him to his cell. While normally he would be on the lookout for the niggas that slung shit and pee on the regular when you walked by their cell—at the moment his mind was in a deep haze.

For months he had been paying the phone bill at his grandmother's house because he knew his sister April was in and out of jail. She always needed someone to call so he kept the phone on for her.

AC shook his head as the cell door slid back trying to clear the confusion from it. He had so many questions, but they would have to wait another twenty-three hours.

When the door closed and the handcuffs were removed he walked to the square window that overlooked the yard. Sometimes he would stare out of it to take his mind off things. Today It wasn't working.

His emotions were everywhere. He could handle the grief and the sadness that came with death. It was the shame and regret that threatened to undo him.

He had missed the birth of his nieces and nephews and now the death of his grandmother. Angola had taken something from him that he would never get back. Time.

AC had been so focused on making it out alive it never crossed his mind that he wouldn't have anyone to make it out too.

****

Hours later Phatz was still on a natural high after his visit with Denise and Twin. Already he was anticipating their next visit with his son. A smile touched his face at the thought. Little Dino was four almost five now and Phatz had witnessed his growth from afar through pictures and phone calls. It was time he had a face to face meeting with his one and only child.

"I take it you had a nice visit with the fam right?" The voice came from behind him.

Peering over his shoulder Phatz stared into Lynnwood's face. Known for his protests and demonstrations against social injustices, Lynnwood was a hardcore activist that found himself railroaded by the system and given a thirty-five-year sentence for felony gun charges with the intent to cross state lines. Though they had tried to shut him up they underestimated the power he would have on the men behind the walls who knew all about a system built against them. His radical messages vibrated through the camps, gaining him respect and admiration among many, Phatz included. It didn't hurt that he called the shots for the Baton Rouge crew either.

With the ring clasped tight in his hand Phatz closed his locker and spun around.

"Yeah hated to see them leave."

"I know how it is youngin," Lynnwood replied.

Unable to help himself Phatz beckoned for him to move closer.

"Come see this," he said holding the ring up like a kid who had just won a prize from the fair Lynnwood let out a low whistle," Damn this is beautiful man," he said holding the ring in his hand now.

Phatz glanced around to make sure no one was looking. The dorm was unusually quiet for the afternoon and he figured it was because there was a program going on later in the visiting room and the inmates wanted to be on their best behavior. Most were either curled up in bed or in the day room watching television.

"Too rich for my blood," Lynwood joked as he passed the ring back to Phatz.

"Just keep that shit out of sight we got enough problems," he said his voice turning serious.

From the stern expression on Lynwood's face Phatz knew something was up. Quickly he slid the ring on his pinky finger.

"What kind of problems?" he asked, putting his visiting clothes in his locker and slamming it shut.

Before Lenny could respond Chunky interrupted, "Phatz you back?"

Chunky was Phatz next in command. Big D had introduced the two. With Spooky getting shipped to another prison and Big D being in the dungeon, he needed more players in his operation. Chunky was a Piru Blood from Lueders Park Piru in Compton. When Phatz realized he was from a familiar area he immediately began to question him, and it turned out they knew some of the same people. Samoan with a stocky frame and long thick hair, Phatz was the one who coined him Chunky. The two had become close and when Phatz offered him a spot on his team Chunky gave up his hustle of selling his plasma for $7.25 to start making real money.

"Yeah I been back what's up?"

Chunky nodded towards Lenny as he eased near Phatz bed, "Ya boy said he needed to talk to us."

"You owe me another round tomorrow," Ty chimed in from behind Chunky. Ty had been down the walk for almost six months after being thrown out of Camp D for bashing a fool's head in when an argument over a game turned heated.

Phatz had to admit to himself he didn't think Ty would do it, but now that he was Down the Walk he made good on his offer and accepted him into his operation with open arms. Even though Ty's fuck up back in Shreveport had cost them a lot, Phatz couldn't let him starve.

Ty nudged Lynnwood, "I'm talking to you playa."

"It doesn't matter how many times we play chess, you'll never win because you can't think ahead," Lynwood said tapping his temple with his finger.

"Yeah we'll see nigga," Ty responded with a frown. Taking a seat on his bed he looked at them with an expectant look.

"Guess it's serious, if you called these two," Phatz said even more puzzled now. He noticed how Lynwood's eyes briefly focused on something over his head. Before he began to investigate any further the man began to speak.

"A carton of cigarettes was stolen from the locker and I know exactly who did it."

The words made Phatz stand up straight.

Not only was Phatz selling drugs, but he also sold commissary items to the inmates at lower prices. Loose cigarettes in prison were a luxury for many. He raked in just as much dough selling cigarettes as he did weed. But powder cocaine was still his most sought-after product. His good mood from earlier began to dissolve at the thought of someone stealing from him.

"After commissary I went to the locker to put the shit up, and I made sure to take inventory of what we had before I locked up." He paused to make sure he had everyone's attention. "When I went back an hour later, one carton was missing, now I noticed two cats-

"Who?" Chunky asked springing forward, ready for action.

Shaking his head Phatz held up his hand, "Hold up Chunky, let him finish."

When Chunky slowly lowered himself onto the locker, Phatz motioned for Lynwood to continue.

"Honestly, I didn't think anything of it at first cause who in their right mind would steal from us?"

"Some niggas that want their shit broke," Chunky answered balling his fist up.

"Who were these dudes hanging around?" Phatz asked tired of the suspense. He was ready to ride like Chunky.

"Al and Hawk," Lynwood replied.

Immediately Phatz glanced behind him to the spot he had seen Lynnwood looking earlier. The beds that Al and Hawk slept in were empty.

"I just saw em heading to the shower all happy and shit about the program," Lynwood said on cue.

Phatz checked the time on his watch. The program was less than an hour away. That gave them plenty of time to discuss how they would punish Al and Hawk for their ruthless transgression.

****

    The thing about prison was that if you stay behind the walls long enough you begin to recognize the signs of danger before it even occurs. The atmosphere in the dorm began to shift, almost electric like as the inmates roused from their afternoon nap. Just one sniff of the air and they could tell that something was coming. Some took heed and exited, not wanting to be caught up in whatever that was about to go down, while others hung around waiting in anticipation. Phatz lay on his bed with his hands clasped under his head and his eyes closed. The steady beat of his heart filled his ears and mind as he inhaled and exhaled deeply through his nose. Anyone watching would mistake him for sleep, but he was watching and listening. After a few seconds of lying completely still he opened his eyes behind his Ray Bans' and rose slowly, careful not to stab himself with the knife tucked in his pants.

A few beds down he spotted Chunky pretending to read a book and Ty on the phone. The men were in the spots that they'd agreed on. Lynwood on the other hand had gone to another dorm to gather the troops. There was a possible chance that the act of violence that was about to take place would spark a riot between New Orleans where Al and Hawk hailed from and Baton Rouge-the side that was down for Phatz. No matter the outcome blood would be shed. Phatz didn't have to worry about a CO coming in to break it up. Earlier he paid the one usually on duty at this time to stay outside of the dorm. All the man asked in return was that he didn't kill anyone and Phatz agreed.

It was almost time for count. He could tell by line of inmates streaming back into the dorm, but even they knew something was up. Everyone seemed to be aware except Al and Hawk who stumbled in horse playing and laughing after their shower. Chunky was up from his bed in an instant but backed off when he remembered they were supposed to wait until the men had put on their pants.

Hanging up the phone from his pretend conversation Ty eased forward.

Al and Hawk continued to laugh unaware of the danger they were in. It was Al who pulled his pants up over his white boxers first, Hawk followed seconds later.

Giving the signal Phatz walked to Al bed for a better view of the show.

"I guess you muthafuckas never learn huh?" Chunky asked.

Al only a few inches taller than Chunky glanced around confused. Trying to put some space in between the two, his large frame bumped into the bed sending a loud scraping sound through the room. A mask of guilt washed over his face before he quickly concealed it.

"Who the fuck you talking too ni—" Al never got the chance to complete his sentence. Sending a solid punch to his face Chunky knocked him down to the floor, where he groaned and rolled to his side. Gripping the bed Al tried to climb to his feet, but the knee in his face knocked the wind out of him.

"Don't get up motherfucka," Chunky warned as he proceeded to stump him.

Phatz turned his attention to Hawk who stood by watching with a look of shock on his face. When their gazes clashed, he bolted towards the door, only to collide with Ty's fist in his mouth. The impact from the blow made his head snap back and down he went!

"Where the fuck you think you going nigga?" Ty asked standing over him.

Hawk swiped at his bleeding mouth. Staggering he tried to get up as blood dripped down the front of his bare chest onto the freshly mopped floor.

The remaining prisoners on the other end of the dorm room stood on their beds to get a better view. Chunky pounded away at Al, who lay curled in a fetal position.

"Don't stop Chunky!" he yelled.

On the other end Ty smacked his lips as he teased "I should fuck yo hoe ass," he winked sending Hawk in a rage, that was met with a two piece.

Phatz liked what he saw as he looked from one beating to the other. Rubbing his hands together he smiled to himself. It was time to make things a little more interesting.

"Ty and Chunky, switch!" he yelled out.

And just like that Ty was on Al and Chunky was on Hawk, causing double the damage. Only the loud groans and moans from Al and Hawk could be heard as their beating continued At the sound of footsteps approaching Phatz swung around just in time to see the New Orleans crew burst through the entrance.

Stepping out in front of the two beatings happening in the middle of the floor, he eyed the men up and down.

Their faces were a mask of rage. he counted six but knew there was probably more on the way. He had to hold them off until Lynwood returned.

"Get off him!" one yelled taking a step forward.

"Not right now," Phatz said shaking his head as he stood toe to toe with them.

"Nigga get out the way!" Another one commanded, his chest heaving up and down like a mad bull.

A light chuckle slipped from Phatz mouth. "You didn't stop them from stealing out my locker, so you not gonna stop me from making them pay.

Lifting the tail end of his shirt Phatz proudly showcased the knife tucked in his waist. Long as his forearm and two inches wide the knife had deep sharp ridges and curved at the tip. The inmate who made it in the hobby shop had told him that it was used to carve through deer skin. Phatz could only imagine the harm it would do to human flesh.

He watched as their eyes bulged out of their eye sockets at the sight.

The guy in front of him took a step back, then two.

"Yeah that's right, I didn't hear y'all telling them not to steal from me, so sit back and watch the show."

"That nigga gone kill him."

Phatz shook his head, "Nah he just teaching him a lesson."

He didn't have to look behind him to know what was going on. He could hear Ty taunting Hawk as he followed up with punches that echoed through the dorm.

"They'll be aight," he added. The crew standing in front of him looked on helplessly, knowing they wouldn't risk their life for another man. It was worthless.

Phatz heard more footsteps approaching except it wasn't the regular sound of more inmates coming, it was the thundering sound of the CO's boots storming down the walk.

"Let's bounce!" he called over his shoulder. Just like that the beating ended as quickly as it started.

The other inmates scrambled down from their beds as Al and Hawk were helped off the floor. Blood leaked from both men. It looked like a crime scene.

Chunky wiped the sweat from his face. The ponytail he wore had come undone leaving his long hair cascading down his back.

Ty was already at his bed changing out of his bloody clothes. With only seconds to hide the knife, Phatz slid it inside of the mattress next to his where he always kept it. The poor soul that slept on it didn't have a clue.

He sat on his bed watching as the CO's stormed the dorm. Behind them he saw Lynwood lingering in the entrance. Hopping up he went to meet him.

"Told you I was coming back," Lynwood stated. Over Lynwood's shoulder Phatz saw that at least twenty men stood behind him.

Phatz gave a curt nod to them before focusing on Lynwood.

"It's handled."

"You sure?"

"Positive," Phatz responded.

Giving a quick signal with his hand Lynwood dismissed his crew.

Clasping a hand on Phatz shoulder, Lynwood guided him towards the window.

"Let me show you something."

Through the dingy windowpane Phatz could see a large number of men gathered on the yard. If he had to guess it was over sixty, all socializing as if they were at a picnic and not a prison ready to start a war. He could only imagine the weapons that were in their possession.

"My rounds ready to ride, so if them niggas want a war then we'll bring it to em."

Standing back, he regarded Lynwood carefully, he wasn't the peaceful activist that he sometimes tried to portray himself as. This was a man who was about action at all cost. He had people willing to risk their lives for him. Phatz shook his head and smiled.

"You can call the dawgs off for now, I doubt if there's any retaliation, they got caught stealing so they know the rule is take don't steal, you heard me!"

Lynwood smirked, "You know Phatz I respect your gangsta, the only thing these niggas on this river understand is pain and you make them feel it. Respect is pain."

Nodding along to his words Phatz knew Lynwood probably thought that Angola had made him that way, but the truth was that L.A., the land of the body bags had drilled it into his head long before any time in prison could. He was used to bringing the pain.

The two shared a few more words before Phatz returned to his bed immediately he noticed that both Chunky and Ty were nowhere in sight. Their beds were empty. It could only mean one thing. The CO's had taken them to the dungeon.

He cursed as he made his way across the floor. He could feel the stares on his back as he moved.

At the commotion behind him Phatz turned to see Al and Hawk returning.

A long white gauze bandage covered the side of Al's face, dried blood was caked in his nose. Hawk held an ice pack to his mouth; one eye was swollen and a bandage was wrapped around his hand.

At the sight of Phatz approaching they began to sputter out an explanation tripping over their lies.

He held his hand up to stop them.

"I don't wanna hear that shit, if either of you niggas got a problem with me we can do this shit now. Don't get to the outer camps and send back death. It's nothing between us but air you heard me!"

Phatz patted his waist as if he still had his knife.

Their eyes widened.

Al shook his head.

"Naw man Phatz it's not like that."

"Yeah man, we don't know what came over us," Hawk followed up.

Phatz looked between the two. They were a pitiful sight all lumped and bloodied up.

"Al you been down twenty plus years," he turned to Hawk "and you fifteen, so y'all know the rules is take don't steal!"

Again, they tried to apologize. Turning his back in disgust Phatz threw his hand up,

"Just pack yal shit and bounce!" he said knowing that they too were going to the dungeon.

Sitting on his bed he looked around at the damage. Al and Hawk's blood covered the floor. Sometime during the fight beds had been strewn across the dorm. The cleaning crew came in soaking the blood up with the mop turning it into a light pink. As everyone went back to their normal doings and the noise level began to escalate, Phatz thought about how his day had started with laughs and smiles and ended with blood and pain, but that was an average day in Angola. Just like no amount of blood shed or deaths would stop the world on the outside from spinning, it was the same inside of Angola. In a way it helped to keep him grounded and focused and now that he had taken care of the thieves his thoughts returned to the diamond ring on his pinky finger. His mind began to piece together a plan for when he would finally shake loose of his shackles.

****

AC stared at the date circled in pencil on the small calendar in his cell. It was his twentieth birthday. If he were in L.A. he would be partying nonstop with the finest honey's, eating the best food, dressed in the flyest gear with jewels to match. He closed his eyes briefly and imagined it all.

The strong stench drifting up his nostrils and the loud grunts quickly brought him back to reality. To his cell, with his new cellie Bull who was having a bowel movement less than three feet away from him.

Not only was it his birthday, but today AC had accomplished an important milestone. He was celebrating six months out of the hole, in his new dwelling line thirty-six, better known as the working cell block. His longest run of "freedom" since being imprisoned. Freedom from twenty-three-hour lock down came with a price, or rather a cellmate that he didn't exactly get along with. It was times like this when AC wished he had remained in the dungeon, at least he didn't have to smell another man's shit.

"That damn fried catfish not settling right on my stomach," Bull complained from behind the sheet that they used to separate their small living quarters from the toilet.

He listened as Bull began to ramble on about the boxing match that was being hosted by the prison. A once heavyweight champion in his division, Bull didn't mind showing off his skills. He would run through drills punching and sliding across the concrete floor in the cell as he retold stories from his golden days. Let him tell it he was the greatest boxer alive and could beat anyone including Muhammad Ali. For the most part AC entertained him with questions, but then there were times when he wished that Bull would shut the fuck up!

Seconds later the toilet flushed.

"Whew," Bull said. Sliding the sheet back he walked over to the sink and washed his hands.

Removing the tissue grabbed his Walkman and headphones. If he didn't get some fresh air right now, he would suffocate from the smell.

"You got any cigarettes I'll pay you back next week?" Bull asked stopping him in his tracks when he reached the cell door.

AC glanced over his shoulder. Shirtless, Bull had the physique of a man who used to be in shape, but a poor diet of cheese puffs, cigarettes, and homebrew had turned his body into fat. His round stomach jiggled with every move he made. Sweat clung to the thick rolls under his neck. AC watched as he tried to hoist himself on the top bunk. On the third try the man managed to pull his large body up, only he hung in an awkward position. With one leg dangling from the bed his thick fingers curled into the thin sheet, his other hand swiped at the clutter on the bed knocking empty bags of chips ,trash, and paper to the floor. Finally righting himself, he took a deep breath as more sweat ran down his face.

No matter how many times AC tried to keep the small cell clean Bull always found a way to fuck it up. He was a slob.

"No, I'm out," AC finally responded before walking off heading to the rec yard.
****

    The paper in his hand trembled lightly. If it wasn't one thing it was another. Phatz morning had started off bad despite his attempts to have a productive day. First during his weekly call home he'd learned some devastating news, Corey was dead. Murdered in broad daylight at the car wash. The news had left him stunned. It had taken a few seconds for him to regain his bearings before he could speak again. Still Phatz tripped over his words as he shot off questions to Denise. Even while in prison he had remained in touch with Corey. They'd last spoken just two weeks ago and now he was dead. Corey's death brought back memories of Marlon. Phatz couldn't help but feel that both men would still be alive if he were free. It was a heavy burden to bear.

Long after he'd ended his phone call, the news hung over his head like a dark rain cloud ready for release , but Phatz was so numb to loss and pain that not even the death of a close friend could trigger tears. Still, flashbacks of Corey played in his mind: Corey the boy, Corey the tall scraggly teenager, and Corey the man. Phatz had known him for so long it was hard not to imagine that he wouldn't be there to greet him when he returned to L.A. If the news of Corey's death wasn't enough to ruin his day, the letter in his hand certainly was. It was from Ty and this time he had crossed the game. After Al's and Hawk beat down both Ty and Chunky had been sent to the dungeon. Anxiously he had awaited Ty's return so that he could tell him his masterplan for when he hit the streets in L.A. Only Ty never returned. Instead Phatz received the letter he was holding.

He scanned over the handwriting again unable to stop the surge of anger that shot through him.

Pussy ass nigga! his mind screamed out.

Despite Ty's recent disciplinary run in, the slimy bastard had put in a transfer to a lower level prison.

He was leaving them. The news wasn't what bothered him. Phatz was more upset that Ty had parted his mouth to ask him to put in a transfer as well.

Angola was the closest thing to hell on earth that he had ever experienced. It was violent and dangerous, but leaving wasn't an option for him, especially since it meant that he would have to leave AC behind. Because of his frequent trips to the dungeon AC wasn't eligible for a transfer and Ty knew this.

Balling the paper up with his hands Phatz squeezed as hard as he could wishing that it was Ty's neck that he was wringing instead.

This entire time he had been focused on keeping them together so they could all make it back home, instead Ty had been plotting. Waiting for his chance to jump ship like a little bitch. Phatz should have seen it coming, but he had been blinded by his loyalty and now Ty was asking to do the unspeakable. With a sad shake of his head he tossed the crumpled letter into the waste can and spit on it.

****

  Even after two years of being locked up, showering in his prison issued slippers and boxers was something AC still hadn't gotten used to. Every few seconds he lifted his head from the spray of water cascading down on him to make sure he was alone. He knew that fools would wait right good until you were naked and defenseless to sneak in and do whatever they wanted to you. He'd seen it happen too many times to let his guards down. Miraculously after the long day on the yard the showers had been empty, so he stayed in longer than he had intended. The lukewarm water pelted against his skin easing the soreness from his muscles after the workout he had just completed. Squirting a small drop of shampoo from the half empty bottle he massaged his scalp until soap suds began to foam. Rinsing his hair, he repeated the step one more time before soaping his body up. He didn't turn off the water till his fingers began to wrinkle like they did when he was a kid after staying in the tub for too long.

Dressed in a pair of Levi's and a white T-shirt he went in search of the one thing he knew hadn't changed no matter the locations: dice games. The first two dice games brought him small winnings but on his third game located in the cell below his, AC hit the jackpot.

He snapped his fingers loudly as he scooped up over $200 off the concrete floor.

"That's what I'm talking about," he said out loud as he ignored the sad and envious faces around him. Declining to play another game, he laughed to himself as he walked away. He would have played it back, but it was his birthday and there was nothing better than walking around with a pocketful of money. Money that would buy him almost two months of commissary supplies and more stamps to write Shauna back. Shit he may even buy himself a box of cakes to celebrate. At the thought of food his stomach growled reminding him that he still hadn't eaten. After a quick meal in the chow hall he made his way back to the yard to meet Phatz. Landing in the working cell block this time had worked in his favor. For the first time since they had left Elayne Hunt he and Phatz were now on opposite yards with only a fence to separate them. They spent weeks catching up, neither surprised about the others' journey. One thing was for certain, they both had been spilling blood all over the prison.

Outside his eyes scanned the yard. It was the dead of July and the temperatures were in the high nineties and climbing. Most inmates skipped yard time due to the humid heat preferring to stay inside, so only a few lounged around on the workout equipment. Gazing up, AC noticed that the CO in the tower had removed his work shirt and slung it over the rails. The plain white T-shirt he wore was drenched in sweat; a scowl covered his reddening face. He grinned to himself at the CO's misery. Served him right to bake in the heat. His constant run ins with the correctional officers had left a foul taste in his mouth. AC no longer gave them the benefit of the doubt. They were all crooked in his eyes.

Reaching into his back pocket he pulled out an Afro pick and began to fluff out his fro, marveling at how the heat had already dried most of his hair already. He was contemplating braiding it in two plaits when his eyes landed on Phatz crossing the yard. He could tell by the frown on his face that there was something wrong.

****

30 minutes earlier

"You done for the day?"

Nodding his head Phatz handed him the mop bucket and mop. It was the end of his shift and just like every day he returned his supplies to Lynwood who oversaw inventory for clean-up. Normally Phatz would hang around to discuss the latest business move or get the run down from Lynwood, but today his thoughts were in a million places. Lynwood must have noticed his mood as well.

"You aight my nigga?" he asked.

How could he answer that question? One of his closest childhood friends had been murdered and the other one was running scared. Addressing the pain of Corey's death would only make him weak and vulnerable: the two things he couldn't afford to be. Instead, he focused on the sting of Ty's betrayal.

"I'm good," Phatz responded removing the cleaning gloves from his hands.

"Ok I'll catch up with you later," Lynwood said shifting his attention back to his duties.

Moving out of the line Phatz began his trek back to the dorm. He was still in deep thought when he heard his name being called.

Spinning around he watched CO Brian shuffle down the hall towards him with a panicked look on his face.

"Aye, I need to talk to you, it's' important," Brian's eyes nervously darted around the hall that was bustling with inmates. The crews from the field were beginning to file in for lunch.

Waiting until the last inmate had marched by them Brian jerked his head.

"Now!" he whispered in an urgent tone before heading in the opposite direction.

Inwardly Phatz sighed. It was always something. As he followed close behind Brian he stared at the man's large back and wondered if the Oakland Raiders jacket that he'd sent from L.A. fit him. He made a mental note to ask him when they reached their destination. In recent months Phatz drug operation had entered new territory. No longer was he relying on other prisoners to get his work inside for him- he'd been burnt too many times. Through Lynwood he had connected with Brian, a correctional officer in Angola, who lived in Baton Rouge. Phatz had the drugs shipped from L.A. to Brian's house and then the man would bring them in the prison. Because Brain had a lot to lose including his freedom, he was always extra careful in his dealings. No one suspected a thing. It was a beautiful partnership. Though the real icing on the cake was that Brian carpooled to work every day with the captain that was over the walk and a few more correctional officers. Phatz had the inside scoop on everything going on at the prison. Which was how he learned that Captain Perks had a real hard on for him. He and another correctional officer named Jenkins intentionally tried to sabotage Phatz job and his placement in Walnut 4. From surprise shake downs to strip searches. They'd tried it all and still came up unsuccessful and it was all thanks to his inside man Brian. The man's reports helped him to stay one step ahead of them.

A big man that towered over 6'2, Brian's normal smooth brown skin had a clammy look to it when he stopped outside of the chow hall.

"They about to come shake you down in the next fifteen minutes," he said nervously. A bead of sweat dripped from his hairline down his large nose. He wiped at it quickly. Stepping around Phatz he glanced up and down the long hallway before turning to him again.

"Man, Jenkins was the one who came up with the idea, he told Captain Perks you come from money, he saw your sister all dressed up on a visit."

Phatz tensed at the mention of Denise. The news wasn't exactly a surprise, but the one thing he didn't need was punk ass Jenkins paying attention to his sister or anything he had going on.

"What else did he say about my family?"

Brian shook his head. "Nothing, just that he thinks you may be hiding money and other contraband."

"Shit."

Kneading his brow at the sudden sharp pain pounding his head Phatz weighed his options. With such a short time notice there was only one thing he could do.

"Ok let me get to the dorm and get the work and give it to you."

Deep wrinkles appeared in Brian's forehead as his head swiveled back and forth before he spoke in a hushed whisper, "Are you crazy Phatz you can't give it to me, what if they find it?" he asked in a hitched voice.

Phatz shook his head. Brian was a cool dude but sometimes he lacked common sense.

"Fool they searching me not you, how would they find it on you?" Folding his arms over his chest he waited for his words to sink in.

Brian was quiet for a few minutes. Phatz could see the wheels spinning in his head.

"Ok," he said timidly at first then again with confidence.

"Ok."

Patting his shoulder Phatz stared into his eyes.

"You sweating for nothing, let's stop wasting time let me go and get the shit then bring it back to you and you put it wherever. "

"Go," Brian responded.

Phatz had taken two steps before doubling back, "So did the jacket fit?" he asked.

A look of confusion covered Brians' face before he realized what he was referring to.

"Ooooh man yeah I can't believe you sent it,"he said with excitement in his voice temporarily, forgetting their situation. "I really appreciate it."

"You take care of me, I take care of you," Phatz responded before heading off.
****

Present Time

  The powdered white substance left a bitter taste in his mouth. Using his tongue, he tried to scrape at the thick paste that was stuck to the roof of his mouth. After a few unsuccessful tries he finally managed to swallow it all down. The gritty feeling of the headache medicine he'd just purchased from commissary going down his throat made him frown. For a second, he contemplated turning around to get a bottle of water, but AC had already spotted him coming out the door. He was in their usual meeting place at the fence. The only thing Phatz could think of as his sleeping area was being shaken down and ripped apart by Jenkins, was how he would deliver the news of Ty's betrayal to AC. The time spent at CDC had surprisingly brought AC and Ty closer together. It was something that he was once proud of but now he regretted letting the two meet. Phatz should have been celebrating the fact that he had once again made both Jenkins and Captain Perks look like fools in front of the entire dorm. He didn't think he would ever tire of seeing their sour expressions as they stormed out of the dorm empty handed, yet he couldn't shake the unsettling feeling in his stomach as he drew nearer to AC. When he finally reached the fence Phatz opened his mouth to tell him the truth but only one thing came out.

"Corey was killed."

****

AC tried to digest the words that had come out of Phatz mouth. Though he and Corey were never friends, for the sake of Phatz, AC managed to keep the peace. He listened quietly as Phatz gave him the details on the man's murder. When Phatz was done speaking AC shook his head.

"That's fucked up." AC knew there wasn't much he could say to make Phatz feel better. The truth was that death had claimed many of their friends before their time. In L.A., niggas in the streets rarely ever lived to see twenty-five. Either you died or you went to jail. With death hitting so close to home again, AC was beginning to think that maybe Angola was their saving grace.

Minutes passed before either of them spoke, when they did Phatz hit him with more news.

"They shook me down before I walked out here," Phatz nodded his head towards a correctional officer that was standing on the yard, near a check point.

AC glanced in the direction Phatz had nodded in. While a few correctional officers roamed their post, the guard Phatz spoke on named Jenkins stayed glued to one spot watching them.

"Him and that bitch ass Captain Perks thought they would find something; you should've seen the looks on their faces when they didn't."

"Shit if looks could kill right now we would be dead," AC joked. He watched as another correctional officer joined Jenkins, but from the color of his uniform he was in the upper ranks.

"Who's the man standing beside him?"

"That's Captain Perks," Big D said approaching the fence. AC could tell by his reddened skin that he had just come from the fields. Though he had only known Big D for a short time, he liked the man.

"He got the dick," Big D said as he stuck a long cigarette between his lips.

Phatz balled over in laughter. AC looked back and forth between the two men trying to understand the inside joke.

"What you talking about Big D?"

Smiling Big D shook his head. "Before Perks was captain he was a "do boy" just like punk ass Jenkins is now. Thought he ran shit."

Big D took a pull from the cigarette as he continued, "One of them New Orleans niggas got hold to him and put the dick on him."

The words clicked in AC's mind. Someone had raped Captain Perks.

"To keep him quiet and shit, they gave him the position he has now. Put him in a nice office where he can sit back and kick his feet up, the only time he come out is to fuck with Phatz," he said smothering a laugh.

After a few more grilling stares sent in their direction the Captain stormed off the yard with Jenkins trailing after him like an obedient puppy.

Turning to Phatz, AC asked the question that was burning in his mind.

"What did you do with the dope, hide it on you?"

Phatz grinned mischievously. Reaching into his back pocket he pulled out the green substance wrapped in plastic.

"Brian hid it on him until they finished, it was right under their nose."

Big D and AC began cracking up at the genius move.

Growing serious, Phatz stretched out his hand,

"I've been holding on to this for you."

The sight of the weed made AC excited. He could more than triple his money by selling it in the working cell block. The men began to scan the ground for something heavy to tie the weed to so that Phatz could toss it over.

"Got it!" Phatz called out when he located a rocky heavy enough to wrap in the plastic.

They were just about to follow through with the exchange when AC's eyes locked with the guard in the gun tower. He was staring right at them.

"Hold up," he said jerking his head upward. Phatz followed the movement.

"Shit!" he exclaimed. "I bet Perkins told him to watch us."

"What now?" AC asked growing anxious under the surveillance. Eyeballing the plastic, he knew the weed was worth at least two hundred dollars.

"We wait," Phatz responded sliding both the bag of weed and rock back into his pocket.

Forcing himself to remain patient, his focus slid over to Big D who was further down the fence talking to another group of men. He considered calling Big D over to cook up a distraction but from the way the guard stalked them it would be next to impossible. Deciding to wait it out AC began to tell Phatz about his cellie in hopes that the guard would grow bored with watching them. In all honesty Bull was starting to get under his skin more than he wanted to admit.

"He's always begging, right before I left he wanted some cigarettes…" he frowned and wondered if he should put in a request for a new cell mate. The captain in his building wasn't as bad as the others he'd run into, so giving it a try wouldn't hurt.

He ran the idea by Phatz.

"What you need to do is figure out how you can get on this side of the fence, I'll tell you like I told Ty-" Phatz words suddenly cut off.

"What you tell Ty?" AC asked curious.

Waving him off Phatz shook his head. "Nothing never mind, is that guard still watching us?" he asked quickly changing the topic.

AC wanted to press the issue, but he saw how Phatz had shut down. Reversing his position, he shielded his eyes as he gazed up at the gun tower again. The guard's gun rested on the rails as he puffed on the cigarette, his eyes still glued to them.

A tinge of disappointment cursed through him when he realized they would have to wait another day to get the weed across to him. He was just about to tell Phatz this when the image beyond the fence made him do a double take. Weed dilemma temporarily forgotten, AC tracked the man's movement on the other side. Looking vaguely familiar he shielded his eyes from the sun to bring the vision into better focus.

Mookie.

AC had thought he'd recognized the man's profile and he was right.

Mookie had been placed in the cell next to his while he was in the hole. The two often shot dice together. One morning he'd waken to silence and the news that Mookie had been moved. It seemed as if everyone was taking the trip to the paradise that they called Down the Walk. AC knew his time would come soon enough.

He opened his mouth to call out to Mookie when a memory hit him.

Mookie never did pay up on the carton of cigarettes he owed him after losing a dice game. He squinted as he watched Mookie move further away. Today seemed like a good day to get what he was owed. If he couldn't get the weed to sell at least he would have the cigarettes. Consider it his birthday present.

****

Phatz on the other hand thought differently.

"Naw, just leave it alone you can handle it when you make it down here," he responded.

He was in the middle of solving their weed issue when AC interrupted him. Phatz moved away from the huddle he had formed with Chunky and another guy who they'd chosen to throw the weed over the fence. He was banking on the guard being so focused on them that he would miss the play they were about to run. This was a big opportunity for them because If he got the weed to AC on a regular, he could control both the working cell block and Down the Walk. It was an idea that had weighed heavily on his mind, only Ty's presence had stopped him from acting on it. Now that he'd crossed the game Phatz needed more hands and who better than AC to step up. With their window of opportunity quickly closing, Phatz tried to persuade AC to hold off on his business, but from the determined look in his friend's eyes, he knew he was wasting his breath.

"I'ma call him over here," AC stated flatly.

Here we go Phatz thought silently as he homed in on the person AC was referring to.

Mookie was a young cat who looked to be in his early twenties, tattoos covered his arms and his braided hair hung pass his shoulders. Phatz could tell by the way he stalked across the yard expecting people to move out of his way- that AC was unlikely to get anything from him, but AC wasn't trying to hear it.

With a loud shout and a wave of his hand AC managed to get Mookie's attention.

"What up?" Mookie asked once he was close enough.

Phatz could see his shiny gold teeth with every movement of his lips. Instead of answering, AC pointed to the fence where Phatz stood.

"Give my fallie that box of cigarettes you owe me!"

Mookie's face scrunched up, his top lip almost touching his nose in an affronted look.

His expression said it all. Still, Phatz stood off to the side waiting for the signal, aware that they were running out of time. He couldn't stop his gaze from straying to the guard in the gun tower. No longer interested in them his eyes were set on the line that was beginning to form outside of the door in preparation for the end of rec. This was the perfect distraction for Phatz to toss AC the weed. He flicked his hand to grab Big D's attention but stopped short when he saw Mookie's posture go rigid at AC's next words.

"You got what you owe?"

Mookie sucked his gold teeth before answering, "Naw."

A loud thud echoed in Phatz mind. It was the sound of the window of opportunity closing shut.

On the other side of the fence AC's cool demeanor began to crack.

Told him to leave it alone Phatz thought.

"I guess you taking that then?" AC asked, anger evident in his voice.

"I guess so," Mookie replied before spinning around.

He stopped short when his hard chest collided with Phatz stiff forearm.

"Hold up," Phatz warned as he blocked Mookies' escape.

He could see the confusion written over his face as Mookie glared down at his arm. For a split second he could see the slither of fear in his eyes, but it was quickly concealed. Upon closer inspection Mookie didn't look to be a day over twenty-one. He was young and seemingly dumb because there was no way that Mookie thought that Phatz was letting him walk off the yard without paying what he owed.

****

The one thing AC hated more than anything was feeling like he was being played. He admitted to himself that he'd broken his own rule when he let Mookie skirt by with excuses. Though Mookie wasn't what he would consider a friend AC did grow to like the dice games and the shit talking that came with being in the cell next to his but in doing so he realized he had given Mookie the wrong impression about him. Mookie thought he could be played with like a toy.

AC gave a head nod to Phatz.

"What's going on?"

The voice came from the left of him, turning AC stared into the face of the big man that was speaking to Big D only seconds ago. His thick eyebrows formed a unibrow as his forehead crinkled. AC hadn't paid much attention to it before but the man beside him and Mookie bore a striking resemblance. Except Mookie was all muscles where this man was nothing but fat.

"That's my brother you fucking with!" he yelled out to Phatz who still had Mookie rooted in place.

"You know them?" he asked Big D.

"That's Phatz and Awful Clyde," Big D responded. He took two steps back as his hands slapped against each other. "These my niggas and if they got a problem with your brother, I got they slack," Big D responded wasting no time letting the man know where he stood.

Angered, Mookie's brother balled up his fist and pounded it hard against his palm. "Nothing better not happen to my baby brother!" he yelled out realizing what was going on.

His words gained the attention of the inmates on the yard, immediately they began to swarm around in anticipation. Out of the corner of his eye AC watched Big D jet across the yard. That was the signal. He was going to get the knife. AC's was tucked in his shoe in his left sock. He was ready.

****

On the other side Phatz was laying down the rules to how things would go. Glancing up from his watch he let his gaze drift over to Mookie.

"They blow the yard in twenty minutes, you got ten minutes to bring me that box or I'ma come find you!"

The seriousness of the situation finally began to hit Mookie as he looked back and forth between his brother's mean mug and Phatz straight face. Without a word he turned and walked away.

Keeping one eye on his departing figure, Phatz tilted his head in AC's direction.

"You good?"

Nodding AC pointed down at his shoe. "I gotta show these niggas everything that look good ain't to be fucked with."

Though Phatz understood the gesture meant that AC had his knife on him he still didn't like the odds that were quickly stacking against his friend. He noticed that at least eight more inmates had joined Mookie's brother. At the same time, he watched as Big D casually strolled across the yard with a smirk on his face. Stopping beside him Big D slid him the knife, Phatz made a show of tucking it in his waist to let them niggas know what they were up against.

"If he don't pay I'm putting it on his ass then I want you to do it to big mouth right there," Phatz said pointing at Mookies' brother and speaking loud enough for the man to hear him.

AC smiled knowingly ready to get the show started.

"Look," Big D said getting his attention. Returning to the yard was Mookie but he wasn't alone. Phatz recognized the man walking beside him immediately. Cash was one of his foot soldiers. Straight out of Shreveport the young man meant business which was why he was on Phatz team, but he wouldn't be for long if he was siding with the enemy.

Folding his arms, he waited patiently for them to reach him.

Cash was the first to speak, "Aye Cali-Phatz I was just telling this nigga that me and you jam." His head dipped towards Mookie, "Told him you were cool as fuck and everything probably just a misunderstanding." Grabbing the carton of cigarettes from Mookie, Cash stretched them towards Phatz like a peace offering.

Staring down at his hand Phatz understood that because of his loyalty to both sides Cash didn't want to see any bloodshed. And neither did Phatz but he had to speak to the disrespect Mookie had shown. Knowing that AC wouldn't like it, Phatz dropped his guarded stance, and directed his attention to Mookie.

"It's not just about the box, it's about the shit that came out of his mouth!"

Underneath Phatz heavy stare Mookie stood his ground.

"Give the box back to him," he told Cash. Sensing there was nothing more that he could do Cash did as requested.

"Let's take a lap."

Without waiting for an answer Phatz started off around the yard, seconds later Mookie joined him.

All eyes were on them as they walked in silence for the first few seconds.

Producing a rolled joint from his pocket he lit it and inhaled slowly. He had rolled it to smoke in honor of Corey's memory. Now seemed like a good time to put it to use. A mellow feeling washed over Phatz as he pulled hard on the joint inhaling some of the smoke and releasing the rest. His eyelids felt heavy as he looked out across the yard. The corn stalks looked as if they were dancing in the field. Chuckling he stretched the blunt towards Mookie who hesitated.

"It's cool," Phatz reassured.

Pinching it between his fingers, Mookie pulled off the joint twice before lapsing into a coughing fit. After getting his breathing under control he laughed.

"This shit good," he said handing the joint back to Phatz. The weed had done the one thing that Cash couldn't: put them at ease. With the tension melted, Phatz stopped halfway through their lap still aware that they were being watched. He looked in Mookie's' brother direction when he spoke,"You know how you feel about your big brother?" he asked offering up the joint again.

Taking it Mookie nodded.

"Well that's the same way I feel about Awful Clyde, that's my brother and I'll do anything for him."

Brushing a braid off his shoulder Mookie parted his lips to speak, thought better of it, then puffed on the joint some more.

I didn't know y'all were the people running the drugs down through here. I didn't mean any disrespect ya heard me," he said once gathering his thoughts.

Pondering his words, Phatz realized that it was possible that Mookie was telling the truth. He didn't go around broadcasting his status because it was the easiest way to get snitched on. Still most inmates knew who was running the show even if they never saw him take the stage.

He cut to AC who stood ready to take off, then back to Mookie who wore a look of genuine regret. After a few seconds Phatz stretched out his fist for Mookie to dap up. The man did so immediately, just as they blew the yard. Mookie tried to give Phatz back the joint.

"Naw you keep it, give that carton of cigarettes to Cash for being a stand-up nigga and you get AC what you owe him ASAP."

Mookie looked relieved as he his head bobbed up and down. "I got you."

It would've been easy for Phatz to stick Mookie up with a knife for his perceived disrespect, but he thought about how the niggas like Spooky Black and Big D had welcomed him in and earned his respect. He was giving Mookie the opportunity to do the same.

With a few parting words Phatz rushed over to AC, explaining everything. Though disappointed that he wouldn't be using his knife today AC cheered up when Phatz slung the weed over the fence.

Slipping it into his pocket AC pat his large fro, "Shit was about to get real." He paused staring Phatz in the eye, "He didn't know it was more to me than just me."

"Well he knows now. I gave him the rules. We playing it like it go."

"Just some mo of it," AC responded naturally before reaching down to readjust the knife in his shoe. The move made Phatz hand go to his own weapon at his waist. He had been so close to using it. With the threat no longer lurking he was able to think clear. Had the knife hit Mookie the wrong way he could've ended the man's life. That meant he would never go home. His eyes briefly shuttered close at the thought. More than his pride was on the line, so was his freedom. He turned to share the revelation with AC weighing his words carefully as he spoke.

"Listen don't go and kill one of these clowns or you'll never get outta here, we gotta get back to Boss Angeles…together." He said hoping his friend understood that they would have to start retaliating smarter.

Gripping the pic in his hand AC thought over the words. "You right, can't get stuck on this river."

"That's right," Phatz responded happy that AC had heard his message. It didn't meant that they would stop punishing niggas, but it did mean they would move more careful from now on .

AC jerked his thumb behind him where the yard was almost cleared out. "I'll catch back up with you tomorrow, thanks for looking out and I already know what to do with this," he said touching his pocket where the weed was.

Spinning to head into the building Phatz stopped mid stride.

"Happy Birthday!" he called out.

Beaming AC gave a slight wave of his hand before jogging away.

As Phatz crossed the yard thoughts of Ty's betrayal returned to his mind. Phatz had meant what he said when he told Mookie that AC was like a brother to him. AC would never replace Marlon, but he was as close as a brother that he would ever have again. He hadn't been able to protect Marlon, or Corey, but he wouldn't fail AC and he wasn't leaving him. He couldn't.

■■■

The soft moaning in his ear almost made him lose control, shifting on the bench Phatz could feel the crotch of his pants straining against his growing erection. When her wet tongue grazed the inside of his ear, he took a deep breath. If they didn't stop now, he wouldn't be able too. Mentally counting to ten in his mind he pulled away immediately missing the heat from her body.

"You good?" she asked a hint of laughter in her voice.

He pecked her on the lips before settling against the bench.

Scanning the crowded visiting room Phatz used those seconds to bring his hormones under control. He hadn't felt that horny since he was a teenager. He shook his head to himself. The things prison could do to a man.

More in control now his eyes raked over her body. Silky was glowing. The burgundy silk dress that stopped just above her knees hugged her in all the right places. Prison had been good to her in the weight department taking her from a skinny girl to a voluptuous woman. The thin material stretched over her plump ass. Her soft round breast felt heavy in his hand when he caressed them. Even now he could see the outline of her hard nipples. He shook his head and inhaled but the sweet-smelling perfume she wore drifted into his nostrils as images of the last time they'd sex came to mind. A guard in the visiting room had warned them once already. Yet Phatz couldn't keep his hands to himself. His hand began to roam up her inner thigh.

Facing her now he watched her full lips stretch into a smile.

"We better stop before our visit gets cut short."

He laughed before removing his hand. Nuzzling her neck, he pulled back to stare at her again. He couldn't get over how good she looked. Silky had visited with him twice under Louisiana's Common Law marriage rule that recognized them as married, but today was different. This would be Silky's last visit as a prisoner of the state. In less than three days she would be a free woman.

"What you got planned?" Phatz asked before biting into a honey bun. The sweet taste filled his mouth and he cringed. Visitation was the only time he allowed himself to indulge in the delicacies. Just last week his mother Kathi and his son DJ had visited and between the three of them they'd eaten almost every item at the snack bar. It had taken him a while to come down from the sugar rush. With that in mind Phatz tossed the cake in the small trash can near them.

"I'm going back to school for hair remember?" Silky responded running a hand down the front of her skirt. The move drew attention to her still hard nipples.

"Yeah, I remember, you want to go school and own a shop right?" he asked snapping out of it.

Silky rewarded his memory with a kiss.

How could he forget? The closer it had gotten to her release date the more she'd spoken of her desire to become a beautician. With her skills Silky had started a nice hustle fixing the female prisoner's hair for a fee. Even her hair was neatly styled with fluffy curls that fell below her chin shaping her pretty face. He listened as she talked about all she would do once free.

"I just don't know where I'ma get the money from," she said with frustration.

Phatz knew Silky was a hustler, but the last thing he wanted to see was her jammed up behind bars again for boosting. It was time for her to turn a new leaf.

"Listen you're smart and you got your whole life ahead of you, this time I want you to stick to the sidewalk leave the streets alone for a while, get in school, get a job."

Silky sighed.

"You're right."

Intertwining her fingers with his, she pulled him closer, lost in their own world they talked and laughed for the remainder of the visit.

You have five minutes until visitation is over.

The voice over the intercom announced. The crowded room grew even busier as visitors scrambled to collect their things and tell their loved one's bye. It was the moment Phatz had been waiting for.

Silky made a move to stand, but Phatz stopped her.

He wrapped his arms around her, his body shielding hers. Pulling her in for a quick kiss he nibbled on her ear.

"Open your legs," he whispered.

He heard the quick intake of breath as Silky's legs parted.

"Wider," he commanded.

He continued to kiss her as his hands snaked up her warm thigh. Still kneading her flesh, he took a quick look around. The place was in chaos kids running everywhere. The correctional officers stood at the front trying to gather everyone.

Returning to his task he could feel Silky's heart thudding against his chest. The look on her face looked as if she was about to climax. Her eyes were squeezed shut; her mouth slightly parted. His fingers brushed against the soft fabric of her panties making her moan.

Silky's leg began to tremble as he slid his hand inside.

"You like that?" he asked in her ear.

He swallowed the moan on her lips.

Visitation is now over.

The voice announced again.

Phatz slid the small bag that was in his hand inside of her panties.

Silky's eyes snapped open as he removed his hand.

He saw the confused look on her face.

"That's $500, gold chains, and weed to help you get on your feet and when you get back call up Billy, he has more for you."

Flinging her arms around his neck Silky embraced him in a tight hug. Hot tears leaked from her eyes onto his face.

He could barely understand her words as she mumbled against his skin.

"Don't cry," he said untangling himself from her. Correctional officer Jenkins started to approach them. Phatz stopped him with a hard stare. Jenkins folded his arms across his chest returning the stare.

"Hurry it up," he said annoyed.

Except for the prisoners the visiting room was almost empty.

"I promise to come back to see you," Silky said as she threw the light jacket around her shoulders.

Phatz gave her one last hug and a firm squeeze to her ass. She wiped at the tears as Jenkins led her away. At the door she turned and smile.

"Thank you" she mouthed.

When she disappeared from his view Phatz reclaimed his seat on the bench. He couldn't let Silky go home empty handed. Not after all they'd been through. Billy would set her straight with a whip, shopping, and more money once she arrived. He only hoped that she followed through in her plan to become a hairstylist. He knew ultimately it would be up to Silky to make that change. A part of him felt like a hypocrite for encouraging her to leave the streets alone especially since it was the one thing that he craved every waking minute. He was on pause for now, but soon enough it would be time to press play on the game, but this time he wouldn't get caught.

****

The cold steel handcuffs pressed into his skin as he made the long walk to the room where the board meeting would be held. Every footstep felt heavy as the chains on his cuffed legs drug behind him.

"Sit here," the guard escorting him instructed when they made it to the door. Seconds later he disappeared behind it. Instead of sitting, AC propped his foot on the edge of the chair. The time to decide his fate had come again. It wasn't his first appearance before the board members and if they didn't free him from the hole this time, it wouldn't be his last. Of course AC had expected to be sent to the hole after knocking Bull out when he caught him stealing from his locker, but what he didn't expect was for Bull and the guards to pin a weapon on him. What was supposed to be only a three month stay in solitary had turned into eight long months. Today would be his second time going before the board and unless he confessed to the knife like they wanted him to, he would be tossed back in the dungeon.

To AC the trip was a waste of time because he wasn't admitting to anything he didn't do. Sitting down he drummed his fingers on his leg, ready to get it over with.

"Alright, come on," the guard stated opening the door.

With his eyes fixed straight ahead AC moved down the narrow aisle as quick as his chained feet would allow him.

When the guard behind him tapped him on his shoulder halting him in his steps he took the time to survey his surroundings. The row of tan metal chairs to each side of him were empty. White concrete walls lined with gray paint gave the room a sterile feeling. His first time inside AC remembered feeling like a kid at the doctor's office waiting anxiously for the nurse to come stick a needle in his arm. Back then he dreaded the shots and would give chase until he was captured by either his grandmother's firm grip or someone else. But now closed behind four walls, shackled at the wrist and ankles, there was nowhere to run. And at the end of this visit there would be no lollipops or stickers to ease his pain. His eyes fixed on the four faces sitting at the table they were the same ones that were keeping him from reentering the general population.

The guard motioned for him to approach.

"State your name and booking number?" a gruff voiced asked.

Quickly he rattled off his information.

"You may be seated."

Schooling his face, he lowered himself into the metal chair in front of the table. This shouldn't take long he thought to himself. His vision strayed to the rays of sunlight shining through the only window in the room.

"Mr. Scott you are here today for your annual review, correct?" the white major in the middle asked.

AC's response was cut short by a voice at the far end of the table.

"Scott?"

For the first time he realized that there was a different Black man at the table than last time.

The Black man rubbed his eyes before placing his glasses on his face. He leaned back in shock "Well I'll be…"

A door closed somewhere in the distance as AC looked in the man's smooth brown face. His graying hair was beginning to recede at the hairline. Behind the glasses his eyes were sharp and his face held the same smug expression it had when he met him in 85'. It was a face he could never forget. Still he pretended to not remember.

"You know me?" asked AC.

The lieutenant leaned back in the chair in disbelief.

"I'm Lieutenant Bill, we met when you first got here."

Turning to the man beside him Lieutenant Bill let out a short laugh. Removing his glasses again he scrubbed a hand down his face, "Remember the kid I told you about that jumped across the table on me and knocked me out of the chair."

Dropping the act, AC sat up straight, "You asked me if I was a hoe. You don't ask no man nothing like that," he said cutting in. "Just cause I'm handsome don't mean I can be fucked with." A tinge of anger began to swell up in him as he thought back to the encounter.

"So you do remember," Lieutenant Bill smirked.

Shrugging AC ignored the comment wishing that they would get things moving. As if reading his mind, the white major at the table spoke up, "In all fairness it's a routine question that we ask everyone." He cleared his throat before speaking again, "Let's get things started."

Immediately AC noticed that Lieutenant Bill was reading his file.

Lieutenant Bill glanced up at him, "I see you've been busy man your file is full of write ups that date all the way back to your first day here." He shuffled through the papers shaking his head as he went.

AC rotated his neck; he was growing stiff sitting in the chair. "You were the one who sent me to the cell blocks," he said stubbornly.

That first day set the pattern for how AC would spend most of his time at Angola. Punishing anyone who dared disrespect him. He had no regrets.

When Lieutenant Bill spoke again it was with deep remorse in his voice. He clasped his hands in front of him.

"Believe it or not I was doing my job, that was three years ago and all I could see was a young kid that didn't know what he had gotten himself into."

AC scoffed. He had heard that before.

The lieutenant gazed back at the open file in front of him.

"Based on what I see you've been holding up for yourself."

Pretty damn well too," he added.

The remaining board members looked on with interest. They had given up handling the case. It was obvious it was personal to Lieutenant Bill.

Closing the file, the lieutenant sighed. His head hung low for a few seconds. Raising it, he stared AC in his eyes. "Whoever accused you of having a knife to get you sent to Camp J is lying."

Shocked, AC rubbed his ears thinking he had heard wrong.

"I can tell that knife wasn't yours, someone set you up."

Never in his twenty years did AC think he would ever agree to anything the prison staff said. But here he was agreeing to the very words that left the Lieutenants mouth.

A stretch of silence passed. AC was still trying to digest what he heard. Silently he questioned if the laws were truly on his side now? Or was it a set up?

No matter how much the lieutenant agreed with him he could never forget that they were on two separate sides. Glancing down, the shackles on his hand served as a reality check.

The sound of the door closing behind him jolted him out of his thoughts.

"Mr. Scott, I know it's been a long ride for you, but you're almost done. I have to admit that I am pretty impressed with how a young man like yourself managed to survive around the wolves."

Motioning to his board members he said, "My colleagues can tell you that we don't see that very often a lot of young men like you that come in don't survive."

The men at the table all nodded in agreement.

With a stiff spine AC spoke up "I'm different." He could have told them how his whole life had been about survival, instead he had showed them.

"I can't argue with that," Lieutenant Bill said to AC's response. He tapped the folder "This file tells me the exact same thing. Now since I'm responsible for all of this I am going to try to fix it." He paused to sip from the glass of water on the table. Wiping at the corners of his mouth he continued, "You made it this far and I wanna make sure you continue to do so. I will be calling for a dismissal of those weapon charges against you."

Removing a pen from the pocket of his shirt he quickly jotted something down in the file.

"In the meantime, tell me where you want to go?" he asked as he continued to write in the file.

AC couldn't believe his luck. He had resigned himself to being locked away until the end of his sentence and now he was being released by the same person who had started it all. The irony of it made him shake his head.

"Home," AC answered sarcastically.

Lieutenant. Bill looked up from his notes and laughed "Well that's coming but I'm talking about in Angola, where would you like to serve out the remainder of your sentence?"

AC pondered the question the lieutenant asked him. While he was half joking about his home response the other half of him was serious, but he knew that was impossible. He had caught one break already that day he wouldn't push his luck. Until he could reach L.A., he would settle for the next best thing.

****

"Freeman!Freeman!"

The man's shrill cry bounced off the walls of the shark one left tier located inside of Camp J as members of his crew banged on the doors of their cells in hopes of fending off the brutal attack that was playing out in front of their eyes, but it was too late. Fear slowly began to creep in as they witnessed in shock, the take down of their infamous leader.

"I see you not so bad now," Phatz gritted out driving the ice pick into the inmate who went by Ape Man muscled forearm causing another round of cries to rush from his mouth.

A strangled sob tore from his throat. "Please," he pleaded, but his pleas fell on deaf ears as Phatz plunged the weapon deeper into Ape Man's black skin.

The sight of blood oozing down his victims arm slowly like water brought a satisfying grin across his face. He would show no mercy because Ape Man had planned to do much worse to him. From day one his presence had not been welcomed on shark tier one left: the home of the most disgraced, uncivilized inmates at Angola. It was AC who had warned Phatz about the animals locked up in Camp J. Hard headed he'd dismissed the warning figuring he would never see the place, but one incident with Officer Jenkins changed all of that. When Jenkins cornered him outside of the dorm and threatened to expose his drug operation if he didn't give up half the money on every deal made, Phatz had snapped. He wasn't upset that someone had once again ratted him out, he was fuming because Jenkins of all people thought that he could take his hard-earned money from him. The money he risked his freedom for almost every day. With no hesitation Phatz had beat the man into a bloody pulp a move that hadn't gone over well with Captain Perks. While he didn't regret his actions, he hated the fact that he had played right into their hands and gotten kicked from down the walk landing himself in a new hell. Now here he was two weeks into his year sentence punishing a fool.

"Don't call for them now bitch ass nigga they can't help you," Phatz breathed out drawing more blood with the icepick. As Ape Man squirmed to get out of his firm grasp, Phatz thought back to how it all started. Now AC had told him all about the shit slinging crew on shark tier one left who hoarded shit and piss in milk boxes and slung it at the CO's and inmates as they returned back to their cells, so he was already on high alert when he arrived. He hadn't been in his cell a good thirty minutes when he heard the scratchy voice

"Who that in cell nine?"

The voice sounded like it was coming from the cell beside him. Leaning forward on his small metal bed Phatz tilted his head to the side.

"Raphael," he answered deciding to give an alias just in case it was one of many enemies he'd made at the prison.

"You a hoe?"

The question made him jump to his feet. just as he parted his lips to release his wrath the CO's were returning to escort him to the shower. Without a word, Phatz grabbed his things and followed.

Fifteen minutes after his shower and phone call he stood on the tier in front of the big mouth nigga's cell ready to breathe on him. Black and ugly the man smiled revealing his yellow teeth.

Getting to it, Phatz took a step forward, "Do I look like a hoe?"

His smile waned a bit as he spoke, "My bad dawg I thought you was somebody else. What you said ya name was again?"

"Raphael."

Ducking his head, he chuckled under his breath.

"I'm Ape Man."

The name fit him well Phatz thought to himself as he listened to Ape Man continue to talk, but something felt off. Maybe it was the way Ape Man kept laughing to himself like there was an inside joke being told. Listening to him shout down the other inmates with threats and name calling Phatz peeped how no one responded, realizing that the man was showing off his power.

"Nigga you big do you work out?"

Phatz nodded once.

Disappearing for a few seconds Ape Man returned with a stack of books held together by a leather belt.

"I do too. I use these heavy ass law books," he said before launching into a set of arm curls.

Phatz listened to him talk until it was time for him to be locked in for the next twenty-three hours again.

"Tomorrow when I come out for my shower, Ima show you a cold ass routine with those law books."

Ape Man lit up. For the next two weeks after his shower and phone call they worked out with the law books. Little by little Phatz began to feed him information. Like where he was from, how he had codefendants. Small shit to make him think they were friends, but he could tell that as ugly and stupid as he was Ape Man was playing the same game. Despite his friendly attitude, Phatz could see through the ugly mask he wore, that he couldn't be trusted. Even more importantly though he couldn't let him off the hook for calling him a hoe.

One night when darkness had washed over the tier. Phatz lay wide awake going over the phone call he'd had with Silky earlier in his head, when Ape Man's laugh made him sit up. Going with his instincts Phatz had pretended to be asleep when the man called out to him twice that night. The move turned out to be a smart one. Creeping to the door of his cell he listened as Ape Man spoke with the prisoner next to him. Together they plotted to throw shit and piss on Phatz when he went out for his next shower. Ape Man's mask had finally come off! Biting down on his bottom lip Phatz forced himself to continue listening, growing furious at the thought of feces touching his body. Ape Man laughed as he called Phatz another hoe and made fun of his California accent. Phatz took it all in and when the tier grew silent and he heard Ape Man's loud snores he began to form a plan of his own.

Phatz plans lined up like clockwork the next day. First, he had finally received his property, including the ice pick that he had glued in between his slippers. He would need that to set it off. Secondly to throw Ape Man off Phatz had slid him a pack of the butter scotch candy he loved so much before he headed to the shower. When he made it back to his cell unscathed of piss and shit, he knew that his plan was working. Ripping open his slipper he removed the ice pick tucking it in his waist before pulling his shirt down.

"You ready?" he asked as he stepped out on the tier.

"Hell yeah," Ape Man responded. Like usual Phatz went first with the workout routine. Sliding his arm through Ape Man's cell slot, at the feel of the two heavy law books being placed in his hand Phatz launched into his arm curl, half listening to Ape Man's chatter. Forcing himself not to rush through the routine Phatz concentrated on his breathing.

"Alright man I'm done he said after four reps, pretending to be exhausted."

"That wasn't shit," Ape Man teased.

Pushing the books towards Phatz, he slid his hand out the slot in anticipation of his turn.

"Let me show you how this shits done, come on nigga," he urged.

"Aight, you gotta slide your arm out some more," Phatz instructed, maneuvering the icepick from his waist. Feeling someone watching him he glanced up, a few cells down his eyes connected with an inmate by the name of Foster watching his every move.

Fuck he thought to himself hoping the man wouldn't call out a warning to Ape Man.

On second thought Phatz tucked his weapon. He had to pace himself. Placing the law books in Ape Man's hand he watched him lift the books up and down.

After a few minutes he could hear him began to breathe heavy.

"Ok, rest a minute then we'll switch to the other arm. Oh let me use that radio y'all be listening to," Phatz requested.

Without hesitation Ape Man called out, "Lil Tee, let him get the radio!"

Walking to Lil Tee's cell Phatz retrieved the radio and dropped it off in his cell on the way back.

"This time when you stick your arm out make sure your elbow is out too so you can get the full effects," Phatz coached when he stood in front of the cell again.

When Ape Man's arm extended far enough for his liking Phatz removed the ice pick.

"My other arm already feels that shit," Ape Man commented.

You about to feel something else.

Grabbing Ape Man's wrist firmly, with one hand Phatz raised the law book as if he was about to place it in his hand. "On the count of three."

"1..."

His eyes went to Foster who was still watching.

"2..."

He carefully lowered the law book to the ground.

"3..."

With all his strength Phatz slammed Ape Man's outstretched arm against the tray slot. The painful sound that left his mouth was quickly followed by screams as Phatz began sticking him with the ice pick.

The cries brought him back to the present. Minutes had passed since he had launched his assault and Ape Man was still hollering.

"Don't holla now nigga play it like it go clean up this blood like y'all wanted me to clean up that shit."

Every time Phatz thought about the gruesome plot he'd overheard he stuck him.

"They can't help you now lil bitch," Phatz taunted. His chest heaved up and down. Sweat covered his brow as he tried to keep his grip from slipping. But the slick blood was making it nearly impossible. Striking out Phatz felt the sharp end of the ice pick collide with bone as he stuck him in the elbow.

"Freeman!" Ape Man choked out in a guttural voice. This time It was enough to alert the correctional officers of his distress. Phatz could hear them assembling at the front door but he knew they wouldn't come to the stairs unless he was inside of his cell.

"Lock it down!" the CO shouted through a megaphone.

Phatz head swiveled back and forth down the tier. Faces were pressed against the bars of the cell watching.

Finally releasing Ape Mans arm he stood and wiped the blood on his pants. Stepping back, he admired his handy work. From the awkward angle Ape Mans arm hung, he could tell it was broken. The deep gashes made by the ice pick revealed the tissue of his skin.

He wouldn't be throwing shit on anyone for a long time. Looking down Phatz stared at his blood-stained hands.

Frantically he searched for a way to get rid of the weapon. In all his plotting it was the one detail he hadn't figure out in his plan.

A light whistle got his attention. Whipping his head around in the direction it had come from he stared at Foster who pointed to the ice pick in Phatz hand. Blood dripped from it as he gripped the handle of it.

Give it here he mouthed.

In one fluid motion Phatz slid the weapon across the concrete floor under the door of the cell. He saw long fingers reach to pull it further inside. Seconds later he heard a flushing sound and Fosters smiling face appeared in the door. Outnumbered by the New Orleans niggas on the tier Foster had been in a shit fight daily.

With the evidence gone Phatz knew that the only thing they could do was extend his sentence at Camp J.

"Bradley get to your cell!"

Following instructions Phatz made his way inside of his cell, but there was one last thing he had to do.

Grabbing the small portable radio off his bed he walked out on the tier, not stopping until he reached Lil Tee's cell.

Without a second thought Phatz slammed the radio into the wall, pieces scattered everywhere before landing on the floor. Picking the remaining parts up he slung it into Lil Tee's cell.

He stabbed at the air with his finger as he spoke, "If I ever catch you lil coward ass niggas in population I'ma bring it to you hard so have it on your mind."

The pounding began again. Ape Man's posse yelled threats at him from behind the door, but Phatz knew that it was all they were. Threats. The cowards were nothing without their leader and they would never leave Camp J in fear of him and others making good on their words.

Returning to his cell he grabbed his property that was still in the bag.

"You ready to go Bradley?" Three CO'S stood outside on the tier dressed in riot gear. Shrugging a shoulder Phatz grabbed his bag and let them handcuff him. By the time he was ready to be transported Ape Man had been taken to medical. Phatz caught sight of the pool of blood in passing. Averting his gaze, he looked straight ahead but the CO had already caught him. "Looks like you got Ape Man pretty good, that's a lot of blood," one commented as they escorted him off the tier.

Remaining mute he kept looking forward. They were halfway down the stairs when Phatz heard the unapologetic voice of the CO on his left.

"About damn time."

****

Down the Walk in Pine 2 dorm, the inmates were swarming with an excitement that could be felt all over the prison. The noise level reached heights the CO's had never heard before as they struggled to gain order over the rowdy bunch. For months, this day was anticipated among the prisoners but even the CO's who tried to hide their excitement behind steely glares were having a hard time doing their jobs. There was never any true happiness behind the concrete walls that caged them in shutting them off from their loved ones and the rest of the world, but today was special. The rodeo was in town. For prisoners who participated it separated the boys from men, for those who watched it provided an opportunity for them to pocket a little money through the bets they held. Everyone took a part in the day in some form. Well almost everyone.

Laying on his bed AC tried hard to block out the noise. The more he tried the worst it became until he gave up all together. Sitting up straight he removed the headphones to his cassette player that was blaring Eric B and Rakim's hit song *Paid in Full*. Pressing the stop button, he quickly wrapped the cassette player up and stored it away in his locker. His eyes settled on the inmate in front of him dressed in a spotted black and white cowhide suit with cowboy boots. It was AC's first time ever seeing something so ridiculous up close. He'd had a lot of first since making it Down the Walk, the place he'd requested Lieutenant Bill to send him.

It was the first time he had been housed in a dorm with dozens of men instead of the solitude of the hole. It was different, and he couldn't decide if he liked it or not. In that exact moment he leaned more towards extreme dislike. Still, AC had managed to adjust to his new living quarters as best as he could. The prison was always doing something to keep the inmates entertained, just a few months ago in February, they'd celebrated what was called Mardi Gras. Being from a big city like Los Angeles, AC was familiar with the holiday, but never did he experience it on the level that he had while in Angola. AC mentally recalled how pounds of cooked sea food had covered the tables in the chow hall. Steam rose from the big pots of gumbo. He'd taken one bite of the jambalaya on his plate and closed his eyes as his taste buds exploded with euphoria. When his stomach was full of king cake and crab meat, he moved to the day room where more festivals were being held. He'd sat on the edge of his seat mesmerized at the performance occurring. The prisoner's usual blue jeans and denim shirts had been traded for colorful purple, yellow, and green costumes that resembled Indian clothes. The floor in front of the makeshift stage had been turned into a battle ground and for the first time it didn't end in blood shed. Members of the Disco Jazz and Rolling 12's went head up in a fierce dance off displaying some of the most intricate foot work known to man. AC watched a Rolling 12 shuffle his feet as if he were dancing on hot coal. Spinning around on the heels of his shoes he leaned forward before dipping back never once losing his balance or missing the beat. Soon a Disco Jazz strutted up waving a white handkerchief in his hand. It wasn't long before the two were sliding across the floor as if their bodies were possessed by the music. On more than one occasion AC had caught himself nodding his head to the upbeat tempo the band played on stage as the groups battled. He resisted the urge to snap his fingers when the trumpet player got on one knee and blew air into the instrument. His fingers glided over the keys belting out smooth notes. In the back the persistent tapping on the snare drums added edge to the jazzy sound. When AC questioned the performance, he learned that it was called second line. It was a tradition that the Louisiana natives took pride in. He walked away impressed with Louisiana for the first time that day.

The rodeo was an entirely different story. AC couldn't believe that the inmates were willing to risk their lives riding a bull for one hundred dollars. It was play money to him. Tired of the antics going on in the dorm he drifted over to Walnut 4, where Chunky was knee deep in a dice game. The two had become close friends thanks to Phatz. Chunky being from Cali was a plus.

"You want in on this or you tryna be a cowboy?" Chunky joked.

AC shook his head. His eyes scanned the dorm for Phatz, but all he saw were more inmates dressed in boots and hats.

"Where Phatz?" AC asked as Chunky pushed up from the floor as the game ended.

"He had to make a call," he stated as he strolled over to his bed where he peeled off a few dollars before carefully stuffing the rest of his money in his pocket. Chunky motioned to AC

"You gotta get in on this bull riding shit that's where all the money at today."

"Is that right?" AC responded. He himself, would never ride a bull for chump change but on the other hand that didn't mean he couldn't place a bet and benefit from someone else's ignorance.

****

"You gotta talk to your boy, he fucking up," the words spoken in anger made Phatz frown as he stared at the man that was blocking his path back to the dorm. He only recognized him because he was one of his frequent customers. An accused killer with a nasty coke habit, usually laid back, it appeared as if someone had rattled him. He paced in front of Phatz.

"He tripping if he think I'ma let him get away with that weak shit," he huffed out. Around them the hall bustled with inmates, but the man seemed oblivious to it as he talked to himself in a low voice. His strange behavior made Phatz wonder if he was high off a line.

"Ima fuck that nigga up!" he declared with a wild look in his eyes.

Phatz was still puzzled as to who he was speaking on. Admittedly he was distracted by the phone call he'd just abruptly ended. Even now her words echoed in his head.

Silky gone do what Silky wanna do.

It had been over six months since her release. The last time they'd spoken ended on such a high note, with her telling him she was in school that Phatz hadn't expected the sudden change of attitude when he phoned this time and asked about her progress. Her sharp words were all he needed to hear before hanging up. It was the reason he was on edge and the coke head pacing in front of him wasn't making it any better.

"What's up man, who you talking about?" Phatz asked no longer in the mood for craziness.

His head snapped up; glossy eyes fixed on him.

"That bitch ass CO Brian shaking ever body down, nigga took my shit."

Brian?

Phatz shook his head as if he were hearing him wrong. He had to be because Brian was everyone's favorite CO. The man's face was the first that he had seen after his year long stint in Camp J. Though they had tried to extend it after his attack on Ape Man, with no weapon it became Ape Mans words vs. his own and just like that the case was dismissed! Meanwhile back on shark one left tier Phatz had earned a few more stripes after taking the notorious shit thrower down. Now he was back Down the Walk with AC and Chunky and things were going smooth, at least he thought.

"What you don't believe me?" the dope head asked incredulously.

And why would I? Phatz thought to himself.

The man took two steps backwards as if reading his thoughts.

"Follow me." Without another word he spun on his heels and swiftly walked down the hall. When he made it to end of the hall, he beckoned for Phatz.

Phatz wanted to turn the other way because he had a lot on his mind. Something else was troubling him, but curiosity got the best of him and he found himself covering the short distance to where the dopehead stood.

"What the fuck!" he yelled at the sight in front him.

"Told you his ass was tripping."

In the hall three inmates were being patted down by Brian. Phatz watched Brian shove one out of the way once he finished his search.

Rubbing his temple with his forefinger Phatz tried to calm down. This wasn't like Brian. Quickly, he tried to recall if Brian had mentioned anything bothering him that week. The two talked about everything. Their latest topic: money. Lately, the man had been down on his luck, often coming to work hungry and broke. Phatz gave him the combination to his locker where he kept his food. He couldn't have his workers going hungry and after that everything seemed fine, but it obviously wasn't.

"Get out of my sight!" Brian yelled as he shoved the last inmate away pocketing whatever he had found during his search.

He exhaled deeply. He couldn't let it down go like this. Brian was the best help that he had.

Approaching him from behind Phatz tapped him on the shoulder.

"Get back inmate!" Brian yelled his hand flying to the can of pepper spray on his side.

Phatz tossed his hands up. "Relax, its me."

His words did nothing to calm the man.

"What you want?" he asked in a hard voice.

Stunned Phatz swiveled his head back and forth to make sure it was him who Brian was talking to. Except for the dopehead that stood at the end of the hall they were alone.

Closing off the remaining space between them he got in his face,"We need to talk."

Brian scoffed. "I'm at work I—"

Phatz cut him off, "I'm the reason you made it to work this morning," he stated knowing that it would remind Brian of the money he'd given him to get back and forth to work. The men that he was carpooling with had started complaining about Brian not pitching in on gas enough. Phatz had taken care of it, throwing him a few extra dollars. That was just the other day.

Brian jutted his chin out and crossed his arms. It was obvious his friend was power tripping. After a few seconds Brian dropped his brave front.

"We can't talk now we gotta do this later," he tried to move pass him, but Phatz grabbed his arm.

"Naw, it's now or never," he said pointedly hoping that Brian would get his meaning.

The walkie talkie crackled on his hip. Turning the volume down Brian threw his hands up in the air and moved closer towards the wall.

"Ok what's up?"

Moving him out of the sight of the dope head Phatz folded his arm across his chest pinning him with a stare.

"You tell me?"

Brian shrugged, "I'm just doing my job."

Bullshit.

"You haven't been doing your job," Phatz responded. Suddenly there was a loud sound. It was the signal for the rodeo to begin. Then came the feet of the inmates stomping down the hall out onto the yard. When the noise died down, he turned his attention back to Brian. It was obvious the man was having a bad day but roughing up the inmates wasn't the way to go. Phatz had to wake his game up because Brian was playing with his own life.

"Listen don't get caught up in all this job training."

Brian opened his mouth to interrupt but he cut him off "When they hired you, they didn't tell you to be disrespectful because you having a bad day."

A frown creased Brians' face and he pretended to be occupied with his badge but Phatz didn't let up.

"We have bad days in prison as well in fact every day is a bad day."

It was true. No matter how much money Phatz made, it didn't take away from the fact that he was still fighting to survive in a place where a person's life wasn't valued. Every day he opened his eyes he was blessed, but it also meant that it was another day that he had to fight.

He seemed to have Brian's attention now, the man was no longer fumbling with his badge. Phatz could hear the cheers from the crowd at the rodeo. He briefly wondered if AC and Chunky were in attendance. Turning his thoughts back to the situation in front of him he placed a hand on Brian's shoulder and leveled him with a stare.

"Most of these prisoners have life, that means they gone die here and be planted on Point Look out. Do you think they give a fuck about you going home safe to your family when they can't leave?"

He waited for Brian's response when he didn't get one he continued, "We determine if you go home every day, not the Captain, you have everything to lose but we already lost."

The words must have struck a chord in Brian because suddenly he dropped his head.

"Don't use your authority to fuck over these inmates, just do your eight hours and go home, stop the bullshit."

With a heavy sigh Brian raised his head, "You right Phatz I'm tripping."

He wiped at the moisture underneath his eyes.

"My bad man."

The two shook hands.

Stepping back into the middle of the hall Phatz saw the dopehead still rooted in the same spot.

"Give him his shit back."

Brian laughed before reaching into his pocket.

The dopehead mumbled something as Phatz passed by but he paid no attention. He was lost in his own thoughts. The game that he'd just given Brian had potentially saved his life. Phatz hoped that he took heed to it because he wouldn't be able to get him on the right track if he fucked up again. An unsettling feeling roiled through his body. Instead of going through the double doors that would lead to the yard Phatz moved towards the dorm. He was half relieved to see neither Chunky nor AC there when he entered. Grabbing a change of clothes, he headed for the shower. He needed time to think. There had been a heavy weight on him since he'd found out the news. While Silky's call had put him in a foul mood the truth was that he had been on edge way before then. Though it was out of his control Phatz was about to do the one thing that he'd swore to never do: leave AC behind in Angola.

****

He'd won. AC couldn't believe his luck. He let out the breath he didn't realize he had been holding as he stared over into the arena. A few rodeo workers rushed to the side of the prisoner now lying flat on the ground as the other men struggled to lead the raging bull back into his cage. The dust that the bull and rider struck up during the contest still lingered in the air. Loud applause and cheering erupted from the stands when the prisoner stood and began to limp away from the arena. The man had held on as long as he could on the back of the bull before being bucked off. AC had bet on the prisoner on a whim, thinking that if he didn't win at least he would get some good entertainment, but he was wrong. He did win and it was enough to make him stick around to bet on a few more prisoners. In the end he'd walked away with more money than he started with. Who knew that bull riding was an extreme sport in Louisiana? Though he shouldn't have been surprised. Louisiana seemed to have its own culture separate from the rest of the world. AC had experienced most of it from the food to the unspoken codes behind the walls. He knew that he and Phatz had the odds stacked against them the moment they were sentenced to Angola, but they were hustlers from some of the worst parts of LA and in the end they'd survived, now this chapter of their lives was almost over. Under the new Good Time Law, they could exchange their earned wages for a reduced sentence cutting down their original seven years to three. The countdown was on; the two were finally going home. AC couldn't contain his excitement when he learned the news, even after discovering that he would be released thirty days after Phatz. It was Phatz who seemed to be bothered by their short separation. AC on the other hand was just glad that he had a release date. It didn't change his routine behind the walls. He and Phatz had spent the last eight months together Down the Walk and it was almost like being back in L.A. Together they watched each other backs while hustling. Now freedom was on the horizon.

****

"What up Phatz you going to the rodeo?"

Phatz reached for the handle of the shower turning off the water. Grabbing his towel, he pat his face dry before responding to the voice. It was Black Gal formerly known as Marvin.

"That country shit don't excite me."

Black Gal laughed, "Oh yeah you from the big city."

Gathering his clothes Phatz wrapped the towel around his wet boxers. The shower had done him some good and cleared his head. He wasn't even angry at Silky anymore. He'd learned long ago that people rarely ever talked the talked and he couldn't blame her. Hustling was all she knew, just like him.

He was almost out the shower when Black Gal called out to him, "You got any more of that last batch of weed?"

He shook his head. Black Gal had been one of Ty's loyal customers when he was around in fact all the hoes loved Ty. Phatz and Big D would often joke about it, but he knew that Ty would never trade his manhood. To Phatz it didn't matter who the weed was going to because all money was green so when Ty left the hoes started seeking him out for the product. As long as they didn't disrespect him things were good.

"Check back with me next week," he tossed over his shoulder before walking out.

On his way he passed one of Big D's friend who was heading into the shower the two exchanged head nods. Big D who had been shipped to a lower level prison had sent word to Phatz that he had his photo album in his possessions. When he was released Phatz would make sure to send Big D his address so that he can have the pictures. He needed the memories to help him remember all that he had overcome and why he would never make the same mistakes again.

Dressed and finally ready to join AC and Chunky on the yard. He noticed Brian was sleeping at the table. His loud snores vibrated through the room. The talk he'd had with him earlier calmed him down and he was back to doing what he did best. Turning a blind eye and not giving a fuck about his underpaid job. Phatz was nearing the door when he heard commotion near the custodian closet.

Two men he recognized from his dorm were gathered around a table.

"Let us through," a voice said from behind him.

Turning his head Phatz saw a horrified Black Gal being led towards the two men. From their sinister expressions something really bad was about to happen. Phatz wanted to move but it felt like his feet were glued in place.

"Hoe you disrespect this man even when I told you that dick you got don't work no more!" The words came from Black Gals lover Hank.

Wide eyed Black gal looked back and forth from Hank to the man accusing him named Bo.

"No, I didn't do nothing." There was light tremor in his voice as he spoke.

Bo shook his head before slamming his hand down on the table "When I came in the shower you had yo dick out and was facing me that's disrespectful to a real man."

Wide eyed Black Gal turned to Hank pleadingly. A tear rushed from his eye, "Baby I didn't di-"

Whipping out his knife Bo pointed it at Black Gal who was openly crying, "So what you tryna say hoe I'm lying?"

Black Gals shoulder shook as sobs raked his body. Hank had pulled out his knife as well.

Phatz blinked hard. Leave his mind told him. But his feet wouldn't move. In Angola, the hoes had a different set of rules to live by. They had to piss sitting down and leave or turn their backs when other men where in the shower. A rule that Black Gal was now being punished for breaking.

Slap.

The sound of Hank's hand connecting with Black Gal's face echoed down the hall. Black Gal grabbed the side of his face that had been struck as more tears poured from his eyes.

"I'm sorry," he sobbed out.

"I bet you is hoe."

Removing his boot Hank grabbed Black Gal by the neck. "Put yo dick on the table hoe."

Black Gal tried to ring himself free only angering Hank more.

"Hoe if you move again I'll stab yo ass, now I said put yo dick on the table."

He handed his boot to Bo who stared down at it confused.

"I-"

"Naw he disrespected you so you gotta teach him a lesson, whip his dick," Hank said cutting him off.

At the sound of Black Gals pants unzipping Phatz finally pried himself from the spot and turned to leave.

He was only a few inches away when he heard the loud sound of a boot coming down hard on the table followed by Black Gals agonizing screams.

He squeezed his eyes shut wishing he could block it out. The further he walked the louder the screams became. Bang! Bang! Bang! The boot slammed down on the table. By the time Phatz reached the doors to the rec yard there was silence. He reasoned Black Gal had lost conscious. A feeling of anxiousness built up inside of him. He was ready to leave Angola. He knew he would be able to put some things behind him but other things like Black Gals' loud screams would remain with him long after he walked out the gates.

****

The next day Chunky, AC, and Phatz stood on the side line enjoying the last of the festivals together. It was the championship football game between the prisoners down the walk and the prisoners in the camp. Angola's field looked completely transformed. A section of the yard had been marked off to look like a real football turf. White lines covered the surface, stretching from one side to the other. Two goal posts were placed at the end zone. There were even referees dressed in the signature black and white uniforms with shiny whistles dangling from their necks. Even the players' uniforms looked real. The bronco's players dressed in orange and blue ran exercise drills before the big game. The reigning champs, the bulls dressed in black and red uniforms were huddled at the other end going over plays.

A ref blew the whistle signaling the beginning of the game as the teams faced off on the field.

The bulls would get possession of the ball first.

The acting quarterback signaled down' set' hut' before the ball was tossed in his hands. Scrambling to tackle him a bronco's player plowed forward just as he sent the leather football sailing through the air. On cue the wide receiver stretched his arm forward catching it. First down bulls the announcer yelled in the mic from the sideline as the wide receiver was tackled to the ground.

When half time rolled around the bulls were leading by ten points.

"What I tell you," Chunky smirked knowingly in AC's direction. AC had betted against the bulls despite Chunky's advice.

Seeing the score did little to ease the tension in his body. The bulls were playing one hell of a game but so was the broncos defense line. Wiping his sweaty palms on the front of his jean shorts AC noticed the dryness in his throat. No doubt caused by the loud yelling he was doing from the sidelines. He was beginning to feel like he was the coach. Beside him Chunky and Phatz were having a heated discussion about the game. Slipping away to the refreshment tent AC chugged down a cup of water enjoying the nice shade the tent provided. While the players were trying to rip each other apart on the field, the game had created a relaxed environment at the prison. He'd never seen Angola like this before. Guards freely fraternized with the inmates telling jokes and exchanging stories. A few tossed a football back and forth while others turned a blind eye to the excess smoking and drinking that was going on.

The game had resumed with the bulls still leading. Deciding to enjoy the rest of it from underneath the tent he was refilling his cup when a glimpse of a familiar face caught his attention. Booman's large profile was hard to miss. He joked with a few prisoners across the yard. AC wondered when he made it back down the walk. More importantly if Phatz knew.

Booman had managed to sneak off the walk without paying them the money he owed after allowing the man to borrow an eighth of cocaine on word alone. AC had told Phatz not to trust him. He got a bad feeling when Booman came around. Abandoning his spot under the tent he walked over to Phatz

"I want you to look over my shoulder and tell me who you see," he said to him.

"Anybody in particular?" Phatz asked as he searched the crowd.

"Booman," Chunky spoke the name venomously spotting him first.

Pressing his lips together AC nodded.

"Oh yeah I see that snake ass nigga, when did he get back down here?" Phatz asked when he finally located their target in the crowd.

"Shit that's what I want to know," AC said turning around.

Watching Booman slither around like he didn't have a care in the world angered him. If Booman thought he could get away with stealing from them he had another thing coming. Apparently Phatz and Chunky had the same idea. AC considered waiting until the game was over since the broncos were closing the small lead the bulls had over them.

His eyes darted to Chunky, who lifted a thick eyebrow.

"I'm down."

"Let's ride!" Phatz responded.

Chunky shook his head "Don't worry bout it—"

Phatz stopped him, "The fuck you mean don't worry about it? You already know how I get down Chunky this game shit going on don't mean nothing too me."

AC understood Phatz anger, but he was too close to going home. He and Chunky could handle Booman, Phatz would have to sit this one out. Expressing his concern, he watched Phatz think it over.

On the field the crowd booed. The ref had just thrown a flag on the play completed by the bulls.

"Ok y'all handle it," Phatz said a little resigned.

"Good," AC said putting the plan in motion. During half time the three of them moved towards Booman stopping only a few feet away.

Too busy running his mouth Booman wasn't aware of the deep shit he was in.

Fear jumped in his eyes when he turned to find them standing behind him.

Relaxing his face into a smile AC tossed his hand around Booman quivering shoulders. Not wanting to alert the guards around them. "It's good to see you."

Booman blinked fast "Uh yeah man y-you know," he stuttered.

"Look," stopping to gather his words his head swung back and forth between Chunky and Phatz "I- I -was gone pay you back but when they kicked me out they took all my shit you know man."

Pretending to understand AC eased away from him. "That's too bad man don't you hate that shit."

Rubbing the back of his neck Booman laughed nervously. "Yeah I hate that shit."

"You know what don't even worry about it."

AC watched the relieved expression wash over his face.

Booman let out a long breath. "Really?" he asked hopeful as his eyes bulged out of his head.

Letting the smile slide off his face AC closed in on him, "No motherfucker you owe us."

With one hard shove he sent the man flying into Chunky who caught him with a hard right to his rib sending him sprawling to the ground.

Squatting down AC got eye level with him, "I don't play about my fucking money." It was the same thing year after year beating niggas about money or disrespect. Just because he had a release date didn't mean he would let up. He just wouldnt kill em.

Chunky kicked Booman hard in the same spot making him ball up as Phatz looked on.

When the guards realized what was going on Booman's front teeth were lying somewhere in the grass. As they were being escorted off the field AC tossed his head back to look at the score board. Damn the bulls had won.

****

"Let me holla at you for a sec, skinny," old timer Fo Five said approaching Phatz. Leaving AC to look over the list of items he would be giving Chunky who was back in the hole after their fiasco with Booman, Phatz followed Fo Five to his bed. Fo Five was a lifer that Phatz had befriended when he moved to Pine Unit. A New Orleans native, the old man had been caught with a bundle of heroin in the early 70's. He was always calling Phatz skinny, but besides that he was full of game and wisdom so when he spoke Phatz listened.

Pulling up a chair next to his bed. Phatz watched Fo Five ease onto the mattress. The little hair that remained on his head was snow white. His skin like brown tattered leather, hung loosely around his face. Phatz could hear his labored breathing as he tried to get comfortable. Finally settled, he folded his hands across his stomach and stared at him. A small smile played at the corners of his lips.

"Hand me that box right there," he pointed to the table.

Grabbing the light blue box Phatz placed it in Fo Five's outstretched hand and watched as he opened it. Inside was his new dentures. Popping them in his mouth he reached for the mirror underneath his bed. Just watching him made Phatz aware of the reality of the situation. Fo Five would never be leaving Angola. He had grown old in the place. His only entertainment was watching television every day. Not only that but lately Phatz had begun to think about Chunky who was also a lifer. He couldn't imagine his friend growing old like Fo Five and never getting to see outside of those walls again. It was heartbreaking. He couldn't stomach leaving Chunky behind no more than he could leaving AC. The only difference was that he knew AC would be following behind him. Chunky wasn't.

"Skinny I like how these dentures look but these motherfuckers hurt my mouth," Fo Five commented.

"Let me see," Phatz said standing from his chair.

Removing the dentures, he placed them in the box and gave Phatz some rubber gloves.

"Right there," he said pointing to the spot where it hurt.

"I probably can fix em," Phatz said inspecting the dentures. The water in Angola had long ago rotted Fo Five's teeth. The new dentures were a replacement to his older ones that had also rotten.

"Skinny, don't mess up my teeth," he called out.

Phatz grinned. "I won't."

Moving over to the sink where the hot pot was, he noticed one tooth was higher than the rest on the gums. Filing it down on the edge of the sink he washed them and handed it back to Fo Five who put them back in his mouth.

Fo Five ran his tongue across his teeth, "Yeah that's what I'm talking about. Good looking out skinny," he winked.

Reclaiming his seat he waited until Fo Five was settled again. The movement in the dorm was beginning to slow down, it was almost time for lights out.

"Skinny listen to me, I know you bout to jump port, I saw you with that knife three days ago and I knew you was gonna take them niggas down through there."

The incident he was referring to was a result of the Booman situation that happened weeks ago. A few of his friends didn't like that AC and Chunky had beat his ass. They wanted to retaliate, not just for that, but Phatz knew they were still smarting from what he had done to Ape Man in the hole. Everyone knew about it now. Phatz was ready to take it to them, but Lynwood talked sense into their heads and Phatz had almost hoped he hadn't. It would be the last time he got to stab a man freely without landing in prison.

Fo Five moved to the edge of the bed "Listen to me boy if you kill one of those silly ass rabbits you at home right here on this river."

Phatz had told AC similar words when they confronted Mookie.

"You already know the captain try to catch you at every turn," he said referring to Captain Perks.

Phatz nodded. They were still after him even knowing he was about to go home.

"You know I got you, but listen to me, shut down that dope shit, because all these niggas on the river know you gonna take em down through there over yours."

Fo Five settled against his pillow again. "Never let none of them know when you go home."

He had been listening, but it was the last statement that got his full attention. Besides AC, Chunky and Fo Five were the only two who knew about his pending release date. Phatz was considering letting Lynwood and a few others in the operation know but he was still on the fence about it. He sat up straighter now.

"Why?" he asked.

Fo Five shook his head before responding. "You didn't let them know when you were coming. Not just that, but if these niggas know your mind is on the streets and you focused on getting back home, they will play games with you."

His words made sense to Phatz so he leaned in closer as he spoke.

"They'll do something so that you can retaliate and get more time. I know that's not what you want so play it like it go. Don't give them the upper hand."

In agreement he nodded. Phatz had never thought about it that way. In fact, he had made his mind up to stay slinging and fighting until they let him out but now…

He looked at Fo Five who had a knowing look on his face.

Fo Five was right. If he gave them the upper hand he would never get out.

"Just let them niggas see your names on call out list that's how you make the announcement."

The first set of lights began to dim over their heads.

Fo Five Reached out his hand. Phatz took it and gave it a firm shake.

"You right old time," he said.

Fo Five winked. They exchanged a few more words before Phatz sauntered over to his own sleeping area. AC had gone to bed. Lying back in his bed. Fo Five words replayed in his head. He was so close to home. He wouldn't let anyone get in the way. Not even himself. He made up his mind that first thing tomorrow he would give Chunky full control of the drug operation. It was time for him to refocus on his return to the streets.

3 weeks later

His younger self was back in Mother Dears living room at the table feasting on every kind of food he could ever want. The smell of Church's Chicken wafted up his nose, homemade biscuits, sweet potatoes, collard greens, and spaghetti covered the table. No matter how much he ate, he couldn't seem to get full. Phatz took a sip from his drink just as his Uncle Kenny swept in.

"Damn nephew I see you been hitting that iron at Y.T.S.," he smiled.

"Yep," Phatz responded proudly as he made a muscle. His uncle tossed his head back and laughed.

"Yeah you big but I'm fast," Marlon said coming from the back wearing a smile. He was dressed in designer clothes from head to toe.

"Watch this," Marlon said. He threw a few air punches. Moving in closer he punched the air above Phatz head. "See you not fast like me."

Setting his meal to the side Phatz stood.

Behind him Mother Dears laughter drifted in his ears. He glanced over his shoulder to where she was sitting on the couch and winked at her.

"You can't whip me no more," Phatz said challenging his big brother. "I got that knockout punch," he raised his fist.

Marlon began to bounce on his heels like they'd seen the professional boxers do in the ring.

"Come on," he said putting his own fist up.

Phatz smiled. In a quick move he grabbed his brother in tight hold.

"Let me go!" Marlon half laughed as he wiggled to get out of Phatz hold.

"You fast get loose."

Not giving him time Phatz went under Marlon's leg and flipped him on the floor. He landed with a soft thud. Holding him down Phatz kissed the top of Marlon's head. They rolled around on the floor before Marlon was finally able to get free. Standing he held his hand out to help Phatz up.

"Man you strong," Marlon said when Phatz was on his feet. There was a hint of admiration in his voice.

"I told you," Phatz said. Their laughter intertwined carrying him further and further away.

It took Phatz a few seconds to get his breathing under control as his heart thudded against his chest. He wiped at the tears that had managed to escape from his eyelids. It was a dream. A dream that he never wanted to wake up from. No matter how hard he wiped the tears wouldn't stop. He was glad for the cover of darkness in the pitch-black dorm room. It had felt so real. All these years and he had never allowed himself to cry for Marlon. Tonight, he let it out. Silent tears began to flow. Not just for his brother, but for Mother Dear who had died suddenly in her sleep a few months earlier. That blow was almost fatal to Phatz. He had just spoken to Mother Dear the day before and the next day she was gone, with no goodbyes. He would never see her smiling face. Never eat Church's with her. Never hear her laughing at his jokes again. It was the worst pain he'd ever felt. Phatz had taken loss after loss in Angola. He'd lost his brother, his friend, and now the backbone of the family. Things would never be the same again. Finally, able to get his tears under control he cleared his throat as he rose up. Checking the night watch on his table it was 11:30 P.M. In less than thirty minutes he would be signing his release papers. He stood and began to put on his clothes. The dorm was eerily quiet. Just loud snores vibrating through the room. Sliding his feet into his shoes, he snapped the buttons on his shirt together. It would be his last time wearing his prison uniform. He wasn't leaving with much, most of his things he'd given to Chunky. Sitting on the bed he let his eyes adjust to the darkness as he waited for the guard to come get him. Phatz had given him strict instructions to come to his bed to get him instead of waking up the entire dorm by shouting his departure. So, he waited.

****

At 12:01 A.M. Phatz walked out of Angola's prison gate a free man. His skin tingled as he breathed in a lung full of fresh clean air. Glancing up he looked up at the dark sky. It had been years since he'd seen stars. They twinkled so bright he felt as if he could reach up and grab one. Behind him the sound of the squeaky gate rolled back closing with a finality. A swarm of emotions overcame him. He'd stabbed, fought, and hustled his way out of the deadliest prison in the world. Taking one step forward he glanced over his shoulder. In the dark he could see the outline of the prison and the guard that he knew was in the gun tower watching. Keep moving, the voice inside his head urged. This time when he stepped forward, he didn't look back. Phatz walked towards the headlights of the cab that was waiting on him. The door swung open, there was a loud squeal before Denise jumped out and flew into his arms. Dropping his bag, he lifted her off the ground and swung her around like he used to do when they were kids.

Denise laughed hard. Finally, he stopped spinning and placed her on the ground. Still she didn't let him go.

"I'm so happy to see you,"

"Me too," Phatz said.

Lifting his head, he noticed Twin standing on the other side of the cab.

"What up?" Phatz called out in greeting. Twins' face split into a wide grin.

"Come on," Denise said pulling him along. At the cab he and Twin embraced before Phatz slid inside. Denise climbed in the middle of the two, snuggling close to her big brother. It still felt unreal. Suddenly his hands began to sweat. What if they'd made a mistake and let him out early? Well they would have to come get him this time.

"Ok you can go now," Phatz said patting the headrest of the driver's seat.

When the cab began to ease forward Phatz felt the tension in his stomach dissolve. He let out a deep sigh. It was over.

****

He couldn't sleep. For the past two hours Phatz had tossed and turned on the soft mattress. It was as if his mind was working overtime as it processed every new sound and smell. From the doors closing and shutting in the hall to the low hum of the air conditioner in the room. He could even smell the coffee brewing in the front lobby. Every time he managed to doze off to sleep, he would jerk awake thinking it was time for count. It took a while for his brain to realize that he wasn't in Angola anymore. It had been almost four hours since he'd left the place. His first stop had been to Brians' house where the two had spoken for over an hour. Brian would continue bringing in drugs for Chunky. After leaving they grabbed a bite to eat and checked into the hotel. Inside his room Phatz had taken a hot shower. Hoping that it would cleanse him of all the prison filth and grime over the years. He stayed under the spray of water until the water had turned cold. Then he'd dressed for bed intending to grab a few hours of sleep before their flight. But he couldn't sleep; he was too wired. His mind turned to AC and if he was honest with himself, that was the reason he couldn't sleep. It still didn't sit well with him that AC was behind those gates without him. Even though he would be making the same trip home soon, Phatz knew that a lot could happen in the span of thirty days. Phatz had spoken to Chunky briefly before he left who promised to make sure that AC got home to him safely. He was counting on Chunky to keep his word, other than that there was nothing he could do.

Untangling himself from the sheets he climbed out of the bed, giving up on the idea of sleep. He glanced at the clock on the nightstand it was 4 A.M. It was time for count in Angola. He hated how his body couldn't shake the routine. He clicked on the TV feigning interest but after a few minutes he gave up on that as well. While checking in Phatz had noticed the Hotel had an indoor gym. It was exactly what he needed. Dressing in a pair of sweats and tennis shoes, he found his way down to the gym where he worked out until he saw the sun rays shining through the glass window. Feeling a little better afterwards he helped himself to a few muffins and a bottle of water before returning to his room where he showered again and changed into a Polo shirt with the pants to match. The shirt hung loosely off his body and he needed a belt for the pants, but he still looked good in it. He stood in the mirror checking out himself. When he'd gone into Angola, he was husky, now there wasn't an inch of fat on his toned body. He'd fallen in love with working out while in prison. It was the one positive thing that came out of his sentence. After all he needed to stay fit to rock niggas to sleep.

Unwilling to stay in the room any longer he packed his bag and headed a few doors down where Nell and Denise slept.

In the hall he tapped lightly on the door. A few more taps and he heard the knob turn.

A half sleep Denise appeared, in her pajamas.

"Dino boy its five o clock what you doing up so early?" she asked, rubbing the sleep out of her eyes.

Behind her Twin flicked a lamp on flooding the room with light.

"Sis it's time to go," he glanced at the Rolex on his arm that Denise had given him.

"But our flight doesn't leave until eight," she complained.

Behind her Phatz saw Twin climb out of the bed and began gathering their things.

"You heard what your brother said," he called out.

He smiled at the annoyed look on his sister's face. One hour later they were checked out and headed to the airport in Baton Rouge. When Phatz got on the plane he stared out of the window as thoughts raced through his mind. In less than eight hours he would be in the one place he'd longed for, for the last four years: Boss Angeles.

Touching A Dream

The First 72 hours

Phatz had learned a few things in Angola. The most important being that the world kept spinning no matter what happened. Got fired from your job, the world kept spinning. Lost someone you loved; the world kept spinning. Spend the last past four years of your life locked up behind bars, the world kept spinning and only an act of God would stop it from doing so. Which was why seated in the back of Denise's gray Nissan Maximum he was beginning to see life through new eyes. It was almost as if he could feel a shift happening inside of him. The shift from small to big. Amateur to professional. His eyes focused on Denise in the driver's seat of the car. Phatz had plans to take care of his entire family and there was only one way that he could do it: hustle. Yet, one would think that after coming out of Angola he would want to walk the straight and narrow. But it was the exact opposite for him. Angola had done nothing to quell his hunger for the hustle because it was planted deep in his veins. Images of his childhood where he'd gotten his first taste for hustling flashed in his mind as they drove past the Inglewood neighborhood, he and his siblings had grown up in on 9614-1/2 and Redfern Street.

At night while his mom Kathi worked, Phatz would sneak out and ride his bike up and down Century Boulevard. The busy street came alive at night and he got to witness it all. Prostitutes dressed in tight skirts, bras, and heels strolled the street soliciting men for sex. Sometimes he and his friends would get bold and try to cop a feel as they raced pass them on their bikes. They would laugh as the hookers chased behind and shouted curse words at them. When they weren't clowning around Phatz and his crew would steal bikes from the hotels, break into the newspaper stands, and pickpocket wallets off of unsuspecting victims on the stroll. Even back then he was a bad ass trying to get money.

One year for Christmas he'd begged his mom for the $2,500 Honda motorcycle that he'd seen outside of Bill Cruise Honda Motorcycles on Century and La Brea Boulevard. Every day after school he would go and sit on the dirt bike and daydream until one of the workers would come out to chase him away. It only made him more determined to have it. Except Kathi had told him no and closed the case on the subject. It didn't take a rocket science to figure out that she didn't have the money for it. Still he would visit the shop and imagine taking the dirt bike home. He could almost feel how smooth it would ride underneath him. Phatz knew that he would be the envy of every kid on the block. Even his friends had spoken on how dope it would be if he could get the dirt bike, but deep down inside he knew it was just a pipe dream.

One day after being chased off by a worker Phatz had claimed a seat at Bob Big Boys restaurant right across the street to keep the dirt bike in his sight. He munched on a burger and fries as he watched the shoppers go in and out the shop. At one point a little boy around five had hopped on the dirt bike, his feet barely touching the gears. Phatz had watched with dread as the little boy pretended to ride it. He felt like his dream bike was slipping away right in front of him and there was nothing he could do about it. Only when the boys' parents came out to make him get off did Phatz began to breathe again. It was a close call. Too close. All day he watched the dirt bike hoping for a Christmas miracle, that would end with the motorcycle being at his house. Maybe his mom would come up with the money, but he knew that wasn't happening and even if she did, she would spend it on bills. Providing for her children was one of Kathi's greatest pride and Phatz knew it. He also knew that eventually someone would recognize the dirt bike for what it was – a true prize- and buy it. He hated the thought. Hated the idea of someone getting what was meant for him. As he watched the workers load the bikes in a room outside of the shop during closing time, Phatz made up his mind. He was getting that bike. Making a quick trip home he retrieved a flat head screwdriver. By the time he made it back it was dark outside, and the Honda shop was closed. Under the cover of darkness, he made his way across the street to the door where he'd seen the workers place the dirt bikes. He had thought about including his friends but decided not to. He couldn't wait to see the look on their faces when he rode down the street on the brand-new bike. Sliding the screwdriver inside of the locked door, he heard an audible click before the door popped open. For a second, he couldn't believe his eyes. All the motorcycle bikes were there, and they were unlocked. His heartbeat hard in his chest as he walked over to his dirt bike and wheeled it out of the room.

    The prostitutes were out in full effect that night, but no one paid attention to the kid walking a motorcycle bike across the street. Removing a lock from his pocket, Phatz locked the motorcycle on the bike ramp at Bob's Big Boy. It stood out against the other plain bikes on the rack. His mind raced as he thought about what he should do next. There was no way he was leaving the other unlocked dirt bikes in that room; the only problem was that he couldn't ride all the bikes home. He would need help. His big brother Marlon came to mind. But he would need proof. Marlon always wanted proof. Gliding back across the street to the shop Phatz grabbed the closest dirt bike near the door. A XR-75 Honda motorcycle dirt bike. Pushing It out the door, instead of taking it to Bob's he retreated to the alley and started it up. The engine purred to life. He couldn't stop the smile that spread across his face as he hopped on the motorcycle and rode down 99th Street west towards home. By the end of the night he, Marlon, and Marlon's crew had wiped all seventeen dirt bikes from the room. It was then that Phatz realized he didn't have to wait for his miracle to happen when he could make it happen himself.

****

    His thoughts drifted to the present as the city came into focus. It hadn't been a full twenty-four hours since he'd received his walking papers, yet Phatz was already thinking of his next move. He was returning to the hustle only this time he was swapping out his hammer for one of the most sought out drugs on the streets: cocaine. In the past he had dabbled with dealing cocaine, but it never could keep his attention long enough Things were different now. The Columbians, who were the main suppliers of coke, were bringing in the drugs by the boat load flooding the streets of Los Angeles, changing the game in ways people couldn't imagine. From the rich to the poor everyone seemed to be hooked on the potent drug. Dealers were caught up in the riches that cocaine provided while users were strung out on its high. At the thought of dealers his gaze shifted to Twin in the passenger seat. Twin, Billy, Big Mac and a few more guys were some of the biggest players in the game now and it was all thanks to Phatz plugging them in. Everybody had a slice of the pie and it was past time for him to get his slice.

"Why we stopping?" he asked as the Nissan came to a crawl on Century Boulevard and Inglewood Ave. Glancing out the window Phatz realized they were pulling into a car wash.

"My car has been sitting at LAX for almost two days, it needs a good scrubbing," Denise tossed over her shoulder while unbuckling her seat belt.

Sitting back against the seat he began to drum his fingers against his thigh. Though Phatz was ready to jump into action, he knew better than to rush his sister. He had a hunch that she was up to something based on the sly smiles she kept giving him. Whatever the case he was just glad to finally be home. *Home* he tossed the word around in his head as he gazed out of the window. Not much had changed except a few new buildings here and there. One being the new gym he had peeped out that was on the corner. Had he been in Angola he would be working out. It was the other thing Angola had taught him: discipline and routine. Phatz was determined to keep up his appearance. He liked the way the clothes molded to his fit body and how the sleeves of the shirt wrapped around his bulging biceps. Stepping out of the car he removed his jacket. Though it was February, the weather was warm. Figuring checking out the gym wouldn't hurt while they waited for the car to be finished, he motioned for Twin to follow him.

A blast of cold air rushed over Phatz as he opened the glass door to the gym.

"Welcome to Guys Gym," The blonde hair blue eyed attendant at the desk greeted with a friendly smile.

"Is there any--" her words were interrupted by the shrill ringing of the phone next to her. Snatching it up quickly she spoke into the receiver. Taking advantage of the distraction Phatz moved across the gyms shiny floor. It was midafternoon, but the place was packed with bodies. And women were everywhere. On the treadmills in front of the tall glass windows, the bicycles, the stair master. It was a glorious sight to see. A white woman dressed in a sports bra and hiking shorts glided pass him, her long blonde ponytail bouncing after her. Phatz let his eyes roam over her washboard abs, toned thighs, and tight ass before the familiar sound of metal striking metal pulled his attention away. On the other side of the gym the men were doing the heavy lifting. It was just what Phatz had come for, he needed equipment ideas for when he started putting together his home gym.

"Come on," he said nudging Twin who stood beside him taking in the scene. Together they moved pass the attendant's desk-who never stopped to look up- to the weight machine. Running his hand over the metal bar Phatz began piling weights on it noting that the equipment was like the rusty Olympic weights he'd worked out with in Angola.

"There," he said as he placed the last of three hundred- and fifteen-pound weight on. To him that was light work.

Turning around he laughed at the wide-eyed expression on Twin's face.

"That's a lot of weight," the man commented.

Instead of answering Phatz hitched his shorts up before sitting down on the bench. Lying flat he wiggled around until he found a comfortable position.

"Come spot me," he said to Twin.

With Twin standing over him, he gripped the bar with his hands and lifted his feet off the floor. He was preparing to raise the bar when the sound of someone clearing their throat caught his attention. Standing to the left of him was a white man dressed in slacks, and a tie. He smiled at Phatz.

"Hi, I'm Guy."

Immediately Phatz made the connection. Guy was the owner.

Tapping on the weights Guy asked, "You looking to join the gym, we have really good deals this month for new members?"

Shoving his hands in his pockets he rocked back and forth in his penny loafers as he waited for an answer.

Phatz knew Guy was making a sales pitch, it was too bad he wasn't interested, but he didn't let the man know that.

"Yes, I'm looking to join a gym I just need to see if I can hit this," Phatz responded slyly.

Guy nodded his sandy blonde head, "Absolutely, go right ahead," he said as if Phatz needed his permission.

Inhaling deep he pushed the bar straight up over his head with ease. Exhaling, he repeated the move, losing himself in the rhythmic movement. Peering through slit eyes he saw that Guys mouth was gaping. Pursing his lips together Phatz smothered the laugh he wanted to let out.

Bringing the bar down in one quick motion he let it rest on his chest, while in his head he began to count to five.

"You ok?" Guy asked, the concern evident in his voice.

Mistaking the brief pause for a sign that he needed help Guy made a move towards the weight just as Phatz pushed five more reps out. Racking the weight, he hopped up, and bounced on the heels of his shoes. He felt energized as adrenaline rushed through his body. Pulling in a ragged breath he realized that most of the men had paused their workout to look at him. Now they all stared with appreciative glances.

"That was great!" Guy said with excitement. He stuck his hand out. Phatz looked at it for a few seconds before taking it.

"Where'd you learn to control your breathing like that?" he asked.

Releasing Guy's hand Phatz looked him square in the eye as he spoke, "Prison."

****

Back in the car he and Twin howled with laughter as they repeated the story to Denise.

"Sis you shoulda saw the look on his face," Phatz said before cracking up again.

"He wanted to run back in his office," Twin chimed in.

"Boy you can't be doing that," Denise said cutting her eyes at him. Unwrapping a car freshener shaped like a tree, the sweet smell of strawberries permeated the interior of the freshly clean car.

"So how much can you bench?" Twin asked seriously, turning around in his seat.

"Four fifty max," Phatz answered proudly.

Twin looked shocked. Pulling his safety belt across his chest Phatz began to tease him, "The only thing you been lifting is money."

Smiling Twin faced the front once more as Denise started the car.

"So where to next?" Phatz asked as the car merged into traffic.

"Beverly Hills," Denise called out in a sing song voice.

He smiled at the mention of his old stomping grounds. Maybe they were taking him shopping. The thought made his smile widen even more, but Denise quickly dashed his hopes with her next words.

"I'm going to get a MCM bag."

Beside her Twin groaned. "You have enough bags Chanel, Gucci, Louis Vuitton," he said listing them off.

"And now I'm adding MCM to my collection," she said with a wink.

Phatz was quiet as he struggled to mask his disappointment. A shopping spree would have been nice. This was just another reason why he had to put a few plays in motion, so that he could spoil himself with the things that he wanted. He remained quiet for the rest of the ride as Denise gushed over her future purchases. He had no idea what a MCM bag was but based on his sisters taste he knew that it was expensive.

When the car stopped outside of the MCM store on Rodeo Drive in Beverly Hills, he decided that this was where they would part ways. Getting a few quarters from Denise, Phatz headed towards the payphone only a foot away from the store. With his back facing the concrete wall he picked up the receiver as he slid quarters into the slot. Dialing in a number he had committed to memory he cradled the phone to his ear as he watched Twin and Denise enter the store. As the phone rang on the other end Phatz scoped out his surroundings.

Beverly Hills was still full of money and under heavy surveillance. There was a squad car at every corner. His lips tilted up. They still hadn't learned that if a young cat like himself wanted something, the presence of police wouldn't stop him. He would just find a smarter way to get it.

"Hello," the gruff voice answered after what seemed like the hundred ring.

"Bout time," Phatz said at the sound of the voice of the man who he had stayed in contact with while he was away.

The man laughed "You're finally home?"

"Damn right and you know what time it is," Phatz said as he eyed a squad car that had come to a slow creep in front of him. Switching the receiver from one ear to the other he ignored the polices presence.

"Billy, I need you to come scoop me up."

"Where you at?" Billy asked. After rattling off his location Phatz quickly ended the call. Weaving through the crowd he made his way back to the car just as Denise and Twin exited the store. Denise looked radiant as she clutched her purse in her hand. Phatz still couldn't believe how much she had grown. His sister had both her own car and apartment. The last bit was news to him. But knowing that she and Twin lived together put his mind at ease a little.

Denise was laughing at something Twin said when Phatz made it to them.

"You ready to go?" she asked pulling out her keys.

Phatz shook his head. "No, I need forty dollars."

A confused look covered her face as she moved closer to him. "Bro you do know we're in Beverly Hills right, I doubt if forty dollars can buy you a shirt."

At her response he tossed his head back and laughed. He knew that.

"All of them clothes and jewels I used to give you came from here."

"Ok so what you need with forty dollars then?" she pressed further.

Still smiling Phatz shook his head at his baby sister. He gazed up and down the block before looking at her "Don't worry bout that I'll meet up with you and Twin later."

"But mama has to see you she's cooking a big dinner for you!" Denise blurted out. She covered her mouth the second the words were out. Behind her Twin shook his head. It was just as Phatz suspected; they were planning something for him. Again, he smiled before glancing down at his sports watch.

"Mama at work girl."

"I know, but still." A look of guilt washed over her face for ruining what was supposed to be a surprise. At the sound of a siren everyone's head whipped around. The same squad car from earlier had circled the block and was now pulling over a car.

"Here," a resigned Denise said, after realizing that she couldn't change his mind.

Folding the forty dollars Phatz stuffed it in his pocket.

"I'll be fine," he said before planting a kiss on her cheek.

With a nod she slid behind the wheel of the car.

"Don't be late," she warned as the car started.

With a promise not to, he watched as they drove away. At the sound of another Beverly Hills police arrive his attention quickly switched to the situation across the street What looked like a routine traffic stop had turned into much more, but Phatz didn't stick around to see the scene unfold or the unlucky bastard be carted away.

30 minutes later

> *How could I move the crowd*
> *First of all, ain't no mistakes allowed*
> *Here's the instruction, put it together*
> *It's simple ain't it, but quite clever*
> *Some of you been trying to write rhymes for years*

But weak ideas irritate my ears

Phatz bobbed his head along to the words of Eric B & Rakim's *Move the Crowd*. He'd listened to the rappers a lot while on the River, but this was a song that he'd never heard before. One that expressed his exact feelings, because he was about to move the crowd in a major way. His eyes cut to Billy in the driver's seat of the big red dually truck. Clicking the signal light Billy switched lanes before coming to a stop at the red light. Reaching under his tiger print suit jacker he pulled out a 9-millimeter. Never once taking his eyes off the road, he handed the gun to Phatz.

"Put that in the glove box," he said sliding him the key to unlock it.

Doing as instructed Phatz was about to close the glove compartment when Billy removed a .25 automatic from his gator boots.

"Where mine?" Phatz asked seriously after locking it up.

Easing off the brakes Billy drove through the green light.

"At the house."

They rode in silence, but Phatz couldn't stop his eyes from straying back to Billy. He could tell the lifestyle was paying off for his friend based on his new wardrobe.

The man had exchanged his signature T-shirt and jeans for Armani suits and gator boots and Phatz liked it.

Clicking the dial to turn off the radio after the song ended Billy glanced in the rear-view mirror before breaking the silence.

"It's good to have you home."

"Good to be back my nigga."

And it was. thoughts of his friend came to his mind at that exact moment. Phatz still didn't like that his boy was left in Angola, but there was nothing he could do about it other than get things in order for when AC returned.

Needing to know what he was dealing with, Phatz turned to Billy.

"You gon' give me the run down?"

Billy tilted his head.

"Glad you asked," he said, switching lanes getting on I-10 west.

"It's the same game with new players…"

****

Two hours later when they pulled up at Billy's gated house in Northridge, Phatz knew everything he needed to know, at least about the players of the game. Getting out of the truck he grabbed the bags off the back seat. He had gotten his shopping spree after all when Billy had taken him to the store in Hollywood and broke bread. Instead of choosing the Fila sweatsuits he was so accustomed to Phatz had taken a page out of Billy's book and opted for Linen suits and gators. He didn't miss the look of approval in Billy's eyes at his choices. Phatz understood that he was entering into a grown man's game and in order to play the part he had to look it. He was serious about shifting things to another level and apparently so was Billy because wardrobe wasn't the only thing that he had changed. Walking up the winding driveway he took in the large houses that lined the clean quiet block of the rich suburbs in the valley neighborhood. His eyes grazed over the neat lush green grass in the yard before he moved up the concrete pathway flanked by blooming flowers. The brick two story house looked like it could be on the cover of *Better Homes and Garden Magazine*. The inside was no different. Placing his bags down he looked around as Billy disappeared behind one of the closed doors. African art lined the white walls. His eyes climbed higher to the tall ceiling where a crystal chandelier hung, the light from its diamond shaped light bulbs reflected in the marble tiles of the floor. Expensive crème colored furniture pieces were neatly arranged in both dining areas. He poked his head inside a room that he assumed was Billy's office due to the wooden desk and chairs before continuing to the kitchen where there were stainless steel counter tops , an island in the center and every high tech kitchen equipment imaginable including a TV. Phatz had to admit he was impressed not just with Billy's taste in décor either. This was yet another testament that the game was treating his friend good. Walking past the long table that seated eight people, Phatz stood peering out the sliding glass doors that led to the patio. Outside were two 300 CE Benz's and a four door Benz.

Suddenly Billy appeared at his side cradling a glass of liquor in his hand. From the strong smell Phatz could tell it was Hennessey.

"Whose toys?" he asked pointing at the cars.

Sipping out the glass, Billy waited until the sting of the liquor rolled down his throat to answer.

"Couple niggas owe me money, they can't pay I take what they prize the most." He shrugged his shoulders at Phatz as he peered over the rim of the glass taking another sip.

"You want some?" he offered.

Phatz shook his head. Drinking was never his thing.

"Follow me I wanna show you something," Billy said spinning on his heel.

Admiring the cars with one last glance he followed Billy into a room, that had a small bed and dresser in it. His shoes sunk into the plush beige carpet the minute he stepped inside. Going to the closet Billy removed a large Louis Vuitton bag and placed it on the floor. He nudged the bag towards Phatz with his foot as he retrieved his glass from the dresser.

Kneeling, Phatz unzipped it. His pulsed sped up when he looked inside. The only thing that had been on his mind since he set foot off the plane at LAX was money. And here he was staring into a bag full of it.

"Its $500,000 in there," Billy responded casually before taking a sip from the glass.

Phatz eyes widened.

"Here."

Glancing up Phatz stared at the 45 Uzi Billy was offering him.

Though he wanted guns what he wanted more was the money. Taking the 45 Uzi from Billy's outstretched hand he gazed down at the money again. His fingers tingled to touch it.

"Fruits of my labor." Billy grinned.

Storing the money away, the men exited the room as Billy rambled on about guns.

Meanwhile Phatz mind was spinning. If Billy had five hundred g's just laying around like that, he knew he could make more.

The two men sat in the living room talking as the sports channel played in the background. At the sound of the front door opening Phatz glanced up just as a soft voice called out,

"Babe?"

Rounding the corner, a woman dressed in a denim jean skirt, a white halter top that exposed her flat stomach and a pair of heels came into view. Removing the sunglasses covering her eyes she smiled as Billy waved her over.

"Come meet Phatz."

Phatz watched her long brown sienna legs carry her to them. He knew that the woman was no other than Le Le Billy's girl. Whenever he would call to the house and Billy wasn't there it was Le Le who would deliver messages for him. Sometimes they would talk for hours and now he was finally able to match a face to the voice.

Instead of a handshake Le Le embraced him in a warm hug. Pulling back, she swiped at the loose spiral curl falling into her eye.

"It's so good to finally meet you." Lifting her head, she quirked an eyebrow at Billy.

To which he responded, "He already knows about the party."

"And I see you've decided to start early," she said referring to the drink in his hand. He was on his third glass, but Phatz didn't let Le Le know.

"Well since the surprise is out, I'm going to fix me a light lunch before things get under way, either of you want anything?"

"No," both he and Billy said in unison.

Leaving them alone, Le Le walked into the kitchen. It was almost 3 P.M. when they decided to get ready for the party. Showing him the bathroom where he could shower, Billy left him alone with his thoughts.

Inside Phatz rested his hands on the marble sink counter as he looked in wall length mirror. Physically he'd changed a lot. Fit from head to toe, the big afro that he wore in Angola had been exchanged for a low haircut. His handsomeness hid the scars well. Not just the ones from Angola, but from life. He let out a deep breath. It wasn't worth dwelling on. Besides today was his day. A day to celebrate his survival and soon what would be his return to the game.

****

Outside of the white house on 43rd and St. Andrews Street, cars lined the block. The people inside mingled in anticipation of the arrival of the guest of honor. There was a faraway look in Phatz eyes when the black stretch limousine that Billy rented stopped outside of the house, he had grown up in. He swallowed deeply as he felt his eyes gloss over.

"Shit!" Billy said pulling Phatz attention to him. Droplets of champagne had spilled on the linen suit Billy was now dressed in. Hurriedly Le Le handed him a few napkins to wipe at the spill. Phatz looked down at his own suit. He had exchanged his polo fit for grey linen pants like Billy's and a light sweater, since the temperature had dropped. Seated next to Billy, Le Le wore a silk dress that looked as soft as her skin. Diamond droplets hung from her ears and an expensive watch draped her wrist. She smiled when she caught Phatz staring at her.

"The two of you go ahead, let me clean up in here," Billy said frustrated. He brought the bottle of champagne to his mouth and took a big gulp from it. With a shrug, Le Le opened the door. Phatz stepped out first and stretched his hand out to help her.

His head whipped back and forth, nothing about the street looked as if it had changed, but he knew better. Above them the stars were beginning to twinkle against the darkening sky as the two walked side by side up the concrete driveway. With every step he could feel his heart pounding in his ears. Pausing at the door Phatz took a deep breath. Beside him Le Le gave him a reassuring smile before he reached for the doorknob.

"Surprise!" The loud voices erupted as he stepped over the thresh hold into the living room. Party streamers hung everywhere. A huge sign with his name and the writing Welcome Home was strung on the wall. A sea of familiar faces from family to old friends gathered around clapping him on the back and shaking his hand. Trying hard to greet everyone Phatz maneuvered through the crowd in search of one person. Suddenly the bodies parted like the Red Sea and there she was standing off to the side with her hands clasped over her mouth. The tears began to fall from Kathi's eyes as she embraced her son in a hug that only a mother could give. The kind that melted the worries away and made you feel like everything was going to be ok. Phatz couldn't stop the tears from falling from his own eyes as he rocked from side to side with his mom in his arms. Even the spectators watching the heartwarming moment dabbed at their eyes.

Kathi pulled away from Phatz before placing a hand on either side of his face. She wiped at his tears with her thumbs.

"I've missed you so much baby."

Phatz managed to mumble out the words to her. Using the flat of his palms he dried the remaining wetness from his face. The water works had caught him by complete surprise unlike the dinner.

A wobbly smile crossed Kathi's face as she sized him up. "You look good."

He could say the same for her. As usual his mother's hair was neatly styled and the outfit she wore complimented her figure. She didn't look at all like the forty-eight years that she was.

"Nephew!"

At the sound of the voice Phatz turned to see his Uncle Kenny smiling with his arms stretched out. The two embraced.

"I see you slimmed down a lil bit."

He flexed his muscles, "I still got it."

Kenny tossed his head back and laughed. Lacing her fingers through his Kathi pulled him around the room, introducing him to some of her coworkers. She only left his side once and that was to check on the food. Speaking of food Phatz hadn't seen that much in a while. There were aluminum containers of ribs, hamburger meat, and Italian sausages in the kitchen. His mouth watered just looking at it, but it was too bad he had given up meat almost two years now. It was tempting and as much as he liked meat, Phatz didn't like how it made him look over the years.

Kathi seemed to read his thoughts, "Don't worry I made greens and yams too," she winked at him as she removed a pan from the oven. His stomach growled in approval. He was helping her carry the food to the dining area for the guest when the phone rang. Kathi rushed to grab it. Seconds later she tapped him on the shoulder.

"It's for you."

Picking up the receiver Phatz spoke into the phone.

"Hello."

A wide grin covered his face at the sound of the voice coming from the other end.

****

Angola

Hanging up the phone AC stood shaking his head. He was glad that Phatz had made it home safely.

"Everything good?" Chunky asked as he sat down on the weight bench.

"Yep."

"You decide what you gone do when get home?" Chunky asked when he was finished benching the weights. The question made AC smile.

"My nigga you know what I'ma do."

He was so close to home he could taste it. In his mind he envisioned himself eating at Fat Burger, taking a hot bath, and laying up with a woman- but not just any woman Shauna.

"Wipe that stupid smile off your face," Chunky joked.

Howling with laughter AC took his place on the bench he was about to launch into his workout when the look on Chunky's face made him pause. Alarmed he sat up and scanned the area. The prisoners seemed engrossed in their own dealings.

"What's wrong?"

Shaking his head Chunky tried to wave him off but AC kept pressing him.

Finally he came out with it. "I'm glad my niggas going home, y'all the realest I met in here." He paused looking AC in the eye "But this is home for me, I'm never leaving."

The heavy reality of Chunky's words hit him in the chest. Chunky was serving life for a crime he didn't commit. He'd exhausted his appeals to prove his innocence with no luck. The system was rigged that way. AC didn't even want to imagine waking up on the river for the rest of his life. Just the thought of it made him shudder. Four years had been enough.

"Listen, we won't let you rot in here, for real we'll get the best lawyers that money can buy to get you out." He Could tell that Chunky didn't seemed convinced, but AC was determined to keep his word. As the moment passed the conversation drifted to lighter matters. Still, AC's mind was made up. He wouldn't let his friend rot in a cell .

∎∎∎

The party was in full swing when Phatz returned from picking up Dino Jr. in the limousine. Grabbing a plate, he finally settled down to eat with the rest of the party goers. He looked out onto the makeshift dance floor as DJ and Kathi bust moves to Marvin Gaye's classic hit *Got to Give It Up*. He couldn't help but laugh at his son's smooth dance moves. They definitely didn't come from him. Not to be upstaged by her eight-year-old grandson Kathi had a few moves of her own. It didn't take long for the others to join in. Over the loud music he heard the phone ringing. It had been doing that since he arrived. The news of his homecoming was spreading like wildfire. Phatz snatched up the phone just as Denise and the twins walked through the door.

Sticking one finger in his ear to hear over the music he shouted into the receiver.

"Hello!"

"I see y'all started the party without me," the man responded with humor in his voice.

Phatz immediately recognized that the voice belonged to Big Mac. On days when he phoned home from Angola and Billy wasn't available to talk, Big Mac was who Phatz spoke with. It was through those calls that they'd formed a close bond. Big Mac was once in charge of all of Billy's crack houses, but a bout of jealousy made Billy's ugly head rear and he fired the man. Only twenty-two years old, Big Mac was an ambitious hustler so being fired hadn't stopped him, it just gave him more reason to go into business for himself. From Angola Phatz had plugged Big Mac with one of his older Jungle homeboys who was dominating the game and the rest was history.

"My nigga you should have come," Phatz responded.

"I knew ole boy would be there..." Big Mac's voice trailed off.

Phatz clocked "ole boy" Billy sitting next to Le Le, clutching the champagne bottle with a death grip.

Though he was aware of the tension that existed between the two men he had decided to not get involved.

"But check this out, I got something for you, just tell me when and how to get it to you," Big Mac stated.

Minutes later Phatz disconnected the phone feeling excited. Big Mac would be giving him a whip and some money. While he appreciated both he was happier about the money because as of now all he had to his name was $14.57 of the forty dollars Denise had given him. He was about to reclaim his seat when *Paid in Full* begin to blare over the speakers. Allowing his mother and Dino Jr to pull him to the dance floor, Phatz tried to mimic some of the dance moves he'd seen Dino Jr do earlier. The laughter and loud cheers from the guest let him know he wasn't doing too bad. When Denise and Uncle Kenny joined them, it became one big dance off. Old School versus new school. In the end Dino Jr. would walk away as champion of the dance off. Hours later the last of the guests walked out the door.

Tucking Dino Jr. in his bed Phatz helped his mother clean and put away food before she too turned in for the night. Now all alone he finally had time to think. The day had gone better than he'd expected but the highlight of his day was when AC called. Hearing his friends voice put his mind at ease and motivated him even more to get things ready for his homecoming. Maybe he would throw him a party like his family had done for him. What he really wanted to do was put money in AC's pocket. His thoughts continued to roam until he found himself dozing off in the chair. Jerking awake he stood to stretch as he stifled a yawn with the back of his hand. He decided to turn in for the night so that he would be well rested especially since the next few days would be busy for him. Beginning with a flight to Chicago with Billy tomorrow and after that Phatz had to start the ongoing pain of pissing in a cup for his parole officer for the next three years. A requirement of his release. Double checking that the doors were locked he flipped out the light in the kitchen. A chill shot down his spine as his eyes swept over the darkened house and memories flashed in his mind. Today had been a bittersweet moment for him. While Phatz had finally made it to the one placed he longed for, he knew that after the death of Mother Dear and the murder of Marlon, home would never quite be home again.

(Phatz. First day out!)

****

"How many you want?"

Phatz eyes widened at the sight of the two hundred and fifty kilos of cocaine wrapped in plastic and duct tape on the floor. Across from him Big Mac leaned back in the chair with a smirk on his face. They were in the lower level of the man's house in Pasadena Hills, where Phatz had stayed the night before. After years of talking over the phone the two finally met face to face to pick up where they had left off: business.

Big Mac crossed his ankle as he reached for the Cuban cigar sitting on the desk. Lighting it he puffed on the cigar twice before offering it to Phatz who declined.

Instead of answering his question Phatz asked one of his own.

"You getting these straight from Pablo's people?"

He needed to know who the plug was just in case shit ever got funky.

With a nod of his head Big Mac tapped the cigar in the ashtray.

"The Colombians supply damn near everybody, we got niggas from every coast coming to Cali to make purchases." He pointed at the mounting tower of drugs in front of him, "Twice a month by boat the big man sends his henchmen to deliver them."

Big Mac frowned as if remembering something then shook his head. "These birds can make your wildest dreams come true."

Pinning Phatz with a stare he asked, "You ready to make that happen?"

Drawing in a deep breath Phatz stared at Big Mac through the haze of sweet smoke. 6'2 and over two hundred pounds, Big Macs face held a hardness to it that made him look older than his twenty-two years.

"Not right now," he answered truthfully.

While Phatz knew that Big Mac would front him the work, he still would have to secure buyers and that could take time. Meanwhile he was putting together a team of loyal people to move the work for him and the only thing they were missing were the buyers. He had a feeling all of that was about to change especially after his short trip to New Orleans a few days ago where he'd reconnected with his knife man Pocket, Big D's cousin. Both men had been happy to see each other outside of that river in Angola and while his friend Baby Boy had partied at a local club, Phatz and Pocket discussed starting their own operation in New Orleans. See Pocket had did the math and realized that buying birds in L.A. would be the best thing to do since they were going for $10,000, while in his home state a bird was $30K. Phatz liked the idea and came up with an even better one to increase their profits. Instead of charging the full thirty he and Pocket would let the birds go for $27,000 each. To the locals in New Orleans it would be a steal from the original price of $30K. It was a win win situation for them both. Looking at the work on the table, Phatz mind drew up a mental image of money to replace the vision in front of him. Cautioning himself to slow down he shook clear of the image. First thing first, get a few buyers. With any luck Pocket would be calling him today to tell him that he'd done just that.

"They'll be here when you ready," Big Mac replied stubbing the cigar out. With a flick of his wrist he beckoned for one of his workers to come remove the product from the room. Standing he pushed away from the desk.

"It's still a little early you want some breakfast?"

Glancing down at his Omega watch Phatz saw that it was almost 9 A.M. He thought about declining, but the growl from his stomach answered before he could. Leaving the lower level Big Mac lead him up the stairs to the second level of the house where they took a seat at the table on the balcony. An older maid placed two covered plates in front of each man.

"Thank you, Martha," Big Mac curtsied. When she returned with a glass of apple juice for Phatz he removed the silver lid covering the plate. A slice of perfectly browned toast, avocado, poached runny eggs, pancakes, and fruit made up his meal. It was hard to believe that just a few days ago he was eating in a crowded hall off a plastic tray. Now he was sitting in a house worth over a half a million dollars that overlooked the sprawling Pasadena Hills, being served by a maid like he was royalty. Phatz scoffed to himself before digging into his food. Washing down a bite with a sip of apple juice he dapped at his mouth with the embroidered handkerchief.

"Did you like your welcome home present?" Big Mac asked lathering his toast with strawberry jam.

The present in question was a fully loaded Astro van and $5,000 which he had all of $2,000 remaining from. He'd spent most of it on clothes even after Billy had taken him to Chicago and spent $7K on him, Phatz still found himself scouring the stores in Hollywood for all the high-end fashion items. Even now he was dressed in dark blue linen pants with a black Bill Cosby sweater, with a chain around his neck and a pair of alligators on his feet. The outfit had cost almost five hundred alone.

"The van is a good undercover ride," Phatz said slicing into his fluffy pancakes. It had been his first thought when he received it. The Astro van was fly, but not too flashy. Fresh out, Phatz didn't want the ride drawing attention from the wrong people especially since he would be moving birds in the van so for now, he needed to be able to fly under the radar.

Big Mac grinned giving his hardened face a more youthful appearance. "I figured you would like that. I knew from the first time we spoke you would want some fly shit."

"Ima a fly nigga can't you tell," Phatz said spreading his hands wide.

Big Mac tossed his head back and laughed.

Phatz voice grew serious "I meant what I said earlier, you need me to get your money back just say the word." Big Mac had revealed that a few people had gone into hiding after owing him money. Phatz wanted to go get it back, either they would pay up willingly or he would make them. Nobody played with his friends' money.

With a slight nod Big Mac changed the subject.

"I don't think Billy gonna like me working with you," he said draining the water in his glass.

Phatz waved a hand dismissively. "Don't worry about Billy, any moves I make is my business."

The words seem to put Big Mac as ease as they flowed into another conversation, but his concern flopped around in Phatz mind. He respected Billy's grind, but compared to Big Mac he was getting crumbs. Big Mac's was getting three and four hundred birds at a time. There weren't too many in the game doing it like him, Billy included. And if Phatz wanted to make any noise he had to play with the key players. Billy would have to understand that it was business nothing personal.

"So what's the move?" Big Mac asked.

They were standing in the doorway after finishing their meal. Phatz gripped his overnight Gucci bag in one hand and his keys in the other.

"Gotta go see my parole officer in a few hours," he answered stepping out into the hot sun. He walked down the driveway where his van was parked beside Big Mac's brand-new Rolls Royce and his slant nose P- Car.

All I need is ninety days and we'll have all this shit.

Tossing his bag in the backseat he slid behind the wheel of his van.

"That's right," Billy nodded, "they still tryna keep up with you."

"Key word is try," Phatz said sticking the key into the ignition. Pissing in a cup wasn't a problem for him, at least it beat being back in Angola. His only hope was that his PO would be cool.

After a few more parting shots, Phatzz pulled out of the driveway and settled in for the short ride back to L.A.

∎∎

ANGOLA

AC knew it wouldn't end well the minute he stepped foot inside the game room and overheard the Shreveport nigga name Ken high signing during a heated game of Tunk. Posting up at the door he split his attention between the game and the showers. Once Chunky was finished showering it would be his turn until then he focused on the two men in front of him.

"How you like that shit," Ken bragged, slamming a card on the table gaining another book. "Sho' can't wait to smoke them cigs," he said nodding towards the prize that he was close to winning. Across from him his opponent Daryl's face was blank, but his death stare said it all.

"You NO niggas don't know shit about Tunk so let me school you," Ken said before winning the next few rounds.

He tossed his head back and laughed in victory. Grabbing the carton of cigarettes Ken leaned back in the chair staring up at Daryl, a sly smile crossed his face as he taunted,

"Go get you some more money if not I'm gone!" he said giving Daryl a chance to redeem himself.

The chair scraped back as Daryl stood and stormed out the room, brushing up against AC in his quick exit. At the table Ken gathered his prize.

"Stupid nigga," he said loud enough for everyone to hear.

"Anybody else wanna go," he challenged his eyes darting around the room before landing on AC.

"What about you Solo?"

With a calm shake of his head AC passed on the opportunity to put Ken in his place, not because he didn't want to, but because he knew Ken was about to learn his lesson soon enough. And if he hadn't been so busy bragging, he would've recognized the signs as well, instead Ken strolled to his bed in the dorm and laid down. Meanwhile across the dorm on the other side, Daryl stood by the coffee pot eyes boring a hole into an oblivious Ken. The CO at the front of the room paid no attention to Daryl walking towards Ken with the coffee pot in his hands. From where AC stood, he could see the steam rising from the pot.

Shit he cursed under his breath. With Chunky still out of sight he watched the scene unfold.

Daryl stood over Ken undetected for what seemed like minutes. In one quick move he dumped the hot water onto a sleeping Kens face and body. A blood curling scream echoed through the dorm. Beside Ken, his bedmate John sprang up when some of the scalding water touched his exposed skin. Ken on the other hand lay flat screaming, his brown skin already beginning to peel from his body revealing pink flesh underneath.

"Talk that shit now," Daryl bit out before whacking him twice with the steel mop ringer knocking him out cold.

At the front of the room the CO fearfully pressed the panic button to alert the workers up front. Most of the inmates tried to remove themselves from the scene as Daryl paced the floor still screaming at an unconscious Ken. AC shook his head at the sight. Shit talking was one of the easiest ways to lose your life in prison especially during gambling, because you never knew what was running through the next man's head. From the looks of it, Daryl had a lot on his mind.

"What I miss?" Chunky asked coming up beside AC just as the goon squad stormed the dorm apprehending Daryl.

With a shrug AC tucked his items underneath his arm.

"This just some mo of it up in this bitch," he said before heading to the shower.

****

10 days later

Everything was falling into place for Phatz. After ending his call with Pocket, he was in a considerably good mood, in fact he had been since returning from Chicago. The men had finally found a couple of buyers. True to his word Big Mac had fronted him fifty birds with no hesitation and in turn Phatz had taken twenty and sent them to Pocket while selling the remainder to his buyer in Chicago. When Pocket phoned to say that he would need a re up just ten days later Phatz could barely control his excitement. After phoning Big Mac to get things in motion, Phatz wandered aimlessly around the house, money clouding his thoughts. In less than two weeks he had made over a half a million dollars- not counting the money he would have to pay Big Mac for fronting him the work. He smiled to himself. He'd made it back to the big league and was ready to make his wildest dreams come true for he and his family. Finally shaking himself free he sat on the edge of his bed and thought about his plans for the day. When he heard the front door unlock, he glanced at his wrist. Only a quarter to eleven, being that his mother was still at work Phatz knew that it had to be either his sister Denise or his Uncle Kenny. His suspicions were confirmed when he heard Denise voice outside of his bedroom door.

She knocked and pushed the door open.

"I didn't say come in," he joked.

One look at the stormy expression on her face and he knew something was wrong.

"I need you to come with me right quick." Not waiting for an answer, she spun around on her heels and stomped out of the room.

Abandoning his plans Phatz followed Denise outside where she stopped and paced in the driveway. Today she was dressed in a light grey silk Chanel pants suit with matching heels and a Chanel purse slung over her shoulder. She looked like she had just stepped off the runway. Her fingers gripped the keys in her hand repeatedly. Drawing in a deep breath, Denise pointed to her car parked on the street. It was the first time Phatz took notice of it. He could see the outline of person inside but before he could ask who it was, she began talking.

"After you told me about daddy and all our people out in Shreveport I decided to call him myself to check on him?"

Phatz nodded as Denise paused, "Anyways to make a long story short he told me that we had cousins out here and that he would pass my number along to them just in case they wanted to meet up."

The slamming of a door drew their attention to the neighbor's house next door. After exchanging greetings with the old woman and her husband, Denise rushed on, "An hour ago I get a call and it's her." She pointed to the passenger seat answering Phatz question from earlier. "She's our aunts' daughter," she said filling him in even more.

A lot more interested in Denise story now Phatz walked over to the car and tapped on the window. The girl lifted her head.

"What's up lil cousin, I'm Phatz."

Cracking the door, she spoke in a soft voice "I'm Retha." Phatz smiled at her southern accent.

Brown skin with dimples she was cute and couldn't be any more than seventeen. And from the looks of her red rimmed eyes she had been crying.

At the feel of Denise tugging on his arm Phatz moved away from the car.

Lowering her voice so only Phatz could hear Denise continued her story.

"Her sister put her out because she wouldn't fuck her boyfriend, I guess they were tryna be on some pimp shit," she said with disgust in her voice.

His jaw clenched tight as his head snaked back to Retha. Now he understood the tears.

"I go over there to pick her up and straighten out her bum ass sister and the sister's boyfriend bitch ass wants to play tough, he grabbed m—,"

Phatz was halfway across the yard before she could finish her sentence. He didn't need any convincing. Bump the fact that it was his first time meeting his little cousin, she was family and the thought of a nigga putting his hands on his sister made him see red.

Back inside his room he grabbed the .45 he kept tucked underneath his pillow. Removing the clip, he checked to make sure it was loaded before sliding it back into the gun.

Denise pushed the door open just as he tucked the weapon in the waist of his pants.

"He needs his hat handed to him."

Despite the serious look on her face Phatz couldn't stop the smile from crossing his own. Mother Dear would've been proud of her statement. Smoothing his shirt down over his pants to hide the bulge from the gun Phatz walked out the house, Denise close behind on his heels.

"We'll take my car, but I want to drop her off at my apartment first."

With a lift of his head acknowledging her words, he eased into the backseat of the car ready to handle business.

Twenty minutes later the two of them sat in the parking lot of the apartments on El Segundo and Crenshaw. Phatz had been in this neck of the woods a few times in his earlier years. He watched a group of kids race their bikes back and forth in the streets.

"I told that nigga I had somebody for his bad ass," Denise stated brushing her hair behind her ears. She had calmed down but not enough to change her mind.

He zeroed in on the door of the apartment Denise had pointed out when they arrived. No one had come or gone, and he was tired of waiting. Removing the .45 from his waist he turned to Denise.

"You ready?"

Without a word she got out of the car and proceeded up the steps leading to the second floor. Her heels clicking angrily over the concrete with every step.

Behind her Phatz beamed. Whoever the guy was that touched her was in for a rude awakening…from the both of them.

When they reached the door Denise tilted her head to the side.

"Stand over there," she whispered.

Standing off to the side where he couldn't be seen, Phatz watched her remove a .380 from her purse. He figured she must've gotten it from the house when they dropped off Retha. He chuckled to himself. Denise was mad.

Balling up her fist she pounded on the door.

No answer.

After a few more pounds Phatz decided to peer through the windows. Inside all of the lights were off, but he could see the outline of furniture thanks to the sunrays.

"Don't look like anyone's home sis."

Refusing to give up Denise banged on the door a few more times.

Tucking his gun back in his waist Phatz realized they had an audience. Not only could he see the neighbor peeping out of their blinds but the kids on the bikes had gathered around to watch the show.

At any second the cops could come.

"Come on," he said grabbing Denise mid pound.

"I'll slide back through tonight you just tell me how he looks so I can pistol whoop his ass."

Denise sucked in a lung full of air and let it out. Her nostrils flared with anger.

"She got a gun," Phatz heard one of the kids say.

As if realizing where they were Denise quickly slipped the gun back in her purse. With a stiff nod she walked back down the steps.

"No, you come and get me if you sliding back through I wanna kick him in his big ass mouth."

Snatching the door open she climbed behind the wheel. Making sure the coast was clear Phatz slid on the passenger side and waited until they were a safe distance from the apartments to start laughing.

"He fucked with the wrong one," he said playfully taping Denise's arm.

"Damn right," she finally said cracking a smile.

Suddenly Phatz had a flashback of something Denise had told him during a visit once.

"Remember those guys who knocked at your door with that noise."

Her neat eyebrows crinkled. "Yeah what about em?"

Phatz gripped the cold metal in his hand.

"Let's go see them," he said mischievously.

He placed the gun on his lap as Denise happily drove to her old apartments. Big Brother was back, and he was knocking on all doors about his.

****

"AAHHHH you gone break my arm!" The man face down on the desk yelled. Hitching his arm up higher behind his back Phatz enjoyed the howl that left his mouth this time as Baby Boy roughed the man up.

Baby Boy moved his lips close to his ear "Ima break more than that if you don't pay what you owe," he snarled.

"What's yo name?" Phatz asked as Baby Boy squeezed his arm tighter.

"Shawn," he bit out between clenched teeth.

Nodding to Baby Boy to let go, Phatz yanked Shawn up by his shirt and slung him in the white chair.

"Ow!" he cried out.

Wiping at the light perspiration that had gathered on his top lip he gazed in the corner where Big Mac was sitting with a satisfied smirk on his face. Outside the closed door Phatz could hear the bass of the music pulsing through the walls of the Phone Zone shop that Big Mac owned on Olympic and La Brea Boulevard. The music was just a cover up to keep the customers from hearing the man's loud screams. When Big Mac finally called in the favor to retrieve his money that people owed him, Phatz had been more than happy to oblige. While he didn't want to get caught up in no one else's game he felt like he had to send a message and set the tone in the streets. If you owed money you paid. Simple. He turned his stare back to Shawn. Not only did the weasel owe money from drugs that was fronted to him, but he still hadn't paid off the car that was sold to him. The red 5.0 Mustang was outside in the parking lot. Picking up the keys to it Phatz tossed it in the air and caught it before placing them in the pocket of his jacket.

"Come on don't take my car," Shawn whined, to which Phatz scoffed.

"You never paid it off so how is it your car?"

Putting his hand behind his ear he waited for an answer. When one didn't come Baby Boy kicked the leg of the chair startling the man. Liking the fear that he saw in his eyes Phatz unbuttoned the jacket of his suit, putting the .45 on his hip on display.

Shawn eyes rounded as big as saucers when he spotted the gun.

"I-I can get the money," he stuttered.

"Is that right?"

"Yeah, yeah," Shawn nodded eagerly.

Locking eyes with Big Mac, Phatz signaled for Baby Boy to move closer.

Removing the keys from his pocket he tossed them to him.

"Pay what you owe then you back in good standing, but I'm keeping these now get yo ass out of here."

Grabbing him up from the chair Baby Boy shoved him towards the door.

"Don't play no games," he warned before kicking him in the ass.

Phatz laughed. "Tell them to turn down the music when you get out front."

Nodding Baby Boy closed the door as he left. Seconds later Phatz heard silence on the outside.

"Anybody else?" he asked turning around.

Big Mac paused then shook his head.

With a nod Phatz moved towards the door.

"Listen Phatz," Big Mac called out behind him "Whatever you need I got you and I mean whatever."

"Just make sure the reup is ready tomorrow."

"You got it."

Buttoning up his jacket to conceal the weapon on his hip Phatz made his exit. Only a few customers were inside the shop. Spying Baby Boy flirting with the young cashier he proceeded to his car. Adjusting the side mirror as he pulled out of the parking lot his eyes grazed over the mustang. He would give Shawn twenty-four hours to produce the money or he would send Baby Boy to knock on his door, only this time he would tell the man not to let up. Phatz caught his reflection in the mirror and winked. He was glad to be back in the land of the body bags!

•••

A few hours later he pulled up to GG's jewelry store on Sixth and Hill in downtown L.A. He'd gotten so caught up with getting everything in place for when AC got home that he almost forgot the jewels he'd given GG to melt down and remake before he went to prison. That was one of the things Phatz loved about gold: It could be remade over and over again, helping him to get his money's worth. Climbing out of the van he entered the store only to find GG bent over the counter showcasing jewelry to a customer. When he raised his head, the man looked as if he had seen ghost. Removing the jewelry loupe from his left eye GG scrubbed a hand down his face to clear his vision.

"Phatz?" GG asked hesitantly.

Stretching his hands forward Phatz did a slow spin. "In the flesh," he stated with a smile.

"Where's AC with that hammer?" GG asked looking around wildly as if he would magically appear. Phatz tossed his head back and laughed as the memory of GG and AC's first introduction came to mind. It had ended with AC bashing in his cases and GG pulling a shot gun on them. The day had been wild, but before they left out of the store, they all had come to an agreement. GG wouldn't try to shortchange them for their jewelry and AC wouldn't use his hammer. It was a deal that turned out to be a win for them all.

"He'll be home in three weeks, " Phatz said as he moved further into the store

Winking GG smiled, "I have a gift for him when he arrives."

Noticing that his customer was growing impatient, he waved his hands towards the cases on the other side of the store.

"Why don't you check out our new merchandise over there, while I finish up here."

Returning to his customer GG left Phatz to explore on his own. Inside of the case a diamond ring caught Phatz eye.

"Find anything you like?" GG asked coming up beside him minutes later. They were the only two in the store now.

"That diamond ring right there."

"Good choice," he commented before rounding the case and removing the diamond ring.

"You got the loupe on you?" Phatz asked.

Digging into his pocket GG handed him the jewelry loupe.

The cluster of diamonds sparkled brightly under the loupe.

"I gotta have this," he said when he was finished examining the jewelry. With a smile GG began to get the ring ready for purchase.

Now that he was closer Phatz could tell that GG had aged a bit. He could see strings of gray sprouting from his hair line. He still wore a gold ring on each finger on his left hand with a gold Cuban link around his neck.

"Still got that shot gun under there?" he asked.

"Two," GG replied humorously.

"And my jewels?" Phatz asked, getting around to the main reason for his visit.

GG wagged a finger in the air.

"Wait right here."

Phatz tracked his movement as he darted behind the purple drape that sectioned off the back of the store from the front.

Seconds later he returned and waved for Phatz to follow.

In the back GG removed the jewels from a safe and placed them in front of him.

"You like right?"

Phatz eyes roamed over the chains and rings, each one made from a past jewel heist. He more than liked it. Picking up the heavy gold Turkish rope he was about to place it around his neck when GG came to his aid.

"Let me help you with that. You have to be careful with this," he said as he slowly placed the Turkish rope around Phatz neck and locked the clip.

Patting Phatz shoulders firmly GG stepped out of the way. As he looked at himself in the mirror Phatz gazed over his shoulder at GG who was stroking his graying beard. There was a distant look in the man's eyes.

"You know when I heard what happened, I said those guys will be fine they're tough. And I kept your jewelry safe for you all those years."

Phatz remained quiet as GG spoke. He slid on the ring that he had remade out of diamonds and gold that he'd taken from the mall during a heist.

Beside him GG gushed. At the sound of the bell that alerted him of a customer, he hurried from the back, while Phatz continued to try on all his jewels. The sight brought back memories he'd tried to keep at bay. For weeks now he had felt restlessness in his body. It was his old life calling him back to the hustle. As tempting as it was Phatz had to remind himself that there was a new game to master. Though sometimes he swore he could almost feel the weight of a hammer in his hand. Heavy like the rope around his neck.

Damn he missed it.

Gathering his jewels, he carefully placed them in a bag and stepped from behind the drape. There was no sign of GG but Phatz could hear his voice coming from somewhere in the store.

"Do you know one of the biggest jewel thieves in Los Angeles The Phatz?

Puzzled, Phatz tried to creep around to the other side to see who GG was talking to but the man spotted him.

"There he is now Phatz come here I want you to meet someone," GG stated waving him over.

The woman GG was speaking with stood with her back facing Phatz so he could only see the long waist length braids cascading down her back. Skinny and dressed in a light sweat suit there was something familiar about her. Curious Phatz moved in their direction, just as he was getting close, she spun around stopping him in his tracks.

Her eyes widened as her hand flew to her chest. A smile stretched across her full lips. When the shock wore off she spoke, "Phatz, it's me Vivian."

Phatz blinked almost in disbelief.

Standing in front of him was the last person he expected to see. Corey's widow.

****

He struggled to keep his heavy eyelids open as his head lolled back against the soft cushion. Seconds later the day's events finally caught up with him and Phatz lost the battle with sleep as darkness wrapped around him like a tight blanket.

"Found it!" the voice called out.

Jerking awake it took him a second to get his bearings as he looked around the unfamiliar room, then he realized he was in Vivian's two bedroom home in Brentwood right next to the Inglewood Forum Phatz had promised her he'd stopped by after bumping into her at GG's because according to her, they had a lot to catch up on. Scanning the dimly lit living room he took in the modest designs and scarce furniture throughout. He knew from hearsay on the streets that before his untimely demise Corey had been making bank. From the looks of it he hadn't left much to Vivian or maybe he had Phatz thought to himself remembering the red two-seater Benz parked in the double garage.

He was just about to stand and stretch when he heard her footsteps approaching.

"This was hidden in one of the boxes I still haven't unpacked yet, look at my baby," she said placing the book that she held in her hands in his lap as she slid in the spot next to him.

Phatz flipped through the book -that turned out to be a photo album- with indifference. Sitting around looking at old pictures of his dead friend wasn't something he wanted to do at almost two in the morning. Besides that, he had clubbed most of the night away with Big Mac at Carlos and Charley's in Hollywood and had seen a few honeys he wanted to get at. It was going on two weeks since he came home and still hadn't sexed anyone yet.

"And that's the car he had before he was killed," Vivian pointed out breaking into his thoughts.

Just then the pager on his hip vibrated saving him from anymore trips down memory lane.

"Can I use your phone?"

Nodding towards the phone on the table, she closed the photo album.

"I'll go check on Corey Jr," she said rising.

Phatz waited until she disappeared behind the door before he picked up the phone and dialed the number.

The voice on the other end sounded like smooth silk to his ears. He'd met Tiffany during his first visit with his PO. He and the brown skinned cutie had been silently peeping each other out when Phatz decided to make the first move. One thing led to another and they had exchanged numbers with plans to meet up later.

"When are you coming over?" Tiffany asked.

Liking how she had cut straight to the point, he took a cue and did the same .

"Soon but I wanna make this clear, I've been home for two weeks and I haven't had sex in four years so don't ask me to come over right now unless we're sexing."

The line on the other end grew quiet. Phatz thought he had struck out until she spoke again in a raspy voice.

"How about this?" she paused, " you pick me up, take me to dinner then bring your A game."

"Girl it's no A game," he shot back smiling from ear to ear.

Rattling off her address, Phatz promised to come scoop her up the next day.

Ending the call, he noticed Vivian was standing behind him. Unlike last time he hadn't heard her creep up.

With a smirk she dropped down beside him on the couch again. Phatz took the time to study her. Make up free, dressed in black pajamas with her long braids wrapped in a head scarf, Vivian looked young and innocent, but he knew better. Vivian or Viv as they called her had been on Corey's arm for a while it was how she and Phatz formally first met but even before then she was considered community pussy by a lot of niggas in the hood. He remembered seeing her dancing in front of cars on Marvin Street, when she was younger, and he couldn't forget how she and Dino Jr's mom would go fight girls over him and Corey. Viv as a young girl had been wild, still Corey saw fit to wife her and it was for that very reason that Phatz even bothered showing up to her house that night.

Tucking a leg underneath her bottom she rested her chin in her palm. A long pause of silence stretched between them before she spoke,

"You know Corey use to talk about you a lot, he thought of you as a brother."

Phatz nodded "I know."

Memories of Corey that he tried to keep at bay began flooding his mind. Mainly the time Corey called him with the police on the phone. It wasn't his best memory of Corey, but it was one that he'd thought about a few times while he was in Angola. He wondered if Viv remembered the incident since she too had been on the phone that day. Just as he was about to bring it to her attention, her shoulders suddenly began to shake.

Viv clasped a hand to her mouth to smother the cry coming from it.

On instinct Phatz pulled her into his embrace where she buried her face in his shirt.

"I miss him so much," she choked out.

Trying his best to comfort her Phatz ran a hand up and down her back as sobs racked her thin body. Then the tears stopped as suddenly as they had started.

Pulling away she swiped at her eyes with her fingertips before releasing a shaky breath.

"You must think I'm weak huh?" she asked, giving him a wobbly smile.

Shaking his head Phatz peered into her face. Eyes swollen from crying; he saw the pain in them. He could also see the vulnerability she struggled to hide.

"You lost your husband crying for him doesn't make you weak."

Bobbing her head up and down Viv let out a deep breath.

"Just didn't think it would end this soon we had so many plans…" she let her voice trail off.

Death was one of the reasons Phatz was determined to live his life to the fullest. There was no telling when it would come calling for him and he didn't want to leave this life with unfulfilled plans.

Clearing her throat, she reached up to tuck a loose braid that had found its way from under her head scarf.

Her voice was much stronger when she asked, "Where you staying?"

"I'm living off the fat of the land, wherever I lay my hat is my home," he answered reciting the famous line from the The Temptations.

Her lips twisted as if she was thinking about something.

"You can stay here if you want,'" she tossed out casually.

Caught off guard by the suggestion Phatz opened his mouth to speak but she rushed on

"You're like family," she glanced up at the clock on the wall, "and it's almost 3 A.M., I know you're tired."

He took a minute to think about it. Granted it was late. And though he had a key he didn't want to risk waking up his mom at the house. Deciding it was harmless he went to retrieve the overnight Gucci bag that he always kept in his van. Now showered and dressed in his black nylon boxers he had every intention of sleeping on the couch for a few hours, but when Viv pulled him towards her room, he didn't stop her. Call him crazy, but Phatz had a feeling that had been her plan since he walked through the door.

In the quietness of her room he lay wide awake on her cool sheets listening to them both breathe. Though there was a decent amount of space between them he could feel the unease creeping in. Afterall he was in his boxers sleeping next to his dead friends' wife.

What you doing Phatz? The voice in his head asked.

It was a question he couldn't answer, instead he listened to Viv's breathing grow shallow. Only when he was sure she was sleep, did he finally give in to the sandman that he had been fighting all night.

-----

3 weeks later

She was late. Glancing down at his watch for what felt like the hundred-time Phatz walked away from the window he had been peering out of.

"She's still not here?" Kathi questioned asked from the kitchen. He heard the sizzling sound of bacon frying in the pan followed by the tantalizing smell that still made his taste buds tingle despite it being over two years without meat.

"No," he answered before planting himself in a chair.

The "she" in question was his parole officer Ms. Williams. Phatz had prayed and hoped that he would get a nice parole officer. He realized his prayers would go unanswered the minute he laid eyes on the black woman's pinched expression as he entered her office. Ms. Williams who Phatz guessed was in her mid-forties had been a pain in his ass during their first meeting, starting with her condescending attitude and insults. Even so he had kept his cool- that was until she called him a mama's boy, then he'd let her have it. He took great pleasure at the sour expression on her face when she realized that the limo outside was for him. Leaving the office with the instructions for a home visit as their next appointment, he knew he was in for an uphill fight. But no matter how much of a bitch Ms. Williams was he was determined not to slip up and get sent back to prison. Pushing the unpleasant thoughts of her out of his head, his gaze settled on the black and white cowboy flick playing on the TV, he tried to tune in, but the fact of the matter was that his mind had quickly taken off in another direction. Weeks ago, if someone had told Phatz that he would be in cahoots with Corey's wife, he would've laughed at them. Not only because it was crazy, but because he'd known Viv for as long as he could remember, and she had never crossed his mind in that way. It was a given that she belonged to his friend, so that made her off limits, but those limits had been broken and burned. One night of staying at her tip in Brentwood had turned into two then three and so forth. Viv had even given him a key. Eventually the two fell into a quiet routine, Phatz would play the streets all day and return in the wee hours of the morning when she and her son were fast asleep. By the time they woke he was gone again. Everything was going well until he woke to find her sliding his dick in her mouth. Still in a sleep daze Phatz had tried to push her away, ignoring the feeling rushing through him as her wet tongue ran up and down his shaft. His resistance crumbled when she took him fully into her mouth. When she mounted on top of him Phatz didn't stop her. Instead he gripped her waist as she worked her hips in a slow rhythm. She was different from Tiffany the hot thing he had sexed at the motel for hours just a week before. True to his word Phatz had brought his A game, it was Tiffany who hadn't brought hers.

Viv was more experienced as she clenched her muscles with every thrust he made inside of her bringing them both to an eruptive climax. Just like that they had a new routine that started with breakfast in the morning and ended with sex at night. Soon any wrong that he felt about the situation began to fade away. It was just another part of the game and the way Phatz saw it, at least he wasn't fucking over her and beating her like the men from her past. Corey may have been high signing while he was alive, but his death had left Viv broke and living on scraps to get by. With only a high school diploma and a mouth to feed, she'd turned to the same game that planted her husband six feet deep. Corey had forgot to teach her the number one rule of the game, never mix business with pleasure. Fucked and tossed to the side like the prey that she had become, Viv was living on her knees when Phatz swooped into the rescue. That was one of his downfalls he would later learn; he hated to see a woman in need. Yet, the game wasn't the only thing that had fucked her over.

One morning Phatz had awaken to the sound of angry voices drifting up the stairs, immediately reaching for the .45 he kept on the night stand he slowly crept down the hall. Peeping his head into Corey's Jr. room he saw that the boy was still asleep before proceeding to the edge of the steps with the cold steel clutched tightly in his hand. From his position he could see Viv standing at the entrance of the house. The thin white silk nightgown she wore to bed that night molded to her round ass. He knew for a fact she didn't have any panties on underneath it. The thought had made him glance down at his own lack of clothes, a nylon tank top and matching boxers. Leaning forward to get a better view of who she was speaking to he stopped short when he heard her yell in a shaky voice.

"Get out my house!"

To make his presence known he cocked the .45. The loud noise made Viv glance up at him as he quickly traveled down the remaining stairs. Fear clouded her usually clear brown eyes.

"Phatz, its ok," she said stretching out her hand to stop him.

With a better view Phatz shook his head at the sight standing in front of them. Her brother Derrick was a stone cold crackhead. The man had some nerve coming to her house after what happened the day before. If it wasn't for Phatz roughing up

Mikey, another crackhead, for scamming Viv mother out of her rent money, the nice old woman would have gotten thrown out of her house that day. Luckily, Phatz had stepped in and put his foot down and it looked as if he would have to do the same with Derrick.

Only Derrick had taken one glance at Phatz who was perched on the last step with his .45 resting against his thigh and backed out of the house. That was the last he'd seen of Derrick. Phatz was making it clear that he would take care of his people by any means and in a short time Viv had managed to fall in that category.

Pulling his thoughts back to the present, Phatz couldn't wait to get started with his plans for the day. That was if Ms. Williams ever decided to show up. The credits of the show were rolling across the TV screen when the sound of squealing brakes pulling into the drive way grabbed his attention. Sliding his finger through the blind he watched Ms. Williams climb out of a beat up, loud yellow bucket. She struggled to close the door and after a few seconds used her hips to slam it shut. A smile washed across his face. Now he knew why she was upset about the limo. With the folder tucked underneath her arm, he watched as she made her way up the walkway. Instead of the tweed suit she wore when they first met, this one was red and polyester.

"That her?" Kathi asked venturing from the kitchen. Untying the apron from around her waist she pat her hands dry just as the doorbell rang. He moved to answer it but stopped at Kathi's voice.

"I'll get it," she said firmly. Taking a seat in Mother Dears chair Phatz folded his hands in his lap. Outside he was the picture of calm, but inside he was grinning like the Cheshire cat who ate the mouse.

Pulling the door open Kathi relaxed her face into a warm smile.

On the other side the pinched expression that Ms. Williams normally wore eased into what could be assumed as a smile.

"Hello, I'm Ms. Williams, Dino Bradley's parole officer." She stuck out her hand.

"Why are you late?" Kathi asked dropping her smile and ignoring the outstretched hand. A supervisor for DPSS, Kathi had called in late to be present for the appointment. Due to Ms. Williams tardiness her attitude was more than justified.

Taken back Ms. Williams mouth dropped open. A shocked expression covered her face as she struggled to find the words.

"Well I-I-."

Crossing her arms, Kathi pinned her with a stare.

"If the shoe were on the other foot and my son was late for his appointment I'm sure you would have had him escorted to jail and being the momma's boy that he is I would have to come get him out right?"

Behind her Phatz struggled to keep a straight face. Kathi had tossed the same words Ms. Williams had said to him back in her face. He had silently anticipated this day. After telling his mom what occurred at the paroles office and how she was breathing down his neck Kathi had put it in her mind to set Ms. Williams straight and she was doing a damn good job of it.

Ms. Williams eyes darted over Kathi's shoulder to Phatz. He could see the silent plea in them for help. Averting his head, he pretended to be watching TV. Seconds ticked off before she finally found her voice.

Shoulders sagging underneath the cheap polyester suit, she let out a deep sigh

"Mrs. Bradley, please forgive me for being tardy."

She hung her head like a child being scolded.

Without a word Kathi stood back and allowed her to finally enter. Phatz suspected that if it weren't for their nosey neighbors, his mom would have stood right there and continued to grill the woman.

Sitting up straight he watched Ms. Williams eyes dart around the living room.

"Smells good in here," she commented nervously as she struggled with the folder underneath her arms.

Finally, she turned to Phatz.

"Mr. Bradley how are you doing today?"

He could tell it was killing her to be polite to him.

"Same as I was doing the last time I saw you," he stated flatly, enjoying the uncomfortable look that crossed her face.

With a stiff nod of her head she turned to Kathi.

"You can have a seat," she offered.

Dropping into a chair at the table she shuffled through the papers in her folder. Above her head Kathi and Phatz gaze locked. She winked.

His mother always had his back no matter what.

"What do you need to see in my home?" Kathi asked, already knowing the routine since this wasn't Phatz first parole stunt.

Ms. Williams head snapped up from her search. "Uhhh," she glanced back down to the papers in front of her, "his living area."

"Follow me," Kathi said moving towards Phatz room not once bothering to look behind to see if she was following.

Jumping up Ms. Williams shuffled down the hall. Phatz lingered in the doorway as the woman asked more questions and inspected his room. She was talking so fast he barely understood her.

"Ok I've seen everything," she said slamming his drawer shut.

Stepping back so that she could exit, Phatz was confused when she stopped in the middle of the hall.

"What's in that room there?" she asked, referring to the closed bedroom door.

Behind her Kathi cleared her throat.

"I'm not on parole Ms. Williams so you don't need to worry, because that's my room."

Kathi nodded to Phatz, "Lead her back to the front."

Phatz watched Ms. Williams lift her head high in the air as she tried to salvage her remaining pride. Back ramrod straight she followed Phatz into the living room where she asked a few more questions before making a hasty retreat.

"She'll know better next time," Kathi said standing beside Phatz at the door as they watched her back out of the driveway, brakes squealing.

Phatz turned and hugged his mom, planting a kiss on her cheek.

She laughed loudly.

"Come on and eat before you go pick up AC and before I go back to work."

While Phatz hadn't forgotten his important plans, seeing Ms. Williams squirm had made him temporarily block out anything else. AC would be arriving home in less than two hours and Phatz had everything in place. Starting with a shopping spree to Chicago. He couldn't wait to see the look on AC's face when he told him. Dining on the breakfast she'd cooked he and Kathi laughed as they rehashed the events of the day. With only an hour remaining til AC's flight arrived Phatz helped Kathi clean, before changing into a Gucci linen suit.

Kathi beamed when he walked out the back.

"You look nice."

"Thank you, ma" he said sliding on his Omega. He made a mental note to stop by GGs for AC surprise when they returned from shopping. Calling up the stretch limo and Le Le, Phatz was almost out the door when Kathi handed him a pen and paper.

"What this for?"

"Read it," she said sitting down at the table again with a serious expression on her face.

Phatz huffed. "I don't want to be late picking up AC."

Outside he could see the stretch limo pulling up to the curb.

"Read it," Kathi said again more sternly. At that voice he plopped down and skimmed over the words on the paper. It was a life insurance policy.

Without a second thought he grabbed a pen.

"Mama you're wasting money, I'm not the one that's going to die in these streets. I'll be judged by twelve before I ever be carried by six," he said after signing on the dotted line and handing the policy to her.

"Never know when it's your turn to go son."

Kathi had already lost one son suddenly to the streets, but she had had the insight to insure the family long ago. When the time came to bury her child, a feat that she thought she would never have to face, the expenses had been the least of her worries. Now she was doing the same for her youngest son. Phatz knew that his mother had an idea of what he did. It was impossible to hide his flashy lifestyle and honestly he wasn't trying. He gave her money and presents every chance he got. She never asked questions, but he knew that she wasn't a square. He understood the reason for the policy. It was her way of preparing for the unexpected. Planting another kiss on her as he headed out the door, he touched the .45 at his waist. He had no intentions of letting his mother bury another child.

****

"Passengers your flight will be landing at the LAX airport in approximately five minutes, we ask that you please stay seated until the captain gives clearance," the flight attendant announced.

Lifting the shade near the seat window, AC stared at the clear blue skyline, not a cloud in sight as the plane began its descent. Briefly closing his eyes, he exhaled slowly. AC imagined that this was how a baby felt when they took their first breath of life. It was almost like a new world to him. His mind flashed back to his last hours in Angola, most of them spent with Chunky, whom the courts were determined to keep caged until he died. Even with the promise that he would do all he could to get his friend released, AC's heart still felt heavy as he walked out of those gates underneath the dark sky to freedom. Tucking his sadness away, he set his mind on carrying out the steps that he and Phatz had discussed upon his release.

When the door to the cab that was waiting on him swung open and out stepped Shauna, he felt like his heart would explode in his chest. Scooping her up off her feet, he lost track of how long they stood with their arms tightly wrapped around each other as if the other would disappear if they let go. Eventually they managed to untangle themselves and climb inside, still he kept her soft body pressed against his. Phatz had outdid himself by sending Shauna as a surprise to pick him up at 12:01 A.M. He couldn't stop smiling. After giving directions to the cabbie to Brian's house, they tried to squeeze four years of letter writing into one conversation often fumbling over their words and giggling like teenage lovers. AC couldn't get over how pretty she looked. Even in the darkness of the car he could see her yellow skin darken as he whispered in her ear. All too soon their flirting was cut short when the cabbie stopped outside of their destination. One-minute AC was laughing it up with Brian after transferring the money that they made down the walk into his hand and the next he was on a plane back to L.A.

At the sound of the light snores coming from beside him he glanced down at a sleeping Shauna, her head slightly resting on his arm. A tinge of regret hit him as he thought back to the way he reacted once they made it to the hotel after leaving Brian's place. Obviously after four years of being locked down and love letters AC was expecting some action. He was disappointed when she revealed that it was that "time of the month" so sex was off the table, but he'd waited four years, five more days wouldn't hurt.

Shaking her lightly, he waited until her eyes cracked open before planting a kiss on her soft lips.

"We're homeeee," he said grinning. AC's smile quickly turned into a frown when he tried to stretch his long legs. He was happy as hell the minute he saw the outfit Phatz had sent for him to return home in. The peach silk shirt and white linen pants fit perfectly. The shoes were another story. Cabin pressure from the plane had caused his feet to swell twice their size in the alligator shoes. He winced when pain shot up his leg when he tried to wiggle his toes. Around him passengers were gathering their things as the wheels of the airplane screeched on the runway. Pain momentarily forgotten AC tried to control his excitement as he glanced out the small window again. In the distance he could make out the tall outline of what he knew to be L.A.'s signature palm trees. Just the sight of them made his heart flutter.

"You got everything?" Shauna asked standing as the pilot's voice came over the intercom.

Not everything he silently thought drinking her body in with his eyes. When he'd met Shauna, she was a teen girl, body still budding like a flower. Now she was in full bloom. The denim shorts clung to her shapely hips and thin waist like a second skin. Even at 5'11 she had to stand on her tip toes to reach the overhead compartment, the move exposed the smooth skin on her flat stomach.

Just a few more days AC told himself, as he reigned in his raging hormones.

Inside the crowded airport he followed closely behind her, the swarming bodies making it impossible to walk side by side. But he didn't mind it gave him a nice view of her round ass as her hips swayed with every step. He wasn't the only one caught up in her sexiness. AC realized that men were openly staring at Shauna as they breezed through. He couldn't blame them. She looked as if she were floating on air instead of walking. Head held high, shoulders squared ready to take on the world or anybody that got in her way. She looked like a goddess. Any other man would have been jealous to see other niggas gawking at their woman, but AC's chest swelled with pride. She was all his. Shauna wasn't the only one turning heads. AC had caught a few appreciative stares from the women as well. He bit back a grin when one woman winked at him in passing. The attention was nothing new, he'd kept himself up while in Angola and it showed. The fro was gone and so was the nineteen-year-old body he once had. He was ripped. If his looks didn't make them stop and stare the thick gold rope- courtesy of Phatz-hanging from around his neck did. AC looked like money and felt like it too.

Though the chains of prison were off there were some habits he couldn't shake, like people watching. The skill had come in handy in Angola, teaching him to always watch his surroundings. As they walked through the airport, he tried to digest everything around him as he took in the smiling and friendly faces going to and fro. A warm feeling settled in his stomach when he witnessed a little girl run into her father's arm. His gaze cut to Shauna, maybe that could be them in a few years. When they passed the payphones lined on the wall he considered stopping to phone his aunt, but quickly dismissed the idea. On a day like today he figured she was probably at work anyways. He would have plenty of time to get to her, besides AC had a reputation for bringing gifts whenever he showed up and after four years, he couldn't show up empty handed. At the baggage claim he scooped Shauna's Louis Vuitton luggage up and continued their trek.

"Look like you in a lil pain playboy."

AC had been so busy watching everyone he hadn't noticed the person walking beside him.

He glanced over once, then did a double take.

Stopping in his tracks, AC stared at the man now in front of him. Dressed in similar clothes as his own, it felt like years had passed between the two when it had only been a month. Suddenly a swarm of emotion gripped at his chest. Angola had tested everything they stood for. They could have died in a strange land, away from everyone they loved and knew. Instead they stood tall, back to back and fought for their lives. If he had to do it all again, he would do it with the one person that had held him down from day one. The Phatz.

The two shared a quick but warm embrace as people tossed curious glances at the two men dressed to the nines. AC had a quick flash back to the moment the two finally met face to face on the yard after years of being separated in Angola. Word had gotten back to Phatz that a cat named Solo was inquiring of him. Not hip to the many alias that he used, Phatz had sent a few of his soldiers to check him out. When their search turned up nothing, Phatz was forced to go seek this Solo cat out for himself. By the time he made it to the other side of the yard every eye was trained on him, when AC finally spun around a smile as wide as the Grand Canyon stretched across Phatz face. AC knew that Phatz enemies were probably hoping that he would be the one to take him out, but they were sadly mistaken. When the two men were apart they were dangerous, put them together and they were unstoppable.

"Boss Angeles baby," Phatz said pulling away and removing the Ray Ban shades from his face.

"No place like it."

Just then a black flight attendant strutted pass, sexy calf muscles on display in her six-inch heels. The uniform hugging her in all the right places caught the attention of both men.

"You right about that," Phatz replied watching until she disappeared down the flight corridor.

"Ahem" at the sound AC turned to see an amused Shauna staring at him. Her lips slightly poked out with an eyebrow raised.

"See something you like?" she asked as her feet tapped the floor.

Laughing he pulled her to his side and kissed the attitude out of her. When he was finished, he draped an arm across over her shoulder.

"You got me good with this," AC said nodding his head as he pulled Shauna closer.

"I knew you would like it," Phatz responded with a smirk.

Glancing around AC noticed the airport was twice as packed now. He couldn't wait— His thoughts were cut short by the pain slicing through his foot. Shifting from one foot to the other he grimaced.

"What's wrong?" Phatz asked. AC could hear the laughter in his voice.

"Shoes too little," he admitted with a bashful shrug.

"That would explain why you walking on your tip toes," Phatz said breaking into laughter.

AC chuckled.

"Damn I forgot about the cabin pressure," Phatz said with a hint of laughter still in his voice.

"Next time go two sizes up."

Above them the intercom crackled announcing a flight arrival. Placing the Ray Bans' on his face, Phatz motioned towards the bag in his hand.

"That's all y'all got?"

"Yep."

"Cool, let's go get you some more shoes." Phatz mimicked how AC walked sending them all into another round of laughter as they moved through the airport and out the doors.

Outside, AC eyes widened when Phatz walked up to the stretch limousine waiting at the curb.

Beside him Shauna bounced excitedly. He could count on one hand how many times he'd rode in a limo. IT was only once and that was during a family members funeral. He and his younger cousins had fought about who would sit next to the window. In the end he'd won. Despite the tear's AC had felt like a movie star that day on the short ride to the church. It was his last ride in the limo, but it wouldn't be his last funeral.

"Damn we doing it like this now?" he asked walking up to the limo, his reflection clear in its tinted windows. A few people began to hover around in hopes that they would see a movie star exit. Phatz and AC were the stars of the show, the people just didn't know it.

"Bigger than this, you'll see," Phatz stated before climbing in.

Shauna bounced in next and AC slid in right behind her. He was surprised at the pretty brown skin girl sitting on the other end, but her warm smile quickly put him at ease.

"I'm Le Le," she said giving him a hug.

AC tried to recall where he had heard the name before. Then it came to him. She was Billy's girl. Music came from the speakers as the limo's engine started. AC found himself rapping along to the words. It was a song that he'd played a lot during his last days at Angola.

"Move the crowd."

"That's right," Phatz said joining in.

Tapping on the partition Phatz waited for it to roll down. The black chauffeur turned his head in their direction.

"Driver take us to the Fox Hill mall."

With a nod he eased the limo from the curb.

AC had all but forgot about his aching feet. Settling against the leather seat he gazed around as Shauna and Le Le began chatting it up.

Phatz nudged him.

"How's Chunky?"

Chunky. The thought of his friend brought a dark cloud, then AC remembered his plan. Make enough money to get Chunky a real lawyer for his case and not one of those fake ass public defenders. Perking up he nodded his head.

"He's good, but we gotta get him out of there."

Phatz nodded in agreement. "One step at a time."

AC was relieved to know that they were on the same page, but then again, he knew Phatz would be. As the limo driver pulled out of the airport, he closed his eyes and said a silent prayer for his friend for protection, until they were able to get to him.

"Here."

Eyes snapping open AC looked at the champagne glass stretched towards him. Phatz had produced a bottle of champagne. Neither of them was drinkers, but today was a special celebration. Pouring champagne into the girls' flute, Phatz raised his glass in the air, with everyone following suit.

"I'm glad you made it out that jungle my nigga."

"We," AC said correcting him.

"That's right, now it's time to kick shit up you heard me."

"Of course," AC responded. They had gone over their plans so much AC could recite it in his sleep. Phatz had kept him tuned in to everything that was going on. The game, the drugs, everything. Now that Phatz had claimed his place in the game it was time for him to do the same.

"To life," Phatz toasted clinking their glasses together.

AC had an even better one.

"To freedom, to getting this money…"

He locked eyes with Phatz, they had taken on the bloody war in Angola together, now it was time to take on something different.

"…To family and some mo of it."

(AC. First day out!)

****

Red, green, and blue party lights moved over the gyrating bodies on the dance floor as the DJ pumped out Heavy D's hit song *Overweight Lovers* from the speakers on the stage. Phatz was no longer overweight but his body rocked along to the beat. When a short woman in a little black dress began to grind against him, he matched her move for move. Pretty soon the two were caught up in their own world like many of the dancers on the floor. A quick scratch on the record and the song smoothly transitioned into another classic, breaking their daze.

All that dancing had made his throat dry.

"I'm going to the bar! You want something?" he asked over the music. The cutie with the banging body shook her head. Mouthing for her to wait for him, Phatz made his way through the crowd to the other side of the club.

"Water no ice," he ordered when he reached the bar.

The bartender, a man dressed in all black with tattoos covering his arms, quirked his eyebrow at the foreign request. After a few seconds he shrugged his muscled shoulders, produced a cup, and squirted a spray of water into it, before setting it in front of Phatz and returning to his customers.

Leaning on the bar with one hand he used the other hand to dab at the sweat that had gathered on his forehead with a napkin. Nursing his water like it was a shot of brandy, he sifted through the sea of faces in the dim lit club in search of AC, not surprised when he found him lounging on a chair with two beautiful women right next to him. There was always a trail of ladies following behind wherever they went. While Phatz liked to think that it was because they were fly good-looking men, caution wouldn't let him ignore that the real reason was money. Women could sniff out money like a blood hound who'd caught the scent of an escaped prisoner. The reality was that money was the first thing that came to anyone's mind when Phatz and AC were mentioned. A year had passed since their release from the hell that was Angola and in that time, they'd taken a hold of the dope game by its throat. They were on a major level now, moving over 100 to 150 birds at a time. The duo had a flawless operation system, while Phatz set up shop and became the plug for Atlanta and New Orleans, AC had conquered Ohio and Chicago. With the recent drought forcing the Columbians to go up on their prices making birds jump from ten thousand to thirteen thousand dollars, Phatz and AC had no other choice, but to increase their prices as well . It was the classic supply meets demand approach. The dealers in the other states understood this, so there was hardly any backbite when the prices changed. Phatz was proud of the empire they were building and like all emperors he was looking to conquer new territory. Next up was Oakland. He made a mental note to run the plan by AC, before they met with Big Mac later in the week.

His gazed fixed on AC again. A third woman was comfortably positioned in his lap now, she tossed her long hair over her shoulder as her hand stroked the gold chain around AC's neck. He smiled to himself at just how much a lot could change in a year. They were living life to the fullest, making up for all the time that they'd spent locked down, macking on women and partying at a new club every night. Tonight it was Geraldine's on Imperial and Crenshaw located in Inglewood. He had plans to attend Club Paradise, but it was Viv who talked him into coming to Geraldine's to celebrate her friends birthday party. The birthday friend in question Edna, sat a few feet away from AC in the V.I.P. section. Edna was the wife of long-time hustler, Fast Eddie. The man sat next to his wife and Salty who was Phatz friend and Inglewood family. Seeing Salty's face in there had come as surprise to him. After playing catch up they'd spent most of the night taking pictures and making memories. Viv gloated in her friends faces as she showed both Phatz and AC off to the older crew, like they were prized trophies. She, herself was back shinning thanks to AC and Phatz, still she waltzed around looking for another lick to score. Along with the drug game they'd picked up another hustle: jacking. Using Viv as bait she would fuck and suck big time dealers and because most niggas liked to pillow talk it wasn't long before she knew all of their secrets including where their safe houses full of kilos were located. That was when Phatz and AC would step in and hit the lick, sometimes walking away with more than fifty birds and large sums of cash. The dealers never saw it coming and no one had ever linked Viv to the treachery. It was another reason why Phatz had attended the party, he knew it would be full of old ballers with long money and any one Viv hooked tonight, would become their next target. Finally gulping down the water, he scoped out the scene a little more. Earlier he'd been eager to get to the dance floor now with the crowd thinning out, he could see better. Viv was perched at the end of bar making conversation with a woman. Her long braids that she once wore had been replaced with equally long weave. The shiny black metallic dress she wore matched the Gucci pumps on her feet. When they made eye contact, she subtly shook her head. Phatz knew that meant she hadn't been successful on locking in on a mark yet. She averted her eyes continuing her conversation with the woman. *Oh well maybe another night* he thought. Checking the time on his Omega he figured if he and AC left now, they would still have time to make it to Club Paradise to really party. Spinning to the bar to ask for another water his body stiffened when he felt soft hands rub over his back. Figuring Viv had decided to join him he spun around.

"Long time no see," the woman said rubbing her body against his.

Phatz dick hardened in his pants.

"Silky," he hissed out between his teeth.

She nodded running her tongue across her lips. His gaze raked over her body. The skintight dress she wore barely left anything to the imagination. Phatz could see her nipples tighten through the thin material. They'd dealt with each other once or twice since he had been home and even though Silky would always have his respect for how she rode out with them in Louisiana, his feelings for her were no longer the same. He couldn't say when they had changed, he just knew they had. He looked at her again, but that didn't mean he would turn her down if she offered.

She threaded their fingers together.

"You're looking good."

He watched the lust jump in her brown eyes before he glanced down at his attire. The tailored tan suit he sported were compliments of his tailor. Before he could respond to her a hoard of people began to rush the bar. Pulling her out of harm's way, he flattened her back against the wall. Out of his peripheral he noticed Viv watching them like a hawk. The corners of her mouth turned down. She knew all about Silky and their past. Several months after he and Viv had started their thing, Silky had called him up on his car phone. Vivian being the jealous hearted woman that she was told Silky in these exact words "If you would suck his dick more and stop spreading his business maybe he'll see you more!" Before hanging up in her face. The situation was humorous to Phatz, women had been fighting over him all of his life, but Viv had taken it to another level. That was the last he had heard of Silky until tonight.

"And where have you been?" Silky asked, pulling his attention away. Her hands continued to roam over his body.

"I been around," Phatz said locking her hands in between his own, stopping her exploring.

She snatched away.

"Well why haven't I seen you?" she asked with an eye roll. Folding her arms under her breast Silky cocked her head to the side waiting for an explanation.

Instead of responding Phatz edged closer and nipped the sensitive skin on her neck. Immediately she pressed closer to him. He slid his hand up her warm thighs, before moving his mouth over her lips. The loud music drowned out her moans. Suddenly she broke away, Phatz eyes popped open.

"What's wrong?" he asked.

With a smirk Silky nodded her head over his shoulder. Glancing behind him he saw Viv. Her eyes were spitting fire in their direction.

"Call me when you get done playing house," Silky said swatting his hand away. She pulled down her skirt before walking off. Phatz dropped his head to conceal his smile, Silky was playing hard to get. If it wasn't for the fact that they were in the club he would have had her out of her clothes in no time. Adjusting his pants, he made his way across the floor toward Viv, AC had joined her and another woman stood off to his side.

"What's up?" he asked coolly stopping in front of them.

"I wanted you to meet someone, but I see you're busy," she bit out between clenched teeth. Her eyes narrowed into thin slits. Lately, Viv had become possessive. Asking his where a bout's, checking his pager. In the beginning they shared a mutual understanding. Sex with no ties while they made money together. That was all, but more and more it seemed like she was losing her sight of their agreement. One part of him found it sexy, the other part annoying. He wanted to address it but knew that tonight wasn't the right time. Behind them a round of cheers went up as Edna and her birthday crew continued to celebrate her with another round of drinks. Viv must have come to her senses because her face slowly shifted into a smile. She moved to his side.

"Phatz this is my friend Karol."

She motioned towards the woman standing beside AC.

Karol was a shapely woman who looked to be in her early thirties. It wasn't her pretty heart shaped face framed by curls that got Phatz attention, it was the thick gold chain that glistened around her neck. When Karol reached out her hand for him to shake, Phatz zoomed in on the diamond rings on her fingers. Now there were two things he liked to think he was an expert on and that was jewelry and money. Phatz could count money with his eyes closed and he knew fine jewelry when he saw it. Based on what he was seeing, Karol had at least $50K dollars' worth of jewelry on her persons.

"It's nice to meet you Phatz I was starting to think you and your friend were just a figment of old girl's imagination," she winked at Viv.

"Oh no we're very much real as you can see," Phatz responded meeting her stare.

"Well you should know you're all miss thang talks about, maybe all of us could go out sometime after this."

She slanted her eyes at AC, who stood by quiet, but Phatz could see the interest in his gaze.

"Just name the time and the place and we're down," AC jumped in on cue.

Viv opened her mouth to say something, but quickly shut it. Phatz watched the color drain from her face as she looked over his shoulder. Turning to see the cause of her sudden distress, he watched a man dressed in an off-crème suit approach them. Tall and brown skinned with a low haircut, Phatz had seen the face many times after the street races he attended on Adams off Crenshaw at Johnny's Pastrami.

"There's RL," Viv rushed out just above a whisper confirming it was who he thought it was. He watched the man stop to shake hands with the players at Edna's table.

Thanks to Viv Phatz knew all about the woman beater. He was a car thief and he also happened to be Viv's ex-husband. The marriage had ended, mainly due to the fact that RL couldn't keep his hands to himself. The scar underneath Viv's eye was a testament to the harsh beatings he'd given her. Phatz ground his teeth together. He couldn't stand a woman beater, but even more he hated a fake and RL's whole demeanor screamed fake. If Phatz memory served him correct he owed Viv money. RL and her had set up a few licks because the dope game wasn't paying off for them. Their first lick was stealing three birds from a well-known dealer named Corvette Mike. Their next mark was another dealer by the name of Franny. Providing RL with the information to break into his stash house and steal $70,000, Viv had waited patiently for the signal as she dined at a restaurant with Franny. She had felt like a mastermind when they pulled off the double scheme, but things started to fall apart when RL learned the real game, that Viv had fucked both of the men in order to gain access to their riches. A furious RL beat her viciously before running off with her cut of the money. Though it had been years since it happened Phatz could see that she was still affected by it.

Motioning for AC to move closer he leaned in and whispered.

"Follow my lead, I'm about to get us to Club Paradise." With a nod AC waited for his signal.

"Viv, baby how you doing?" RL stretched his hands out in a hug gesture when he reached them.

She slid further behind Phatz. Confusion washed over his face before he quickly concealed it with a phony grin. Clearing his throat, he nodded his head at Phatz.

"Phatz what's up I heard you was home," he said, going in for a handshake, dismissing all the warnings around him.

Taking his hand Phatz pulled him closer. Patting him on the back he squeezed his hand as he moved his lips near RL's ear.

"Nigga for Corey I'ma fuck up yo eye like you did Viv."

RL inhaled sharply and tried to pull away, but Phatz held his hand in a crushing grip.

"You have twenty-four hours to pay her that $10,000 you owe her." To get his point home he moved RL's hand to the .45 in his waist.

Clapping him on the back Phatz finally let him go.

RL swallowed hard his eyes bugged out his head. He looked from Phatz to Viv.

"I-"

Phatz held up his hand. "Fuck all that talk lets go outside."

"You good?" AC asked jumping in on cue.

"Talk to him please," RL pleaded with desperation in his voice.

AC scoffed. Reaching inside his waist he produced the twin .45 and cocked it.

"It's no talking to Phatz when he's like this, you gone need this to even out the odds," he said holding it out towards RL.

RL's mouth moved but no words came out. He was shaking in his boots.

Phatz walked off. Outside in the parking lot he leaned against the car knowing that RL wouldn't come out, instead a worried Edna and a jolly Viv rushed out in his place.

"Please don't turn my party out," Edna said coming to a stop in front of him.

"What yo-?" he caught himself at the realization of her words. Edna had noticed the small altercation between he and RL. He glanced at her pleading face and swallowed the laugh in his throat. It was all for show if he had really wanted to take it there with RL, he would've done it right there. Instead he had used the man's presence as an excuse to leave the club that he had grown bored with. It was time to make his way to Club Paradise with the young honeys. That was if AC ever brought his ass out, he thought realizing the man was still lingering inside. Focusing on Edna he pulled at the sleeves of his jacket playing along.

"Ok I'm gone."

He turned to Viv but before he could open his mouth she jumped in his arms and gave him a kiss.

She wrapped her arm around his neck.

"RL's paying the 10K first thing tomorrow."

Of course, he would if he knew what was best for him Phatz thought.

Peering up at him she used her finger to rub off the lipstick on his lips.

"Cut it in half," he said, referring to the cut that he would take for getting it back. It was a part of their agreement. With a giggle she kissed him again.

Phatz slapped her on the ass before pulling away.

"Now go enjoy the party." He looked at Edna and winked, "Happy Birthday."

The two women strutted back inside just as AC was coming out the door with a knowing look on his face. Phatz had given them all some game, now the real partying was about to start.

(Phatz & Awful Clyde with friends)

****

      The next day Phatz stood at the kitchen counter shoving sticks of celery and carrots into the blender. Pressing the button, he winced at the sound of the blades grinding the vegetables up into a smooth concoction. Transferring the mixture into a cup he held it under his nose before taking a deep breath, the strong scent of celery made his nose hairs tingle. Exhaling deeply, he downed the cup in one motion. Immediately his face scrunched up at the bitter taste. Still he kept chugging until there was no more. Plopping the cup down on the counter he reached for a bottle of water to wash the taste from his mouth.

"Shit," he spat before swishing the water around in his mouth.

He knew that it would be a while before his taste buds returned to normal, but it was the cost of discipline. Every day before the break of dawn Phatz woke to start his morning workout routine that included five hundred pushups, five hundred sit ups and weightlifting. There were some days the energy pulsed so fast through his veins that he went further, pushing his body to the limits ignoring his screaming muscles. Phatz knew that if he could get his mind use to the pain, eventually his body would fall into line. So he pushed, pumping out set after set until his mind became numb, until his loud breathing was the only thing he could hear. To him he wasn't just training his body how to respond in stressful situations, but also his mind. Now if only he could do the same for his stomach.

He gagged once as the vegetable cocktail threatened to come up. Squeezing his eyes shut he brought his fist up to his mouth and inhaled deeply before exhaling. He repeated this step a few times, until the queasiness in his stomach began to subside. When he could breathe again, he busied himself with preparing for the day. He had just reached for his buzzing pager when Viv, Corey Jr, and Dino Jr breezed through the door.

"Daddy!" Dino Jr yelled before throwing his arms around his waist. Clipping his pager on his hip Phatz leaned down to return the hug.

"What's up lil man?" he asked Corey Jr, before giving him a high-five.

"Dad Viv took us to six flags!" Dino Jr said excitedly.

At the mention of her name she appeared in the archway of the kitchen. Setting her purse on the table she handed him the newspaper before kissing him on the cheek.

"We had a lot of fun!" She announced winking at Dino Jr. who took off to join Corey outside.

Returning her attention back to Phatz she pecked him on the lips.

"Miss me?"

Silky's words ran through his head at the exact moment. They were in fact playing house. Viv had even started looking after his son who was staying with them for summer vacation. He scanned her up and down. The sex was good and she made sure his son was straight when he wasn't around. Maybe playing house wasn't so bad after all, as long as she remembered who was in charge. Squeezing her small waist Phatz moved away.

"You weren't gone long," he responded.

Tucking the newspaper underneath his arm he moved into the living room with her in tow. With a flick of his wrist he slid the curtains back allowing the sunlight to filter inside. Outside the window the boys raced on their bikes.

"Those boys ran me ragged today so much energy," she said flopping down on the couch. Slipping out of her tennis shoes she tucked her legs underneath her. The red paint on her toenails matched the color on her nails she ran through her hair.

"They're boys that's what they do," Phatz nudged her to the other side of the sofa.

A faraway look appeared in her eyes as he flipped through the paper.

"Maybe they need something to soften them up."

Half listening Phatz turned the page.

"Maybe they need a sister."

His hand froze on the sports section. He blinked hoping he'd heard wrong.

"We can have a baby girl for them," Vivian stated happily. She clasped her hands underneath her chin.

Baby?

He would have laughed if the expression on her face wasn't so serious.

And just like that their playing house had went up in flames right before his eyes, but Viv wasn't the only woman who wanted to have his baby. At one point Silky was desperately trying to have his seed, calling him to sex her during the times she was ovulating. She went as far as making an appointment for him to make sure his equipment was working properly. And it was. After seeing her last night, he was glad a child had never entered their situation. Children complicated things. He was about to tell Viv this when the door alarm sounded pulling his attention away to AC strutting inside.

"What's up?" he greeted dapping Phatz up before nodding at Viv. Taking a seat opposite of them he looked back and forth between the two.

"Did I interrupt something?" he asked with a smirk.

"Nope," Phatz spoke up quickly. Placing the newspaper down on the table, he suddenly had lost interest in reading it.

Turning to Viv he tilted his head.

"You said you wanted to talk to us about something."

Her perfect arched eyebrows furrowed for a few seconds. She slapped her hands together.

"Right, damn I almost forgot."

Her eyes darted to Phatz, he read the look in them. She wasn't done about the whole baby situation. That was too bad cause he was. At the nod of his head he motioned for her to continue.

"Ok remember the friend Karol that I introduced y'all to last night right?" she asked. Edging to the end of the couch she placed her feet on the floor.

"How can I forget baby was stacked," AC grinned.

"In more ways than one," Viv responded standing up. She moved to the window where she slid the curtains down. Though only a slither of light remained, Phatz could still hear and see the kids. Facing them she placed her hands on her hips.

"A few months ago, homegirl hit the lotto she's racking in at least $50,000 a month."

Phatz let out a low whistle. He'd been dead on the money when he summed up all the jewelry on her last night.

"Not only does she have money, but the other day when I was over her house, I saw her nigga put twenty birds in the closet."

Both he and AC sat up straight at the mention of the birds. She had their attention now.

"Twenty?" AC repeated.

Viv nodded.

Phatz liked where things were going. They didn't care anything about the jewelry. It was the drugs they were interested in. Viv on the other hand couldn't keep her eyes off of Karol's jewelry all night. Ole thang didn't care shit about loyalty or friendship. Though he smiled at the thought, he also tucked it away in his brain for safe keeping.

His pager buzzed again. Same number. He would get to it later he thought motioning for her to continue.

"Ok so she got a real fly ass apartment in West L.A."

"Give us the address we can get to it now," AC said jumping up.

Phatz could always count on him to be ready but there was one problem.

"We don't break in houses," he leaned back to let his words sink in.

It wasn't just that they didn't break in houses but there were too many additional problems that came with home invasions. For all he knew there could be someone waiting in the closet ready to blow a hole threw them. He preferred to stick to the script.

Easing back into his seat AC shrugged.

"Well how are we going to get the drugs?" he asked voice laced with frustration.

In front of him Viv wrung her hands as she paced back and forth.

"She copped a new 190 Benz too…" she let her words trail off. Stopping she rotated her shoulders as in deep thought. The room grew silent. After a few seconds

AC slapped his hands together and stood again "Ok well most women have their car keys and house keys on the same chain" he looked at Phatz to make sure he was following along.

"Lure ole girl out and I'll take the keys and car from her, we won't have to break in if we have the key."

A sinister smile crossed his face.

Phatz was still uneasy about the plan.

"How do we know the place will be empty and the work will still be there niggas move twenty birds all day on one deal?" he questioned.

Viv huffed out a deep breath.

"Becaussee" she said stretching out the word. "I wouldn't set us up on a dummy mission." She clicked her tongue when she realized the excuse wasn't good enough for Phatz or AC. "Her nigga is out of town and won't be back until Sunday. Her tip is basically the stash house, so the drugs are there."

Phatz tossed his hands up. Why hadn't she included that information the first time. Still his mind tossed the scenario around in his head. If they had the keys, they wouldn't look suspicious when they went in. Easing to the window he peeped out the curtain, Corey Jr. and Dino Jr were having the time of their lives on the bikes. His mind focused back on the opportunity in front of him. Only one person needed to get the kilos. The other two would distract Karol. He shook his head at Karol's boyfriend naivety. You never left precious cargo around without protection, but his misstep was about to be their gain.

He locked gazes with AC.

"Suit up."

****

      The cars whizzed by on the busy street of Crenshaw and Adams as the nine to five workers rushed to their destinations after a long day of work. At the bus stop a man sat with his head bent forward, the bulky navy-blue mechanic jump suit hid his muscular figure. With his chin resting on his chest and his eyes lowered to the ground he appeared to be sleep to the outside world. Just another helpless bum of the city, but the keen eyes hiding behind the pair of tinted sunglasses on his face said otherwise. The familiar buzz of the pager going off in his pocket made him glance down at the flashing digits. Right on time he thought. Wiggling his finger around the collar of his shirt he let out a deep breath. The sun was beginning to set in the sky, but not fast enough. Underneath the jumpsuit he could feel the T-shirt begin to stick to his skin. Lifting his head, he honed in on the store across the street. Briefly he considered crossing over to grab him something to drink but quickly dismissed the idea. He would stick to the plan as he always did. Over the years he'd learned to master the art of stillness of the mind and the body, no matter how uncomfortable the situation was. He knew first-hand how one miscalculated step could cause a chain of undesired consequences. So, he waited. It wasn't long before more people begin to crowd the bus stop. Most of them kept a safe distance from the man in the jump suit who was now slouched on the bench. In L.A. you never knew what could happen when you came in contact with the homeless. Some would attack you in their drug induced state, while others badgered you with their pity stories in hopes of getting money. Whatever the case most people avoided the homeless like the plague and the man knew this. He stretched his long legs out further on the bench, unbothered by the looks of disapproval on the people's faces. From behind the shades he silently dared anyone to say anything, when they didn't he chuckled to himself first softly then loudly. The sound mixing in with the approaching bus squealing brakes. They didn't know that he was giving them some uncut game. When the pager in his pocket buzzed for the second time he stood and began to walk in the opposite direction as the people began to pile on the bus. Like clockwork a red two-seater Benz, followed close behind by a 190 Benz, turned sharply into the 76 gas station. Slowly crossing the street, he noticed that traffic was beginning to thin as the bus pulled away from the curb. Locking in on his target, he slid the ski mask over his face and slid the shades back on. With her back facing him she never saw him coming.

"Aaaahhhh!"

A loud scream tore through the air as she turned around coming face to face with her assailant.

Placing a slim finger to his lips he shook his head.

Her gaze swung around wildly as she looked for help. Realizing they were the only ones in the parking lot she resulted to the only thing that would save her life.

"P-please don't hurt me" she pleaded, squeezing her eyes shut. Every inch of her body shook as she tried to prepare herself for whatever was coming.

He almost laughed. He'd heard the terms "knees knocking," but witnessing it was another thing

Making quick work of her fear. He snatched the keys from her tight grip. , pausing when he heard the quick intake of breath.

"Please don't hurt me" she repeated with tears streaming down her cheeks.

Ignoring her pleas his eyes scanned over her body until he found what he was looking for. Snatching the diamond earrings out of her ear he moved to the gold Rolex around her wrist next. The fact that she didn't put up a fight made everything so much smoother and to think he didn't even have to utter a word.

Firmly pushing her to the side he slid behind the wheel of the Benz. In one quick motion he put the car in drive, skating out of the parking lot. The whole thing had taken less than thirty seconds.

****

"Help, Help!"

Phatz turned at the sound of the loud distressed voice as Karol stumbled through the gas station store doors. He stood at the cash register paying for a bottle of apple juice and a pack of gum. Seconds before his eyes had been trained on the small TV broadcasting the evening news behind the counter.

"Oh my God Karol!" Viv yelled rushing up the aisle. She made it just in time to catch Karol as she crumbled to the floor.

A dark trail of eye shadow rolled down her tear stained face as she tried to gulp in air.

"I've been robbed," she choked out followed by a loud wail. Her lips trembled as she tried to speak again.

"You want me to call the police?" The cashier asked with wide blue eyes gazing at the two women on the floor.

With a subtle shake of his head Phatz kneeled beside Viv who cradled a hysterical Karol in her arms.

"A m-man in a mask just took my car."

"When?"

"N-now," she stuttered. "He took my car and my earrings,

she glanced down at her naked wrist, "and my Rolex." She said before bursting into another fit of uncontrollable tears.

Dropping the items in his hand Phatz grabbed his keys from his pocket.

"What are you about to do?" Viv asked with a glint in her eye.

"Ima try to go get her whip back."

Not waiting for a response, he rushed out the double doors ignoring when she called after him.

Hopping inside of the Benz, Phatz flipped the switch and stomped the gas.

****

     A few blocks away the 190 Benz swerved in and out of traffic. Snatching the shades and mask off his face AC drew in a lung full of Karol's flowery perfume that still lingered in the interior of the car. Glancing wildly around he checked both side mirrors for any signs of police before his gaze focused on the red plastic cherries swaying back and forth around the rear-view mirror. That had been the most excitement he'd had in a while. Snapping out of his daze he read the code coming through on his pager.

Perfect

With one hand still on the wheel AC shrugged out of the hot jump suit until it was bunched around his waist.

"Let's see what else you got in here."

Easing his foot off the gas as he approached the red light, AC popped the glove compartment open. Eyes still trained on the road he rummaged through the papers slightly disappointed when his search turned up empty. The light was still on red when the familiar sounds of Frankie Beverly and Maze *Look at California* reached his ears. Cutting his eyes to the Benz in the next lane, he admired his reflection in the cars shiny red paint job. Slowly the window of the Benz rolled down.

"Took you long enough," AC joked head angled out of the window.

"Had to make it look real!" Phatz shouted above the music.

"Tell Viv I got the watch and earrings she asked for." And to prove it, he dangled the Rolex watch out of the car before tossing it and the earrings into Phatz car. The car in front of him nudged forwards as the light turned green.

"You know where you going right?"

With a nod of his head AC eased his foot off the brake.

"Catch you back at the house," he said before punching the gas. Fifteen minutes later he entered Karol's apartment like a thief in the night. AC stumbled through the darkness until his hand found the switch. Light flooded the plush apartment. Careful to not leave any fingerprints, he took in the upscale furniture with the great view. Karol was living in style and he liked it. Making his way down the well-lit hall he tried two closed doors before he found the master bedroom. The kilos where in the closet just as Viv said they would be. AC shook his head at the carelessness of the man they belonged to. Transferring the twenty kilos into his own bag, he left as swiftly as he had come.

● ●

Meanwhile Phatz mind replayed the events of the day as he steered the Benz. Just hours earlier Karol, Viv, and him had feasted on seafood and shrimp scampi at the new Cajun restaurant Harold & Bells on Ninth Avenue and Jefferson Boulevard. During dinner Karol had sung Phatz praises for taking care of Viv. So much that he'd almost felt bad for what was about to happen. Except for the fact that he'd already made the deal to sell the birds for $20,000 each and there was no turning back. He watched closely as Viv laughed and joked with Karol over the dinner table. Once or twice she'd caught him staring and gave a careless shrug. There wasn't an inch of remorse on her face for what she knew was about to go down. He thought It was funny how trust worked. It was the key to most successful relationships and friendships, but if given to the wrong person trust could be a dangerous thing. Karol trusted Viv so much that she walked right into the trap they had set for her with her eyes wide shut. Though lucky for Karol, he and AC were a set of principled criminals who didn't seek to hurt naïve women. Just rob them. The only thing that had been hurt during the incident was Karol's pride.

When the mini mart came into view Phatz shifted his attention.

Parking the Benz, he put on his game face as he made his way over to Viv and Karol who were now standing outside. He could still see the shock on Karol's face. Her eyes widened when she saw him approach.

"My car?" she asked in a breathless voice.

Jumping into actor mode Phatz dropped his head. "I'm sorry I lost him on the freeway." The lie rolled so smooth off his tongue he would've believed it if he didn't know the truth. Just then the store attendant burst through the door.

"I can still call the police if you want me to, we have cameras out here but it didn't get much," she said apologetically. Phatz shot the woman a death look, but she was staring directly at Karol. Biting her lip Karol shook her head.

"No police," she croaked out.

Good girl, Phatz thought. She may have wanted her car returned, but Karol knew the rules of the streets. With a bewildered look the store clerk retreated inside the store knowing there was nothing more she could do.

"Just take me to my boyfriends' house," Karol said eyes shining with unshed tears.

The request made Phatz pause. Above her head he glared at Viv who hadn't said a word. Her perfectly arched eyebrows wrinkled into a deep v.

Running her hand down Karol's back Viv began leading her to the car.

"I thought you said your man was gone out of town," she finally spoke.

Karol shook her head as she slid in the back seat. "He changed his mind at the last minute," she said before bursting in tears.

The confession made Phatz angry. He could feel the skin around his neck begin to tighten. *Shit* his mind screamed as he slammed the door. AC could be in trouble. Reflexively he reached under the seat feeling for his .45. When his fingers brushed against the cold steel, he relaxed a tinge. Punching in the code on his pager he pressed the button sending a message to AC. It felt like hours had passed as he waited when in fact it was only seconds. An audible sigh left his mouth when the digits appeared on the small screen. The triple threes meant that AC had reached home. Shifting to drive he locked gazes with Viv in the rear-view mirror. She averted her gaze still trying to console Karol. Phatz bit down on the inside of his cheek to keep from exploding with anger. Next time he wouldn't let AC go alone.

****

Standing on the steps of the Barstow Police Department AC shielded his eyes from the glaring sun that bore down on him. A dull pounding settled in his head as he tried to determine how much time had passed since he'd last eaten. On cue his stomach growled. Too much time he thought. The last few hours had been a blur, what had started as a night on the town quickly turned into an almost overnight stay behind bars for perjury. He chuckled to himself as he thought about the game they'd given to the police. It would've worked if not for one person. His eyes darted to Phatz and Ty coming out the swinging glass doors. From the look on Phatz face he was pissed, and he had every right to be. Reconnecting with Ty was proving to be a headache.

"What made you tell them your name was Julius Quinn stupid?" Phatz asked Ty as they stopped beside AC. Back in Angola Phatz had come up with the idea for them to adopt an alias. He even went so far as to get them California licenses with their new identities. AC's new I.D. read Carlos Quinn, while Phatz had claimed Ralphael Quinn and Ty Julius Quinn. When they were pulled over outside of Las Vegas a quick search revealed that neither driver Carlos nor Raphael had a history of a California license. AC knew they were fucked, but it was Ty who had chosen to volunteer his alias, giving the police all the ammunition that they needed to haul them to jail.

Ty glanced in his direction, a plea of help on his face. AC shook his head. He was done helping the nigga. He wanted answers just like Phatz.

"Well?" he asked.

Before Ty could open his mouth to respond their bail bondsman G.C. walked out followed by Viv. She tossed a glance in Ty's direction. AC tilted his head in amusement. If looks could kill Ty would be dead on the spot.

"Thank you, gentlemen, for the business." GC shook each of their hands before bouncing down the steps to his car. AC watched after him. The man had a slight spring to his walk, no doubt the result of the share he'd gotten off the $15,000 bond that they'd place. $5,000 for each one of them, including Ty's bond that they had to pay as well. He turned his gaze to Ty eager to hear the reason for his fuck. Then again, he didn't care. It was done with. Heading towards the van Viv had driven in he left them on the steps to hash it out on their own. Instinctively his hand went to his pocket where his Benz keys should've been. It was empty. Squeezing his eyes shut he swore under his breath. AC had become somewhat obsessed with purchasing himself a Benz after hitting a lick in one. So, when the opportunity came, he jumped at it. While he had chosen an all-white Benz, Phatz had gone with a two-seater slant nose Porsche. Both the showroom cars now sat in the impound.

Angrily he banged his fist on the hood of the Astro van. A pair of uniformed officers walking by glanced curiously in his direction. Reeling in his anger he slid inside. It wasn't long before the others joined him. Except for the music coming from the radio, the ride to L.A. was quiet. While some of AC's anger had died down, he was still seething about his car. When Viv pulled over into a gas station to buy gas Phatz turned towards them in the back seat.

"When we get home, I'll send Denise and Viv back to pick up the cars."

With a stiff nod AC turned to Ty who hadn't said a word.

Feeling eyes on him Ty turned to meet AC's hard glare.

"I'm sorry I-I don't know what I was thinking."

AC sucked his teeth. That was thing. Ty never seemed to be thinking.

"Nigga sorry don't cut it you owe us $10k or did you forget about how we saved your ass at the hotel last night," Phatz barked.

It was true. Last night after selling twenty-five birds Phatz and AC sat at Viv's tip thumbing through stacks of hundred dollar bills. Loading the money in two bags to drop off to the safe at aunt Be Be's house AC was sidetracked when Ty paged him. Over the phone he'd learned that Billy had left Ty high and dry with a $5,000 hotel bill after binging on drugs for days. His first mind told him to hang up especially since he knew that Ty hooked up with Billy after Phatz sent him on a run. Only Ty never completed the mission and instead chose to chase after Billy and sniff powder. Surprisingly in the end it had been Phatz who talked him into going to retrieve Ty and pay the outstanding bill so that he would avoid jail time. Now AC wish he had ended the call when he had the chance.

"Ima pay you back," Ty declared.

"How? You gone call your friend Billy?" he asked, shifting in his seat.

"No man I told you he said yal—"

AC snapped. "We don't give a fuck what he said about us! You weren't defending us when he was talking shit so don't tell us nothing he said now!"

"Real talk," Phatz echoed.

Viv was heading back to the car now. When she got in her head swiveled back and forth at the undeniable tension in the air.

"Everything ok?" she asked before cranking the car.

No one said a word. Shifting into drive she eased into traffic.

Thoughts rushed AC's mind as they made their way home. He wasn't so much fucked up about the money-hell not even the car anymore. It was just that every time Ty came around some bad shit happened. He was beginning to think the man was bad luck. He cut his eyes towards him and shook his head to himself. Maybe it was the drugs that was fucking Ty up. He couldn't remember ever seeing him so pathetic and desperate. Even so, letting him off the hook wasn't an option. Ty would have to pay one way or another. A smirk creased the corners of his lip as a plan began to formulate in his mind.

****

"Relax, you're doing fine," Phatz whispered in Viv's ear. His hand tightened around her waist as they walked through the airport. Glancing over his shoulder he spotted AC following close behind. Dressed in their signature linen suits neither man looked as if they'd spent the last two hours on a plane. Behind the Ray Ban shades Phatz eyes were sharp and alert. Viv on the other hand was a walking bag of nerves. He could see the sweat stains seeping through the light pink Chanel blouse she wore. Reaching up he swiped at the strands of hair that were beginning to plaster to her neck, revealing the diamond earrings that AC had lifted off Karol in her ear. Making eye contact he slowly slid his hand to the small of her back, feeling the moment the tension began to ease from her body. Still she chewed on her bottom lip nervously.

Once outside Phatz inhaled sharply at the breathtaking view of the towering mountains against the night's skyline. City lights and shining stars twinkled all around. The image looked like a painting out of a museum. Instead it was the backdrop of Denver, Colorado their next lick. While Phatz thought that he was the only one struggling to put the jewelry licks behind him, AC's plan said differently. Sending Ty to Denver where his brother lived to scope out three jewelry licks sounded like a golden opportunity for them all. On one hand Ty would have the chance to redeem himself from his unloyalty and pay them the money he owed, on the other the jewelry bandits had the chance to shake the dust off their hammers and get back active. Phatz smiled at the thought, but it disappeared just as quickly when he remembered that they'd only spoken to Ty once in the past three days and that was to confirm that he'd completed the mission. Still, Phatz hoped for Ty's sake he wasn't bullshitting because this time there would be no more second chances.

"You got the rental car information, right?" he asked Viv.

Nodding she fumbled through her Chanel bag before removing a piece of paper.

"This is the registration."

"Ok go right through those doors," he pointed behind her, "and show them the papers, get the whip and bring it back here."

"Ok," she said before sucking in a deep breath. Spinning on her heels she headed in the direction that Phatz had pointed.

"What's wrong with her?" AC asked coming up beside him.

Phatz stared after her. He wanted to introduce Viv to another part of the game, one where she didn't have to set up her friends to get jewels, but he was beginning to wonder if he had made the mistake of bringing her along.

"She not cut like Silky, she's used to laying on her back to get what she wants."

"Ouch," AC winced playfully.

He shrugged carelessly.

"Shit, it's the truth."

Phatz focused his mind on the jewelry lick ahead of them. He could feel his heart begin to speed up just thinking about it. The dope game was elevating them to new heights, but it could never give him the thrill that came with bashing cases. He closed his eyes and imagined the sound of the glass cases cracking from the force of the hammer but the noise from the ascending plane in the night sky drowned it out. That was alright, because he would get to hear it up close and personal soon enough.

****

"Look at this fool," AC muttered under his breath as he watched Ty stumble out of the rundown looking apartments. Like any other city Denver had its slums and Ty's brother lived in the center of one. Once he woke from his drug induced stupor and returned their phone calls, Ty claimed that he'd found three jewelry licks. AC scrutinized him from the passenger side and wondered how true it was.

"Hope he's not wasting our time with some small ass stores, we only hit life changing licks no small shit." He ran his hand down the front of his Fila sweat suit he'd temporarily changed into.

In the driver's seat Phatz scoffed. "He knows we're in the big leagues besides," he said pausing to adjust the rear view mirror. "He's broke so the finer the jewelry the bigger his cut, ya heard me?"

"I heard you yea." The two erupted in laughter at the Louisiana lingo they'd learned in Angola. Tilting his head back against the seat Phatz gripped the steering wheel.

"Billy had him playing with his nose fucked him up even worse."

"Well he better have his shit together today," AC replied right as Ty reached the car.

"What's up" he greeted, sliding in.

"Where ole girl?" he asked glancing around wildly.

Old girl he was referring to was Viv and they had left her at the hotel, but Ty didn't need to know that.

Turning around in his seat to face Ty, for the first time AC noticed that he had cleaned up, donning a similar sweat suit as the ones they wore. At least he remembered the dress code, he would give him that much.

"You got the licks lined up right?"

Ty's head jerked up and down. "Yeah man I told you already," he responded defensively. AC studied his face for any signs of deceit when Ty didn't waiver under his stare he faced forward just as Phatz put the car in drive.

"Let's give em some real game so they know we really do this shit in any state. They caught us once because of another nigga mistakes not ours," he added pointedly.

In the mirror he watched Ty tuck his head into his chest.

Phatz slapped the steering wheel in excitement.

"Like old times!" he yelled out speeding through the city.

Like old times AC thought.

****

Can you feel it nothing can save you cause this is the season for catching the vapors.

Phatz repeated the words to himself as the beat to the Biz Markie song played in his head. He slid the leather gloves on his hand before stuffing them in his pocket. Up ahead he could see the jewelry store that Ty and AC had entered seconds earlier. Pacing himself he pretended to linger at the food court of the packed mall as he began a mental countdown.

29...28....

He removed a hand to clutch the Nike tote bag at his side as he weaved through the bodies of people surrounding him. It always amazed him how oblivious people were to the things that were happening right under their noses. By the time he made it to ten he was only inches away from the door. A couple of teens dressed in black darted in front of him momentarily breaking his stride. The loud group hadn't even glanced in his direction. No one paid much attention to the man dressed in the Fila sweatsuit, with the cold calculated look in his eyes. If they had they would have run for cover.

3...2...1....

He entered the store swiftly, locking the door at the bottom as it swung shut. He counted nine customers on the floor face down, another two were crouched behind the counter with their faces buried in between their knees. A thrill of excitement went through him as he watched Ty move from case to case, he realized that the man hadn't lost his touch. AC caught his eye and gave him a nod. Without hesitation he pulled out the hammer. Stepping over the trembling bodies on the floor he made his way over to the glass cases where diamond watches winked at him. Raising the hammer over his head he brought it down on the glass with all his might until it cracked into tiny fragments freeing the treasures inside.

****

"Scoop, Scoop, Scoop!" AC's voice boomed.

His eyes darted to the watch on his wrist, sixteen seconds had passed. They were doing good. Only two more cases to go. If they kept it up, they would set a new record. He ignored the silent pleas and muffled cries coming from the customers and focused on the door. Outside the crowd moved along like a herd, but AC knew that all it would take was one person to try to enter the store to set the alarms off. He turned back to Phatz who was cleaning out one of two cases remaining. On the other side Ty was moving like he was in a marathon; AC wasn't surprised that he finished first. Stuffing the pillowcase full of jewelry in his tote bag Ty moved towards the door with Phatz close on his heels. The two exited the store just as quickly as they had come in. It had taken less than two minutes to pull off. It was glorious!

"Thank you all for your cooperation, remain on the floor," AC said, easing backwards toward the door. His eyes lingered over the crime scene of broken cases. This was what he missed. The excitement. The control. The reward. By the time he slid into the backseat of the stolen car with Ty and Phatz inside AC wondered how he had ever given up this part of his life.

****

The line for boarding crept along at a snail's pace making Phatz more anxious. He scratched at the tingling spot behind his ear. It was never a good sign when the spot tingled. Still he tried to compose himself. Fumbling with the button on the linen suit he had changed back into, he peered over his shoulder. Five spaces behind him was AC, he gave a small nod before focusing ahead again. As beautiful as Denver was it was time to leave. Ty had done well picking out the jewelry licks, now he was back at his brother's spot doing God knows what. Meanwhile their treasure from the three jewelry stores were tucked safely away in Viv's Louie bag. Returning to the hotel where they stashed her away only to find it crawling with police had raised all the alarms in Phatz head. Still he forged ahead to retrieve her. He didn't believe in leaving people behind. It went against his code. They came together and they would leave together. But even he was relieved when the front desk attendee explained that it was a police convention occurring at the hotel. He had bitten back laughter at the irony of it. What were the odds that they would book the hotel on the same weekend? Instead of pondering what could have turned into a nasty situation, he quickly fetched Viv and checked out. Now it was time to head home.

Phatz sighed when the pace of the line finally began picking up. He slid his hand around Viv's waist. He could tell she was still worried by the way she was gnawing on her bottom lip with her teeth again. He wanted to tell her that her worries were for nothing, it was over…

"Mam there's a bundle of something showing up on our screen," the white woman stated as the bag rolled through the scanner. Beside him Viv inhaled sharply her eyes darted to him as she stumbled over her words.

Phatz had instructed her to remove the glass and wrap the jewelry in one bundle. He even went as far as watching her do it. When she placed it in the Louis duffle bag, he was certain that it wouldn't be detected.

"Mam?" the woman asked again with an expectant look on her face.

Viv licked her lips before opening her mouth. No words came out. He swore silently to himself. They had been so close to making it home.

"I froze."

The words were uttered by Viv as she slid her soft body against his in the bed. Her lips pressed into his before she rose on her knees and straddled him. The black lace panty and bra set complemented her small figure. Grinding her hips into his she started a slow pace before abruptly stopping.

"I don't know what came over me, if you hadn't…" her voice trailed off. He could see the goosebumps rise on her arms. She had frozen like a deer in headlights when the airport security stopped them. For a split second he thought it was all over and his mind immediate went to how much time they would face. With no priors Viv would get off with a light tap but being that he and AC were still on parole the outcome wouldn't be in their favor. Knowing the odds were against them, Phatz sprang into action. When he finished explaining to security that Viv was a jeweler who had just come from the safety convention at the hotel, they were allowed to pass without further inspection. His quick thinking was the reason they were all safe at home. Gripping the sides of her waist he leaned forward.

"Stop talking and finish what you started."

Her hand snaked around her back to unsnap her bra freeing her big breast.

"I wanna make it up to y'all." She placed a kiss on his bare chest. His body tensed at the move.

Phatz gripped her chin firmly.

"What you mean y'all?"

A sly smile spread over her lips. He could see the mischief in her eyes. Kissing her way up his body she stopped at his ears.

"Remember I told you I always wanted to do something wild," she whispered.

He did. It involved them and another woman, but there was no other woman in the house with them. She couldn't mean…

"Call AC," she stated putting an end to any doubts he had.

Jumping up he was halfway across the room, when he glanced over his shoulder.

"You sure?"

Viv let out a throaty laugh as she slid her panties down her legs.

"Damn sure," she said with determination in her eyes.

Phatz had to only call out AC name since he was already there. When the door to the room he was staying in opened he waved him over.

"Viv wants you to come in."

AC's eyes widened when he peeped into the room to see Viv spread eagle on the bed.

Phatz saw the question in his stare.

"It's all good," he grinned.

Flipping off the light in the room he made his way back to the bed. AC lingered outside for a few moments before entering. Firmly grabbing Viv's head, he pushed her face down into his boxers. She moaned before taking him into her mouth. Phatz closed his eyes and enjoyed the feeling.

****

Ole thang Viv was a freak, AC thought as he entered the dark room. He could hear her moaning as her ass wagged back in forth. Stepping out of his boxers he touched her waist to test her reaction. When she spread her legs wider revealing her glistening crotch, he ripped the package off the condom he'd doubled back to grab and slid it on. In one quick motion he entered her. Her moans grew louder as he pounded in and out of her with force. She met him stroke for stroke grinding into him. AC wasn't surprised when Phatz finished his business and left the room leaving the two alone. Viv wasted no time switching positions. They took each other for a pleasurable ride.

****

Sometimes it would hit him unexpectedly like when he was making a drop off at one of the many safehouses he controlled or out hoeing. Or like now when he was driving, no matter the time, the feeling was always the same. First it would start with a memory that triggered the thought of Marlon, then his chest would tighten up as the grief settled deep inside almost taking his breath away. Pulling into the driveway of Viv's tip Phatz parked the slant nose Porsche and waited for the pain to subside, but not before his eyes grew heavy with tears. Blinking furiously to clear his vision he breathed deeply through his nose. His hands gripped the leather steering wheel as he fought off his emotions. Marlon had been the reason he'd purchased the P-car. Phatz had kept his promise even if his brother was no longer alive to see it. He squeezed his eyes to stop the tears from falling. He knew that Marlon wouldn't want him sitting around crying for him. Pulling himself together Phatz exited the car and entered the house relieved that no one was home. Climbing the stairs, he stripped down to his workout gear hoping to take his mind off the dull ache that was still in his chest, but his mind didn't want to follow. He should've been basking in all that he'd accomplished. He had money, jewels, a pick of any woman he wanted, and they'd just accomplished one of the biggest heists yet. Just like the other cities they'd taken by storm. Denver was no different. He should've been out celebrating, but his brothers' murder weighed heavily on his mind and heart. Though his killer had been caught it didn't make it any better. Phatz stood and wiped the sweat from his body.

Launching into a set of pushups his thoughts strayed to Viv.

Ole Thang.

Neither of them had spoken on what went down in the bedroom that night after the lick in Denver. They went about their business as usual. Except Phatz could feel her feelings growing deeper for him. Especially after the recent Mother's Day dinner Viv held in honor of their mothers. Both Phatz and Viv had showered the women with flowers, diamond rings, and Audemars Piguet watches from their latest heist. The two mothers were ecstatic. Phatz didn't miss Viv cozying up to Kathi all throughout the dinner, trying to paint the picture of the perfect girlfriend. It was a farce. No matter how much she claimed to love him, Phatz understood that Viv was only loyal to money. And in many ways, he respected that. It showed they were more alike than different. But on the flip side Viv was beginning to break her own rules. Letting thoughts of babies and love cloud her judgement. What they had was about sex and money. He wasn't willing to give her more especially with her history. Phatz wasnt blind to the fact that Viv liked to sleep around and was considered community pussy. As a proud man he couldn't have her on his arm for that very reason. Cold? Yes, but it was the game. If he didn't give her a reality check now it wouldn't end well when it was time to walk away. Shelving thoughts of Viv he shifted his focus back to his workout. The once burning pain began to sizzle out to its usual numbness. By the time he was done his arms felt like rubber, but his grief had been locked away to deal with for another time.

He had just finished dressing after his shower when Viv and AC strode inside laughing. She paused when she noticed him standing at the top of the stairs. Coming down he dropped a kiss on her lips.

"We need to talk."

She searched his face, a look of concern etched into her owns.

At the sound of the chair scrapping back they both turned their heads towards AC who took a seat at the end of the table. Tugging on her hand Phatz was about to pull her along into another room when she snatched it away.

"Wait I need to show you something," she blurted out before quickly disappearing.

He cast a curious glance in AC's direction. With a boyish shrug AC leaned back in the chair.

Phatz glanced around at the sound of Viv making her way back to him.

"Y'all been shopping?" he asked, looking at the bags in her hand.

He watched Viv and AC share a look right before she darted away again, returning with two more bags all from the cheap shopping center a few miles away. The suspense began to mount. Viv would never shop there; her own wardrobe was full of the latest name brands from Gucci to Chanel.

With a lopsided grin AC motioned to Viv who sat the bags down on the table.

Digging inside, she pulled out a black hoodie. She lowered her voice.

"I know you said no more burglaries, but this one owes me."

****

"He has three kids, one girl, two sons, ages twenty- five, twenty -three and twenty-one," Viv was hunched over the armrest from the backseat where she sat. She popped her grape flavored bubblegum in Phatz ear before tossing her hair over her shoulder.

"What?" she asked at the look of annoyance on his face. She had wiggled her way out of their talk with this new info, but he would save it for another time.

Drumming his finger on the steering wheel his eyes cut to the side mirror that gave him a perfect view of the towering castle like house they were staking out in the San Diego neighborhood. It had taken them two hours to reach their destination and, in that time,, Viv filled them in on their lick.

Gerald a lead singer in a once popular black 60's and 70's group, who was famous for their soulful harmonizing and jazzy dance moves, had gotten himself mixed up in some shit. With their music sales tanking and their accolades slowly fading away due to the new hip hop sound overtaking the industry, Gerald turned to slanging dope to pay his bills. It was Viv who fronted him the kilos to help keep up his rich and famous appearance. Now he was $20,000 in the red and from what Phatz had learned it didn't look as if he ever intended on getting himself out. All that was just fine with him though. This would be an easy come up. What surprised him was how Viv had taken to the lick, normally she was nervous. He figured she was still trying to make up for her misstep in Denver. Today was her chance.

At the sight of the woman jogging on the sidewalk he whispered out a warning,

"Duck!"

Everyone in the car slouched down a few inches at the warning. Seconds before she reached the car the woman crossed over to the other side of the street never once glancing in their direction. Phatz let out a sigh of relief. Being out in broad daylight in a high-class neighborhood like this one was risky. It wasn't like hitting a jewelry store, where they could easily blend in with the shoppers or where he knew the layout of the store like the back of his hand. Home burglaries required more planning, more attention to detail which equaled up to a lot of time; time that they didn't have.

"Are they in the house?" AC asked from the passenger side, like Phatz and Viv he was dressed in a black hoodie with matching sweats that she had gotten from the shopping center.

Rising from her slouched position she peered out of the back window.

"Nicki's the only one home right now."

"How you know?"

She pointed to the shiny new Benz in the driveway.

"That's her car."

Glancing around Phatz removed his pager from his hip.

"W—"

"The cars' leaving," AC pointed out cutting him off.

Sure enough the Benz was easing out of the drive way. It was now or never.

"Let me out," AC stated reaching for the door.

Phatz gave him a quizzical look before hitting the unlock button.

Smoothly AC exited the van and began jogging in place.

"What's he doing?" Viv asked crouched in the backseat again.

AC began throwing light jabs in the air as if he was a boxer. Phatz watched him pivot from one foot to the other.

"Giving them some game," he said starting the van up just as the Benz pulled into the street. Eyes fixed ahead he drove off, passing Nicki who never glanced in their direction. When Phatz reached the park only a few feet away from the house he shut off the engine.

"Wait here," he said to Viv

"Ok," she answered.

From his position he could see AC nearing the house, seconds later he cut off into the driveway. Thinking quick on his feet Phatz grabbed the green trash can on the curb. He would need an excuse just in case someone was inside. To passersby's he looked like the trash man. Removing the hood from over his head, he sprinted in the direction he had seen AC disappear to, but AC was nowhere in sight when he finally reached the door. Not wasting time, he raised his hand and knocked on the door.

"Nicki, I got the trash cans you home?" He asked already knowing the answer but playing it smart.

There was dead silence.

"Patio door unlocked but they got a stupid ass dog that won't stop barking," AC said suddenly appearing beside him out of breath. Sweat shined on his forehead that he wiped at with the back of his hand.

"Did it chase you?" Phatz asked.

The two shared a laugh at the question.

"Forget the dog and the back door," he said as his hand gripped the golden handle of the door, testing his luck. Slowly it opened.

"We'll just use the front door," he said with a smile.

Inside the house the smell of food permeated the air.

"This is nice," AC said gazing at the art on the wall. He stopped in front of the platinum plaque hanging and began to hum the words of one of the groups songs. He hit a fancy footwork that caused Phatz to double over in laughter. After a few seconds he grew serious.

"Come on, we got work to do." He eased through the house, letting his nose guiding him to the kitchen where a pot was boiling on the stove. Across from the kitchen in the living room the TV was tuned in to Oprah.

Phatz swore under his breath. The food cooking and the television only meant that Nicki would be back soon. They had to move quick. Kicking it up a notch he motioned for AC to follow him as he led them up the narrow staircase following the exact directions Viv had given him. Twisting the handle to the last door at the end of the hall he moved towards the closet where he pushed pass the expensive clothes. Gerald had good taste he thought as he fingered the all-white linen suit. He made a mental note to ask his tailor about one next time he was fitted. When he reached the back of the closet annoyance covered his face. The floor was empty.

Behind him AC sucked his teeth.

"Not there," he said knowingly.

Phatz repeated Viv's directions to himself. They were at the last bedroom at the end of the hall like she said. The box of money was supposed to be in the back of the closet, but it wasn't.

He let out a deep breath as frustration began to seep in.

"Go check the other rooms and closets."

"Wait no," Phatz said stopping AC just as he turned. They didn't have time for that.

"Stay here," he said before jogging down the steps and out the door. Grabbing the trash can he pulled it after him just in case. It only took him seconds to reach the car.

"It's not there."

Startled Viv jumped at his voice.

Sliding across the seat she gave him a confused look.

"What do you mean it's not there?"

"Like I said it's not there. Listen we don't break in homes you know this, and the girl is set to return at any second."

Without another word she flung the door open. One minute she was getting out the car and the next her feet were hitting the pavement. Phatz watched stunned at her speed. He had forgotten that she was a track star in high school. At the sound of a dog barking he snapped out of his daze and jotted behind her silently praying that Nicki would stay wherever she was for a little longer.

Inside the house Viv bounded up the stairs. Posed to follow her, Phatz paused at the bottom step when the sound of the TV caught his attention. He made a move to follow but stopped when he heard AC's laughter coming from the kitchen. When he neared he saw the reason for his laughter. AC had made himself at home, fixed a sandwich and was now taunting the dog with it.

Upstairs he could hear Viv moving around. Seconds later she bounded down the stairs with a black box underneath her arm.

"Got it," she said coolly.

Phatz pumped his hands in the air victoriously.

"Let's go!"

On command the three of them headed out the door and towards the van. Phatz had just driven off when Nicki's Benz turned on the street. Like the first time she kept looking straight ahead.

"Shit that was close," he said cutting his eyes to AC who was still chomping on his sandwich.

"Too close," Viv said from behind him.

Two hours later they sat at the table as Viv counted out the money.

"$172,000," she said pushing the green bills to the center of the table.

Phatz palms tingled at the number. Maybe home burglaries could become a thing for them. Who knew? Then he thought about how close they had come to getting caught and shook his head. He would stick to the drugs and on special occasions the hammer.

"Cut it up three ways."

"Three?" Viv echoed her eyes rounding like marbles.

He nodded. After all this time Viv still wasn't used to them splitting the pot with her. She had been fucked over so much she expected everyone to do her wrong.

"You did good back there," he commented.

Her head snapped up as a smile split her face. In the blink of an eye she was on her knees in front of him and his pants were around his ankles. Money left on the table pleasing him seemed to be her only concern at the moment. Phatz wondered if she would continue once she found out they were moving out.

****

      The warmth of the sun rays beaming down on him through the slit in the curtain caused him to tentatively crack one eyelid open then the other. Rubbing the sleep from his eyes It took a few seconds for him to realize that he wasn't in the comforts of his own room. For one the mattress under him was nothing like the bed at home that seemed to mold to his body, this one was lumpy and had caused a fitful night of sleep. The white walls, beige carpet, and mini bar was another reminder. Easing from underneath the covers he pulled himself into a sitting position as he stared down at his rumpled clothes. The same ones he'd worn the night before as they traveled to the one place he never thought he would see again, but business had come calling. Fifty birds priced at $27K each was on the table. It would've been foolish for them to turn down the deal. Instead, they called the airport and booked flights to leave the next day. Using the formula, they'd use in Denver to smuggle the jewelry through the airport, they wrapped the kilos in thick white bath towels to pass through the x-ray machines. When the plane landed in New Orleans at 3 A.M. that morning there was a stillness to the city that AC wasn't used to. Flashbacks of the last time they'd crossed state lines had entered his mind, making him leerier of the deal. That and the drugs stashed away in the trunk of the rental car was enough to put them away for life. Louisiana was the last state he wanted to get jammed up in again. Sometimes he could still feel the burning sensation in his shoulder blades from working in the fields all day. No matter what happened he wasn't going back on that river.

Standing AC stretched his arms above his head before forcing his socked feet into his tennis shoes. He crossed over the beige carpet, pass the unmoving body in the bed next to his, and into the bathroom where he completed his toiletries. Deciding to shower he exchanged his rumpled clothes for a silk shirt and linen pants. When he exited out the hotel in search of breakfast, Phatz was still sleeping soundly.

Slipping the Ray Bans' on his face he headed towards the Waffle House restaurant. When he returned with hot breakfast for them both AC noticed the empty bed just as the toilet flushed and the water from the shower came on. Settling in the chair, he sipped from his cup of coffee, his eyes closing as the hot liquid washed down his throat. The exchange was still hours away so he hunkered down and waited for what he hoped would be an uneventful night.

****

"Soon as those clowns get here I want you and AC to rob me for the money." Pocket looked in between Phatz and AC as they stood outside of the restaurant.

So much for uneventful AC thought regarding the man carefully. This was his first-time meeting Pocket but Phatz had filled him in on the role he'd played while they were in Angola. Pocket was now one of the main suppliers in New Orleans thanks to them. Still AC studied the expression on his face, wondering how serious the man was.

"Why you wanna jack him?" AC asked curiously.

Smiling Pocket flashed a mouth full of gold teeth in his direction. "This nigga that's coming tonight shorted me on a deal last time we met up, so he got it coming. Plus, he's from Shreveport so fuck him." He spat the last words making AC realize that the beef that he'd witnessed between the two cities while locked up extended outside of Angola.

He and Phatz shared a look. He was down with it, especially if it meant they got to keep the money and the birds.

"What's the plan?" Phatz asked.

Pockets smile was back. He moved towards the old school Chevy Nova parked beside their rental, retrieving a bag he sat it at their feet.

"Everything you need is in there, now here's how it'll go…"

****

"They coming?" AC asked when Phatz placed the receiver back in its cradle.

"Yep," he answered.

Rising from the bed. AC surveyed the room that pocket had chosen to tuck them away in at the Ramada Inn. His vision drifted to the closed door on the other side that lead into the room next to theirs where the men were meeting. Any second now they would be coming through.

Tucking the .45 in his waist, he gave Phatz a nod just as a knock sounded at the door.

"Come in," Phatz answered.

Pocket appeared with a fixed smile on his face followed by another man. Each one carrying a large black duffle bag in their hands.

Pocket stretched his arms out towards them in greeting.

"My niggas how was the trip?"

"Long," AC responded following along with Pocket's role playing.

"This my round Gee," he stated introducing the man behind him.

AC sized him up. Dark skinned and short with a mouth full of gold like Pocket, Gee seemed skeptical as he glanced around the room. Finally, his eyes landed on AC. He lifted his chin towards the two Louis Vuitton duffle bags on the floor.

"That's the work?"

"Sure is," Phatz stated just as he blindsided the man running at him full force, sending his body slamming into the wall. An oof sound left his mouth as they slid to the floor and began to wrestle. Pulling the .45 from his waist AC trained it on Pocket who was about to interfere.

"You move and its over for you," he said in a lethal voice.

To make it more real he cocked the gun. From the corner of his eye he watched Phatz subdue Gee in a choke hold.

"Damn I didn't know y'all was rolling like that I thought we was better than this," Pocket expressed in anger.

"Well now you know," AC responded. He waved the gun towards the bed motioning for Pocket to take a seat on it. "Keep yo hands up," he commanded as Phatz removed Gee's gun from his waist.

"Seem like your friend over there had the same idea we just beat him to it."

"You niggas dead," Gee grunted out.

Phatz socked him in the head causing the man to scream out in pain.

"No, you and ya boy gone be dead if y'all try some slick shit."

Removing his gun Phatz aimed it at Gee. "Now get up and don't forget what I said."

He pressed the steel to the middle of Gee's back to get his point across, "One wrong move."

The words seemed to settle the man as he rose from the floor with his hands raised.

"Sit down on the bed," AC commanded.

With the two men sitting they moved to the next phase in the plan. Ignoring the daggers Gee was shooting in his direction Phatz tied both of their hands behind their backs with the sheets off the bed they'd ripped up.

"Y'all niggas got some nerve to pull this fuck shit in my city, this ain't---"

Slapping a strip of duct tape over Pocket's mouth he put an end to his speech.

AC glared down at him, "You should take a page from ya friends' book and shut the fuck up."

Pocket words were muffled behind the tape.

Behind him Phatz let out a low whistle as he counted a million dollars in each Louis duffle bag.

Grabbing up their things he tapped AC on the shoulder.

"Let's roll."

Gun still trained on their victim's AC grabbed the duffle bags with the money in them.

Gee's eyes narrowed to thin slits as he began mumbling behind the tape. Feeling humored AC ripped the tape back causing him to wince.

"I respect the game, but just know it's coming back on you." His chest heaved up and down.

AC chuckled before shaking his head.

"Liked you better when you was quiet," he said sealing the tape over his mouth again.

They were headed to the door when Phatz paused.

"Wait," he said glancing over his shoulder at the squirming men.

Dropping the duffle bags, he went to the bed.

"This not good enough."

Confused, AC was about to ask him what he meant when Phatz laid Gee on the floor. He bit back his laughter when he realized what was about to happen.

Five minutes later Phatz stood and brushed off his pants.

"There," he said surveying his work.

The men were hogged tied with Pocket laying on top of Gee. The sight made AC laugh uncontrollably. He was still laughing when the door closed.

****

The train ride was smooth. Phatz stared out the window as AC dozed in and out of sleep in the seat next to him. Miles and miles of trees were making his own eyelids grow heavy with sleep. Shaking himself he stared at the Louis Vuitton duffle bags underneath his feet. When he'd seen the money in the bags, he silently thanked Pocket for coming up with the plan. After dropping Pockets half off at his girls house like he instructed, they turned in the rental and fetched a cab to the Amtrak station. An hour later they were headed to L.A. His mind went back to Pocket and he wondered if the men had found their way free yet.

"We should've flown," AC said stretching his arms over his head.

It was Pockets idea for them to take the train since it was the quickest way out of the city. Shifting in his seat Phatz looked out the window again. The sun had come up only an hour ago, they still had six more hours left on the train.

"Shit I see why Jesse James robbed trains, its nothing back here, but trees and woods hell I would've done the same thing," Phatz grumbled.

Beside him AC chuckled before crossing his feet at the ankle and lacing his hands together. Shortly after his eyes drifted closed again.

Phatz thought he was sleep until he spoke, "Man we gone retire with this money."

Day in and day out they had been putting in work. From moving weight to hitting licks. Each one bigger than the next, but this one had topped them all. He thought about AC's words. They'd hit the ground running since returning from Angola. Phatz realized that they were touching the dream. Settling back against the seat he let his eyes close.

"Yep we won, it's time to live now."

2 YEARS LATER

It was funny how one minute you could be on top of the world rocking the flyest gear, pushing the latest whips with the baddest women at your side and in that next minute have everything you ever hustled for snatched away from you. It was how Phatz imagined the players in the game felt when the drought hit in 88'. The drugs that were once so plentiful had dried up sending the streets into panic mode. A little too late did some of them realize that the game was a business and in true form the Colombians did what any business would do when the demand for coke went up- Increase the price on a kilo. Not only that but frontin' the work had suddenly become a thing of the past. The Colombians new order of business was simple: If you wanted to play you had to pay.

The rules didn't go over too well with everyone, mainly because it separated the real hustlers from the fake ones. Only those who had been really putting in work over the years were able to pay the price up front. Those who couldn't were forced to sit on the bench and watch, making them greedy and envious. But that wasn't the worst of it. With the drug laws tightening up, the game was changing. Niggas used to be able to take a sentence, get out and return back to the hustle, but not this time. The government was throwing life sentences at almost every dealer caught up in its nationwide federal sweep. Faced with the thought of spending the rest of their life behind bars the hardest men in the game began entertaining the worst ideas, like snitching. Suddenly friends who had grown up together were now competing with who could tell the most in exchange for the lightest sentence. Loyalties were being broken, no one was sure of who to trust anymore and without trust there was bound to be bloodshed. Just like that the glory years were behind them now replaced with something darker and more dangerous.

Phatz was watching it unfold right in front of him. The threat of going back to prison was becoming more real with every passing second. So real that he began planning their exit. While he and AC had saved most of their money from jewelry licks, it wasn't enough to comfortably retire with. Phatz was thinking about moving the entire family out to Calabasas or some other rich suburb of Cali. It would be a welcome change from the city that was quickly turning into a war zone. In order to do that he knew that they would have to keep playing this dangerous game a little while longer because timing was everything.

Speaking of timing he was running late. Shoving the thoughts in the back his mind, he focused on the one thing that mattered in that moment as he weaved in and out of traffic. Tonight, was all about Kathi. His mother Kathi was turning the big fifty and to celebrate he was hosting a party at Monty's Steakhouse in Westwood. Phatz turned his head toward the fine honey in the passenger seat of the Benz. 5'5 with a model face and a killer body, Bonnie looked like she could have just stepped off the cover of *Vogue* magazine. He had her to thank for the party. While Phatz had paid for everything it was she who had taken care of the details.

"I hope your mom likes everything," she commented, fingering the hem of the black Chanel dress that fit her body like a second skin. Taking his eyes off the road for a second, he grabbed her hand.

"She'll like it, my mama is not hard to please so relax," he said focusing his gaze ahead.

"She'll like you too," he added with a wink.

Bonnie squeezed his hand lightly before giving him a smile that lit up her pretty face.

Thirty minutes later they were walking hand in hand inside of the restaurant. Phatz let his gaze sweep over the arched ceilings and sparkling chandeliers. Situated on the twenty first floor Monty's was a high-class restaurant that overlooked Westwood. The popular dinning spot normally required its patrons to reserve months ahead of time, but that wasn't the case for Phatz being that he gambled with the owner Mike. He removed his Ray Ban shades, tucking them into the pocket of his off-white Armani suit as they followed the hostess to their waiting party. Kathi's face broke into a smile when her eyes landed on them approaching.

"Happy Birthday Mama," Phatz said greeting her with a hug and a kiss.

"Baby I can't believe you did all this for me," Kathi said pulling back from his embrace. She swept her arm at the tables that had been reserved for her.

"I had a little help," he said giving Bonnie a gentle push forward.

"Mama, this is Bonnie she was the one who made all the---" Before Phatz could finish his words Kathi had pulled Bonnie into a hug. She swayed back and forth with her.

"Thank you for this."

Kathi wiped at her eyes. "My son sure knows how to pick them."

Bonnies' brown skinned darkened as she blushed.

"I'm glad you like everything, Happy Birthday."

Taking her hand Kathi pulled her along to sit beside her. Phatz had been right Bonnie had nothing to worry about. Soon the other attendees began to arrive, and it was party time.

Monty's was filled with laughter and applause as each person took turns wishing Kathi a Happy Birthday. Phatz chest swelled with pride as he looked on. Both his sister and Uncle were in attendance. AC, Shauna, Aunt Be Be and Twin sat at another table. The atmosphere was filled with love most of it directed towards Kathi who had shed more than a few tears during dinner. A table close by overflowed with gifts, including the one with fifty single hundred dollar bills inside. Phatz couldn't wait to see her face when she opened it.

The night was going perfect. In the middle of Be Be's speech Phatz slipped away to make a call, only to be intercepted by his Uncle Kenny on the way back.

"Nephew, I wanna thank you for handling that situation for me the other day." Kenny said pulling him aside. Peering over his shoulder Phatz could see Bonnie still enjoying herself, she tossed her head back at something Denise said.

Directing his attention back to Kenny he noticed the cut on his lip was healing, but the bruises on his face were still apparent. Phatz had to still himself to keep the anger from returning. When Kenny had called him in a rage, he could barely make out his words, but the ones that he did manage to understand was "hurt." That was all he needed to hear to rush to his aid. A few youngin's had thought it was wise to beat up on Kenny and take his money from him. When they discovered the group walking just a few blocks away AC and Phatz had happily gotten revenge, knocking them around and emptying their pockets.

"No need to thank me unc, them lil niggas know better now."

Kenny nodded his head, "But you know had it been one on one." He threw a few punches in the air.

Phatz laughed. "I already know unc."

"You're not leaving the party, are you?"

Shaking his head Kenny pulled out a joint. He nodded his head towards the balcony. Understanding his meaning Phatz slid out of the way. The laughter was growing louder now as he continued his trek. He was nearing the party when Twin came out of nowhere almost smashing into him.

"Whoa!" Phatz called out as droplets of the champagne Twin was holding in his flute spilled on his hands.

"Shit." Handing him a cloth napkin from an empty table Twin helped him wipe up the spill.

"Your mom told me to come get you and Kenny, it's almost time to cut the cake."

Clutching the napkin in his hand Phatz nodded his head towards the direction Kenny had gone.

"Kenny's on the balcony."

Sidestepping Twin he halted when the man called his name. Phatz rolled his eyes to the ceiling.

What now he thought as he turned around.

"Stop by the house on 108th soon I need to run something by you." Phatz could see the seriousness in Twin's eye as he spoke. He could only imagine what it was about. Though Twin was still selling coke the drought was shaking everyone up. Big Mac had gotten shot three times in the arm on Crenshaw in his BMW, niggas was getting kidnapped and all because of the drought and crack laws. Shit was funky in Boss Angeles!

"Ok I got you," Phatz responded after a few seconds. By the time he finally made it to Bonnie she was doubled over with laughter.

He slanted his eyes in Denise's' direction.

"What you tell her?"

Giving an innocent shrug she fluffed the curls on her short and fly haircut.

"Nothing bro-ski, relax."

Bonnie inhaled deeply just as another round of laughter followed. This time Denise joined.

"Ok I told her about the time you beat those kids up for messing with me when we were kids."

He gave her a disapproving look as he eased down beside Bonnie.

"I can imagine you beating the crap out of some kids."

"That's right," Phatz said slipping his hand around her shoulder to pull her closer.

"I'll do anything for my family."

Phatz winked at Kenny who was returning with Twin in tow. Across the table AC and Shauna were cuddled together. Everyone continued to enjoy themselves filling up on champagne and cake. He couldn't recall seeing his mom smile like that in a long time. When they'd learned that their father had passed earlier that year, he witnessed the sadness return in her eyes. Even so Kathi and Denise traveled to Louisiana to pay their respects and say their farewells. Phatz decided to forgo the funeral and cherish the memories they'd shared instead. He wasn't surprised that his dad had left them money in his will, Harry was a man that had given his last to take care of his family and he had instilled the same thing in Phatz.

****

      Grabbing the two Louie duffle bags out of the trunk of the Benz he still couldn't believe that he'd agreed to the meeting, but with Los Angeles being dryer than a desert Phatz had to make a move. Waiting for Big Mac to find buyers would only slow his money flow down and that was the last thing he needed. When Viv called and revealed that RL knew a buyer in Oakland that wanted to buy some work, Phatz first thought was to turn him down. Though he'd paid Viv her money RL was still a pussy in his book. Just being near him now made him frown in disgust. But the pussy nigga had something he wanted so he'd set his personal feelings aside for the sake of business and made the trip to Oakland. Traveling in separate cars they pulled into the parking lot of the nice apartments where the meeting would be taking place. Securing each bag that held ten birds each over his shoulder he motioned for RL to lead the way. Walking up a flight of steps Phatz kept his eyes and ears open. The beef between Oakland and L.A. ran deep, but the recent drought had escalated it even more. So much to the point that niggas had taken to robbing those from the opposing city. As they stopped in front of beige door Phatz slid his hand to his waist again, hoping that he wasn't walking into an ambush.

RL raised his hand and knocked twice before the door slowly opened.

"Damn you act like you didn't wanna let us in!" He barked shoving his way inside. Slightly taken back by how quickly his attitude had changed, Phatz almost missed the beauty standing in the door. The pink tight shorts that she wore gripped her thick yellow thighs, while the thin matching shirt molded to her firm breast and flat stomach. His eyes skirted over her heart shaped face pausing on her shiny lips that were turned down in a frown before stopping at her pretty brown eyes that she lowered.

"Come in," she said stepping aside.

Hesitating for a split second he stepped over the threshold. The small apartment smelled of warm vanilla. At the sound of the door closing he spun around, hand on his gun. Phatz didn't know much about the woman standing in front of him, only that she played a small role in setting up the deal. This was part of the game that he hated. The blind trust part, still When she breezed by, he followed. From the splashes of pink seen throughout the décor he assumed that it was her favorite color. Plopping down on the crème colored sofa she grabbed a magazine from the table and began flipping through it.

"You don't have any manners, you not gone introduce yourself to the man?" RL asked bringing the glass to his mouth.

Pushing her bone straight hair off her shoulder the woman looked up from the magazine.

"I'm Tonya," she said before returning to her task. Baby was cold. He chuckled.

"Rude bitches," RL mumbled under his breath.

"Make ya self at home Phatz."

Spying a bar in the corner Phatz dropped the Louis bags in one of the bar stools. It was time he laid down some rules.

"Give me your gun."

RL sputtered on the liquor he was drinking. Wiping his mouth, he stared wide eyed

"What you need my gun for?"

Instead of answering Phatz stretched out his hand.

With a sigh RL handed him his small .380.

"Now when they get here, I want you to check each and every stack of money that they have—"

"Why I gotta do all that?"

Phatz rolled his eyes in annoyance.

"To make sure that it's all money and not mixed in with paper." He said feeling as if he were speaking to a small child.

It took a few seconds for RL to process what he was saying.

"Awwww, that's right," he said wagging his finger.

"Move the couch out the way and put these in the floor, I want it to be the first thing they see when they walk in," he said handing him the bags.

With little complaint RL did as he was told. Afterwards he turned to Phatz for more directions.

"What next?"

"How much am I getting?" Tonya cut in. She looked back and forward from Phatz and RL.

"Nothing if you don't shut up, and where these niggas at?" RL asked irritated.

At his question, Tonya and RL began to argue. Phatz hung his head.

"Be quiet!" He yelled silencing the room.

"Y'all can talk that shit over when the deal is done."

Removing his gun from his waist he pulled the bar stool out and took a seat. Picking up the .380 he rested each against his leg.

"Now what?" RL asked skeptically. Phatz noticed the nervous look in his eyes.

"Now we wait."

•••

"They're here," Tonya announced as she slipped from the window Phatz had instructed her to watch from.

Jumping up RL ran a hand down his face before standing.

"Remember what I said," Phatz said before spinning around on the stool, his back facing the door.

A knock sounded shortly. Closing the distance between him and the door, RL pulled it open.

When the door closed Phatz spun around, gun raised in each hand. The two men dressed in plain T- shirts and jeans carrying a Nike bag halted at the sight of the gun.

"These guns are for your protection and mine," he said at once.

Behind them he saw the shock on RL's face. The seriousness of the situation was just now registering to the man. RL was too caught up in the idea of eating the pie that he hadn't considered the dangers. But Phatz had and he hadn't come this far to get robbed or killed so he was playing it like it goes.

"Any weapons?" he asked.

The men shook their heads hurriedly. The answer wasn't good enough for Phatz.

"Lift up the shirts and turn around."

Sitting the Nike bag on the floor the men lifted their shirts and slowly turned in a circle. When Phatz was satisfied he gave a nod, but kept his guns trained on them.

Tilting his head towards the Louis bags he spoke,

"One of you give the money to RL and the other grab the Louis bags."

He watched carefully as the men followed instructions. His gaze wandered over to Tanya who sat mesmerized. When their eyes locked, he winked at her before turning his attention back in front of him.

"It's three zip locks inside so cut open any three kilos you want or all twenty but all I have is three."

With another nod of his head he motioned for RL to begin counting.

Everything was going smooth. As anticipated the men were already inspecting their merchandise. Phatz hadn't expected anything less.

"We cool?" he asked when he noticed them zipping the bag back up.

"Cool," the short dark skinned one stated. The tall light skinned man at his side remained quiet.

Phatz turned to RL who had a big smile on his face.

"Did you make sure all the money is there?"

"Yeah," he said grinning again.

The spot behind Phatz ear began to tingle. Something wasn't right. He watched the man through slit eyelids. His gut told him that RL was lying and so did his giddiness.

"Check it all to make sure."

Never lowering the guns Phatz kept one eye trained on their guest and the other on RL.

"It's cool, I told you," he said reaching his hand inside pulling out a stack of cash. He glanced at the wad of bills and tossed it back inside. The move made Phatz insides boil. Stupid ass nigga was only looking at the bills on top.

"Nigga I said check it all! Run your thumbs through that shit!" Phatz said exploding unable to hide his anger any longer.

RL flinched at the loud command before fumbling with the bag. He began to inspect each stack closely.

Phatz shook his head at his ignorance.

Minutes later RL glanced up. "It's all here."

The room that had been filled with tension seemed to relax.

"Let me walk y'all to the car."

When the dark-skinned man looked towards his partner Phatz knew who was the boss. Spinning on his heels he watched the tall man head for the door. Outside the trio walked to the corner were their car was parked. Gun still cocked in his blazer, Phatz waited for the tall man who he knew was the plug to speak. He didn't have to wait long.

"You did right in there with that clown," the man said speaking for the first time as he slid behind the wheel.

Phatz nodded.

"I'm Ink by the way," he stated sticking out his hand.

"Phatz," he said returning the handshake. The two shared a knowing look as Ink closed the door and his partner slid in the other side. Reaching into his pocket Phatz pulled out a piece of paper with his number written on it. He had taken the liberties to write it down when he was sitting at the bar.

He passed it to Ink.

"How bout we cut all this middleman shit out and get to the money?"

Ink stared at the paper for a few moments.

"I'll call you."

With those words he crank up the car and pulled off. Phatz headed back towards the apartment in high spirits. He didn't need a middleman and RL had been too stupid to see it. He paused outside as loud voices rose from the apartment. Phatz was glad that the day was coming to an end. He had what he wanted, the money and now one of Oaklands' biggest connect. But crossing RL out had been the best part of all.

∎▪▪∎

A loud animal sound tore from his throat as he released himself inside of her warmth with one final thrust. His body sagged onto the damp cotton sheets. Heart pounding Phatz let his eyes drift shut until his breathing returned to normal.

A giggle made him slit an eye open.

"What the hell?" he asked springing up.

Beside him Viv was a sight to see. Sweat from their steamy fuck session still clung to her naked body—which at the moment was upside down. Using her arms to hold her body weight, and her head to stabilize her, Viv's long legs lie flat against the wall. She looked like an extension of limbs.

Untangling himself from the sheets he stood as he surveyed the room for his discarded clothes. He tossed a glance over his shoulder at Viv who was still upside down and shook his head.

"I saw it on this old movie once that if you stay like this the sperm could find its way to the egg faster."

At her explanation Phatz doubled over with laughter. So that's what it was. She was still trying to have his baby.

When her arms buckled, she tumbled softly to the bed.

Righting herself she huffed as she pushed the long hair off her face.

"What?" she asked innocently.

"Nothing."

In the closet he sifted through the suits that he kept at her house. He could tell by the extra space left in the closet that Viv was still hoping that he would return. She'd done everything possible to keep them from moving out starting with the big crocodile tears she shed when Phatz broke the news. In attempt to get him to stay she offered to put his name on the lease and when that didn't work she'd stolen the car full of clothes they had packed up- only to return it later. Her efforts were a waste because Phatz mind was made up. He needed his space to hoe more. It wasn't like he could bring women under her roof, she was too jealous, so he got his own. Still they did their thing. Viv was always on call for him.

Settling on his usual linen attire he made his way to the bathroom where he hopped in the shower, seconds later Viv joined.

An hour later the two emerged satisfied for the second time that morning.

"RL's been calling said he needs to talk to you," she commented as she sat at the vanity brushing the tangles from her weave.

Shrugging into his shirt Phatz laced up the gators on his feet.

RL

The man still hadn't gotten the message that he was no longer needed. Phatz didn't have to wait long for Ink to call and since then he had made two trips to Oakland on his own. With the game in awry he understood that in order for he and Ink to do good business they first had to build up trust. Apparently, Ink thought the same because his first move was crossing out Tonya. Her spot was no longer needed. Which was all good considering that Phatz had to punk RL after arriving back inside the apartment to find her crying because he was refusing to give her half of the cut. He didn't need that kind of drama.

Instead he and Ink met at Inks sisters house, a teacher married to a firefighter. Ink even introduced them to Phatz. The move was significant because a man who didn't trust you wouldn't bring you around his family. Slowly the two began to form a bond that went deeper than the beef between the two cities. While the men still had a long way to go one thing was for certain in their eyes: RL was pointless.

"What you want me to tell him?" she asked at his silence.

Clipping the beeper on his hip Phatz glanced at her.

"Whatever you want to."

When Bonnie's number flashed across the screen he smiled. They had been kicking it a lot lately. Tonight, they were going out for a dinner and a movie and maybe something extra. Bonnie did crazy--

"Can you help me cut this out?"

The voice made him snap out of his musings.

Viv held the outstretched scissors to him. A look of defeat had etched itself into her face as she struggled to no avail with the tangled hair.

Lifting a flat strand Phatz let it drop against her bare shoulder. Stepping back, he scratched at his head.

"Uh what you want me to do?"

Eyeing the watch on his arm he concluded that he had time to help. His date with Bonnie was a few hours out.

"Just cut it like this," she said taking the scissors and snipping at the long strands.

Hesitantly Phatz held the scissors and a patch of hair.

"Cut it," Viv said with humor in her voice. "Trust me you're not cutting my real hair."

At her words Phatz began to snip away at the hair. It fell in heaps to the floor.

After a few seconds he wiped his brow with the back of his hand. His fingers were beginning to cramp, but there was still a lot of hair left. Viv worked on taking down the braids underneath as he cut.

"This a lot of hair," Phatz said voicing his thoughts.

"Expensive too."

"How much?" he asked inquisitively as more strands began to drift to the floor.

"This brand of hair can run anywhere from $500 to $700 depending on the length."

His brows furrowed as he looked down at the hair now.

"You telling me that every time you're at the beauty shop you spending that much money on just the hair?"

"Mmmm hmmm."

"But that's not including installation, which could be another five hundred," she added.

He thought back to the many women he would see inside the hair salons. While it wasn't hard to believe that women were spending almost a stack on hairweave, he wondered why he had never looked closer at the hair business.

"Is this a good brand of hair?"

Viv laughed.

"French Refine, only the best like you." She winked at him in the mirror before she launched into explaining the different hair brands. Phatz was cutting out the last patch when she wrapped her explanation up.

"Why got something in mind?" she asked with a raised eyebrow.

The pager buzzing on his hip interrupted his response. It was Billy. The last he'd heard from the man he had been going through a serious stage of drug induced paranoia. Billy had called him and AC up in a panic with claims that there was a hit out on him. When they met in front of Harold's & Bells, Billy revealed that the person responsible for this hit was a player by the name of JJ from Pasadena, Phatz knew then that he was trippin' off the drugs that he was inhaling like water. For one JJ was currently during time in the feds after being swept up by the alphabet boys and was facing football numbers under the new crack law. Secondly there was still the fact that Billy hadn't revealed why there was a hit out on him when Phatz questioned him. After declining Phatz help to breathe on JJ's brother who he was jam with, Billy had gazed at them with an empty look in his eyes and patted the gun at his waist.

"I'm ready!" he declared before racing out of the parking lot. That was over a month ago. Telling Viv that they would discuss it later he grabbed up his things and hoped this wouldn't be another blank meeting.

****

"What was so important that I needed to be here?" Phatz asked Billy as they stood in the kitchen of his house in the Valley.

When Billy's head began to nod forward, and his eyes glossed over Phatz realized that the man was high. It was nothing new in fact it seemed to be his usual state these days. Being so near made Phatz realize just how bad the drugs were doing him. Billy's normally fitted clothing now hung loosely off his frame. Dark circles and heavy bags rested under his eyes. With hair growing all over his face it looked as if he hadn't shaved in weeks. The cravings for the drug had him neglecting his hygiene and everything else in between. Dirty dishes piled high in the sink trash overflowed from the waste bin. For a brief second Phatz wondered where Le Le could be?

He shook his head sadly as Billy stumbled forward, reaching out to grip the countertop to steady himself. Snapping out of his stupor Billy grabbed an unwashed glass and filled it with liquor from the cabinet. He motioned for Phatz to follow him. In the dining area clothes were scattered all over the floor and furniture. It was hard to believe that it was the same place Phatz had visited when he first got out. Cleaning off a spot for himself Phatz sat opposite in the chair from Billy.

"Where's Le Le?" he asked.

Hitching up his pants as he leaned forward Billy shrugged. He clicked the button on the remote. With his eyes fixed on the TV screen, he barely glanced at Phatz when he spoke.

"You know how bitches get, only around as long as the money is good bitches—" he cut off. Phatz could tell Billy hadn't meant to reveal what he already knew. That he was broke. Billy tried to coverup his mistake, "I buy her anything she wants, and she still trips out."

He cleared his throat after taking a sip from the glass. Finally looking at him he smirked.

"To answer your question from earlier I got a proposition for you."

Seemingly out of thin air Billy brandished a .45. Stilling himself Phatz saw a twinkle leap in the man's eye. Running a finger over the steel Billy smiled. The move made his already dark features look sinister.

A muscle in Phatz eye twitched as Billy gaze bore into him.

"What's the proposition?" Phatz asked not liking the fact that the man had his gun out and his was in the car.

Placing the .45 on his lap Billy rested his head against the back of the chair. His high was beginning to wear off.

"I got a few guys in route," he paused to drain the glass.

"They just dropped twenty five birds off in L.A. over to my safe house on Pico and High Point."

When Billy suddenly stood and crossed over to the patio Phatz never took his eyes off the gun that now hung from his hand.

"They're coming to pick up the money, but I got another plan in mind," he said with a faraway look on his face.

"Like what?"

Though Phatz knew where the conversation was headed, he still wanted to hear Billy say it.

Piercing him with a stare Billy asked in a hitched tone, "Do you know why Corey was killed?"

"What?" The question took Phatz by surprise. Before he could question him any further Billy quickly switched subjects.

"You know what I'm on…" He let the words hang in the air as he retreated to the kitchen, leaving Phatz alone with his thoughts. Billy was so desperate after taking a big loss in New Mexico that he was ready to rob his own workers. Now that part didn't come as a shock to Phatz. Billy was full of grime these days, robbing anyone that came across his path to feed his habit. Old and new friends had severed ties with him afraid that they would be next. Phatz had chosen to stick around hoping that Billy would see the light, but by the looks of things he was a long way from it. And what was up with him talking about Corey's death, it was the first time he'd ever heard Billy speak of it. When Billy returned Phatz tried to steer the conversation back to Corey, but Billy was focused on his plans.

He cocked his gun at the sound of an engine outside. Placing the gin bottle down on the television he eased towards the patio door.

"Ok so you're going to rob them and then what?" Phatz asked sitting back ready to watch the spectacle.

"Kill em."

The words made him sit up. Billy hadn't said anything about killing earlier. The fool was watching too many mafia movies and now thought he was a killer. The most Phatz ever seen Billy do with a gun was wave it.

Bright lights flashed through the window of the house as the car eased into the driveway steering around to the back.

Seeing the determined look on his face Phatz moved to his side.

"Who these niggas you gonna plant?"

At the sound of car doors slamming Billy tucked the .45 in his waist.

"See for yourself," he nodded.

Three men moved through the darkness up the driveway. When they reached the door, Billy pasted a smile on his face.

"What's up?" he greeted.

Phatz inhaled sharply as he watched the three men walk in.

"What up Phatz what you doing here?" Twin asked when he spotted him.

Instead of answering, Phatz searched Billy's face. Surely he couldn't be this stupid, but as they locked gazes Phatz felt as if he were staring into a dark empty hole. They stayed that way for what seemed like hours until Billy broke the stare.

"Y'all can get the bags in the kitchen," he said ushering Twin, his brother and Keith their childhood friend further inside.

Phatz waited until the men were no longer in listening distance. Cornering Billy he gripped the man's arm.

"Nigga have you lost yo mind?" he gritted out between clenched teeth.

"What?" Billy asked innocently snatching away from his grasp.

"You know what—that's my sisters' man in there you tryna kill?"

Billy huffed out a breath. "Them niggas about to get $325,000-"

"I don't care," he said cutting him off.

Phatz took a deep breath to calm himself down. He couldn't believe it. Twin was like a lil brother to him. Billy and Twin wouldn't even know each other if it weren't for Phatz, and now the man wanted his help to kill him.

"I thought you was about getting money," Billy stated in a raised voice.

Money. The green light weight paper had corrupted Billy so much that he had forgotten the number one rule. It was family over everything, and Twin was family to Phatz. So was Billy at one point but he couldn't say the same now.

"Find another way," he said with finality in his voice.

Spinning on his heels Billy stormed towards the kitchen. Phatz kept his eye on Billy the entire time they did the transaction. When it was over, the men left unaware of the danger they had just escaped. Phatz was still trying to process what Billy had suggested when he left. Racing to the twin's safe house he hoped like hell they would be there when he arrived. His date with Bonnie popped in his mind and he quickly dismissed it. He had more important things to deal with. Phatz released a sigh of relief when he turned on 108th and Crenshaw and noticed the cars in the driveway. At the door he could hear them moving around inside. Knocking twice he peeped the slight movement of the blind before the door swung open. Twin stood in the entrance with a wide smile.

"You was supposed to stop by two weeks ago after your mothers party," he said moving aside to allow him access.

Twin motioned for Phatz to follow him to the backroom where Keith and the other Twin was counting the money they had just picked up from Billy's house. Scrubbing a hand down his face he let out a deep breath. During the drive over, he had thought about what he would tell the twins and Keith. Though the news would fuck up their connect Phatz knew that he would be able to plug them with another one.

"What's up? We're headed to club when we wrap this up. You coming?" Twin asked breaking the silence.

Phatz shook his head. The man had no idea how close to death he had just come.

"Listen don't ever answer Billy's call again when he put in for work, don't do no more business with him," he stated without going into detail. Keith stopped counting money to stare at him as Twin sat with a confused look on his face.

"What you mean?" he asked.

Before Phatz could answer Keith stood and walked towards them.

"That's his friend, so if he says don't answer we don't answer," he said pointedly.

Glancing between the two, Twin shrugged his shoulder. "Ok," he said accepting Phatz word. After tossing out a few names to replace Billy, Phatz slipped out the house leaving the men with much to think about. He was settled in his car when the car phone began to buzz. A strange feeling rolled through him as he answered.

"Hello?"

On the other end he could hear heavy breathing. Phatz knew who it was before the man even opened his mouth.

"Nigga you gone say some or just keep breathing?" he snapped after a few seconds of silence.

"You said find another way and I have," Billy spoke in a low tone.

Shaking his head to himself Phatz pulled the phone away from his ear. Billy just wouldn't give up.

"Ok I'm listening," he said. A noise pulled his attention away from the conversation. Looking up he watched as the Twins and Keith exited the house and piled into their cars. When they drove off, he shifted his attention back to Billy who hadn't said much.

"Meet me somewhere and we can discuss the details." Rattling off a location to meet up, Phatz hung up the phone.

Drumming his fingers against the steering wheel he thought about blowing Billy off. Neither of them had to say it out loud, but tonight had changed the dynamics of their friendship. Phatz was really seeing Billy for the snake that he was. Keeping this in mind he slid the .45 in his lap and steered the car towards their meeting place.

****

That same .45 now was tucked securely in the waist band of his pants as he sat in the passenger seat of Billy's Benz while they drove through the streets of Los Angeles crossing into uncharted territory. The car ride had been quiet but the tension inside was evident. Phatz could feel the side eye coming from Billy. The man was obviously up to something more than he was letting on. Tilting his head slightly he assessed Billy's profile. With his shoulders hunched up to his ears, he gripped the steering wheel tightly, anger vibrating off him as he muttered lowly to himself. Phatz strained his ears to listen but gave up after realizing Billy was high again so his words were incoherent. He focused his attention outside of the window. Even in the darkness he could make out the hilly landscape of Hollywood Hills. That alone was the first flag that went off in his mind when Billy told him about the lick he wanted to hit in the area. The view only confirmed what he already knew. It would be impossible to reach the house through the rough terrain. He suspected Billy knew this as well. Phatz knew Billy well enough to know that all of this "lick" shit was a cover up for the fact that he was still fuming over his hit on the twins being stopped. This was all a front and he saw right through it but instead of calling Billy out on his bullshit, he waited for the man to play his hand. When the car slowed down on Mulholland Drive, he discreetly touched the steel at his waist.

Beside him Billy cleared his throat.

"We can go up the back way and get to the house I was telling you about," he pointed to the outline of the million-dollar houses nestled in the hills.

Pretending to look off in the direction. Phatz took note of the absence of traffic on the street. Between the almost deserted street and the hills that stretched on for miles this was the perfect place to leave someone.

Cutting the engine and the headlights off, Billy shifted in his seat towards him.

"If you get out you can see what I'm talking about."

Phatz could feel the man burning a hole in the side of his head with his stare. Realizing that he wasn't getting out Billy grunted and swung the door open and stood. Studying his silhouette Phatz could make out the print of the gun at his waist.

He chuckled to himself. Finally, he exited the car and rounded the front to stand beside Billy whose eyes were fixed on the hills. The warm night air blew across Phatz face as he leaned against the hood and crossed his arms.

"I'll wait here while you go check it out," he nudged his head towards the hills.

Glancing at him Billy clamped down on his teeth making the muscles in his jaws flex. They shared an intense stare off before Billy dropped his shoulders.

"Yeah you do that," he stated before taking off between the bushes.

Removing the .45 from his waist Phatz gripped the gun, his finger on the trigger. He wasn't stupid. The look in Billys' eyes said it all. He wanted to kill him. Just like he had wanted to kill the twins and Keith and anyone else that he thought was doing better than him. To Billy, Phatz had made a grave mistake by taking the twins' side. He'd stopped him from getting the one thing he loved the most besides drugs: money. Phatz shook his head to himself. Billy could no longer be trusted and apparently the man had come to the same conclusion about him, hence this little set up. This was the perfect place to take him out. With eyes trained on the bushes Billy had disappeared through, he listened for any sound of movement, but was only met with the chirping of insects that filled the night air. Phatz could feel the tension in his thumb from gripping the gun so hard, still he didn't relax his hold on the steel. If Billy thought he was about to get the drop on him he would be sorely mistaken. Minutes had passed when he thought he saw the bush move. Cocking the gun. He released a steady breath through his nose as he took aim. One wrong move and Billy was dead.

At the sound of laughter his brow furrowed.

Was this a trick he thought to himself still aiming his gun.

A string of curse words followed before Billy appeared. His head was down as he inspected the ground.

"Shit man I think I pissed on my shoes."

Peeping that his hands were nowhere near his gun, Phatz quickly tucked his piece back in his waist releasing the breath he didn't realize he was holding. Billy seemed oblivious to what had almost happened as he continued to stare down. Finally, he glanced up and smirked.

"You were right man we can't get through there," he said with a shrug before heading towards the driver side. Phatz starred after him. Billys' mouth said one thing but the flat cold look in his eyes had said another. He guessed somewhere during the hike Billy had come to his senses and decided not to kill him. It was either that or Billy had saw him holding the gun. Either way he had made the right choice because he had been minutes away from being a cold stiff body left on the side of the curb for all the animals who roamed the hills to feast on.

For the second time that night Phatz found himself back at the twins' house, only this time AC was lounging against his Benz when he pulled up. Phatz had paged him after parting ways with Billy. Hopping out the two men dapped up. He gave him a quick rundown of what all had happened. Including the part about Corey which Phatz still didn't know what to make of.

"You didn't put no led in his ass? he asked when Phatz was done.

Phatz shook his head and leaned on the car.

The two lapsed into a comfortable silence. Phatz mind was still reeling from the nights events when AC's voice broke into his thoughts.

"What we gone do about him?"

****

The question echoed in Phatz mind three days later. He knew that he couldn't let Billy get away with trying to kill him and the Twins. It would send the wrong message, one that he was sure would only encourage the man to try again. Billy had knocked at his door now all Phatz had to do was decide when he would answer. He was still putting together his plan when he arrived at Silky's apartments. Somehow after that scene at the club that night the two had found themselves back in each other's arm, or bed rather, reigniting their on again off again dealings.

Aware that he was running on a tight schedule Phatz hurried his steps up to her door and knocked. At the sound of her voice, he twisted the knob and entered at her directions. Immediately the smell of weed engulfed him before his eyes scaled up Silky's toned body perched on the couch in nothing but a red and black bra and panty set. Feeling the stirring in his slacks, he shut the door before he began shedding his clothes right there in her living room. Careful to put his .45 in a safe spot, the two made a beeline to her room. Phatz had just slipped inside of her and found his rhythm when a sound caught his attention making him pause.

Silky's eyes popped open as a moan died on her lips.

"What?" she asked at the concerned look on his face.

Head tilted to the side Phatz listened for the sound again. He was about to chalk it up to his imagination when it became loud and clear.

"Shit my alarm!" he yelled as he scrambled up. Snatching the .45 up as he dashed into the living room, he swung the door open and peered down at his Benz. Noticing his door was cracked, he saw the top of a figures head.

I'm not getting jacked today he thought as he took aim. When the figures head popped up and looked in his direction Phatz saw the fear on the boy who couldn't be no older than eighteen face, when he realized he had been caught.

BOOM!BOOM!BOOM!

Firing three shots in the boys' direction, Phatz watched him get low and try to scramble away. Knowing that the shots had bought him time he slipped into his clothes just as Silky came rushing out of her room. His gaze swept over her naked body again. It was just getting good.

"What the hell?" she asked.

"Some lil fool tried to take my Benz, I gave his ass a few warning shots though."

Leaning in he kissed her on the cheek before slapping her on her soft ass.

"I already know one time on the way," he paused "We gotta do this at a safer place next time."

His words caused Silky to laugh. Rushing down with the .45 in his hand Phatz scanned over his Benz to make sure nothing was missing. Satisfied he jetted off. Pulling up at Viv's tip he figured he would grab a quick shower before their meeting started. Pushing Billy and his almost carjacking to the back of his mind he focused on more pressing matters.

He had just stepped into the spare bedroom when Viv appeared in the door with a smirk on her face. He knew that look. They had just parted before he made his pit stop at Silky's place. She was on him before he even had time to blink.

"Whoa slow down," he said between kisses as she attacked his mouth hungrily. He could smell the fruity alcoholic drink she had been sipping on her breath.

Instead of slowing down Viv dropped to her knees with lust in her eyes. Phatz tried to stop her from pulling his pants down. He knew Silky was still all over his manhood which was why he was trying to hop in the shower. He couldn't tell her that though. After wrestling with Viv for a few seconds he surrendered and laid back on the bed. When she freed him from his boxers and took him in her mouth, he was certain she would smell the other woman's scent on him. Surprisingly, she made no comment as she slurped on him with her wet mouth. Closing his eyes, he enjoyed the feeling of her lips wrapped around him.

Damn she got some bomb ass head he thought as he laced his fingers through her weave. Ten minutes later he was drained.

"You can go take your shower now," she said standing to her feet with a wink.

Doing just that, Phatz donned a matching Polo shirt and short set afterwards and made his way down to the living room.

"AC here right?" he asked spying Viv stretched out over the couch.

"Yep," she replied as he leaned over to brush her lips inhaling her sweet scent.

"He's in the kitchen," she responded lazily when he pulled back.

In the kitchen Phatz found AC leaning against the counter holding a bowl.

"You eating cereal?" he joked.

Shoving the spoon in his mouth AC shook his head.

"Out of milk so I improvised."

Pushing the bowl towards him Phatz frowned at the captain crunch cereal and the thick white substance mixed in.

"What is it?"

"Vanilla ice cream," AC, responded around a mouth full.

"Try it it's better than milk."

Skeptical, but curious Phatz made himself a bowl surprised at how the flavor meshed perfectly in his mouth. When they were finished, they joined Vivian in the living room.

"You did your homework right?"

Viv bobbed her head eagerly as she jumped up from her seat. While AC slipped from the room Phatz listened as she repeated the latest street gossip. Not much for gossip Phatz listened with one ear, sometimes the information could be useful most times it wasn't like now.

When AC returned, with a Nike bag clutched in his hand Viv switched topics quickly.

"From what I found out the best hair vendors are in Italy," she began.

Phatz nodded along to the conversation. The three of them were starting a hair business. The idea had come to him while cutting Viv's hair. After doing some research of his own Phatz learned that it was a lucrative business, but even more so, the hair business provided an even better opportunity for him. It was their end game. He and AC had talked about this, getting out the game, cleaning up their money, and living the rest of their days feasting off the fat of the land. Well the time had finally come.

"So how much is it going to cost?" Phatz asked when Viv was finished.

Hesitating, she tapped a finger against her lips, "About $50,000."

Standing AC dropped the Nike bag on the table.

"It's $75,000 in there, do what you gotta do, but remember what I told you," AC stated in a serious voice.

Viv's hand paused on the money. Her eyebrows wrinkling in question.

"We don't need you setting up no more licks for us, you let us worry about the streets and you handle the hair business."

By the expression on her face Phatz could see that she was struggling with the decision. Viv didn't care who she had to set up as long as she got money, but they needed her hands clean if she was going to be the face of the company.

With a deep breath she agreed.

"Alright good, now how soon can you have things up and running?" AC asked clasping his hands in front of him.

"I can search for flight schedules to Italy today."

"Well get to it," Phatz stated playfully swatting at her ass.

Money in tow Viv set off to complete her task.

Alone now, Phatz and AC discussed the loose ends that they had to tie up. A few more months and they would be entering into another world. One where they didn't have to carry a .45 to make money. The plan was perfect, so much that neither man accounted for what was coming next.

(Phatz, Keith, and the Twins)

3 Months Later

Cincinnati, Ohio

Cold. He hated the cold and couldn't understand for the life of him why it was fifty degrees in May, but one peek out of his hotel's window and he had the answer. It had been less than a week since he arrived in Cincinnati to tie up those loose ends and already he was missing the feel of LA's warm sunshine on his face. On the other hand, at least, he was dressed for the weather in his Bill Cosby sweater and wool slacks, but despite his clothes the cold blast of air chilled him to his bone as he stepped out of the door forcing his feet to move swiftly across the tar parking lot to the black rental car. Sliding inside his hands instinctively went to the heat button as the engine purred to life. With the heat on high, he surfed through the stations before settling on a hip-hop station. Head bobbing to the sounds of DJ Jazzy Jeff coming from the factory speakers, AC navigated through the streets that had become familiar over the last two years. He passed the liquor stores which seemed to be on every corner. The churches in the city were just as plentiful. At a red light he let his gaze wander across a row of abandoned houses. Most places had been hit by the crack epidemic. Crack destroyed thriving communities turning productive citizens into walking zombies. The American dream had been abandoned like those houses, for their next high. As the light turned green a twinge of regret shot through him. How many of those abandoned homes were he responsible for? AC couldn't be more ready to leave the game behind. Maybe he would buy land in Cincinnati and build new homes, give them a new hope.

First thing first though, bringing the car to slow stop he shifted into park before checking the clip of his .45 automatic. Happy with the full clip he reinserted it and shoved the gun in the back of his pants. Next, he checked the small .22 holstered to his right leg. When he was finished, he inspected the 9-millimeter in his waist. Everything was good. Removing the bag from underneath his seat he reached for the door handle. It was go time. As AC made his way up the steps of the white house, he didn't miss the added security. Two men paced the front porch, another lingered on the side just out of sight. Briefly he wondered if there had been any trouble lately, in all his time visiting he never encountered any guards.

Surprisingly neither of the two men guarding the house paid him any attention as he walked to the door. With their eyes focused forward they seemed to be alert to another enemy.

AC heard the metal bolts slide back as he waited to be given access inside. When the ironclad door finally opened, the strong scent of weed hit him in the face.

"AC." A gruff voice stated rather than asked. When the door widened, he crossed over into the dark dining room. His curiosity was even more piqued. Months ago, the room had been decked out with furniture and the latest appliances now it was bare. Newspapers covered the window making it impossible for light to seep inside. The spark from the loose cigarette dangling from the man lips was the only light in the room.

"Gotta pat you down," the man with the gruff voice said. Though AC could barely see him he could make out his figure. He couldn't be any taller than five feet, but from the sound of his heavy breathing he was big.

AC shook his head at the news.

"No need to I'm locked and loaded."

He heard him draw in a deep breath that turned into a hacking cough. After catching his breath, the man responded, "Wait right here." Then there were footsteps. AC didn't care about the extra security the fact remained that no one was taking his guns from him. When a light flipped on illuminating the room, he swung his gaze around.

"Come through here," the man motioned. AC was right he was fat and short, but the darkness had hidden the ugly scar that ran from the corner of his eye to underneath his chin and the scars on his hands. Following the man's lead he walked down the creaky basement steps. Instead of weed, the room smelled of wet cement. Colorful bulbs hung from the floor planks like a fiesta party. In the center of the room a cheerful familiar voice called out to him.

"Awful Clyde," Peter stood behind a table with three other men. Forty with a low haircut, Peter had a slim build. The men locked gazes before Peter stuck his hand out, pulling him in for a shoulder bump.

"Good to see you my nigga," he said in that funny accent that only northerners could speak. He and Peter had been in business for years. Peter as the buyer and AC the supplier. Not just that, but Peter was the biggest dealer in the small city and all moves went through him. And in a city like Cincinnati, Peter was doubling the profit, when he sold to other dealers. The smaller the city the higher the price of the kilo, was the name of the game.

The latest shipment was one of their largest. It had taken weeks to arrange things then days to transport it, but all twenty-five birds were there. Just not all with AC now. He'd only brought ten. The remaining would be exchanged tomorrow. Then it was goodbye Cincinnati.

"Let me introduce you to the boys," Peter said clapping his shoulder.

He waved his hand around as he introduced each man in the room.

"This is Awful Clyde," Peter said slapping him on the back. Murmurs went around as the men spoke.

Leaning in closer he nodded at the bulge in his waist.

"I see you came prepared."

"Always," AC responded.

"Good, good."

Peter crossed over to makeshift bar and poured himself a drink. After motioning for AC to pull up a seat at the table he reclaimed his seat.

"Couple lil niggas thought that it would be cool to try to run up in here." He slammed a card on the table before tossing his drink back.

"Know that's not happening."

His words explained the men outside and the guns AC had peeped near the bar.

"You got that?" Peter glanced up from the game.

"Most of it."

The man bobbed his head. Though Peter tried to play it cool, AC knew that the words weren't what he wanted to hear. If you do business with a person long enough you'll start to learn a few things about them and the one thing that AC had learned about Peter was that he was sneaky. AC had always gotten the feeling that Peter would have tried him long ago if he thought that he could get away with it, but he knew he couldn't. Sneaky and manipulative, Peter would try to talk the prices down, but AC had only to tell him once that his prices were nonnegotiable. Either he had it or he didn't.

"You want in?" Peter asked referring to the game of poker they were playing.

He took one look at the stack of money next to Peter and realized the other men at the table were losing sorely.

"We'll handle that other business after we finish playing here."

Another thing about Peter was that he liked to pretend that he called the shots, but this one-time AC decided to let it slide. Besides, taking him for all his money would be more fun.

Loud music floated from the party to Phatz ears as he paralleled parked his Porsche behind the long line of cars on 112th and Western. After many nights of planning and executing their company Hair Distributors was fully in business and thriving. Phatz and AC had even rented a building to store and sale the hair that Vivian purchased with their money from Italy. What better way to celebrate their success than partying? When word got back to him that an old friend was hosting one of the biggest pool parties of the summer Phatz decided it was only right that he graced the party with his presence. The real celebration would kick off when AC returned from Ohio.

Though a few people loitered the inside of the house, the real party was outside in the backyard. Phatz mumbled along to the Ice T *Colors* song that was blaring from the speakers. He scoped out the scene from behind his ray bans. Smoke from the large grill tainted the air. Topless women tossed a striped beach ball back and forth as they splashed around in the swimming pool. To his left bikini clad chicks in all different shades lounged on the beach chairs on the grass, showing off their toned bodies. He nodded his head to a few familiar faces as he navigated through the thick crowd. Spotting the Twins, Phatz was headed in their direction, when a hand clasped his shoulder from behind. He spun around quickly coming face to face with Duck, the party hostess.

"What's up?" Duck asked smiling. It had been a while since Phatz saw his old friend. The two spent some time catching up and going down memory lane before Phatz pulled him to the side. Keeping his voice low he touched the heavy gold rope and chains hanging from his neck.

"I got on too much jewelry for this hood shit." He glanced around, most of the men that he had noticed were from different hoods. While he didn't see anyone he had beef with, you never knew.

"Let me hold yo strap," Phatz said referring to the weapon he knew Duck always kept on him.

Without hesitating Duck removed the .357 Magnum from his waist.

"You good now?" Duck asked with laughter in his voice.

Tucking the gun in his waist Phatz nodded. After a few more words the two men went their separate ways. Duck to check on the food and Phatz to check out the honeys.

"What's your name?" Phatz asked thirty minutes later. The honey in front of him wore a thin lime green bikini that barely covered her goodies. Short and brown skinned, her hair was neatly cornrowed into braids that fell down her back. She brought the cup to her pink lips, the brown drink inside the same color as her eyes.

"I'm Tiny."

The name fit her small stature perfectly.

They chatted away as she and the other girls in the corner sipped on their drinks. When the drinks ran low, Phatz volunteered to go buy more. Tiny tagged alone. She giggled loudly in the seat of the Porsche as he drove. He could tell she was feeling him. Tiny didn't say it, but Phatz knew she dated a drug dealer. Duck had told him, but the information was nothing to him especially since he liked what he saw and planned to get to know her better before the night was over with. But his plans would have to wait, when they returned, to his disappointment the party was being shut down. Cutting the engine Phatz watched the crowd from the party swarm into the street as a helicopter flew above them shining the bright light. In the distance he could hear the sirens growing closer.

"Damn," Tiny muttered beside him.

She had said the words that he thought. His eyes lingered over her exposed skin.

"Do you see any of my friends?" she asked concern in her voice as she climbed out of the car. Following suit, they searched through the flock of people until she located the girls she had come with. Phatz lingered around talking to Tiny.

Instead of leaving it looked as if the crowd had decided to continue the party in the streets. When a band of police cars arrived, he knew that was his cue to roll. The mere presence of the police made him uneasy. Not to mention the Magnum he had in his waist. Quickly exchanging numbers with Tiny he promised to give her a call later that night to pick up where they left off.

Eager to put some space in between him and one time, Phatz barely paid attention to the group of bangers standing around talking. He was almost to his whip when a loud voice stopped him.

"You got to leave all that jewelry!"

While his mind screamed for him to ignore them and keep walking his body had already spun around to face off. In all his years no one had ever taken his chains and he wasn't about to let it happen now. With the police only a few feet away Phatz wondered how he should play it. He did a quick check over his shoulder first to make sure it wasn't a case of mistaken identity.

"Yea I'm talking to you nigga," a tall dark skinned man said as he stepped from the group.

Letting out a steady breath Phatz sized the man up, pegging him to be the leader. The rest of the crew lingered behind, poised to go at the leaders' command. This was a bad time to pick a fight especially with the police hanging around, but the bangers didn't seem to think that.

"You see the police is everywhere and I know you real bad." He paused to let his words sink in as the group moved closer to the dark-skinned man. It was seven of them versus one of him. The Magnum in his waist would cut them down to one if he could use it, but right now that wasn't even an option. Knowing this Phatz tried another tactic. Reaching into his pocket he dug out the bankroll full of hundreds.

"This about $7k right here, it's $2,000 in my other pocket." He nodded towards his whip "And that Porsche is mine."

Seeing the hunger in their eyes he continued hoping they would take the bait. "I would give y'all all this if the police wasn't in our way." Knowing that he had their attention he placed the money back in his pocket.

"Let's do it like this. Tell me two streets that meet up where it's no police and I'll meet you there right now!"

He swung his gaze to each man face. He could tell they were thinking about it. All except the dark skinned one

"Fuck you!" the man spat venomously.

So much for trying to lure them in Phatz thought. He spun around towards his car again. A sharp pain vibrated through his head. One of the lil niggas had snuck him.

Without thinking his hand reached for the gun in his shorts, but he found himself being restrained by a strong pair of arms.

"Don't do it," the voice pleaded.

It was Duck and behind him was the twins. The crowd had gotten wind of the drama and all eyes were focused on him. Even the police. Embarrassment burned in his face as he looked at the at the dark-skinned man who wore a smile.

"Don't do it," Duck stated again dragging him away and into the house.

Inside Phatz paced the floor.

The blow didn't faze him, it was his pride that bore the bruise. For the first time in his life he had tried to walk away from some shit. This would be the last time he ever did it again.

With his anger growing by the second Phatz had forgotten that Duck was in the same room. The man's voice pulled him out of his violent thoughts.

"I didn't want you to do it outside in front of everybody," he said. Pausing Phatz read the look on Duck's face. By "do it" he meant shoot the man that had attacked him.

"If I was stupid it would have been done." Removing the Magnum from his waist he handed it to him.

Duck could see the fire burning in his eyes. While the bangers had tried to get a come up off Phatz, they didn't know that they'd just marked themselves.

"Twenty-five," Peter counted out. The birds lie flat next to each other on the hotel bed.

With a flip of his finger the fat man with the scar that AC had come to know as June, began to pack the birds up into the duffel bags.

Peter rubbed his hands together, a smile playing at the corner of his lips.

"Awful Clyde, you and Phatz saved the business, y'all about the only niggas that's still able to get their hands on this much work during a drought."

AC tugged on his chin hair already knowing where the conversation was going. He'd been waiting on Peter for hours to show up at the spot. When the man did show, he fed him a story about an attempted robbery at the house. Peter also wanted more birds and AC had only brung the amount that they'd agreed on. He didn't plan on returning to Cincinnati and he let Peter know that.

"This was my last run."

Peter sucked his teeth and was quiet for a few seconds. Slapping his hands together he shoved them in his pockets.

"Ok, how about this time, I come to you," he said raising his eyebrows in question.

The words took AC by surprise, before he could answer a knock came at the door making everyone in the room reach for their guns since he wasn't expecting any company.

"Housekeeping!" An accented voice called out.

"Shit," AC muttered under his breath. He'd forgotten to put the do not disturb sign on the door when he checked in this morning. The room was under an alias and at a different location than the one he slept at. He searched around until he located the sign.

"Be cool," he said to June and Peter as he crossed over to the door. Cracking it open, AC quickly declined the service before placing the sign on the handle and closing the door shut.

He swung around to Peter, the man had eased his gun back in his holster. June had resumed packing.

"Let me check with Phatz," he said getting back to the question at hand.

On cue his pager vibrated. Instructing the men to exit through the closet, where there was a conjoined room on the other side, he punched in the numbers to Viv's house. With his back facing the wall he watched Peter and June with a trained eye. When she answered the phone in hysterics he shifted his focus and cautioned her to slow down. Through her cries he was able to piece together that Phatz was on a rampage after some niggas at a party stepped to him. Hearing the news made, AC eager to get out of Cincinnati. At the sound of the door closing he sat on the edge of the bed gun still in hand, phone pressed to his ear.

"Put him on the line."

AC listened as Phatz recounted the story. He knew Phatz wouldn't rest until he got his payback. The bangers knew that too, which was why they were laying low. AC knew just how to bring them out.

****

Phatz hung up the phone excited. He had been so busy terrorizing the hoods of the bangers that he hadn't thought to do the most obvious thing.

****

Knock knock

Standing on the porch in the banger's neighborhood off 117th and Crenshaw, Phatz swung his gaze left then right as he waited anxiously for someone to open the door. Though it was broad daylight the street was empty. It hadn't taken much to find out where the tall dark-skinned man who Phatz found out name was Jay lived. On the hunt, his first stop had been at the park on 120th and Holly Park were the bangers hung.

They were deep. Phatz had counted at least twenty-five of them on the basketball court and another twenty five in the corner playing a game of craps. With girls prancing around dancing to the loud music and the bangers turning up the 40 oz glass bottles of malt liquor, he realized he had caught them in their element. This was their zone. From his position in the cut Phatz watched them joke and laugh never counting on anyone to cross into their territory. But that's where they were wrong. At the sight of the four cars full of Jungle niggas arriving, headed up by Duck, he got into position. Once he was sure that the park was surrounded by his reinforcement he moved quickly. Vision fixed on the bangers on the court since they were the closest, Phatz stalked across the park dressed in his Italian suit and gator shoes. Once they peeped him coming, with a gun gripped tightly in his hand, they reached for their straps. The move didn't deter Phatz. From the corner of his eye he watched the Jungle niggas fall in step beside him. By the time he reached the court his one-man army had swelled to eight.

He could feel the bangers gaze boring into him as he stopped in front of a familiar face. Mentally Phatz tried to recall his name but kept drawing blanks.

"They told me you hunting them clowns," the man opened his mouth and said.

Not surprised by the news, he checked out the crowd trying to see if any of his future victims were among them. Dressed in khakis and wife beaters they all wore the same mug on their faces, but none of them were the cowards he was looking for.

Directing his attention back to the man he spoke loud enough for everyone to hear.

"When you see any of them tell em' I just want the stupid nigga from the party, and until I get him I'ma keep it funky in they hood."

Phatz wanted them to know that no matter what hood you claimed or set you banged no one was untouchable. With a nod of his head to his Jungle niggas they all fell back retreating in the direction they had come from.

Now here he was still on the hunt. At the sound of footsteps approaching from inside the house, Phatz hand gripped the handle of the .45 tucked underneath his suit jacket. He was ready to dead Jay in front of God and any other witnesses in the house. When the door swung open revealing a small woman in her late sixties, he eased his hand away from his weapon. Moles covered the brown loose skin on her face. Behind the wire framed glasses bright eyes stared at him. The woman brushed at the apron at her waist before cracking the door open.

"May I help you?" she asked.

Clasping his hands in front of him, Phatz relaxed the muscles in his face forcing his lips to stretch into a smile.

"Hi, mam I'm looking for Jay is he home?"

She smiled, her eyes crinkling at the corners.

"That's my son." She brushed at the gray strings of hair around her face studying him closely.

"That's a nice suit you're wearing," she complimented.

Tossing his head back Phatz laugh. "Thank you, mam." He glanced over his shoulder as a car drove down the street. Clearing his throat his focus returned to the woman.

"You wouldn't happen to know where he is?"

She shook her head. "No ,I don't. He's not in any trouble is he?" she asked with concern in her voice.

More than you know.

"No, no," Phatz said trying to assure her.

"I was just stopping by to discuss a little business with him."

The woman stared at him for a few seconds as if trying to determine if she could believe him.

He smiled wider.

"Ok, well no he's not home, he just left in fact."

Damn

Trying to hide his annoyance Phatz nodded his head and stepped back. "Thank you for your time mam."

As he turned to leave, she asked,

"Would you like for me to give him a message?"

Phatz looked up and down the still deserted streets. Jay could be hiding out in either of those houses. He was sure that word had gotten back to him by now. There was no need to hide his intentions.

"Yes, tell him that Phatz is looking for him."

• •

Taking aim, Phatz gripped the Uzi in his hand as he let off round after round at his moving targets. It was 2 A.M. and the neighborhood was wide awake. No one could sleep through the chaos unfolding. Phatz was glad he'd listened to his first mind after leaving the Spinks and Tyson fight that night. He had a strange feeling that the bangers would be out. His feelings proved true when he rolled up to find a group of them hanging out on the corner. Catching them off guard he gave no warning as he started firing. He watched as they ran trying to dodge his wrath, but he wasn't letting up.

Snatching the .45 out of his holster, he clocked his target. Squeezing both triggers he released a hail of bullets into the house they had ran for cover in.

A painful scream pierced the night air. Phatz aimed again but eased up as a girl ran from the house. He didn't want any girls, just those who had wronged him. Gravel crunched under his gators as he walked into the middle of the street. He needed to get closer. When the door swung open and a man shot across the yard Phatz aimed the Uzi, letting another one off. He smiled as the body dropped.

Writhing in pain the man tried to crawl to safety as Phatz neared him. The sound of sirens approaching and the fact that he was out of ammo halted him in his steps.

"Fuck!" he muttered at the sirens getting closer. Reversing in the opposite direction Phatz swung his Uzi into his holster as he tried to map out his escape route. He was considering jumping a fence he had come up on when the sound of squealing tires made him glance up. The Benz that was barreling down on him stopped inches away.

"Get in!" Duck yelled as the door swung open.

Diving inside Phatz slammed the door shut as Duck floored the gas.

Swapping out the empty clip, Phatz turned to Duck.

"Nigga where you been?"

"Gun got jammed." He nodded towards the Uzi on the floor of the car.

Phatz had brought Duck along for backup but told the man to stay in the car until he heard shots. Now he knew why he hadn't showed up.

Duck made a sharp left turn.

"You done?" he asked taking his eyes off the road.

Phatz cocked the gun.

"Just getting started."

****

"Your boy was on the hunt, shooting everything in sight," the man in front of him explained as people from the crowd added their two cents in.

"I heard he ran up in their house."

"Naw I heard he shot the nigga mama-"

The gossip went on and on until finally AC walked away. It was all he had been hearing about since he arrived in the Jungle. Phatz had shaken the city up when he blew through the banger's neighborhood. AC was glad his friend was acting out his revenge, but now it was time to get back focused on the money. Speaking of Phatz his P car rolled into the Jungle sending more whispers through the crowd that loitered the street.

"You the talk of the city, I see," AC said dapping his fist when he reached him.

Phatz tugged on the lapel of his Gucci suit.

"What they saying?" he asked as the two broke into laughter. The crowd was no longer paying attention to them as they dispersed into their usual habit of drinking and laughing.

As he and Phatz updated each other on the happening's AC couldn't help but think how glad he was to be at home. There was a cool breeze in the air, much different than the stiffening cold air in Cincinnati. The atmosphere was different, but the hustle was the same. He watched a crackhead slither up to a dealer for a purchase. No one batted an eye, it was normal, but AC was starting to have a love hate relationship with the game and once again couldn't wait until he was free of it.

"Did you get him?" he asked Phatz who had just finished telling him the real details of his hunt.

"Word on the street is that Jay's mother made him move away." The two shared a look before doubling over with laughter again.

Sobering up AC's voice grew serious. "And Billy?"

Leaning against the Porsche Slant nose Phatz demeanor shifted as he crossed his arms. Minutes ticked off before he finally spoke.

"Missed him."

AC let out a low hiss.

"How?"

"Traffic."

He frowned at the vague response.

"Traffic?" he repeated to make sure he'd heard correctly.

Phatz gave a tight jerk of his head.

AC knew there was more to the story, but decided to drop it. Billy was a liability that they couldn't afford to have roaming the streets since he was trying to plant their friends, but they would have to be smart about their decision to plant him. After all that they had endured in Angola, Billy wasn't worth a life sentence.

"Pass me your gun," Phatz said suddenly.

Puzzled AC nodded before removing the .45 and handing it to him. Phatz stared off into the crowd. When AC realized what was going on, he chuckled.

"You bout to blast this nigga out here?"

"He owes me money," Phatz stated plainly.

Waltzing from the crowd, headed in their direction was Ty. AC hadn't seen much of him since the Colorado lick. Though Ty had paid his debts with him, he was still indebted to Phatz.

"What up?" Ty asked with his hands outstretched.

"Where my money?" Phatz asked in a steely voice.

"M-money?" Ty stuttered.

"Nigga don't play stupid!" Phatz barked.

It took everything in AC not to laugh at the mortified look on Ty's face. Ty had played one too many times about paying Phatz back for the plane ticket he'd bought him in Colorado, now he had to face the music.

"I had to pay my rent," he answered lamely.

"Oh yeah," Phatz eased closer as AC took a step back. He already knew what time it was.

"Ye-"

Phatz socked him in the mouth silencing whatever else he was about to say. Doubling over Ty grabbed at his face. All eyes were on them now. AC saw a few confused looks. Of course they were all thinking that Phatz and Ty were supposed to be friends, but he knew Ty had forced Phatz hand and AC didn't blame him for his reaction.

Phatz pulled the .45 out as Ty righted himself. When he saw the gun trained on him his eyes bulged out of his head. There was a hurt look on his face.

"You need a gun?" Ty asked heatedly.

Phatz handed the weapon to AC.

"Not for you," he said raising his fist.

"Let's get em up and once I beat yo ass I'ma beat yo ass every time I see you til you pay me!"

Ty looked over his head at AC. Though his mouth remained closed his expression screamed for help. AC answered him with a blank stare. In the blink of an eye the man took off running.

"Pussy!" Phatz yelled snatching the gun away from AC and firing.

Zig zagging through the street to get away, Ty was a sight to see, reminding AC of the scene were Scar face zig zagged to dodge bullets in the movie *Low and Fast*. The block was howling with laughter at the spectacle. After dumping nine shots Phatz lowered the gun, letting Ty slink away into the night.

"Guess he got that zig zag shit off TV. It worked too because you didn't hit him not once," AC joked. Laughing about the situation, AC glanced around, everyone carried on as if nothing had happened. It was just another day in the hood.

••

    The waves lapped against the beaches' shore, pulling with it grains of the white sand that stretched for miles on end. With the moon high in the sky reflecting off the water, it was a serene view. Standing on the deck of the luxury condo, that was nestled safely on the beach resort in Puerto Vallarta, Mexico, Phatz mind raced as he stared out into the night. Gripping the rail, he breathed in the salty air as he struggled to get ahold of his thoughts. It was Viv's idea for them to go on a vacation for his birthday. While she had stressed it was because they needed a break, Phatz suspected the true reason was because she feared the bangers would retaliate. That wouldn't be the case. They had waved the white flag after he sought out his revenge on them. Still, when she presented the idea he didn't object. Over the past three days they had water skied, toured different sites, spent a whole lot of money, and had lazy sex on the beach. When they weren't out feasting on the islands cuisines, they spent hours talking about their plans for the hair business. Viv wanted to branch out and begin selling hair to celebrities, Phatz didn't have a problem with that. In fact, he wanted them to go even further. Just like they had dominated the drug game, he wanted to do the same in the hair business. In the heat of the moment she had brought up marriage. Phatz heard the loud brakes in his head scrub at the mention of the word. Steering the conversation away from the dreaded topic he focused on the many celebrity contacts he had accumulated over the years. He just didn't deal to locals, they supplied drugs to the elite as well. Days later Viv's marriage suggestion was still on his mind, but it wasn't the reason for his current unrest. Phatz had realized something much more disturbing and it had all started the night at Billy's house.

    While in the beginning Phatz hadn't given much thought to Billy asking him about Corey's death, unbeknownst to him the seed had been planted. And just like a seed eventually it sprouted taking root in his mind, growing with every passing second making him ask the hard question. Why was Corey killed? It was something he hadn't thought about since coming home from Angola. If Phatz was being honest with himself, at the time it was too much to deal with, first his brother, then Corey. Being trapped in a four walled cell with those thoughts would have driven him insane, so he tucked it away. It was out in the open now, ready to be handled. He knew that Billy was a lot of things, but he wouldn't have brought it up if it didn't matter. Not after all this time. Which lead him to believe that Billy knew more than he let on that night. Phatz had every intention of getting the answer out of him before he planted him, but the man had slipped through his fingers. He'd spent days hunting Billy after shooting at Jay and his crew. Billy's reputation was ruined in L.A., forcing him to keep his game on the road. Knowing that there was a bounty on his head, he never stayed anywhere too long, always in and out. Yet just like most people, Billy was a creature of habit and if his drug addiction didn't pull him out of the shadows his love for bitches did. Phatz knew about the honey he kept in Culver City, so he had someone to stake out baby's spot. He had a hunch that Billy would be showing his face real soon and less than 24 hours his hunch proved him right.

The second he'd gotten the call, Phatz had raced to his car Uzi in hand. Only forty minutes away he'd jumped on I-10 west, but at 5:30 P.M. the lanes were jammed pack with rush hour traffic. Phatz stewed silently as the long lines crept along at a snail's pace, by the time he made his exit to Culver City, Billy had slipped away. He hadn't lied when he told AC that traffic had been the reason.

Deciding to lay it to rest for the time being Phatz had tried to enjoy his vacation still Billy's question gnawed at his mind until he was forced to confront it. The answer took his breath away. It had been staring him in the face for years, but Phatz had turned a blind eye to it, unwilling to believe that someone he loved like a brother could betray him. Yet his mind traveled back to the day Corey had made the frantic call with the police on the line and suddenly the pieces began to take shape and the picture was ugly. If Phatz suspicions were correct, then Corey had done the unforgivable. He'd broken the number one code of the street. Just thinking about it gave Phatz such a nauseating feeling that he gripped the rail until his knuckles turned white. Squeezing his eyes shut he focused on the soothing sound of the waves. When the feeling passed, he took a deep breath exhaling through his nose, past the hurt in his chest. He didn't want to believe it but there were no other options and Phatz had examined it from all angles hoping he'd gotten it wrong. Each time he came up with the same conclusion. Even worse his big brother Marlon came to mind, Phatz gave himself a mental shake. He didn't want to go down that road yet. He lost track of how long he stood on the deck caught up in his thoughts he didn't hear the footsteps. At the feel of soft and warm curves pressing up against him, he stilled.

Coming face to face he watch the moons light illuminate the concern in her eyes.

"You ok?" she asked stroking a hand up and down his spine.

Did she know what her husband had done? Phatz thought to himself.

Instead he nodded. She wrapped her arms around, swaying back and forth. When she tugged at his hand to go inside, he followed. Stripping out of her robe Viv began kissing on his neck, her breathing became labored as she guided his hand between her legs to feel her wetness. Even as he undressed and slipped between her legs his mind was still a million miles away. Stroke for stroke, her moans and breathing grew louder as their bodies began its slide into one another. Bringing them to a complete finish. Fully sated, she curled up next to him before drifting into a peaceful sleep. Phatz on the other hand couldn't sleep a wink. By the time the sun began to rise in the sky shining into the crystal blue waters Phatz had decided one thing. He would uncover the truth at all costs.

● ●

"Corey was a rat?" AC asked with disdain laced in his voice. He skirted over the printed black words on the paper in his hands. It was information from their case. Four years ago the police had been tipped off by a "credible source" about the string of jewelry store bashings in L.A. With the information, they had formed a task squad to go after the perpetrators, only the perps fled before they could apprehend them. The perps in question names were in bold letters.

At the sight of his name next to Phatz, AC shoved the paper to the center of the table. They were having lunch at the Red Onion.

"Yep."

Across from him a cloudy expression covered Phatz face. He had returned from his vacation with Viv in a funk and now AC understood why. "The day he called me with the police on the phone set everything off. Corey gave them us to save himself." At the time Phatz hadn't dwelled much on it, but with the evidence in his face he saw that it had been the tip of the iceberg.

AC digested the words, stunned. Even though Corey's name wasn't on the paper, it didn't take a genius to figure out that he was the "credible source." He was the only one who knew about their bashing sprees. AC examined Phatz closely. The news had to have hit his friend hard, considering many things, the most important being that they never would have left for Louisiana and…

"Marlon would still be here, if that nigga hadn't told on us," Phatz said completing his thoughts. They sat in silence. The words hanging heavy in the air. No longer interested in his salmon and salad AC sipped on the sparkly water in his champagne flute. It failed to wash the bitter taste that had formed in his mouth.

"Corey was snitching on everyone in the game. It was the reason why he was killed," Phatz stated with a shake of his head.

Damn who would've known that Corey would cross the game. AC never cared much for him but, he'd kept the peace for Phatz sake and for once he wish he hadn't.

"You think Viv knew?" AC asked suddenly.

Sucking on his teeth Phatz toyed with the napkin on the table.

"She was on the phone with him the day he called with the police listening in."

AC sighed. Of course she knew.

"But she didn't make Corey snitch he did that on his own, only Corey knew about the shit in that paperwork, he even told them about the spot me and Silky had on 67th and Brynhurst."

Phatz snapped his fingers as if having an aha moment, "Now that I think about it, this one time he rode by the crib while I was charging the batteries on my low rider, except he didn't stop, not even when I tried to flag him down."

Holding up the incriminating paper he waved it in the air, "All of that happened around the same time. That was why they kicked the door in on Silky. He told them where I lived." AC could hear the incredulity in his friends' voice as the picture became clearer.

Massaging his temples, AC wondered what other disloyal acts Corey had committed. Then It dawned on him that they would never know because the dead didn't talk to the living. He was still trying to wrap his mind around the evidence when Phatz flagged down the waitress and began gathering his things.

"I'm meeting Ink at Monty's in a few." He peeled off a few dollars to cover the meal before donning his suit jacket.

"You got everything in place for the meeting with Peter?" Absentmindedly AC nodded.

Phatz stood gripping the back of the chair.

"I know it's a lot, but we'll talk about it later tonight, cool?"

Finally, AC glanced up, he could see the stormy clouds in Phatz eyes. The knowledge of Corey's betrayal did a number on him. Both of them. AC found himself burning with anger. Four years of his life had been taken away because of one disloyal act. An image of a cell flashed in his mind. He had to remind himself that Angola was over. They had survived that jungle and were free. Agreeing to meet Phatz later at the house they parted ways.

Signaling for a refill, AC leaned back in his chair. Corey had tried to fuck them over, but his plan had backfired. In his quest to live the street life he'd broken the code and gotten himself killed. The same dream that he chased, Phatz and AC were living, and they didn't have to betray the ones they loved to do it.

• •

The dope game was full of twist and turns, Phatz thought to himself as he sauntered up to Monty's Steak House. Inside he followed the maitre'd to a table overlooking the city. He barely paid attention to the menu she left or the beautiful picture of the sky as the sun began to set. Corey's betrayal plagued his every thought and even worse his heart was pained. A part of him had hoped that when they returned from Puerto Vallarta that he wouldn't find anything but deep down inside Phatz knew he would. It had taken one request of his case work and there laid out in front of him was Corey's treacherous acts. He hadn't expected the pain to hit so hard, but it did. Phatz tried to put himself in Corey's shoes. And still he couldn't imagine snitching under any circumstances. It went against everything he stood for as a man. There were risks that came with the game and no matter what happened you were never supposed to tell. It was a principle that had been engrained in him since a kid. Phatz was so lost in his thoughts he didn't hear anyone approach.

"Got a lot on your mind?"

At the sound of the voice his head snapped up. Standing in front of him was Ink. Rising, Phatz gave him a fist bump before reclaiming his seat.

"More than you know," Phatz replied trying to push his current woes from his mind.

Ink nodded. "That's understandable," he stated scooting himself up to the table.

Since the meeting in Oakland the two had grown closer. Phatz considered Ink a friend. At the word friend his chest tightened. Corey was his friend, but he had snitched and fucked up everything. Could Ink do the same?

Phatz shook his head clear of the absurd thought. The deep betrayal had him questioning everything and everyone. He focused across the table. The same thing engrained in him was in Ink. He could see it. They were men of principle. It hadn't taken him long to figure that out.

The two talked business as the evening passed. The atmosphere grew more mellow as the once empty tables began to fill.

"It's been a real shake up in Boss Angeles these last few weeks the DEA took down some major crews since that crack law came into effect," Phatz commented as he nursed his drink.

Ink squeezed the lime in his margarita before responding.

"Oh yeah, that's why its dry in the land."

"Not in my land."

Ink paused with the glass half raised to his lips.

"Guess that's just some mo of it then?"

"That's right."

Tossing the margarita back, his face frowned up for a few seconds before relaxing. Slapping his hand lightly on the table he leaned forward.

"I got three big boys that want to win. Can you get 100 birds?"

Phatz smirked,"I thought you said they were big boys?

Big boys want a 100 each," he teased.

Tilting his head to the side Ink gave him a startled look before bursting into a fit of laughter. Phatz joined him. As the laughter subsided Inks' face grew serious.

"Listen I know the ticket is high so tell me your price."

Those were just the words Phatz wanted to hear. Removing the pen from the menu the waitress had brought over he jotted a number down on the napkin and slid it across the table.

A low whistle left Inks mouth.

"Firm?

Phatz nodded.

"Ok, I can win with that.

I need you to come to me this time though," Ink said jumping right into things.

With the streets being dry, Oakland or Cokeland as Phatz liked to call it had become the headquarters. It was the only place dealers could cop from.

"Three of my boys got jacked, I can't afford to take those kinds of losses," Ink said shaking his head. Phatz sighed at the response, though he understood Inks answer. The war between L.A. and Cokeland was full-fledged now. Niggas was dropping because of the drought. Neither man was trying to get caught up in the crossfire. They both had a lot to lose. There were almost no safe spaces in this war at any time things could go up in flames, which was why Phatz was treading carefully. Lately, he had begun to feel like the game was closing in on him. Every which way he turned there was an obstacle that was always bigger than the last one. It was how he knew that the time to make their exit was now. The longer they stayed in, the harder it would be to leave.

Scanning the restaurant, he noticed the crowd growing thicker. When the maître d' seated a couple next to them, Phatz angled his head towards the balcony.

"Grab your drink, let's go out there where I can really breathe on you."

Not waiting for an answer, he headed towards the balcony. Shoving his hands in his pocket Phatz stared out at LA's skyline. The bright city lights twinkled against the dark sky. The sound of the city rushed through him sending a tingling sensation through his body. In that moment he felt more alive than ever. Ink had just handed him a golden opportunity when he accepted his deal. Phatz had scribbled $19K down on the napkin not surprised when Ink had taken it. All he had to do now was make one last trip to Cokeland and he was out the game for good.

"That's a fly suit," Ink said coming up beside him.

Phatz glanced down. The black Armani suit was imported straight from Italy thanks to Viv.

"Thank you." He brushed at the invisible lint as he turned to stare at Ink.

"When I come to you it's gone be a back flip. I leave the same day, that means you need to have all the money on deck."

"I'm on it."

He forged on with his demands. "No hotels, I need a house with a family setting."

Ink flicked his hand in the air dismissively. "You'll trust me like a brother after this," he said.

Phatz could see the seriousness in his gaze. He faced the skyline again. Pulling in a lung full of air he released it slowly.

"The DEA is after all of us in the game, and I know yo boys hungry after the jacking, but I keep it on me." He lifted his suit jacket to reveal the .45 tucked in his waist.

Folding his arms across his chest Ink leveled him with a stare. "You have nothing to worry about." He dropped his stance. "Now let's go back inside, I didn't come all this way to not eat." Spinning on his heel Ink retreated leaving him alone.

Staring after him Phatz knew that he could trust Ink, but he meant what he said.

• •

Back at the townhouse AC found himself dosing off in front of the TV. When the alarm system beeped, reflexively he reached for the gun on the side table. His grip eased when Phatz appeared.

Wiping the sleep from his eye he waved his hand in greeting before pushing himself into a sitting position.

Phatz plopped down in the chair opposite of him. The two were quiet as they watched reruns of *Miami Vice*.

"Got business in Oakland tomorrow, everything still on with Peter right?" Phatz asked breaking the silence.

Reaching for the remote AC turned the volume down.

He clasped his hands in front of him as he leaned forward, his socks digging into the plush carpet. "Yeah everything is in place,"

AC hesitated, "Something don't feel right this time though."

His gut told him that Peter had an ulterior motive for coming to Cali. He had been too eager when AC phoned to give him a go on the deal.

"What you thinking?"

AC couldn't say at the moment, but it would be unwise to ignore his gut. He'd done that with Corey and saw how that turned out.

"That if he play, he lay."

"Damn right," Phatz stated.

"We've run into another roadblock with Chunky," AC stated. True to their word they had hired a lawyer to check out his case, but just like the others before the lawyers kept hitting dead ends with witnesses and evidence.

"We'll keep trying," said Phatz. AC nodded his head in agreement.

Checking his watch, he realized that it was almost midnight, he promised Shauna that he would swing by.

"About Corey?" he questioned, approaching the conversation from earlier. He watched Phatz tense up.

"Nothing we can do about it." From his tone AC could tell that Phatz had made a decision not to dwell on it and so had he.

Stretching his arms above his head AC reached for the keys to the Benz.

"I'll take Ty along to meet Peter just in case shit get funky," he tossed out. He erupted in laughter at the comical look on Phatz's face.

"At least he'll be able to pay you back."

"Yeah, right," Phatz responded flippantly settling on the couch.

Strolling to the door, his hand stilled on the knob at Phatz voice.

"We made it this far."

AC glanced over his shoulder. Truth be told they had made it further than either of them had expected. It had been none stop hustling together since their first meeting at Marshalls. From smashing cases to the dope game, and now the hair business. They were true hustlers and the most important thing about a hustler was that he always knew when it was time to move on. And it was time.

"This is it," Phatz said stretching his hands wide.

"The last run," AC replied with a smile.

****

"I told you everything would work out," Ink stated.

"I'm glad it did," Phatz responded. They stood outside of Inks' sister house in the cul-de-sac neighborhood in Oakland. The squeals of children could be heard coming from the backyard along with the sound of music. Barbecue smoke mingled in the air. To the outsiders it looked like a family celebration.

Will you be able to stay until tomorrow?" Ink asked nodding his head towards the trunk of the limo Big Mac had let Phatz use. Inside were twenty-nine birds. While he hadn't planned on staying, after selling the seventy-one birds to buyers from Richmond, Phatz figured why not? Everything was going smooth and Ink had lived up to his word.

"Yeah I can stay," he responded just as Tiny exited the house. The skirt she wore inched up with every step she took. They had been kicking it since the party. While she was heading out to him on the plane from L.A. Phatz was putting another honey who rode with him to Oakland, on a plane back to L.A. with the money from the seventy-one birds he'd sold. Neither of the women knew of the other and he would keep it that way.

"Thank you for inviting me to your house," Tiny said giving Ink a light squeeze.

"Anytime beautiful," he responded.

Going up on her tippy toes she gave Phatz a kiss before sliding into the limo.

"You keep the bad honeys."

Phatz smirked at the compliment. His hand went to his hip at the feel of his pager vibrating.

"Looks like I won't have to stay until tomorrow after all. The other buyers just hit me up." This time the buyers were in L.A. so that meant they were going home.

As the two walked side by side to the limo, Ink turned to him and asked, "Before you leave I gotta know how you get the money through the airport?"

Swinging the door open, Phatz could see the curiosity in Inks' stare. A lot of niggas were scared to move weight through the airport because it was risky, but since their almost slip up in Denver, Phatz had learned to perfect his technique.

"Wrap the birds and money in thick white towels, the x-ray will pick it up as clothes." He winked as he slid inside of the limo.

Bidding Ink farewell Phatz turned to Duck and Tiny. Duck had been his go to man since AC was handling business in L.A. Phatz made a mental note to page AC once everything was done. They had to celebrate. In his mind he could see himself relaxing on a beautiful island enjoying the rewards of his labor. He slanted his eyes towards Tiny. Maybe he would take Tiny this time. Or Bonnie. Maybe even Silky. Phatz grinned to himself. His options were endless.

He tapped the partition. It rolled down slowly revealing the driver Eric who had come with the limo. During the ride to Oakland they had gotten acquainted. Eric bragged on his highly skilled training in Karate as everyone listened. Eventually Phatz had grown bored, but Duck had been entertained. Giving Eric his next driving instructions, Phatz sat back against the seat as he began to lay out their next move to Duck and Tiny.

■■■

The first clue that alerted him that something was wrong, was the limo was no longer moving. The second was the panicked sound of Eric's voice pulling him out of his sleep. Cracking an eye open, Phatz hand went to the back of his neck as he tried to smooth the crook out. Sometime during the drive, he had drifted off to sleep. But he wasn't the only one. Tiny's head rested against the window, while Duck was slumped over snoring. He turned his eyes to Eric. The fearful look on the drivers' face made him sit up.

"T-The police pulled us over," he said with a quiver in his voice.

"Ok get your ticket and keep it moving!" Phatz barked not trying to hide his annoyance. Pressing the button, he let up the partition. The man had probably been speeding. No sooner had the thought entered his mind did the partition slide back down.

"They have guns out."

For the first time Phatz glanced out the back window. A sinking feeling settled in the pit of his stomach at the sight before him. Over five highway patrolmen had surrounded the limo with their shotguns drawn, while their police cars blocked off traffic.

He swung his gaze back to Eric.

"What you do?" Phatz asked slapping the seat.

Eric winced as if, it was his face that Phatz was slapping.

"Nothing!" he shouted.

He was lying, Phatz could hear it in his voice.

"Shit!" he swore as he reached over to shake Tiny's shoulder.

"Wake up!" he yelled.

Duck was already beginning to rouse from his sleep from the noise. He took one look at Phatz face and sprang up.

"What's wrong?"

Instead of answering Phatz pointed to the back window.

"Shit!" Duck said echoing Phatz exact sentiments.

Dread covered Tiny's face, Phatz watched the fear jump into her eyes. The last thing he needed was a panicked female. Before he could assuage her fears a loud voice came over the intercom.

"Roll down your window and drop your gun out the window, then slowly reach outside and open your door!" The voice commanded.

Gun?! Phatz mind screamed as he glared at Eric who now wore a guilty look.

"We're pulling you over for brandishing a firearm at a motorist on the highway on I-5, south."

"Fuck, Fuck, Fuck!" Phatz began to chant in a state of disbelief.

Pull yourself together he told himself. *Don't panic.* Glancing out of the window again, he realized they were still on the I- 5 , over an hour out of Oakland and the limo was pulled over to the right shoulder.

The voice over the intercom was back.

"I-I gotta get out," Eric stammered.

In one motion he pulled the gun out, dropped it out the window and exited the limo. With his hands raised Eric stretched out on the ground as instructed.

Inside the limo Phatz pulse was racing. The twenty nine birds were still in the trunk along with some money. His hand went to his waist where his weapon rested.

"We gotta get rid of these guns!" he blurted out.

They didn't have much time. He knew what was coming next.

Phatz slid the gun and clips in the trash slot as Duck shoved his under the thick carpet floor.

Scrubbing a hand down his face he stole a glance at Tiny, she seemed to have calmed down. Directing his attention back to the window, he watched the police handcuff Eric after placing the gun he'd dropped out of the window into a plastic bag.

What the fuck was he thinking pulling a gun out? Phatz wondered to himself. All too soon it was their turn.

"Passengers inside of the vehicle, we need you to open the door and exit slowly come out one at a time."

Turning to Tiny and Duck, Phatz said, "Ok be cool, I'm getting out first, no matter what happens follow my lead."

"Ok," they both echoed.

Gripping the handle Phatz slowly pushed the door open.

"Get down on the ground!" The loud voice boomed over the intercom immediately.

Time seemed to stand still as he stretched his hands towards the sky. The scorching heat caused a sheen of sweat to break out across his forehead as his eyes scanned over the decorated officers he faced off with. The five shot guns trained on him were so close he could see down the barrels. Based on the scowls on the faces that held them, he knew that they were ready to pull the trigger at any moment. A chill raced through his body at the knowledge. Swallowing deep, he glanced out of the corner of his eye noticing that traffic on the opposite side of the freeway had all but halted. The drivers watched intensely from their cars at the scene unfolding.

Where they about to witness a murder?

Risking another glance at the patrolmen, Phatz read the silent challenge in their eyes. Just one wrong move and he was done.

"Lay in the dirt!" came the next command.

Turning his head towards Eric who was still face down in the dirt Phatz shook his head. Glancing down at the blue linen suit and gator shoes he wore; he realized their tactic was to try to humiliate him. They had him fucked up. Shaking his head again he stilled himself for the backlash. When none followed, he spoke up, "I'm a passenger, I have nothing to do with what this man did," he said keeping his voice even.

His answer seemed to have caused discussion among the patrolmen as they gathered debating on what to do next.

Taking advantage of their distraction Phatz whistled out the side of his mouth. When Eric's head snapped up, he slid closer to the man.

"Don't panic or trip, I'm not mad. I'ma bail you out just don't tell them shit!" he whispered lowly.

"You heard me?"

Eric's head jerked up and down, but already the man had begun to cry.

Phatz took a deep breath. He needed him to trust him right now. It was the only thing that could guarantee their freedom. There was a strong possibility that they could all walk away untouched. Phatz just had to keep them away from the limo's trunk.

"Ok turn around with your back facing us, keep your hands lifted above your head." It appeared they had come to some type of an agreement. Though the muscles in his arms burned from being raised for so long Phatz did as instructed as they commanded the remaining passengers to exit the limo.

One by one Tiny and Duck climbed out.

"Get on the ground!" the command came again. Immediately Tiny whipped her head around to Phatz.

"Don't do it! Just follow my lead," he said knowing that they needed to be seen as a united front.

"Put your hands up and turn around just like I am," Phatz coached. Behind him he could hear the officer's disapproval. When no one made a move on them, he took it as a good sign. It was time to put an end to this bullshit. He waited until both Tiny and Duck were in the same position as him.

"If you scared shoot!" He called out loudly issuing a dare of his own.

"But we are unarmed." When silence followed Phatz realized that they had the upper hand. There were too many witnesses. The whole I-5 was watching. He used the situation to their advantage.

"I'm going to slowly walk backwards towards you so that you can cuff me."

He put one foot behind the other.

"As you can see my arms are still raised and my hands are empty."

When Phatz reached the nearest officer, he peeked over his shoulder

"I am unarmed," he spoke calmly.

Lowering their shotguns, the two patrolmen shared a look before one grabbed his arm, placing cuffs around his wrist. "Sir I'm sorry for all of this it's just procedure."

Phatz tried to hide his shock at the officer's apology. His plan was working. Quickly he regrouped.

''No big deal, I understand that you all are just doing your job," he said going along.

Next, Tiny and Duck were handcuffed and placed right beside him. They waited with abated breath as a patrolman began to search the front seat of the limo.

Duck caught his eye, with a quick shake of his head Phatz refocused his attention. By now traffic was beginning to move along again.

"Clear!" The patrolman called out after completing his search.

Resisting the urge to sag in relief, Phatz watched them snatch Eric off the ground and place him in the back of the patrol car.

"He's going to Los Banos jail," the officer added as he began to uncuff them.

Phatz rubbed his wrist.

"Ok I'll drive the limo."

"Again, sir we're sorry about this," the patrolmen stated stumbling over their words.

Forcing a grin on his face Phatz waved off their apologies with one of his own.

Keys to the limo in his hand, he tilted his head towards Duck and Tiny who feel in step beside him.

His eyes closed briefly. It was over. Just as he moved another inch towards the limo a voice called out halting him in his steps.

"Wait let me pat around the back to make sure there's no more weapons."

Phatz felt the blood drain from his face at the words.

Swiftly he turned to see a decorated patrolman approaching. The twinkle in his eye said it all. He was a fucking Supercop!

"You guys stand right there and let me do a little more searching," he winked.

Mentally Phatz heard the sound of a cell door slamming shut in his head. He bit down on his tongue. Fuck! His mind screamed out.

Mustering up the strength, he slid close to Tiny lowering his voice so that only she could hear him.

"I'm going to prison you're going home," he stated as the reality began to set in.

Tiny's eyes rounded like saucers. She opened her mouth but Phatz shook his head to keep her from speaking.

"Just don't tell them nothing at all about my business just show them your plane ticket and tell them you flew in last night to party with me." He said giving her a way out. There was no reason for her to take the fall with him.

Her eyes began to water up.

"No tears! Just do as I say."

Tiny gulped hard as she struggled to keep the tears at bay. Finally gathering herself she nodded. Phatz didn't have to say a word to Duck. He knew the game.

When the Supercop popped out of the limo, he was holding Phatz .45 and Ducks gun.

For a few seconds Phatz mind went blank, he couldn't hear the words the patrolman barked. He didn't see the other patrolmen scrambling to the trunk. All he saw was his life over the past few years; the women, the money, clothes and cars. His mother Kathi face came to mind. She had been so happy at her birthday party and he had been responsible for it. It brought him great joy that he had been able to take care of them the way he always wanted. He thought about AC. They were brothers now, born from the same struggle. Together they had touched a dream and shared a lot of good times. But just like everything else, all good things had to come to an end.

A blaring horn in traffic brought him back to the present just in time to see the trunk of the limo be raised. The supercop stumbled back at the discovery inside. Peering over his shoulder his hard stare landed on Phatz.

"Cuff em!"

****

AC was in route to his meeting with Peter when the pager at his hipped beeped. Normally he would ignore it, but the strong feeling that gripped at him made it almost impossible. Following his first mind he made a quick detour pulling into the am/ pm gas station. Eagerly he dialed the numbers on the payphone. When the frantic voice came through on the other end, AC was glad he had listened to his first mind. Jumping in the Benz he steered his car towards Oakland. Peter would have to wait. Phatz needed him.

****

This is Laura with KFSN and we're reporting live today from the Los Banos in Merced County courthouse, where authorities have made the biggest drug bust in history after a traffic stop. Witnesses say that law enforcement received a frantic call around three yesterday of a disgruntled driver brandishing a weapon, threatening other motorist on the I-5. Upon arrival the driver of the limo was detained without incident. But a thorough search of the vehicle, produced $156K in cash and illegal substance that is valued at over two million dollars. Four suspects whose names are not being released right now were detained in *connection and are now being held at the local jail as they await their fate. Back to you Josh.*

3 days later

It was a circus. Every media station in the state was clamoring for the details of the biggest story of the year. Calls went unanswered at the courthouse and jails as the secretary fanned off the press. Authorities were still trying to wrap their heads around what they had uncovered as the details began to unravel with every passing hour. At the center of all the hype was the leading star. Phatz sat at the table across from the lawyer in the small interrogation room. Right out of Fresno, Viv had found the lawyer and already paid the $30K retainers fee for him to represent Duck and Phatz. He listened intently as the man laid everything out. From Phatz understanding, it was the most excitement that the small town had received in years. The news reminded him of another small town he had turned upside down just years earlier. He bit back a smile.

"Mr. Bradley, I have to be honest with you right now, things are not looking good especially now that they've flipped the driver."

The revelation came as no surprise to him. Of course Eric would flip. Phatz blamed himself. He should have gotten someone he trusted to drive them to Oakland. That was a slight on his part that was costing them a lot. The only bright spot in the situation was that Tiny wasn't being charged. She had gotten a DA reject and was being released that very day. Sticking to the script like Phatz had told her she was able to provide them with her plane ticket corroborating her story. As for him and Duck…

"Ok, so who's all in court right now?" Phatz asked.

The lawyer whose name was Smith smiled as his face became flustered, "Lots of media people have flocked to the court, this is big," he said drumming his pale fingers against the table. A big case meant that the light would also be on him. It was his time to shine as well. Smith pulled out a piece of paper.

"The case has attracted attention from the Feds."

At the words Phatz straightened in the chair. "Feds?" he questioned, "I thought this was local jurisdiction?"

Smith nodded, "Right, but your pal Eric took the Feds back to a house near Nolan Park zoo with the claim that it was where you picked up drugs."

He stilled. Nolan Park Zoo… that was Inks' sisters' house.

Oh Shit!

"Luckily, no evidence was found," said Smith. The words brought a great sense of relief to Phatz. Still the Feds getting involved couldn't be good. Smiths 'next statement confirmed it.

"The Feds are looking at trafficking charges."

Damn.

He knew there was no way he could take the case to trial especially with his record. There was only one thing left to do.

"What's the deal they're offering?" he asked hopeful.

Smith's eyes widened as he stuttered "T-there is no deal yet only your arraignment, I-"

Holding his hand up to silence him Phatz shook his head.

"Did you ask for a deal?"

"No," Smith said nervously. He ran his hand through his rusty red hair before touching the rim of his wire glasses. "Listen I can beat this on the basis of an illegal search."

"And if you can't? If we lose, how much time am I facing?" Phatz asked not giving Smith enough time to answer the first question.

"Thirty-five years," Smith answered solemnly.

Tongue in cheek Phatz observed the lawyer from his position. Young and bright he knew that Smith was looking to making a name for himself and what other way than by defending a big drug case. The problem was that was it was more than just a case. This was Phatz life and he wasn't about to let it be played with by some rising lawyer who wanted to use his name to climb social ladders in the corporate world. Fuck that. He knew the game.

"Go ask for a deal."

Balking at the request, Smith's mouth flapped open as he struggled to find the words. Finally, he cleared his throat, "Mr. Bradley--

"No," Phatz stated firmly.

He leaned forward, "I paid and hired you so that mean you work for me right?"

Taking a deep gulp Smith nodded.

"Then you do what I say."

The two men stared at each other before Smith jumped from the table and stalked from the room. Seconds later the door opened and Duck was escorted in.

Phatz shook his head when the man opened his mouth to say something. Catching the hint Duck sank down in the chair. The room was probably bugged. They wouldn't get any more ammunition to use against them.

Instead the men joked around as if their lives weren't hanging in the balance.

When the door opened and Smith stormed in Phatz moved to the edge of his chair. Disdain was etched into the man's face.

"That deal is insane," Smith stated in a huff.

"What is it?"

Removing a pen from his suit pocket Smith began to write on his note pad.

"They're offering seven heavy years for the drugs and a light five for the transportation of narcotics. Also, if you give Los Banos the $160K in cash the DA will prevent the Feds from taking over the case.

Phatz could handle the latter, but the mention of doing twelve years gave him made his stomach knot up. Immediately his mind began to scramble for a way out of what he was facing. He exchanged a glance with Duck.

"Is this room bugged?"

"Not to my knowledge it would be against the law," Smith responded flippantly.

"Good give us five minutes alone."

Begrudgingly Smith agreed. The minute the door closed shut Phatz turned to Duck.

"We gotta take this deal."

Duck kept it gangsta off top and was already in on Phatz plan after he explained it to him.

"Ok, I'll take the drug charge you go to trial and I'll testify that it was all my shit,", Duck said.

Phatz mulled it over. Not once did he doubt Ducks loyalty and he was glad that he was in company with someone who knew how it was, but there was only one problem.

"I can't go to trial the driver already telling, Phatz confessed.

"Shit!" Duck spat out.

"Right," Phatz said leaning against the chair. He stared up at the bright light bulb in the ceiling, his mind being pulled in a thousand directions. Duck's voice interrupted his thoughts.

"I get what you saying big dawg, but I need you out, not in a cell with me," he stated with determination. Though Phatz heard the words it wasn't that easy. He was still fresh out of jail to the system and that was a red flag. To go to trial would be to gamble with his life and something told him that unlike other times, the odds were not in his favor. At the knock he pulled himself up. Smith face appeared again.

The lawyer walked to the center of the room. His head swiveled between the two men. Shoving his hands in his pocket he quirked an eyebrow.

"Have y'all decided yet?"

This time Duck spoke up, "I'm taking the seven," he cast Phatz a look "and he's taking the transportation charge."

Frustrated, Smith loosened his tie before dropping down in the chair. He stretched his hands out in front of him giving it one last attempt.

"Guys I can beat this on an illegal search." He glanced between the two waiting for an answer.

"And if we lose?" Phatz asked again.

"I've told you that the sentence carries 35 years if we-"

"We're taking the deal and that's final!"

Dropping his hands Smith left the room in search of the DA. Five minutes later he returned.

"They accepted."

Duck let out a slow breath as he bumped fist with Phatz. "We got this," he said.

Gathering his papers Smith moved as if he was in a hurry now. His claim to fame had been dashed.

"You have to go before the court."

Standing. Phatz straightened out his rumpled clothes as best as he could. He ran a hand over his hair as he shook his pants legs. It had taken them 72 hours to accept the deal, now he was ready to get on with it. At the door he nodded his head at Duck before being led down the long corridor. He knew Denise and Viv would be somewhere in the crowd rooting for him. AC as well. They were family. And though things didn't turn out the way he had planned Phatz knew that this was just another setback, so he took the lesson in stride. When the knob turned, instinctively Phatz held his breath. The world was about to get their first view of the star that had covered every channel over the last few days. Schooling his face, Phatz walked into the courtroom. It was lights, camera, action time!

****

Los Angeles Times

$2.2 Million in Drugs Found in Limousine

LOS BANOS, Calif. (UPI) — The California Highway Patrol stopped a white limousine on Interstate 5 Thursday evening, arrested four suspects and seized more than $2.2 million worth of cocaine.

Authorities said Friday that the suspects, whose names were not released, may be members of a Los Angeles street gang.

The arrests were made after a motorist flagged down a highway patrolman just after 6 p.m. to report that the driver of the limousine had waved a pistol at him.

Four CHP officers stopped the limousine a short time later on Interstate 5 about 9 miles south of Los Banos and found two handguns in the car.

The officers said they found three athletic bags in the trunk containing 29 kilograms of cocaine with a street value of more than $2.2 million. They also found another bag containing $160,000 in cash.

The suspects are being held in the Los Banos jail with bail set at $1 million each.

400

The day started like any other. AC had woken up to Shauna's soft body pressed against his own. With her working and going to school and him trying to transition to a new life. They hadn't been spending much time together as he would have liked, but as he stared down into her sleeping face, he promised himself that all that would change soon. Slipping a hand under his head, he thought about all that had transpired over the past few months beginning with Phatz. By the time he made to Los Banos, Phatz was being arraigned and had already taken a deal. It would take a few more weeks before the two would finally speak by phone. He couldn't stop the tinge of regret that coursed through his body. Maybe if he had gone along none of it would have happened. But it was too late to ponder the if's.

Together they had brainstormed to come up with a new plan as the Feds began to pick away at their operation. The hair business was the only legal money they had to hustle with, and it was doing so well they had to open a second warehouse. The business was also the one thing protecting them against unlawful seizures of their cars, money, and the townhouse. They couldn't let that happen, so they stuck to the plan of making legit money and slowly the Feds began to back off, but it was still too soon to celebrate. During their last conversation, AC had listened closely as Phatz urged him to leave the game completely before he suffered the same fate. While he agreed, there was still one more last thing he had to do.

Beside him Shauna began to stir to life. When her eyes opened and she snaked a leg around his own, he realized she hadn't been sleeping at all. They spent the rest of the morning making love. By the time he climbed out of bed it was noon. It was rare that they got to sit and eat with each other, AC was usually out the door when the sun rose. Today they shared a late breakfast. Shoving eggs in his mouth he listened to Shauna go over the plans for her birthday party the next week. AC was going all out for his girl. The yacht was rented along with a band. His last task He only had to get fitted for his custom suit in the coming days to square everything away. Dropping five racks on the table for her to cover any more expenses, AC left the house anticipating the party, where he would get to celebrate with his friends and family, the life of the woman he loved.

• •

"Who these cats you fucking with?" Baby boy asked from the passenger seat as AC drove towards the location, he'd given Peter to meet him at. When Phatz was busted he had been forced to push back their plans until everything was settled. Today the time had come to close out his final deal.

"Just some Ohio niggas I been dealing with for a few years now."

"And you don't trust em?"

AC cast him a sideways glance as he switched lanes. He didn't trust anyone outside of his crew, especially since Phatz wasn't around. Even now he had funny feeling in his stomach that he tried to chalk up to nerves. Lately, AC found himself looking over his shoulder a lot more these days. Only thing that soothed his mind was the 9mm in his waist.

"Nope."

A strangled sound came from the back seat, shifting his eyes to the rear-view mirror AC observed Ty's stiff-necked posture. He sensed that the man was still feeling a way about Baby Boys presence, being that it meant he would have to split his half of the share. That was Ty though. Stingy and lowdown. Sometimes he wondered why he still he even bothered with him at this point. After this deal he would be sure to put some distance between them.

He switched his attention back to Baby Boy.

"You strapped right?"

"Just like you."

Good AC thought to himself, easing the car into the near deserted parking lot, he shifted around in his seat. It was time to reveal his plan.

"Alright the meeting is set at the Sizzler's restaurant across the street from the forum on Manchester and Prairie."

"Baby Boy," he pointed, "I need you to sit at the bus stop facing the entrance and the parking lot." He needed eyes in the back of his head and Baby Boy was the perfect person for the job. AC knew he wouldn't blink if shit got funky.

Turning to Ty who was now eager and alert he continued his plan. "I'm checking the money first, then, once I verify that all the money is in place, I'll bring him the twenty five birds." He stared at Ty as he said his next words, "If at any time during the exchange shit gets funky don't think just shoot."

"Got it," Ty responded slapping his hands together.

AC shot off a few more precautions. When he was sure that everyone understood their role, he faced forward ready to get the day over with.

• •

"I can't tell you how much I'm loving this weather," Peter said with a smile.

Just as AC planned, they were in the parking lot of the Sizzlers, only he was alone. At least that was how it appeared. He didn't have to glance over his shoulder to know that Baby Boy was blending with the crowd swarming at the bus stop, Uzi tucked in his pants. Or that Ty sat in the cut of the parking lot in a different car watching and waiting. It was better to let Peter think that it was just him.

"I'm glad you enjoying yourself," AC commented. He tried not to stare at the hideous outfit he wore that screamed tourist the Hawaiian floral shirt with pleated shorts. He even had a camera around his neck and sunglasses June who was dressed casually in a silk shirt and shorts, besides the ugly scar the man looked decent, but AC could tell by the sweat rolling down his face that he was uncomfortable in the heat.

June removed the bag of money from the trunk of the I-Roc. At Peters head nod he handed it off to AC, who checked to make sure it was all money.

"Tell me man, what all is there to do in a big city like Los Angeles?" Peter asked.

There it was again AC thought. The feeling in his gut had returned stronger than ever. Eyeing Peter he watched the man rock back and forth on his heels. AC got the impression that he was stalling him. But for what?

He rattled off a few tourist sites that he knew of. The two talked for a few more minutes before Peter's tone changed from friendly to serious.

"When you coming back with the work?"

"Soon as I go get it, I'll call you and let you know."

Pretending not to notice June's hand resting on the bulge at his waist, AC dipped towards his ride.

"I'll be waiting," Peter called out.

The words sounded ominous.

Spinning around AC locked eyes with the man. Something was there in his eyes. Something he couldn't quite identify.

"Yea you do that," he said before driving away.

****

Back at Viv's tip he gathered the work up. Briefly his mind drifted to Shauna. If he hurried and wrapped this business up, they could still make the appointment for his fitting. AC was almost finished when the phone in the room rang. His head snapped up. Only Ty and Baby Boy knew where he was.

Snatching the receiver off the hook he pressed the phone to his ear.

"Yeah," he answered half distracted still shoving the work in the duffle bag.

"Got some news for you."

He paused at the sound of Baby Boy's voice.

"What's up?"

"It was two old caddies with three niggas in both cars circling the block, the entire time."

AC's hand tightened around the receiver. Shit he hadn't been paranoid. His gut had been right. While that was good news for him. It wasn't for Peter.

"What they look like?" he asked.

"Bangers, from Cali."

He shook his head.

"This nigga done hired people from our territory." He had underestimated Peter.

"So this nigga think we a lick huh?" AC smiled. On the other end he heard the gun cocking back.

Baby Boys voice turned hard when he spoke, "Yep, Phatz told me y'all had some heavy toys, I can't wait to spray this Uzi." AC's hand brushed across the gun at his waist.

"Good, it's showtime."

The crowd at the bus stop had died down. Only a few people remained waiting in the heat for the next bus to their destination, but as shots rang out even they scattered.

"Stupid ass nigga," AC spat as he watched Peter's lifeless body drop to the ground. Blood leaked from the gaping hole in his head onto the concrete. The gun that he had intended to shoot AC with lay right beside him. Peter had been too slow on the draw. The second AC returned to the restaurant; he could feel the change in the air. They were going to rob him and take him out. Keeping up the front he handed over the birds to June, when AC noticed Peter pull a gun instead of the money from the car, he yanked the .45 from his waist and squeezed the trigger. The man never stood a chance. Stepping over his body AC snatched up the bag that June had dropped as he drove away in a panic.

"Come to my city and try to rob and kill me," AC spat in disgust. He glanced back at Peters' body again feeling no remorse.

At the sound of gun fire being exchanged he ducked low in Peters' I-Roc. The bangers had shown up. From his position he watched Ty unload his clip alongside Baby Boy. AC smiled knowingly. He'd chosen the right team. When the Caddie's peeled off in the opposite direction, AC tried to throw the car in drive to give chase, but it jerked hard sending his head slamming against the head rest.

"Fuck!" he winced rubbing his head.

It was a stick shift. He was examining the three petals in the floor when the passenger door swung open. Reaching for his gun he aimed it.

"It's just me!" Ty yelled before jumping in.

"You get em?"

"Not all," Baby Boy answered coming up to the driver's window.

"Look at that bitch nigga," he hocked a wad of spit from his throat, sending it flying near Peter. AC could see the thirst for more blood in his eyes. It would have to wait. He looked over at the drugs and money on the floor, then back to the body. Never mind the bangers, it was time to spread out.

"Baby Boy I need you to follow me in my ride," he responded before tossing him the keys. With a wink the man casually strolled away with the Uzi clutched at his side.

Beside him Ty rambled through the bags. "This a nice lick," he commented. Only AC barely heard him he was too busy trying to operate the car. He placed his feet on the pedal before trying again. When the car didn't jerk forward, he smiled. It still had all the regular parts as a normal vehicle, only with an extra pedal and gears. How hard could it be he thought.

- -

"You're doing it wrong," Ty pointed out for what seemed like the hundredth time. His voice was beginning to annoy AC. He had been driving a stick shift for all of two weeks now, so he was still feeling his way around the car. In his hurry to escape the crime scene AC had taken Prairie Boulevard, cursing silently when they ran into traffic flowing from the Hollywood racetrack. Now it seemed that they were at a standstill, but even worse the car was back to jerking and sputtering again. Shifting gears down he eased his foot on the clutch pedal.

Nothing. He tried again this time he shifted the gear left then right pressing on the accelerator. The move sent them reeling forward. Slamming on the brakes he brought the car to a stop only inches away from the bumper in front of him. Behind him someone laid on the horn.

Frustrated AC slapped his hand against the wheel. This shit not working he thought. He turned his head to stare out the back-shield window in hopes of spying Baby Boy. They would have to abandon the car, but his Benz was nowhere in sight.

"Maybe try pressing on the brake first then shift," Ty suggested. AC didn't want to hear it in fact something else had caught his attention. Something he hadn't noticed before. Three cars away a policeman on a motorcycle waited in the line. The man seemed to be gazing in their direction. Maybe he was imagining things he tried to tell himself. There were other cars in the line. He could be looking at any of them. AC watched the cop speak into the radio attached to his shoulder.

"Don't look but one time on the motorcycle behind us."

Ty turned around in his seat.

"Oh shit!" he exclaimed "Man he's looking right at us."

"Didn't I tell you not to look!" AC yelled.

He checked out the mirror again. Damn so he wasn't imagining things. He realized that by now the cops would be on the scene at the restaurant, looking for any evidence and interviewing witnesses. They'd struck in broad daylight; it wouldn't be hard for someone to identify the I-Roc they'd driven away in. He forced himself to calm down as he tried to focus on putting distance between them and the cop. Ahead of him the light had turned green allowing some traffic to pass through. This was their chance. Sending up a silent prayer, he pressed on the break, shifting into gear. When they began to ease forward, he let out a sigh of relief, but it was short lived, seconds later the car jerked violently.

The sirens followed. Casting a quick glance AC saw the police begin to steer his motorcycle towards them.

"Fuck this!" he said out loud before stomping on the accelerator sending them flying through the lights. Cars scrambled to get out of the way.

"Move, move!" Ty shouted. The race was on. Busting a left on Prairie down 104th street AC tried hard to shake the cop, but in the distance he could hear more sirens coming.

"Got more company," Ty said frantically. Behind them another motorcycle had joined the chase.

AC could feel the beads of sweats gathering on his forehead as he steered. His heart raced inside of his chest. Silently he cursed Peter for choosing a stick shift instead of an automatic. The man's body was probably stiff as wood by now.

Good.

t was his own fault that he was dead. AC had been right to never trust him. Peter ad been waiting on the opportunity to off him all along. He thought that it would be easier to kill him in his own city. AC scoffed to himself at the thought. Anybody trying to kill him would have to work for it, including the cops.

He gripped the wheel tight when they rolled over a curve barely missing the fire hydrant.

Ty hung on for dear life, AC could see the fear on his face. One hand on the wheel he reached for his .45.

"What you doing?" Ty asked in disbelief.

He didn't answer instead turned the wheel to the right, taking them on another street. Above him he could hear the helicopter. Inglewood PD had brought out the big toys.

He swerved to avoid hitting a pedestrian crossing the street. Regaining control of the car AC took a second to estimate where they were at. It was too far off from his safe zone.

He sighed again. In the rearview blue and red lights flashed behind them like a parade. He thought about bussing a U-turn and going towards them but quickly dismissed the idea and made another turn. He quickly regretted it when he saw the gate. It was a dead end.

With the police closing in on them AC looked over at Ty.

"Nigga give me that gun since you not using it."

Fumbling Ty handed him the .45.

AC checked the clip. There were still a few rounds left inside.

"Ok listen you go over the gate on the right I'm going over the one on the left got it?"

Ty bobbed his head up and down.

"On the count of three…"

"1.."

"Wait!" Ty called out.

AC stared at him in confusion. "What?"

"L-Let's take our chances in court," he stuttered out.

Forever trying to cop pleas AC thought to himself.

"Nigga this is court."

Without another word he swung the door open, hopping out the car. He paused just long enough to see Ty curl up on the floor. What the fuck? AC thought just as the sound of gun fire exploded behind him as he began to run. Spinning around AC blindly took aim squeezing the trigger. He watched the police duck for cover. His feet pounded hard against the concrete as he focused on the gate. If he could just make it to the— his thoughts were interrupted by a burning pain in his shoulder.

AC grabbed at it surprised when he pulled his hand back and there was blood. Fucking cops had shot him. Blood oozed from his wound. Gritting his teeth to fight back the pain, he turned his head and fired wildly hoping he'd hit one of them. Refusing to surrender, he pushed himself harder forcing his legs to run faster, ignoring the stinging pain in his shoulder.

Get out while you can. He heard Phatz voice echo in his head.

And he was trying.

Only inches away from the gate AC prepared to leap when another bullet ripped through his body, this time it was his leg.

"Aaah!"

He screamed out in pain as he tumbled to the ground.

Rolling over on his back he raised his good arm up and fired. There was blood everywhere. His vision was beginning to blur making it hard to see, but he kept firing, smile in place. But His smile slowly turned into a grimace as another bullet hit him in the chest sending him backwards. His head hit the ground with an oomph sound as the guns slid from his hands. Blood begin to fill his lungs as he struggled to pull in air. The pain was like nothing he had ever felt before. AC could feel his life slipping from him as the police surrounded him with their guns drawn. Sirens roared all around him.

Get out while you can. The voice echoed again. AC tried hard to fight against the darkness closing in on him. This wasn't how it was supposed to end. He still had so much left to do. When a blinding light appeared, he began to resign to his fate. He waited for flashbacks of his life to play in his head. He'd heard that was what happened when you were dying. That God would show you the good and the bad. Instead, all he saw were bits of pieces of him and Phatz. Then there was Shauna. Young Shauna at the mall where they'd first met, Shauna at Louisiana, Shauna when they made love this morning. He tried to hold on for her. For Phatz. But the pain was unbearable. As he surrendered to the darkness there was one last solemn thought in his mind. Instead of Shauna dressed in all white for her party celebrating life by this time next week she would be in all black at his funeral mourning him.

- -

"Bradley you have fifteen minutes until your visit," the guard standing outside of his cell announced. With a head nod acknowledging his words Phatz sent the guard on his way as he finished getting dressed. He would be spending the next 72 hours on a family visit with Tiny. He had all but expected her to be done with him after getting caught up in Oakland with him, but she had been by his side since his arrival at Solano State Prison in Northern Cali six months ago. Phatz should have been fired up about the visit since he had some steam to blow off, but all that he could think about was Baby Boy who was being buried today. The unexpected loss hit him so hard when he got the news that he couldn't eat for days. Phatz sat in his cell reminiscing on the only thing he had left of his friend. Memories. Yet the memories weren't enough to dull the pain. Nothing was. Every time he ended up behind bars, he lost someone close to him. The only difference this time was that he didn't blame himself. The blame for Baby's Boy death lay with one person and it was someone he had never expected. Viv. She had gone and gotten Baby Boy caught up in her bullshit. When Vivian first came to him with the problem, Phatz considered letting her learn the hard way since she hadn't stuck to their plan to just run the hair business. But true to fashion he found himself coming to her rescue yet again. With him and AC out of the picture she had resorted to her old tricks. Some clown had fronted her two birds after she fucked him. Only problem was that Viv claimed the birds got knocked by the Feds out of town. For the loss that he took the man wanted everything that belonged to her and he'd even gone as far as threatening her to get it. That's where Phatz stepped in. Giving Baby Boy instructions to show up at the man's store so that he could breathe on him, Phatz made it clear that the man was to cut his losses because everything Viv had wasn't hers at all. It was his. And anyone attempting to take from him would be met with harsh consequences. Problem solved. Or so he thought.

     Days later he was just returning from his workout when he got the urge to call Denise. The minute she picked up he knew something was wrong. He listened in shock as she revealed that Baby Boy had been murdered, but that was all Denise could tell him. Numb he had ended the phone call and made a few of his own until he found out the truth. Still pressed for money Viv had linked up with Baby Boy on a lick behind Phatz back. She sent Baby Boy a her friends house that she traveled to Italy with. Viv claimed this "friend" kept $400,000 in her house in Ladera Heights. When the woman came home to find Baby Boy burglarizing her home, she shot him twice. He managed to make it outside of her front door before he collapsed on the lawn where and died. She was hailed as a hero for days by the news. The worst part of all though was that the money was never there. Baby Boy's death opened up the flood works and showed Viv's true hand. She had been using their hair company to ship drugs. The Feds intercepted a few shipments and now she was in the wind. Their money had gone down the drain because of a greedy bitch. She and her husband shared a lot in common including betraying him. Phatz blamed himself for that. He had always known what she was, but he didn't think she would be bold enough to cross the game with him. Not after all he had done for her. And if that wasn't bad enough AC was laid up in a coma fighting for his life after being shot by the police. It was hard to believe that they had been living on top of the world just months ago getting ready to make their exit from the game and now he was serving a five year sentence with no clue if his best friend would ever wake up.

Stepping outside of his cell Phatz made his way to the telephone. With only a few minutes until he went on his visit with Tiny, he wanted to call Denise to ask about Baby Boy's funeral.

She answered on the first ring.

"So how was it?" he asked with the phone cradled between his neck and shoulder blade.

He listened closely as Denise gave him the details of the funeral. A pain hit his chest again. Everyone he loved was seemingly taken away from him in a blink of an eye never giving him the chance to say goodbye. He had tried to balance out the unfairness of life with money, but not even money could take away the sting of death.

"Hold on I have a call on the other line," Denise said hurriedly before clicking over.

Phatz mind was still processing all of what she had told him when her tearful voice came through the line.

Alarmed he stood up straight "What's wrong?" he asked as his heartbeat in his ear.

Denise took a few breaths before speaking.

"It's AC…"

2 years later

"I'm here," Phatz said as he kneeled in front of the marble headstone at the Inglewood Cemetery. The pain in his chest was so strong he found it hard to breathe. He could feel his eyes burning as he read the name carved into the headstone. Blinking back the tears he snatched the Ray Bans from his face. He tried to speak, but the lump in his throat made it almost impossible. It was the first place he wanted to come after being released from prison. Though Phatz didn't have to complete all five years in prison the two years he'd spent behind bars had cost him almost everything. His eyes drifted back to the headstone. When he managed to find his voice again, it sounded strange to his ears.

"Shit got funky when you left," he said touching the cold slab of concrete. Just like the concrete his heart had turned cold and hardened over all that he endured.

"But don't worry I'ma make shit right, I promise," he vowed.

Shoving his hands into his pockets Phatz lost track of how long he stood out there talking. It seemed weird that he was keeping the dead updated, but who else could he turn too? So, he talked about all those that betrayed him. Corey, Ty, Vivian, and even Billy who he had recently learned was on America's Most Wanted for shooting Big Mac and killing the female passenger in the car. Phatz tried to think what he had ever done to deserve any of the betrayals and after pondering long and hard he realized he hadn't done a thing but try to get money with the wrong motherfuckers. And they repaid him with betrayal. When the sky opened up and began sprinkling light raindrops, he forced himself to return to the red slant nose Porsche parked at the curb. Giving one long glance in the rearview mirror he started the car up. Donning the Ray Ban's, he eased down the winding path leading him away from the cemetery. Touching a button, Teddy Pendergrass *Cold Cold World* flooded the car. It was the same song Marlon had driven away listening to the last time he saw him. He hadn't paid much attention to it then but now nodding his head along to the lyrics he felt every word.

Don't let this cold world get you down

When times are hard and friends are few

Don't let this cold world get you down, down, down

(Don't let it get the best of you, don't let it get the best of you)

A small smile began to play at the corners of his lips. Phatz knew one thing to be true: he was coming back harder than ever before and those who had crossed him were about to learn an important lesson. Nothing beat a double cross, but a triple cross.

Awful Clyde

Phatz

Made in the USA
Columbia, SC
22 August 2023

21890827R00224